Decision Support Models to Assist International and Transboundary Water Negotiations

Decision Support Models to Assist International and Transboundary Water Negotiations

Methodologies and Applications

Edited by

MOHAMMADREZA SHAHBAZBEGIAN

Department of Hydro Engineering, Faculty of Civil and Environmental Engineering, Tarbiat Modares University

ARIEL DINAR

School of Public Policy, University of California, Riverside (UCR)

OXFORD
UNIVERSITY PRESS

OXFORD
UNIVERSITY PRESS

Oxford University Press is a department of the University of Oxford. It furthers the University's objective of excellence in research, scholarship, and education by publishing worldwide. Oxford is a registered trade mark of Oxford University Press in the UK and in certain other countries.

Published in the United States of America by Oxford University Press
198 Madison Avenue, New York, NY 10016, United States of America.

Library of Congress Cataloging-in-Publication Data
Names: Shahbazbegian, Mohammadreza editor | Dinar, Ariel, 1947- editor
Title: Decision support models to assist international and transboundary water negotiations : methodologies and applications / edited by Mohammadreza Shahbazbegian, Ariel Dinar.
Description: New York : Oxford University Press, 2026. | Includes bibliographical references and index.
Identifiers: LCCN 2025031935 (print) | LCCN 2025031936 (ebook) | ISBN 9780197802571 hardback | ISBN 9780197802595 epub | ISBN 9780197802601
Subjects: LCSH: Water rights (International law) | Territorial waters | Watershed management—Law and legislation | Water resources development—Law and legislation | Climatic changes—Law and legislation | Decision support systems—Mathematical models
Classification: LCC KZ3686 .D43 2026 (print) | LCC KZ3686 (ebook) | DDC 341.4/4—dc23/eng/20250724
LC record available at https://lccn.loc.gov/2025031935
LC ebook record available at https://lccn.loc.gov/2025031936

DOI: 10.1093/9780197802601.001.0001

Printed by Marquis Book Printing, Canada

The manufacturer's authorized representative in the EU for product safety is Oxford University Press España S.A. of Parque Empresarial San Fernando de Henares, Avenida de Castilla, 2 – 28830 Madrid (www.oup.es/en or product.safety@oup.com). OUP España S.A. also acts as importer into Spain of products made by the manufacturer.

FSC www.fsc.org MIX Paper | Supporting responsible forestry FSC® C103567

Contents

Foreword

by Aaron T. Wolf

Making decisions about water is not trivial. For one, it's not purely a resource, where the invisible hand of the market might drive allocations. Because all life and most livelihoods and ecosystems depend on it, we insist that ethics be included in decision-making. Similarly, water's place in aesthetics and faith traditions often elevates conversations into the emotional and even spiritual realms, well beyond what can be quantified. Finally, there are the vast uncertainties involved in understanding today's hydrologic cycle—orders of magnitude in groundwater, for example—let alone tomorrow's.

Add international borders, and the complexities multiply. As occasional headlines remind us, relations across borders in the world's 313 transboundary basins can be fraught. Just in the last several years, tensions have flared within the Indus, between India and Pakistan; the Nile, between Ethiopia and Egypt; and even within the Columbia, between the United States and Canada. Negotiations can be difficult in the best of times, but it is no wonder that it regularly takes years and even decades to come to terms over transboundary waters. In many basins, agreements remain elusive altogether.

Hence the need for decision support models (DSMs). Mohammadreza Shahbazbegian and Ariel Dinar take up the challenge of surveying the utility of DSMs in transboundary basins with aplomb. Drawing on their vast expertise with modeling and profound, often insider information on hydropolitical negotiations, they are able to offer this lucid and comprehensive volume that explores where DSMs might be helpful and, refreshingly, where they might not. Their assessment includes models developed for individual basins and generic tools for multiple basins. They include those that are applied and those that are theoretical but always with one eye on practicality—what can best support actual international negotiations. As the editors note, DSMs offer a way to bring analytical clarity, scientific grounding, and a structured platform for exploring what-if scenarios in negotiations that are otherwise clouded by political pressures, historical grievances, and deep asymmetries of power and information. In theory, DSMs can help move the conversation from entrenched positions to shared interests, from abstract tensions to tangible trade-offs. Rather than treat DSMs as a panacea, this book treats them as evolving instruments—ones that must be designed, interpreted, and applied with care.

The chapters' authors apply their analyses to some of the most seemingly intractable basins in the world. From the Indus to the Nile, the Mesta/Nestos, the Helmand, the Colorado, and the Congo, no geography is left unexamined. Even without consideration of DSMs, this comprehensive volume works as a primer on the current state of international waters. Add a cutting-edge consideration of DSMs as might be applied in each of these basins, and the world of hydro-diplomacy just got a whole lot richer.

The chapters are organized to reflect both empirical diversity and conceptual evolution. The opening chapter by the editors lays out the stakes: the enduring challenges of transboundary water negotiations and the underexplored potential of DSMs to support more adaptive, inclusive, and sustainable agreements. Drawing on recent negotiations over the Blue Nile, Euphrates–Tigris, and Indus basins, it highlights the gaps between treaty language and changing climatic and political conditions—and how modeling tools might help close them.

Subsequent chapters delve into a wide range of case studies and modeling frameworks, examining where DSMs have been used effectively, where they have faltered, and how they might be better tailored to particular political, institutional, or ecological contexts. The authors highlight not only technical innovations—such as the integration of hydrologic, economic, and legal parameters—but also methodological and ethical considerations: whose knowledge counts, whose data is used, and who controls the assumptions embedded in the model.

The concluding chapter, also by the editors, synthesizes these themes, exploring four critical contexts that shape the evolution of DSMs in international river basins: river basin organizations, multi-track water diplomacy, international water law, and emerging digital technologies. It argues that DSMs are no longer just tools for internal analysis but public-facing platforms that can enhance legitimacy, broker trust, and align negotiations with shared norms and procedural commitments. From artificial intelligence and remote sensing to blockchain-enabled transparency, new technologies are expanding what DSMs can do—but also raising new questions about equity, access, and governance.

A consistent thread running through the volume is that DSMs are not neutral instruments. They reflect the assumptions of their designers, the politics of their contexts, and the priorities of their users. Yet this is not a weakness—it is an opportunity. If developed inclusively and used wisely, DSMs can serve not only to support decisions but to shape the very conditions under which better decisions become possible.

In short, this book is both a technical contribution and a diplomatic intervention. It invites scholars, negotiators, and water managers to take decision support seriously—not just as a computational exercise but as a core element of international cooperation. It challenges us to move beyond simplistic narratives of water conflict or cooperation and to engage with the complex, evolving, and deeply human process of governing shared waters in an uncertain world.

Aaron T. Wolf
Oregon State University

List of Contributors

Carissa Boynton, Vice President, Smartsettle Resolutions Inc.

Daniel Crespo, Postdoctoral Researcher, University of California, Riverside

Ariel Dinar, Distinguished Professor, Emeritus, University of California, Riverside

Gabriel E. Eckstein, Professor of Law, Texas A&M University

Zachary Frankel, Executive Director, Utah Rivers Council

Jacques Ganoulis, Emeritus Professor, Director, UNESCO Chair INWEB, Aristotle University of Thessaloniki

Nickolas Halberg, Research and Policy Analyst, Utah Rivers Council

Najibullah Loodin, PhD Candidate, Texas A&M University

Robert E. Mace, Executive Director, The Meadows Center for Water and the Environment, Texas State University

Nidhi Nagabhatla, Program Lead: Nature, Climate and Health, United Nations University, and Adjunct Professor, McMaster University

Ismail Najafi, PhD Graduate From Tarbiat Modares University

Mehdi Nemati, Assistant Professor of Environmental Economics and Policy, University of California, Riverside

Mahmoud Radwan, Researcher, University of Waterloo and Ecole Polytechnique, CNRS

Padmi Ranasinghe, Research Fellow, United Nations University, and Doctoral Student, University of Texas at Arlington

Graham Ross, Head of International Marketing, Smartsettle Resolutions Inc.

Rosario Sanchez, Senior Research Scientist, Texas A&M University

Mohammadreza Shahbazbegian, Associate Professor, Tarbiat Modares University

Vijay P. Singh, Distinguished Professor, Regents Professor, Caroline & William N. Lehrer Distinguished Chair in Water Engineering, Texas A&M University

Charalampos Skoulikaris, Assistant Professor of Engineering Hydrology, Aristotle University of Thessaloniki

Raya Marina Stephan, water law expert, international consultant; deputy editor in chief *Water International*; International Water Resources Association

Ernest Thiessen, President, Smartsettle Resolutions Inc. and iCan Systems Inc.

Alexandra Turgul, Research Associate, Oregon State University

Anthony Turton, Professor of Transboundary Water, Center for Environmental Management, University of Free State

1

Needs for and Use of Decision Support Models in International Water Negotiations

Ariel Dinar, Mohammadreza Shahbazbegian, and Alexandra Turgul

1.1 Background

The recent tally of international river basins in the world (McCracken & Wolf, 2019; Transboundary Freshwater Diplomacy Database [TFDD], 2024) identified 313 basins on five continents (Asia, Africa, Europe, North America, and South America).[1] Those sources follow an early tally by Wolf et al. (1999). International river basins cover nearly 50% of the total land area and are home to more than 50% of the global population. The size of these land areas covered with international river basins means also that their social and economic performances will significantly affect the welfare of the population in the basins and in the countries that share these basins.

Two hundred thirty-five of all international basins are bilateral, and 78 are multilateral, ranging from 3 to 19 riparian states, or disputed territories, per basin (McCracken & Wolf, 2019; TFDD, 2024). How do riparian states manage the water they share? How many of the basins are considered conflictive basins? Can riparian states improve the way they deal with managing the water in their shared basins? Do riparian states that share a river basin face increasingly difficult situations in dealing with management of their shared water, leading to a higher number of conflicts?

[1] McCracken and Wolf (2019) identified 310 international basins. However, the TFDD has since identified three more. Because no publication exists with the updated number of total international river basins, we will cite both McCracken and Wolf (2019) and TFDD (2024).

Ariel Dinar et al., *Needs for and Use of Decision Support Models in International Water Negotiations*. In: *Decision Support Models to Assist International and Transboundary Water Negotiations*. Edited by: Mohammadreza Shahbazbegian and Ariel Dinar, Oxford University Press. © Oxford University Press (2026).
DOI: 10.1093/9780197802601.003.0001

This chapter sets the stage for addressing such questions by recognizing the weakness of treaties as a sustainable tool to handle water allocation under varying and extreme conditions. Decision support models (DSMs) are useful tools for closing the gap faced by states that interact in complicated negotiation processes over shared international or transboundary water, which increase in complexity with climate change and globalization. However, the development of systematic tools that can assist such negotiations in the water sector has not advanced sufficiently to be applied in real-world situations to address conflicts over shared water in any significant way. The scientific and practical development of tools—DSMs—to assist negotiations over conflicted international or transboundary water still needs more support in terms of methodological developments and empirical demonstrations. This book aims to address that gap. The various chapters in the book aim to demonstrate recent methodological advancements and actual and possible applications to existing international conflicts over international and transboundary water.

The different chapters in this book argue and demonstrate that decision support tools, or models, may serve as a better mechanism to allow riparian states to handle various water scarcity situations in their shared basin. First, this chapter identifies the need to address international water conflicts that arise due to climatic change and other global issues. Using several examples of existing treaties and how they failed to address unexpected shocks, the chapter will highlight the potential value of DSMs as tools that can provide information and assess options in response to unexpected scenarios. Then, the chapter reviews a subset of different DSMs that have been published in the literature and have potential to be used in negotiations to address international water conflicts. Some of these DSMs are further discussed in several of the chapters of this book. Hence, the main limitations associated with DSMs in addressing negotiations in international shared water resources have been highlighted.

With this background we move now to discuss the need for DSMs and their potential benefit in negotiations of international water conflicts.

1.2 The Need for DSMs in International Water Negotiations

The usual method by which riparian states may handle water they share is the agreement, or treaty, they reached after a process of negotiation. Not surprisingly, the number of treaties signed among states that share a joint river basin is relatively small, with 100 of all 313 transboundary river basins lacking a formal treaty (TFDD, 2024; see Figure 1.1). In addition, the majority of treaties in multilateral basins have been signed on a bilateral basis, indicating that even when more than two riparian states share a basin, they find it preferable to enter into agreements in pairs rather than engage in basin-wide dialogue (Table 1.1). A similar finding is reported and explained in A. Dinar et al. (2019).

The data in Figure 1.1 indicates clearly that a significant number of international river basins are still not governed by a treaty as of 2024. Further, Table 1.1 indicates that in most basins, states prefer to enter into treaties on a bilateral basis due to factors such as a lack of trust among riparians.

As can be seen in Table 1.1, only 47 treaties in multilateral basins have been signed by all basin riparians, creating a situation in which even if there is a treaty between riparian states, it may not be satisfactory to all riparians, leading to underperformance of the treaty and tensions between riparians (Brochmann, 2012). Some statistics may help in understanding the problems that are faced by riparian states of an international river basin in the process of managing these waters.

While treaties are a common mechanism to handle water that is shared among several riparian states, treaties, if signed, are not a perfect tool. Given global changes in the economy and in the environment, treaties may fall short of addressing many of the challenges faced by states that share a joint river basin. Treaties may not prepare the riparian states to address extreme fluctuations in water availability in the basin. They may not allow riparian states to address uneven population growth across the basin or uneven economic development among riparians. Both trends affect the demand for water and the position of the state vis-à-vis shared water.

Studies such as those conducted by Yoffe et al. (2003) have documented how states interact over shared waters by following the popular press and formal verbal exchanges. This type of information is coded in "events" datasets that are used to measure the level of conflictive (or acts of conflict) and cooperative (or acts of cooperation) statements/actions made by representatives of the riparian states about their shared water.

A series of studies that used the TFDD at different time periods identified increased trends in both cooperative and conflictive events over time. Yoffe et al. (2003) documented the number of cooperative and conflictive events at the basin level per year. They analyzed the period 1948–1999 and found that during different time periods the number of conflictive events exceeds the number of cooperative events and vice versa. De Stefano et al. (2010)

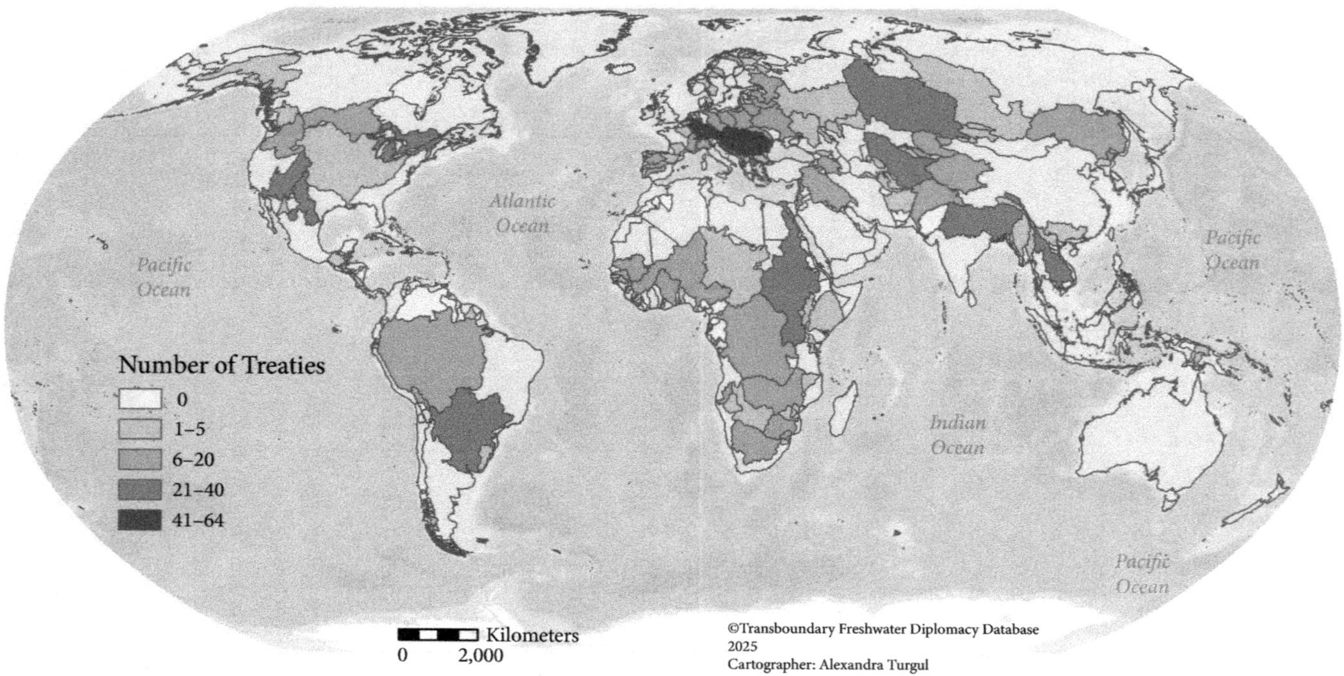

Figure 1.1 Distribution of Treaties by Basin, as of 2024

Note: Elaborated by Alexandra Turgul, using the Transboundary Freshwater Diplomacy Database information.

Table 1.1 Decadal Count of Treaties in Bilateral and Multilateral Basins by Number of Signatory Riparians

Decade	Treaty count, bilateral basins	Bilateral treaty count, multilateral basins	Multilateral treaty count, multilateral basins	All basins states count, multilateral basins
1820	0	1	0	0
1840	1	0	0	0
1850	0	0	1	0
1860	2	4	3	0
1870	0	4	0	0
1880	6	0	1	0
1890	6	4	1	0
1900	6	8	2	1
1910	4	6	1	0
1920	6	28	8	0
1930	8	9	0	0
1940	8	13	1	1
1950	9	57	6	2
1960	21	33	12	5
1970	20	36	24	1
1980	16	31	19	1
1990	25	67	41	11
2000	23	44	27	12
2010	25	24	5	13
2020	3	0	0	0
Total	189	369	152	47

Note: Author's elaboration of data from Transboundary Freshwater Diplomacy Database (2024).

updated the dataset through 2008 and concluded that despite increased water scarcity beyond 2000, cooperative events continued to exceed conflictive events related to shared waters. More recent studies, however, indicate that low-level conflict may be increasing while cooperation is decreasing over time (De Stefano et al., 2017; Kåresdotter et al., 2023; Turgul et al., 2024), pointing to the need for continued research to equip decision makers with appropriate tools to help address future conflicts.

We plot the reported conflictive and cooperative events over time in Figure 1.2 as recorded by the TFDD (2024). While we do not conduct any statistical analysis of trends of the two types of events over time, the conflictive events are kept in a constant range until about the year 1985 and then start increasing until 2008, while the cooperative events show a cyclical pattern until 1985 and then start decreasing until 2008.

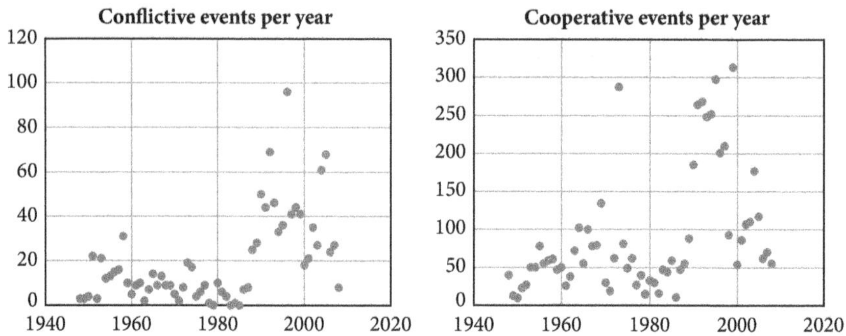

Figure 1.2 Conflictive and Cooperative Events Per Year Among Riparian States, 1948–2008

Note: Authors' elaboration of data from the Transboundary Freshwater Diplomacy Database (2024).

A recent work (Kåresdotter et al., 2023) used a dataset that combines the Oregon State University TFDD and the Water Conflict and Cooperation dataset of the Pacific Institute as sources of data on water-related acts of cooperation and conflict between 1950 and 2019. The water conflict chronology that Kåresdotter et al. (2023) use only reports conflictive events. As a result, much of the data they are using for post-2008 shows only conflict. In addition, they use a different metric to define cooperation and conflict.[2] Their findings (Figure 1.3) suggest that acts of conflict show a trend of increase over time, starting in 1990, and acts of cooperation are of cyclical shape over the analyzed period, with a decline from 1990 until 2019.

Even though there is a difference in the range of number of events per year between the two sources, both present similar trends over time. The most important observation is that over the past two to three decades (depending on the dataset), conflicts increase and cooperation declines among riparian states to an international water source. Does the trend of increased conflicts suggest that states will be less inclined to sign treaties over shared waters?

The history of signed treaties and treaty modifications over time can help answer this question. According to data from the International Freshwater Treaties Database, which is part of the TFDD, approximately 900 agreements have been signed over transboundary waters since 1820 (TFDD,

[2] This may explain the difference in the range of acts of conflict and cooperation (0–45) in Kåresdotter et al. (2023) compared to the TFDD (2024) dataset (0–300).

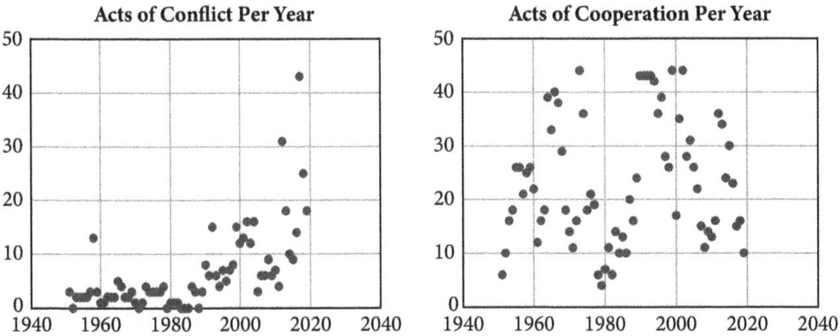

Figure 1.3 Acts of Conflict and of Cooperation Per Year Among Riparian States, 1950–2019

Note: Author elaboration of data from Kåresdotter et al. (2023).

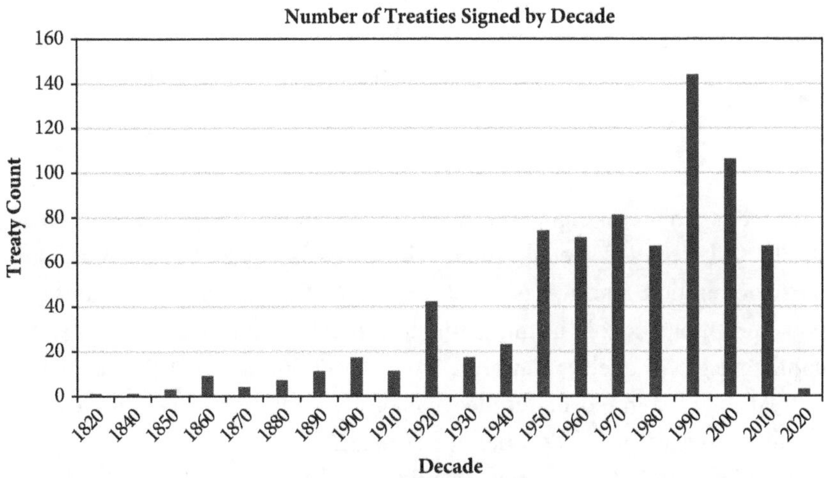

Figure 1.4 Treaties Signed by Decade, 1820–2020

Note: Elaborated by the authors using data from the Transboundary Freshwater Diplomacy Database (2024).

2024). Figure 1.4 displays the total number of treaties that have been signed in each decade between 1820 and 2020.

Between 1860 and 1940, an average of fewer than 20 treaties was signed per decade, while between 1950 and 1980, 60 to 80 treaties were signed in each decade (McCracken, 2024). Treaty signing peaked in the 1990s, coinciding with the peak of the global environmental movement and the culmination of global environmental summits such as the 1992 Rio Earth Summit. Treaty signing has since declined every decade, with only slightly

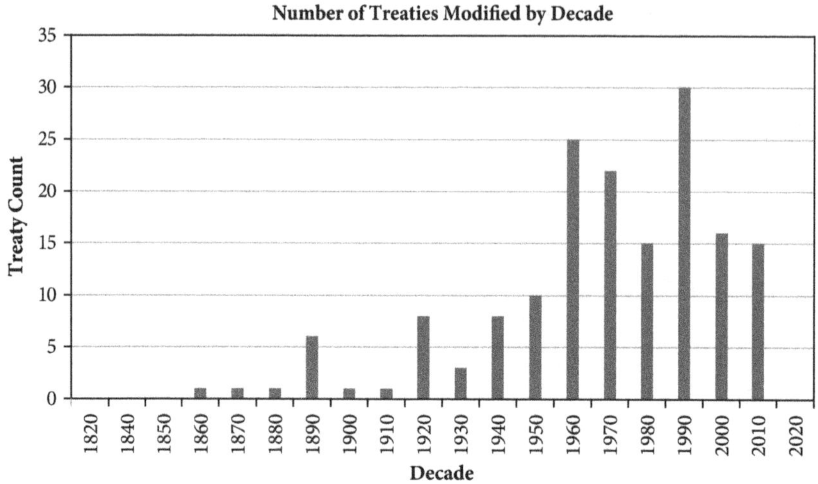

Figure 1.5 Treaties Modified by Decade, 1820–2020
Note: Elaborated by the authors using data from the Transboundary Freshwater Diplomacy Database (2024).

above 40 agreements signed in the 2010s and only three signed thus far in the 2020s (McCracken et al., 2025). These trends suggest that institutionalized cooperation among basin states is decreasing. Given that treaties can play an important role in mitigating and preventing transboundary water conflict (e.g., Mitchell & Zawahri, 2015; Tir & Stinnett, 2012), the decline in treaty signing in recent decades may partly explain the recent increase in conflict reported by Kåresdotter et al. (2023).

A similar trend can be seen in the number of treaties that have been modified per decade (Figure 1.5). A treaty that has been modified is one that either was formally amended or had a protocol added to it after signing. Modified treaties represent cooperative relationships among riparian states. As seen in Figure 1.5, the number of treaties that were modified peaked in the 1990s but has declined since, although the decline in treaties that were modified between 1990 and 2020 is not as sharp as the decline in the number of total treaties that were signed in this same period. Speculating as to what caused this trend is beyond the scope of this chapter; it is important to note that the proportionally higher number of treaties that were modified post-2000 indicates that riparian states prefer to modify existing treaties rather than negotiate new ones.

Climate change and its uncertain impacts on water availability pose a significant threat to transboundary water management. Institutions such as treaties present one mechanism through which basin states can increase their ability to adapt to climate stressors. However, even if treaties exist among riparian states to international waterways, do they allow the riparian states to adapt to external climatic changes that affect the execution of the treaty? If not, how do these states adapt?

1.3 How States Have Adapted to Changes in Conditions That Their Treaty Could Not Address

We will describe two international river basins as examples of the inability of treaties to provide answers to unexpected situations in the basin. The examples are based on S. Dinar and A. Dinar (2017, Chapter 6). In addition to these examples, S. Dinar and A. Dinar (2017, Chapter 6) discuss the cases of the 1998 Bishkek agreement on the Syr Darya (Kazakhstan, Kyrgyzstan, Tajikistan, and Uzbekistan), the 1998 Albufeira Convention between Spain and Portugal on the Tagus/Tajos, and the 1944–1992 agreements on the Rio Grande/Rio Bravo between the United States and Mexico.

1.3.1 The Treaty on the Jordan River Basin Between Israel and the Hashemite Kingdom of Jordan

The 1994 treaty between the Hashemite Kingdom of Jordan (HKJ) and Israel is based on several features to facilitate the sharing of scarce water resources. These include a give-and-take arrangement where 50 million cubic meters are transferred from Israel (the Sea of Galilee in northern Israel) to the HKJ during the summer months in exchange for groundwater pumping rights from aquifers in the Arava Valley in the HKJ. This arrangement has been challenged by recurring droughts that lowered the water level in the Sea of Galilee and prevented Israel from delivering the amount of water it committed to the HKJ. After several years of recurring droughts, the states agreed to an interim arrangement that allowed Israel to complete a desalination project in the Mediterranean, which will guarantee the supply of freshwater to the Sea of Galilee and the annual transfer of the full 50 million cubic meters to the HKJ. While this technological solution helps address uncertainty in water supply, conflict over who should pay how much for the investment in the desalination plants and who should pay for the conveyance costs from the Mediterranean to the Sea of Galilee remains (Katz & Walschot, 2025). This example demonstrates the fragility of the treaty and its inability to provide the riparian states with tools to adequately address future uncertainty.

1.3.2 The Ganges Treaties Between India and Bangladesh at Farakka

The Ganges River basin that is shared between India and Bangladesh (at Farakka) has a long history of disputes and damages from water extremes—droughts and floods. Following the independence of Bangladesh in 1971, negotiations over the Ganges water at Farakka have yielded five treaties between 1971 and 1996 (1972, 1975, 1977, 1982, 1985). All of these treaties were unable to address the severe droughts and water scarcity faced by the two countries. The main reason for the difficulty in reaching an agreed-upon allocation was that the treaties were based on fixed allocations during the dry season that did not address actual water availability in Farakka. The quarter-century between the signing of the first treaty and 1996 was marked by tensions and bitter disputes between the two countries. In 1996, a new treaty was signed for 30 years. The 1996 treaty was based on shares of the flow rather on fixed amounts and varied by subseasons of the dry season (Faisal & Nishat, 2000). While the 1996 Ganges treaty is much more advanced and flexible than former treaties, still Bangladesh claims that it was not able to equitably allocate water during the dry season in 1997, 2008, 2010, and 2016. In addition, Bangladesh claims that between 1997 and 2008 it did not receive its guaranteed share of water during critical dry periods about 65% of the time. This example demonstrates that even a sophisticated treaty cannot guarantee a sustainable handling of extreme water situations.

The couple of examples that we discussed, as well as additional cases of failure of treaties in extreme water availability situations (S. Dinar & A. Dinar, 2017, Chapter 6) and several more examples of treaty failures (Brochmann, 2012), suggest that riparian states that share a joint waterbody may not predict and prepare for all scenarios that affect the agreement they signed. When this happens, the agreement and the relations between the riparian states are at risk, affecting the performance of all riparian states in that basin. A decision support system (including DSMs) can provide the ability to adjust responses to unexpected scenarios and flexibility with the possible adjustments of the agreement between the riparian states.

1.4 The Use of DSMs in International Water

Recent literature demonstrates that DSMs have emerged as valuable tools for facilitating negotiations and promoting cooperative management of transboundary water resources. Nandalal and Hipel (2007) applied a strategic DSM using the graph model for conflict resolution to address water-sharing conflicts along the Syr Darya River in the Aral Sea basin. Comair et al. (2015) developed a DSM that integrated hydrological modeling with stakeholder input to explore various management scenarios in the Orontes River basin, shared by Lebanon, Syria, and Turkey. Pinard et al. (2009) analyzed negotiations in the La Plata River basin, shared by five South American countries: Brazil, Bolivia, Paraguay, Uruguay, and Argentina. Their model helps with understanding the negotiation process and outcomes in this complex transboundary context. The water allocation system in the Jordan River basin has been crucial in negotiations on equitable water sharing, allowing parties to explore various allocation scenarios and their implications (Fisher & Huber-Lee, 2012). Giupponi and Sgobbi (2013) reviewed DSMs for water resource management in Africa, discussing applications in various transboundary contexts across the continent and highlighting the potential of these tools in resource-constrained environments. Madani, Rouhani, et al. (2014) presented a negotiation support system for resolving international transboundary natural resource conflicts, applying their DSM to the Caspian Sea case study involving five coastal states: Azerbaijan, Iran, Kazakhstan, Russia, and Turkmenistan. Khan et al. (2017) developed a coupled modeling framework for sustainable watershed management in transboundary river basins, providing a theoretical basis for DSMs in various transboundary contexts. The application of DSMs in developing countries has received attention as well.

Other researchers have proposed generic models and frameworks applicable to multiple basins. Qin et al. (2019) developed an asymmetric bargaining model for water resource allocation over transboundary rivers, providing a framework adaptable to various contexts. Similarly, Yuan et al. (2023) created a model utilizing strategic concession behavior in a bargaining game for optimal water allocation, addressing water bankruptcy scenarios and offering a tool applicable to diverse transboundary basins. Shahbazbegian and Dinar (2023) highlighted the crucial role of DSMs in enhancing negotiators' understanding of the negotiation landscape. Their research focused on the Blue Nile transboundary river, involving three riparian countries: Ethiopia, Sudan, and Egypt.

Overall, the DSMs range from specific case studies to theoretical frameworks applicable to various basins, showcasing the versatility and potential of these tools in facilitating cooperation and conflict resolution in international water resource management.

DSMs are useful tools to close the gap faced by states that interact in informatic-complicated negotiation processes over shared international or transboundary water, which increase in complexity with climate change and globalization. However, the development of systematic tools that can assist such negotiations in the water sector has not advanced sufficiently to be applied in real-world situations to address conflicts over shared water in any significant way. The scientific and practical development of tools—DSMs—to assist negotiations over conflicted international or transboundary water still needs more support in terms of methodological developments and empirical demonstrations. In this section we present features that are typical of DSMs and provide examples of different DSMs that were developed and applied to ongoing conflicts in international water and are discussed in various chapters of this book.

1.4.1 Pros and Cons of DSMs

Applying DSMs to negotiations over international transboundary water resources can be beneficial, but there are several limitations that have to be considered in order not to raise expectations from DSMs. One significant issue is the complexity of stakeholder interests.

Madani, Zarezadeh, et al. (2014) highlight how each state's unique socioeconomic priorities and political agendas complicate efforts to standardize negotiation outcomes. Islam and Susskind (2018) argue that models focusing solely on water allocation optimization can oversimplify these dynamics, leading to solutions that fail to capture the diversity of stakeholder needs.

The Nile Basin Initiative exemplifies this challenge, where differing developmental goals between upstream and downstream states, such as Egypt and Ethiopia, have proven difficult to reconcile within model frameworks (Wheeler et al., 2018).

The effectiveness of DSMs is heavily dependent on reliable and accurate data. Ray et al. (2015) point out that in many transboundary basins, such as the Ganges–Brahmaputra–Meghna basin, hydrological data is often incomplete, outdated, or inconsistent across national boundaries. Timmerman and Langaas (2005) note that political reluctance to share sensitive data can further compromise model accuracy and undermine trust in the negotiation process. The Indus basin negotiations between India and Pakistan have been particularly affected by data discrepancies (Zawahri, 2008), impacting the reliability of model predictions.

Another significant challenge is the overemphasis on quantitative metrics. Pahl-Wostl et al. (2013) criticize DSMs for their tendency to prioritize quantifiable factors while neglecting crucial qualitative elements. Wolf (2007) emphasizes that factors such as community values, social cohesion, and historical water usage patterns, though difficult to quantify, often play pivotal roles in shaping negotiations. The Tigris–Euphrates basin negotiations illustrate how an overreliance on quantitative data can lead to solutions that fail to address the historical and cultural importance of water to local communities (Kabaroğlu & Gürsoy, 2015).

The impact of climate change and environmental degradation on water resources poses a significant challenge for DSMs. Milly et al. (2008) argue that many models are built on historical data, assuming a degree of stability that may not exist in practice. Brown et al. (2015) highlight how this can result in models failing to account for unexpected variations, such as floods or droughts. The Mekong River basin exemplifies this issue, where models struggled to incorporate the increasing impacts of upstream dam construction and climate change, leading to inaccurate predictions about water availability (Grumbine et al., 2012).

Political and cultural contexts are often underestimated in DSMs. Susskind and Islam (2012) argue that these models frequently undervalue the significance of political and cultural dimensions in water negotiations. Zeitoun and Warner (2006) and Zeitoun et al. (2020) emphasize how historical tensions, power imbalances, and cultural differences between states shape and transform these negotiations. The case of the Aral Sea basin demonstrates how neglecting the political history of resource control among the central Asian countries can undermine the effectiveness of the technical solutions proposed by the models (Micklin, 2016).

Equity considerations present another challenge. Woodhouse and Muller (2017) criticize DSMs for often prioritizing efficiency over equity, particularly concerning marginalized communities with less political power. These communities' water needs and rights are not sufficiently represented in models, which can lead to outcomes that reinforce existing inequalities. The initial negotiations in the Orange-Senqu River basin, which is shared by Botswana, Lesotho, Namibia, and South Africa, exemplify how model-driven approaches can overlook the needs of marginalized rural communities, focusing instead on national development goals (Jacobs, 2012).

Even when DSMs propose viable solutions, implementation can face significant barriers. Fischhendler (2008) points to issues related to legal frameworks, institutional capacity, and funding. Dellapenna (2007) highlights how legal inconsistencies between countries, such as differences in water rights laws, can delay or obstruct the implementation of agreed solutions. The Indus Waters Treaty demonstrates how practical challenges in enforcement and monitoring, exacerbated by institutional weaknesses and political tensions between India and Pakistan (Zawahri & Michel, 2018), have hindered effective implementation of model-driven solutions.

Finally, technological disparities among stakeholders can impact the effectiveness of the suggested DSM solutions. Plengsaeng et al. (2014) note that in many transboundary basins, there are significant disparities in access to advanced modeling tools and the technical expertise required to use them. Sood and Mathukumalli (2011) argue that this technological gap can create an imbalance in negotiations, where more technologically advanced states may dominate the discussion. This is evident in the Nile basin, where Egypt has historically better access to technological resources and expertise, giving it a more powerful position in negotiations compared to some of the upstream riparian states like Sudan and Ethiopia (Cascão, 2009).

In conclusion, while DSMs offer valuable tools for transboundary water negotiations, their effectiveness is limited by various factors including stakeholder complexity, data quality, environmental dynamism, and implementation challenges. Future research should focus on developing more holistic and interdisciplinary models and/or frameworks that can better integrate qualitative factors, adapt to changing environmental conditions, and address equity concerns.

With those limitations in mind, we turn now to a review of different types of DSMs that have been described in the literature to aid negotiations over international water.

1.4.2 The Features of DSMs That Are Aimed to Help in Negotiations Over International Water

Several studies applied or developed DSMs for water negotiation. Some of these DSMs have been developed for and applied to particular transboundary basins. Among such DSMs one can find the water resources yield model that was developed for transboundary rivers in southern Africa (Juízo & Líden, 2008) and has been applied to the Umbeluzi River basin shared by Swaziland and Mozambique. Another DSM, the Danube Accident Emergency Warning System was put into operation as part of the Environmental Program for the Danube River basin (Pintér, 1999). It addresses concerns of downstream riparian states regarding pollution of their upstream neighbors and allows a timely negotiation. Another DSM based on an application of a multi-objective linear programming model, where each objective represents the benefits for a riparian state from using water for agriculture, urban consumption, and energy production, net of conveyance costs was applied to the Euphrates and Tigris River basin and its three riparian countries—Turkey, Syria, and Iraq (Kucukmehmetoglu & Guldmann, 2010). Other DSMs applicable to all transboundary basins include the Conflict Resolution Support System (CRSS) (Nandalal & Simonovic, 2003), the coupled modeling framework (Kahn et al., 2017), and the modeling upstream–downstream interactions using a spreadsheet-based water balance model (Love et al., 2008).

1.4.3 Features of DSMs That Are Based on Hydro-economic Optimization Models

Hydro-economic models (HEMs) are analytical tools that take into account the physical water movements in the basin and the use of that water for production of market goods and for support of environmental needs. Several of the HEMs were applied to address issues related to international water (Hossen et al., 2021). A recent HEM that was developed and applied to the seven states sharing the Colorado River basin (CRB) is the HEM-CRB (Crespo et al., 2023). The HEM-CRB allows individual stakeholders to assess the results for themselves from both changes to natural conditions in the basin and changes to decisions made by any of the riparians (states or sectors). The economic component of the HEM-CRB calculates the benefits of the agricultural users, urban users, and hydropower production.

1.4.4 Features of DSMs That Are Based on Cooperative Game Theory

Cooperative game theory models have been developed and applied to conflicts over international water starting in the early 1970s. We will mention only a few of them in this section due to space considerations. Several variations of a DSM by Rogers (1969, 1993, 1994) were used to address conflicts between India and Bangladesh over the Ganges River basin, including navigation, flood control, pollution, and irrigation issues. A. Dinar and McKinney (2010) extended a simplified (three riparian states) DSM designed to address the conflict in the Aral Sea basin between several former Soviet Union republics. This version of the DSM is built on a full DSM (all five riparian states) that was presented in A. Dinar et al. (2007, 2013). The DSM for the Aral Sea addresses the conflict between upstream and downstream countries over the amount and time of release of water from reservoirs upstream for electricity generation to irrigated agriculture downstream. A similar but much more complicated type of conflict between upstream and downstream states in the Mekong River basin was addressed in a regional DSM by Pham Do and Dinar (2014) and Pham Do et al. (2012) by introducing the negotiation principle of issue linkage. The quantitative values that build the DSM are based on work by Houba et al. (2013).

1.4.5 Features of DSMs That Are Based on Simulations of Hydrology of the River

Several models of water management have been developed to help manage water in the CRB, which is a transboundary/international basin. The US Bureau of Reclamation developed two systems to support the decisions in the CRB: the Colorado River Mid-term Modeling System (CRMMS) and the Colorado River Simulation System (CRSS). The CRMMS and CRSS are basin-wide models that combine water inflows and water demands in a distribution network. These models support simulations for annual, mid-term, and long-term horizons, providing information for temporal and structural water planning. The modeling framework used to develop these models is River Ware, which is a software developed by the University of Colorado Boulder. This software has a module for optimization that provides an optimal solution. The solution is based on the priorities of the water users.

1.5 DSMs Described in This Book

The book presents several DSMs and their application to actual negotiations over management of international river basins.

Chapter 2 presents the Smartsettle Infinity DSM as an innovative tool for enabling collaborative negotiations among riparian states of shared water resources. The DSM is demonstrated using a hypothetical "Kashland" simulation, which is inspired by features of the 1960 Indus Waters Treaty between India and Pakistan. By comparing various aspects of Smartsettle Infinity to those of several other DSMs, the chapter underlines its unique abilities—intelligent suggestion generation, multi-party optimization, and dynamic preference modeling—all of which enable the negotiating parties to converge on consensus solutions along the Pareto efficiency frontier.

Chapter 3 introduces the essentials of the painted water (PW) theory and demonstrates how it can enhance the effectiveness of DSMs in transboundary water negotiations. The PW theory classifies water into red (non-negotiable), yellow (negotiable), and green (unnegotiable) classifications. Using the Blue Nile case the chapter shows how the PW theory can provide realistic and sustainable water-sharing agreements and identifies the institutional arrangements for applying PW classifications in international contexts.

Chapter 4 applies a DSM based on concepts from multi-criteria decision analysis coupled with an eristic-dialectical model (EDM) for conflict resolution in management of transboundary water. The chapter defines several types of conflicts over transboundary water and assigns the multi-criteria decision analysis (MCDA) as a conflict resolution support model and the EDM among the various types of conflicts. Both MCDA and EDM models are applied to the case of the Mesta/Nestos River, shared between Greece and Bulgaria.

Chapter 5 uses the strength–weakness–opportunity–threats (SWOT) DSM for establishing trust among disputed parties to the shared transboundary river water. The chapter demonstrates the use of a cost–benefit decision-making analysis framework for assessing the challenges of trust at the transboundary Helmand/Hirmand River, shared between Iran and Afghanistan. The chapter concludes that to reinforce trust between the co-riparians in the basin, the basin-wide transboundary benefits should outpace national interests in the decision-making process between the two nations.

Chapter 6 analyzes the performance of DSMs in light of the international water law (IWL) that provides guiding principles for states to establish cooperation on their transboundary water bodies. Using core IWL conventions (the 1997 Convention on the Law of the Non-navigational Uses of International Watercourses, the 1992 Convention on the Protection and Use of Transboundary Watercourses and International Lakes, and the 2008 Draft Articles on the Law of Transboundary Aquifers), the chapter identifies one of the calls for cooperation in the conventions as exchange of data between the riparian countries, complemented by the obligation for monitoring. Such necessary obligations can be achieved by designing and implementing adequate policies for sustainable management of these waters. This chapter highlights the requirement for DSMs in IWL instruments by using specific case studies.

Chapter 7 develops a DSM using system dynamics to transform the hydropolitical Helmand/Hirmand Transboundary River discourse between Iran and Afghanistan. Using a dashboard that allows stakeholders to simulate complex water allocation scenarios by integrating hydrological, economic, and ecological aspects, the chapter describes a unique platform for collaborative decision-making that transcends traditional confrontational negotiation strategies. The DSM's key innovation lies in its ability to generate shared understanding through quantitative scenario analysis. By providing a transparent, data-driven framework to analyze complex systemic interactions, the chapter presents a generic approach to augment international water negotiations.

Chapter 8 describes the development of and demonstrates the application of a model to assess the value of cooperation under climate change among the riparian states of the CRB in the United States. The chapter models the water uses for urban centers, hydropower facilities, and irrigation districts under two different climate change scenarios. The analysis assesses the value of cooperation between sectors (agricultural and urban) and states, using different solution concepts from cooperative game theory and several stability indexes. Interestingly, the value of cooperation increases with the severity of climate change impacts on the water resources. Cooperation is preferred for all riparian states, especially for Nevada, California, Wyoming, and Utah.

Chapter 9 demonstrates the use of the Water Security-Oriented Indicator Cluster Matrix (WOSCIM) framework as a DSM designed to address the multidimensional aspects of water security based on the UN Water Security Conceptual Framework (2013). The WOSCIM framework is a participatory negotiation support system (NSS). The chapter describes the application of WOSCIM in the Congo basin. The WOSCIM provides ways to bridge data and information gaps among riparian states. By focusing on participatory, evidence-based strategies, the WOSCIM could serve as a flexible NSS that offers a scalable framework for addressing water security challenges and fostering cooperation among riparian states.

Chapter 10 explores four key contexts that influence the development of DSMs in future international water negotiations: the role of river basin organizations as institutional structures, the application of multi-track water diplomacy strategies, the impact of IWL conventions, and the rise of digital technologies. Drawing on methodological advancements from earlier chapters and on case studies, this chapter illustrates how DSMs have evolved from basic communication instruments into complex analytical frameworks that encompass hydrological, economic, and political factors.

1.6 Concluding Remarks

Managing internationally shared water resources has become more complex and difficult due to the increased presence of globalization effects, increased volume of needed information, and increased impacts on the water system and basin economies from external climatic shocks. All of these affect the ability of decision makers to address and adjust to such complexities (Alemanno, 2013). With more informatic-complicated negotiation processes, the need for analytical support became evident (Spector, 2023).

This book aims to demonstrate the usefulness of DSMs in negotiations over international water management. The various chapters in the book aim to demonstrate methodological advancements and actual and possible applications to existing cases around the world.

The chapters in this book present methodologies and applications of DSMs used for negotiations over international water and apply them to different basins. Several approaches are presented and demonstrated. The Smartsettle Infinity model can be used to renegotiate the Indus Water Treaty between India and Pakistan, resulting in a more stable agreement. Then, the PW concept is introduced to categorize the upstream state's available water flowing in a single time step, by PW classes—green, yellow, and red—to represent levels of difficulty to realize such water. The PW approach is applied to the Blue Nile water conflict between Ethiopia, Sudan, and Egypt. The MCDA model is suggested as a decision support methodology and is applied to the conflict over the Nestos/Mesta River, which is shared between Greece and Bulgaria. Following is the SWOT model, applied to the Helmand River basin between Afghanistan and Iran. The "legal DSM" provides a framework to align the actions undertaken by each of the riparian states with IWL so that legal principles set in international law conventions can be adhered to. Then, a benefit-sharing model is considered for exploring benefit-sharing opportunities in the Ganges–Brahmaputra–Meghna basin between China, India, Nepal, Bhutan, and Bangladesh from hydropower generation, flood control, inland navigation, trade, transit, and land connectivity. Based on participatory system dynamics, the following is a suggested decision support dashboard platform for basin stakeholders to actively participate in informed decision-making. The model is applied to the Helmand transboundary basin.

The DSMs developed and applied in this book include different disciplines, assumptions, analytical methods, and scales. How could such diverse DSMs and basin situations be compared? The book develops, in the last chapter, a metric based on criteria such as the transferability of the DSMs to worldwide transboundary basins, their ability to interact with international databases and negotiation models, and their transparency for and availability to basin stakeholders. The combination of all these factors allows us to compare and contrast the different DSMs and the characteristics of the different basin cases used for the applications, as well as suggest relative strengths and weaknesses of each DSM.

References

Alemanno, A. (2013). Is there a role for cost–benefit analysis beyond the nation-state? Lessons from international regulatory cooperation. In M. A. Livermore & R. L. Revesz (Eds.), *The globalization of cost–benefit analysis in environmental policy* (pp. 104–112). Oxford University Press.

Brochmann, M. (2012). Signing river treaties: Does it improve river cooperation? *International Interactions, 38*, 141–163.

Brown, C. M., Lund, J. R., Cai, X., Reed, P. M., Zagona, E. A., Ostfeld, A., Hall, J., Characklis, G. W.,Yu, W., & Brekke, L. (2015). The future of water resources systems analysis: Toward a scientific framework for sustainable water management. *Water Resources Research, 51*(8), 6110–6124.

Cascão, A. E. (2009). Changing power relations in the Nile River basin: Unilateralism vs. cooperation? *Water Alternatives, 2*(2), 245–268.

Comair, G., Maidment, D., & McKinney, D. (2015). Decision support for improvement of the management and cooperation for the Orontes River. In R. Ballabio, F. G. Comair, M. Scalet, & M. Scoullos (Eds.), *Science diplomacy and transboundary water management: The Orontes River case* (pp. 185–208). UNESCO: UNESDOC Digital Library.

Crespo, D., Nemati, M., Dinar, A., Frankel, Z., & Halberg, N. (2023). *Hydro-economic analysis of the Colorado River basin: A comprehensive framework for water management* [UCR SPP Working Paper Series, WP#23-02]. https://live-ucr-spp.pantheonsite.io/sites/default/files/2023-09/Hydro-Economic%20Analysis%20of%20Colorado%20River%20Basin_0.pdf

Dellapenna, J. W. (2007). Transboundary water sharing and the need for public management. *Journal of Water Resources Planning and Management, 133*(5), 397–404.

De Stefano, L., Edwards, P., de Silva, L., & Wolf, A. T. (2010). Tracking cooperation and conflict in international basins: Historic and recent trends. *Water Policy, 12*, 871–884.

De Stefano, L., Petersen-Perlman, J. D., Sproles, E. A., Eynard, J., & Wolf, A. T. (2017). Assessment of transboundary river basins for potential hydro-political tensions. *Global Environmental Change, 45*, 35–46.

Dinar, A., De Stefano, L., Nigatu, G., & Zawahri, N. (2019). Why are there so few basin-wide treaties? Economics and politics of coalition formation in multilateral international basins. *Water International, 44*(4), 463–485.

Dinar, A., Dinar, S., McCaffrey, S., & McKinney, D. (2007). *Bridges over water: Understanding transboundary water conflicts, negotiation and cooperation.* World Scientific Publishers.

Dinar, A., Dinar, S., McCaffrey, S., & McKinney, D. (2013). *Bridges over water: Understanding transboundary water conflicts, negotiation and cooperation* (2nd ed.). World Scientific Publishers.

Dinar, A., & McKinney, D. (2010). Realizing conflict, negotiation, and cooperation concepts in the context of international water courses. *Journal of Political Science Education, 6*, 188–209.

Dinar, S., & Dinar, A. (2017). *International water scarcity and variability: Managing resource use across political boundaries.* University of California Press.

Faisal, I., & Nishat, A. (2000). An assessment of the institutional mechanisms for water negotiations in the Ganges–Brahmaputra–Meghna system. *International Negotiation, 5*(2), 289–310.

Fischhendler, I. (2008). Ambiguity in transboundary environmental dispute resolution: The Israeli–Jordanian water agreement. *Journal of Peace Research, 45*(1), 91–109.

Fisher, F., & Huber-Lee, A. (2012). *Liquid assets: An economic approach for water management and conflict resolution in the Middle East and beyond.* Routledge.

Giupponi, C., & Sgobbi, A. (2013). Decision support systems for water resources management in developing countries: Learning from experiences in Africa. *Water, 5*(2), 798–818.

Grumbine, R. E., Dore, J., & Xu, J. (2012). Mekong hydropower: Drivers of change and governance challenges. *Frontiers in Ecology and the Environment, 10*(2), 91–98.

Hossen, M. A., Connor, J., & Ahammed, F. (2021). Review of hydro-economic models (HEMs) which focus on transboundary river water sharing disputes. *Water Policy, 23*(6), 1359–1374.
Houba, H., Pham Do, K. H., & Zhu, X. (2013). Saving a river: A joint management approach to the Mekong River basin. *Environment and Development Economics, 18*, 93–109.
Islam, S., & Susskind, L. E. (2018). Using complexity science and negotiation theory to resolve boundary-crossing water issues. *Journal of Hydrology, 562*, 589–598.
Jacobs, I. M. (2012). *The politics of water in Africa: Norms, environmental regions and transboundary cooperation in the Orange-Senqu and Nile Rivers.* Bloomsbury Publishing.
Juízo, D., & Líden, R. (2008). Modeling for transboundary water resources planning and allocation. *Hydrology and Earth System Sciences Discussions, 5*, 475–509.
Kabaroğlu, A., & Gürsoy, S. I. (2015). Water–energy–food nexus in a transboundary context: The Euphrates–Tigris River basin as a case study. *Water International, 40*(5–6), 824–838.
Kåresdotter, E., Skoog, G., Pan, H., & Kalantari, Z. (2023). Water-related conflict and cooperation events worldwide: A new dataset on historical and change trends with potential drivers. *Science of the Total Environment, 868*, Article 161555.
Katz, D., & Walschot, M. (2025). Desalination and the transformation of transboundary water policy. In D. Katz (Ed.), *World scientific handbook of transboundary water management: Science, economics, policy and politics: Vol. 2. Tapping technologies: The role of technological change in transboundary water management* (pp. 51–71). World Scientific Publishers.
Khan, H. F., Yang, Y. C., Xie, H., & Ringler, C. (2017). A coupled modeling framework for sustainable watershed management in transboundary river basins. *Hydrology and Earth System Sciences, 21*(12), 6275–6288.
Kucukmehmetoglu, M., & Guldmann, J. M. (2010). Multiobjective allocation of transboundary water resources: Case of the Euphrates and Tigris. *Journal of Water Resources Planning and Management, 136*, 95–105.
Love, D., Khosa, S., Zaag, P. V. D., Mul, M. L., & Uhlerook, S. (2008). Modeling upstream–downstream interactions using a spreadsheet-based water balance model: Two case studies from the Limpopo basin. *CGIAR Challenge Program Water Food, 15*, 15–21.
Madani, K., Rouhani, O. M., Mirchi, A., & Gholizadeh, S. (2014). A negotiation support system for resolving an international trans-boundary natural resource conflict. *Environmental Modelling & Software, 51*, 240–249.
Madani, K., Zarezadeh, M., & Morid, S. (2014). A new framework for resolving conflicts over transboundary rivers using bankruptcy methods. *Hydrology and Earth System Sciences, 18*(8), 3055–3068.
McCracken, M. (2024, April 12). *New directions and trends: Takeaways from the update of the International Freshwater Treaties Database* [Paper presentation]. International Studies Association Annual Conference, San Francisco, CA, United States.
McCracken, M., & Wolf, A. T. (2019). Updating the Register of International River Basins of the World. *International Journal of Water Resources Development, 35*(5), 732–782.
Micklin, P. (2016). The future Aral Sea: Hope and despair. *Environmental Earth Sciences, 75*(9), Article 844.
Milly, P. C. D., Betancourt, J., Falkenmark, M., Hirsch, R. M., Kundzewicz, Z. W., Lettenmaier, D. P., & Stouffer, R. J. (2008). Stationarity is dead: Whither water management? *Science, 319*(5863), 573–574.
Mitchell, S. M., & Zawahri, N. A. (2015). The effectiveness of treaty design in addressing water disputes. *Journal of Peace Research, 52*, 187–200.
Nandalal, K. D. W., & Hipel, K. W. (2007). Strategic decision support for resolving conflict over water sharing among countries along the Syr Darya River in the Aral Sea basin. *Journal of Water Resources Planning and Management, 133*(4), 289–299.
Nandalal, K. D. W., & Simonovic, S. P. (2003). *Conflict Resolution Support System: A software for the resolution of conflicts in water resource management.* Department of Civil and Environmental Engineering, University of Western Ontario.

Pahl-Wostl, C., Conca, K., Kramer, A., Maestu, J., & Schmidt, F. (2013). Missing links in global water governance: A processes-oriented analysis. *Ecology and Society, 18*(2), Article 33.

Pham Do, K. H., & Dinar, A. (2014). The role of issue linkage in managing non-cooperating basins: The case of the Mekong. *Natural Resource, 27*(4), 492–518.

Pham Do, K. H., Dinar, A., & McKinney, D. (2012). Transboundary water management: Can issue linkage help mitigate externalities? *International Game Theory Review, 14*, 1–20.

Pinard, M., Kempkey, N., Dinar, A., & Pochat, V. (2009). Negotiations over water and other natural resources in the La Plata River basin: A model for other transboundary basins? *International Negotiation, 14*(2), 253–279.

Pintér, G. G. (1999). The Danube accident emergency warning system. *Water Science and Technology, 40*, 27–33.

Plengsaeng, B., Wehn, U., & van der Zaag, P. (2014). Data-sharing bottlenecks in transboundary integrated water resources management: A case study of the Mekong River Commission's procedures for data sharing in the Thai context. *Water International, 39*(7), 933–951.

Qin, J., Fu, X., Peng, S., Xu, Y., Huang, J., & Huang, S. (2019). Asymmetric bargaining model for water resource allocation over transboundary rivers. *International Journal of Environmental Research and Public Health, 16*(10), Article 1733.

Ray, P. A., Kirshen, P. H., & Watkins, D. W., Jr. (2015). Integrated regional changes in climate, water, and livelihoods: Options for adaptive management in the Ganges–Brahmaputra basin. In: E. Craswell, M. Bonnell, D. Bossio, S. Demuth, & N. Giesen (Eds.), *Integrated assessment of water resources and global change* (pp. 339–353). Springer.

Rogers, P. (1969). A game theory approach to the problems of international river basins. *Water Resources Research, 5*, 749–760.

Rogers, P. (1993). The value of cooperation in resolving international river basin disputes. *Natural Resources Forum, 17*, 117–131.

Rogers, P. (1994). *A model to generate Pareto-admissible outcomes for international river basin negotiations.* Nota di Lavoro Fondazione Enrico Mattei.

Shahbazbegian, M., & Dinar, A. (2023). Painted water—A concept to shape water negotiation strategies in shared river basins. *Water MBPI, 15*(19), Article 3343.

Sood, A., & Mathukumalli, B. K. P. (2011). Managing international river basins: Reviewing India–Bangladesh transboundary water issues. *International Journal of River Basin Management, 9*(1), 43–52.

Spector, B. I. (2023). *The dynamics of international negotiations: Essays in theory and practice.* Routledge.

Susskind, L., & Islam, S. (2012). Water diplomacy: Creating value and building trust in transboundary water negotiations. *Science & Diplomacy, 1*(3), 1–7.

Timmerman, J. G., & Langaas, S. (2005). Water information: What is it good for? The use of information in transboundary water management. *Regional Environmental Change, 5*(4), 177–187.

Tir, J., & Stinnett, D. M. (2012). Weathering climate change: Can institutions mitigate international water conflict? *Journal of Peace Research, 49*(1), 211–225. https://doi.org/10.1177/0022343311427066

Transboundary Freshwater Diplomacy Database. (2024). Oregon State University. https://transboundarywaters.ceoas.oregonstate.edu/transboundary-freshwater-diplomacy-database/data

Turgul, A., McCracken, M., Schmeier, S., Rosenblum, Z. H., de Silva, L., & Wolf, A. T. (2024). Reflections on transboundary water conflict and cooperation trends. *Water International, 49*(3–4), 274–288.

Wheeler, K. G., Hall, J. W., Abdo, G. M., Dadson, S. J., Kasprzyk, J. R., Smith, R., & Zagona, E. A. (2018). Exploring cooperative transboundary river management strategies for the eastern Nile basin. *Water Resources Research, 54*(11), 9224–9254.

Wolf, A. T. (2007). Shared waters: Conflict and cooperation. *Annual Review of Environment and Resources, 32*, 241–269.
Wolf, A. T., Natharius, J. A., Danielson, J. J., Ward, B. S., & Pender, J. K. (1999). International river basins of the world. *International Journal of Water Resources Development, 15*(4), 387–427. https://doi.org/10.1080/07900629948682
Woodhouse, P., & Muller, M. (2017). Water governance—An historical perspective on current debates. *World Development, 92*, 225–241.
Yoffe, S., Wolf, A. T., & Giordano, M. (2003). Conflict and cooperation over international freshwater resources: Indicators of basins at risk. *Journal of the American Water Resources Association, 39*(5), 1109–1126.
Yuan, L., Wu, X., He, W., Degefu, D. M., Kong, Y., Yang, Y., Xu, S., & Ramsey, T. S. (2023). Utilizing the strategic concession behavior in a bargaining game for optimal allocation of water in a transboundary river basin during water bankruptcy. *Environmental Impact Assessment Review, 102*, Article 107162.
Zawahri, N. A. (2008). Capturing the nature of cooperation, unstable cooperation and conflict over international rivers: The story of the Indus, Yarmouk, Euphrates and Tigris Rivers. *International Journal of Global Environmental Issues, 8*(3), 286–310.
Zawahri, N. A., & Michel, D. (2018). Assessing the Indus Waters Treaty from a comparative perspective. *Water International, 43*(5), 696–712.
Zeitoun, M., Mirumachi, N., Warner, J., Kirkegaard, M., & Cascão, A. (2020). Analysis for water conflict transformation. *Water International, 45*(4), 365–384.
Zeitoun, M., & Warner, J. (2006). Hydro-hegemony—A framework for analysis of transboundary water conflicts. *Water Policy, 8*(5), 435–460.

2

A Methodological Simulation Using Smartsettle Infinity for Negotiating Transboundary Water Disputes

Ernest Thiessen, Carissa Boynton, and Graham Ross

2.1 Introduction

Transboundary water disputes present significant challenges, particularly in regions where water resources are scarce and multiple stakeholders have competing interests (Dinar et al., 2013). A prominent example is the Indus Waters Treaty, which allocated the waters of the Indus River basin between India and Pakistan (India, Pakistan, and International Bank for Reconstruction and Development, 1960). This treaty has endured for over six decades; however, disputes over water allocation remain a source of tension.

In this chapter, we introduce Smartsettle Infinity, an advanced decision support model (DSM) designed to facilitate complex, multi-party negotiations. To illustrate the system's potential, we use a fictional scenario termed the "Kashland" simulation. Although inspired by elements of the Indus waters conflict, Kashland is a hypothetical model created to demonstrate Smartsettle Infinity's methodology. By using a fictional setting, we can showcase the methodology and negotiation process without implying that the outcomes generated by the simulation could serve as realistic solutions to the actual conflict.

We begin with a review of existing DSMs to highlight their strengths and limitations in transboundary water negotiations. Following this, we provide an overview of Smartsettle Infinity's unique features, including its capabilities for preference modeling, dynamic feedback, and multi-party

Ernest Thiessen, Carissa Boynton, and Graham Ross, *A Methodological Simulation Using Smartsettle Infinity for Negotiating Transboundary Water Disputes*. In: *Decision Support Models to Assist International and Transboundary Water Negotiations*. Edited by: Mohammadreza Shahbazbegian and Ariel Dinar, Oxford University Press.
 DOI: 10.1093/9780197802601.003.0002

optimization. Finally, we demonstrate how these features are applied in the Kashland simulation, emphasizing the model's potential to support equitable, sustainable solutions in international water management.

2.2 Literature Review

Numerous DSMs have been developed to aid negotiations over shared water resources. While many of these systems offer robust features for data analysis and scenario planning, they often lack direct support for the negotiation process itself—a distinguishing feature of Smartsettle Infinity. This section reviews selected DSMs, providing context for the capabilities that make Smartsettle Infinity unique.

1. **Graph Model for Conflict Resolution (GMCR):** GMCR is a conflict analysis tool designed to model multi-stakeholder conflicts by analyzing each party's preferences and available actions to identify potential resolutions. Widely applied in water-related disputes, such as the Nile River conflict involving Egypt, Sudan, and Ethiopia, GMCR provides a structured approach to conflict analysis, emphasizing strategic interactions among stakeholders (Hipel et al., 2003). However, GMCR lacks the dynamic feedback and optimization capabilities that are central to Smartsettle Infinity's approach.
2. **Transboundary Water Interaction Nexus Simulation (TWINS) model:** Mirumachi's (2015) TWINS model provides insights into the simultaneous existence of conflict and cooperation in international river basins, helping to unpack the complex interdependencies at play. TWINS simulates interactions among stakeholders in transboundary water conflicts, such as those in the Jordan River basin. It facilitates stakeholder engagement and encourages cooperation, yet it lacks the preference modeling and real-time feedback mechanisms essential for facilitating real-time, preference-based adjustments.
3. **Mediation Support Project (MSP):** MSP is a suite of tools developed to assist human mediators by providing analytical insights that inform negotiation dynamics. Kittikhoun and Staubli (2018) employed these tools to examine the strategies of the Mekong River Commission,

emphasizing the need for adaptive and flexible water diplomacy in managing transboundary water resources. Primarily focused on data-driven analysis rather than direct facilitation of the negotiation process, MSP complements mediation efforts but lacks dynamic preference modeling and real-time suggestion capabilities useful for negotiation facilitation. This positions MSP more as an analytical aid rather than a comprehensive negotiation tool.

4. **Nile Basin Decision Support System (Nile-DSS):** Developed by the Nile Basin Initiative (see Droogers & Immerzeel, 2010), Nile-DSS is designed to enhance cooperative water management by facilitating data sharing and joint resource planning among basin countries. The system integrates various datasets to support informed decision-making in water resource planning. While Nile-DSS is valuable for long-term resource management and collaboration, it lacks real-time negotiation dynamics and preference modeling, making it less effective in real-time negotiation settings.

Collectively, these DSMs have contributed to transboundary water management by providing frameworks for resource planning and conflict analysis. Compared to these systems, Smartsettle Infinity offers dynamic preference modeling, real-time feedback, and optimization features, which are summarized below. The following sections illustrate how these capabilities equip Smartsettle Infinity to handle complex, multi-party negotiation scenarios effectively.

2.3 The Smartsettle Infinity System

The Smartsettle Infinity eNegotiation and Collaboration System stands out as an advanced DSM specifically designed to facilitate complex, multi-party negotiations. Unlike other models that focus primarily on contextual analysis or scenario simulation, Smartsettle Infinity is a process-oriented system that dynamically models stakeholder preferences, provides real-time feedback, and uncovers hidden value within negotiations. These features enable negotiators to move beyond traditional negotiation methods, achieving optimized and equitable solutions.

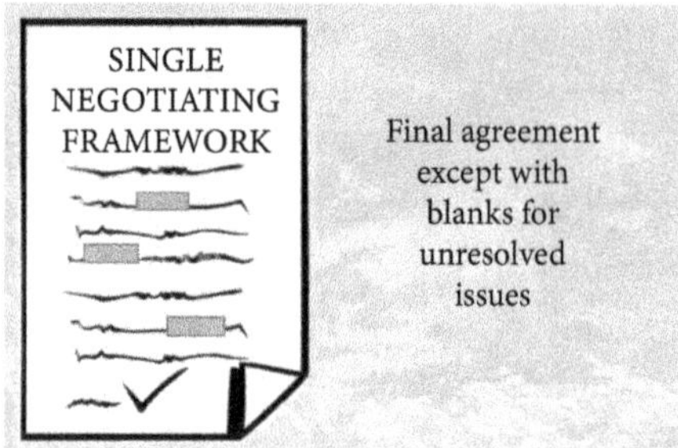

Figure 2.1 Depiction of a Single Negotiating Framework
Note: Elaborated by the authors.

2.3.1 Key Features and Advantages

Smartsettle Infinity's effectiveness is powered by a suite of advanced algorithms that streamline the negotiation process. Each algorithm contributes to transforming stakeholder inputs into a fair and efficient consensus. Below, we outline the key features that distinguish Smartsettle Infinity:

1. **Comprehensive Collaboration Framework:** Smartsettle Infinity supports the entire negotiation process, from identifying common ground to finalizing agreements. A central component is the collaborative development of a single negotiating framework (SNF), which resembles the final agreement but includes blanks representing issues to be negotiated (see Figure 2.1). Modeling the negotiation problem with an SNF allows parties to exchange proposals as complete packages rather than issue by issue, enabling concessions across multiple areas simultaneously. This approach minimizes negotiation time and maximizes value by avoiding piecemeal compromises.
2. **Dynamic Preference Modeling:** Smartsettle Infinity enables negotiators to represent their preferences privately, accessible only to the neutral site, which helps maintain confidentiality and encourages honest input, ultimately leading to more effective negotiation outcomes. This preference modeling of complex issues allows Infinity to generate optimized suggestions tailored to each party's unique interests, all while maintaining confidentiality.
3. **Real-Time Feedback and Intelligent Suggestions:** Throughout the negotiation, Infinity offers real-time feedback, helping parties understand the potential impacts of their proposals. Intelligent suggestions

from the system encourage negotiators to consider mutually beneficial trade-offs, fostering a collaborative and constructive environment.

4. **Multivariate Visual Blind Bidding:** This feature allows parties to submit bids without revealing specific preferences. It incorporates multiple issues simultaneously, enabling a focus on overall consensus and simplifying the negotiation process.
5. **Optimization Algorithms:** At each stage, Smartsettle Infinity applies optimization algorithms, such as Maximize the Minimum Gain, to guide parties toward the efficiency frontier. This approach ensures that the final agreement is Pareto-optimal—meaning that no party can improve its position without reducing another's satisfaction. The result is a fair, sustainable solution for all stakeholders.

These features set Smartsettle Infinity apart from traditional DSMs by offering a comprehensive, real-time negotiation platform that actively engages parties. Unlike traditional DSMs, which often focus solely on data analysis, Smartsettle Infinity provides real-time interaction, facilitating dynamic and effective negotiations. For example, dynamic preference modeling helps negotiators understand the impact of different proposals, encouraging constructive discussions and optimizing outcomes through real-time feedback and advanced algorithms.

2.3.2 Challenges and Limitations

While Smartsettle Infinity provides significant advantages in facilitating negotiations, its implementation does come with certain challenges. The model's success depends heavily on the accurate representation of preferences and priorities by all parties involved. Misrepresentations, whether intentional or unintentional, can affect the quality of the solutions generated.

Additionally, the system's reliance on advanced algorithms and technology may pose a learning curve for some stakeholders, particularly those unfamiliar with digital negotiation platforms. Comprehensive training and capacity-building are essential to enable participants to fully leverage the system's potential.

Although Smartsettle Infinity has been successfully applied to thousands of cases in the past—including live negotiations and realistic simulations—it is true that the platform has not yet been tested in an international transboundary water conflict of this scale. Previous applications have demonstrated its effectiveness in resolving commercial disputes, workplace conflicts, and other multi-party decision-making challenges. These cases provide confidence in the platform's ability to deliver fair and efficient outcomes across diverse negotiation contexts, even if challenges remain when addressing highly politicized or rapidly shifting processes like international water disputes.

Nevertheless, Smartsettle Infinity's structured methodology, preference-based modeling, and ability to guide parties toward Pareto-optimal solutions offer significant potential to overcome many negotiation challenges. Its scalability and adaptability make it well-suited for more complex, high-stakes scenarios in the future, such as those involving transboundary water conflicts.

2.4 Overview of Kashland, Like Kashmir

To illustrate the potential of Smartsettle Infinity in transboundary water negotiations, we conducted a simulated negotiation scenario called "Kashland." A fictional setting (illustrated in Figure 2.2) allows us to showcase the negotiation methodology and process without implying that the simulation outcomes could serve as real-world solutions.

The red line in the figure marks the borders between India, Pakistan, and China, also known as the *Line of Control*, a source of tension for decades. The darker brown areas represent the hypothetical region of Kashland, which mirrors the real-world Kashmir—a territory long disputed between India and Pakistan with complex geopolitical and environmental issues. This region is characterized by its strategic importance, contentious borders, and critical water resources, all vital to the economies and security of both India and Pakistan.

Despite recent diplomatic efforts, the borders around the Siachen Glacier at the northern tip of Kashland remain highly contentious. The glacier's strategic importance and role in regional water resources make it a critical point of dispute. The rivers of this region are highlighted in Figure 2.3, which also displays various water projects at different stages of completion. These projects, essential for agriculture and hydroelectric power, are an additional source of conflict. After a decade of negotiations, the 1960

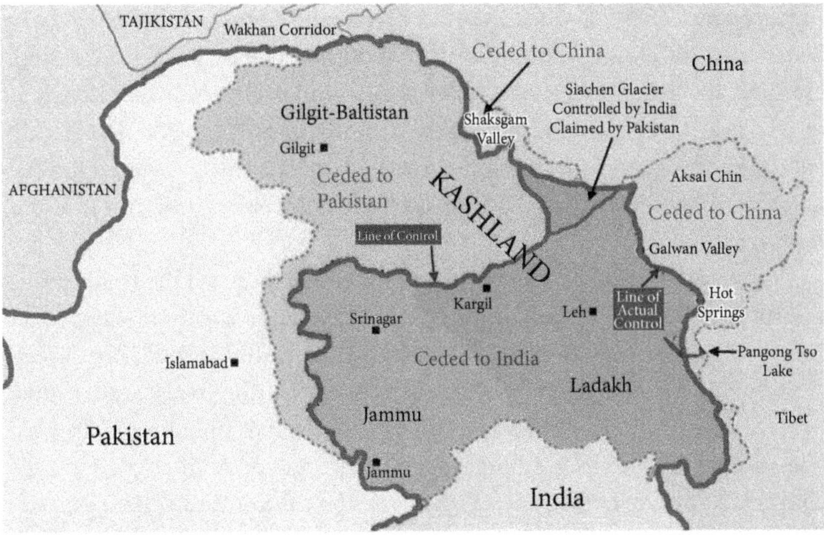

Figure 2.2 Visualization of the Kashland Region, Showing Contentious Areas and the Line of Control Between India, Pakistan, and China

Note: Modified by the authors from image published at https://asiatimes.com/2020/09/an-india-china-reset-is-still-possible/

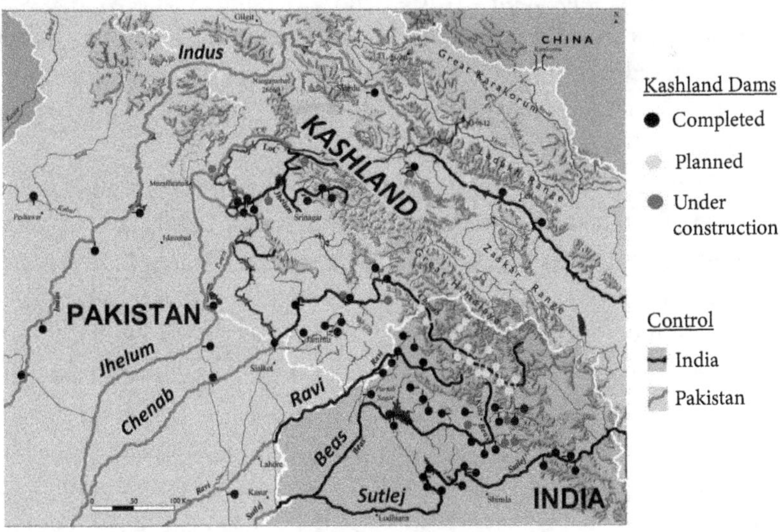

Figure 2.3 Water Projects Controlled by Each Country

Note: Modified by the authors from https://www.dawn.com/news/1292901

Indus Waters Treaty divided the rivers between the two countries (Salman & Uprety, 2002): The southeastern tributaries (Beas, Ravi, and Sutlej), outlined in blue, were allocated to India, while the northwestern tributaries (Indus, Jhelum, and Chenab), outlined in green, were allocated to Pakistan. The current divisions established by the treaty have continued to cause disputes as both nations seek greater control over these water resources.

Regarding the tributaries allocated to India that flow into the Indus, India asserts that it is permitted under the Indus Waters Treaty to divert and consume water from these rivers for its own use. Although the northwestern tributaries are allocated primarily to Pakistan, the treaty grants India limited rights to develop storage capacity, up to 3.6 million acre-feet, for irrigation, flood control, and other specified purposes. Additionally, India is allowed to develop hydropower projects on the western rivers, with a capacity limit of 20 gigawatts, although only a fraction of this potential has been realized.

One prominent example of hydropower development is the Kishanganga Dam, which began diverting water in 2018. Situated on the Kishanganga River (called the Neelum River in Pakistan), this project has sparked controversy due to its impact on downstream water flows to Pakistan. Pakistan raised concerns regarding the dam's impact on its water availability, resulting in international arbitration under the treaty's dispute resolution framework. Other proposed water projects by India have similarly raised concerns in Pakistan (Salman & Uprety, 2002).

The Kashland region is increasingly affected by climate change, particularly due to accelerated glacier melting, which threatens long-term water availability. Scientific studies indicate that annual water flow has increased by approximately 1% because of rising global temperatures; however, as glaciers continue to recede, this trend is expected to reverse, leading to reduced flows and heightened water scarcity in the future (Bolch et al., 2012; Immerzeel et al., 2010; World Bank, 2013).

Both countries are under pressure to adapt by adopting more efficient irrigation practices and exploring alternative water sources, such as atmospheric water generation or desalination, though these solutions may require innovative energy sources yet to be developed. Addressing the challenges posed by climate change, including glacial melt and diminishing water supplies, demands immediate and proactive adaptation measures.

The United Nations Military Observer Group in India and Pakistan[1] was established on the India–Pakistan border in 1949 to monitor the ceasefire called for by the United Nations Security Council and continues its operations today. Meanwhile, both countries have acquired nuclear weapons, a factor contributing to the Doomsday Clock[2] being closer than ever to midnight. Both nations recognize that escalating hostilities—and their development of nuclear weapons—bring them closer to potential disaster. The ramifications of such a conflict could extend globally, and a world without nuclear weapons is widely recognized as safer. Wealthy countries have both the resources and the motivation to support global disarmament and peacebuilding efforts, given the potential consequences of nuclear conflict. However, effective strategies to channel these resources into actions that meaningfully reduce nuclear risks remain elusive.

2.5 The Kashland Simulation

The Kashland simulation was conducted to demonstrate Smartsettle Infinity's capabilities in a complex negotiation setting. This simulation explores issues surrounding water allocation, security, and regional stability, mirroring some of the dynamics seen in real-world transboundary disputes, such as those in the Kashmir region.

The Smartsettle Infinity platform enables each party to model its preferences privately, receive real-time feedback, and consider system-generated suggestions aimed at fostering collaborative solutions. The schematic in Figure 2.4 illustrates the structure and process used by the Smartsettle Infinity eNegotiation and Collaboration System, depicting a negotiation among India, Pakistan, and the World Bank, which participated as an equal party representing the interests of the international community. Skilled facilitators assist the parties in modeling the problem, representing their preferences, and planning and executing their negotiation. Confidential information is managed securely by a neutral site, which maintains confidentiality while using this data to guide all parties toward a fair and efficient outcome.

The simulation is structured in distinct stages, each representing a critical phase of the negotiation process. At each stage, Smartsettle Infinity enables

[1] https://en.wikipedia.org/wiki/United_Nations_Military_Observer_Group_in_India_and_Pakistan
[2] https://thebulletin.org/doomsday-clock/

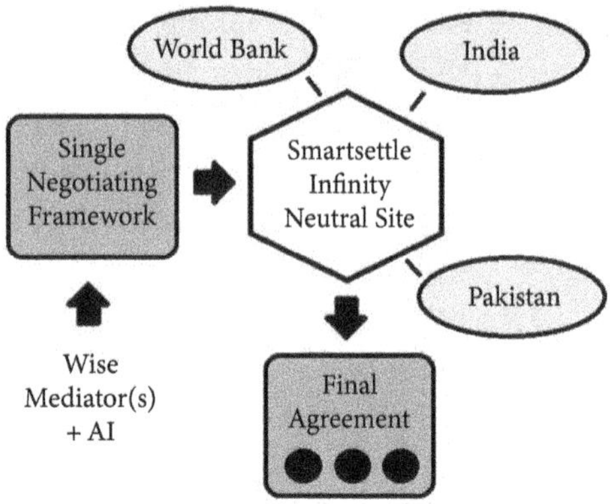

Figure 2.4 Overview of the Smartsettle Infinity Negotiation Process
Note: Elaborated by the authors.

participants to engage in collaborative problem-solving, guided by optimized suggestions generated by the system's advanced algorithms. These stages demonstrate how Smartsettle Infinity's preference modeling, intelligent feedback, and consensus-building tools help all parties move toward mutually beneficial solutions. At various points, we will present details of the simulation from India's perspective; viewpoints of other parties are available on the Smartsettle website.[3]

2.5.1 Simulation Process Stages

The Kashland simulation follows a structured negotiation process, consisting of six stages. Each stage illustrates Smartsettle Infinity's core functions and optimization capabilities in guiding the parties toward a fair and efficient solution.

Stage 1: SNF

The simulation begins with all parties collaborating to create an SNF, a foundational structure representing a new Indus Waters Treaty, with certain key issues left blank to be filled in once a final agreement is reached. The SNF serves as a blueprint for the negotiation, helping parties focus

[3] https://www.smartsettleresolutions.com/post/kashland-videos-descriptions

on the negotiation as a whole rather than addressing issues individually. This comprehensive framework ensures that all relevant topics are included and agreed upon at the outset, establishing a shared understanding and commitment to the negotiation process. Smartsettle Infinity supports this collaboration by allowing each party to contribute its perspectives discreetly, which the system then integrates into a cohesive, balanced structure.

Stage 2: Preference Modeling

With the SNF in place each party privately models its own preferences for each issue within the Infinity interface. This step is crucial for capturing the priorities, constraints, and flexibility of each party. Smartsettle Infinity allows participants to assign values to different options within each issue, reflecting their relative importance. This discreet, preference-based approach ensures that each party's priorities are accurately represented without disclosing confidential information to the other parties. Both India and Pakistan regarded security and economic stability as paramount. The World Bank's primary objective was to create a balanced and sustainable resolution that addresses both countries' concerns as well as the interests of the international community.

Issue Summary and Importance to India

Table 2.1 summarizes the issues that remain unresolved in the SNF, as initially agreed upon by the three parties. The relative importance of each issue, as listed in the table, was determined subjectively by India's representatives in a private breakout session,[4] with the system maintaining strict confidentiality. Later in this simulation, we demonstrate that one point in India's relative scoring system corresponds to approximately $100 million. It is important to note that each party's private preferences remain confidential throughout the negotiation.

To interpret these values, consider the Siachen Glacier issue, which holds a weight of 6 points. This means that permanent control over this territory is almost as valuable to India as the combined benefits of hydropower development and expanded water storage capacity (7 points). Note that the importance of each issue depends on the negotiating range for that

[4] In a real-life negotiation much more time would be taken to make sure that these values represent true preferences.

Table 2.1 Importance of the Issues to India

Negotiation issue	Importance to India Larger number → higher importance
Siachen Glacier jurisdiction (Status Quo, India, Pakistan)	6
India northwestern water storage (3–4 MAF)	3
India northwestern hydropower (15–25 GW)	4
Minimum southeastern flow (1–3 MAF)	1
Minimum Kishanganga flow (6–12 cm)	1
Both eliminate nuclear weapons (6–20 years)	40
UNMOGIP personnel (50–500)	0.2
International contribution to India ($0–$5B)	40
International contribution to Pakistan ($0–$5B)	NA
Net zero emissions target date (2040–2070)	14

Note: GW = gigawatts; MAF = million acre-feet; UNMOGIP = United Nations Military Observer Group in India and Pakistan. Elaborated by the authors.

issue. It is the difference between the best possible outcome and the worst possible outcome. The two most important issues for India have high importance ratings due to each being associated with a broad negotiating range.

India's Preference Representation

Figure 2.5 illustrates India's private point of view within the Smartsettle Infinity interface. On the left side, the issues from Table 2.1 are listed, each with a defined negotiating range. India's preferred values for each issue are indicated on the right side of the issue panel. India has also created several private reference packages by selecting values for each issue. These packages, visible only to India, are listed in the right-hand panel. They are rated based on the assigned relative importances and satisfaction functions for each issue. The names that India has assigned to these packages correspond to their overall ratings, reflecting India's prioritized outcomes.

As the negotiation is still in an early stage, no packages have been published or proposed, so there is nothing yet "on the table" for other parties to see. This setup preserves confidentiality while allowing India to organize and assess its preferences independently.

India ensures that its preferences are accurately represented within Smartsettle Infinity, allowing the system to generate optimal packages tailored to

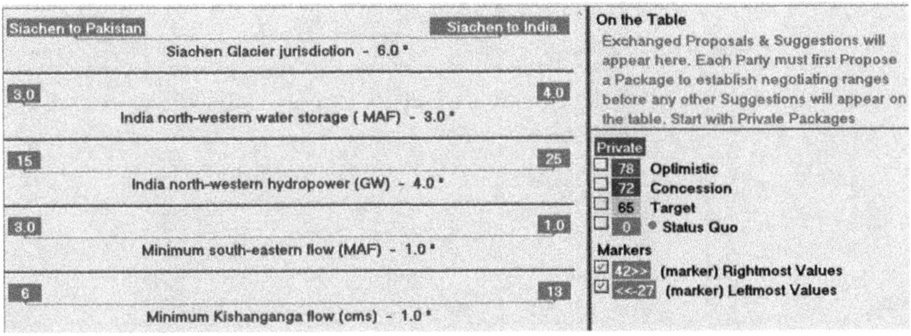

Figure 2.5 India's Private Point of View Within Smartsettle Infinity
Note: GW = gigawatts; MAF = million acre-feet. Elaborated by the authors.

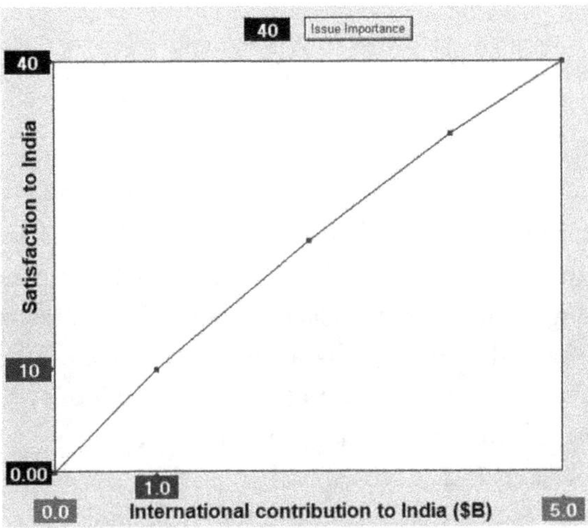

Figure 2.6 India's Satisfaction Graph for International Contribution to India
Note: Elaborated by the authors.

its goals. Behind each issue lies a satisfaction graph, which shows how satisfaction varies with different outcomes. Figure 2.6 illustrates the satisfaction graph for the issue of international contribution to India. This graph indicates that India's satisfaction increases as the contribution amount rises, with maximum satisfaction achieved at the highest possible contribution.

The graph's near-linear shape suggests that the importance India places on this issue is almost directly proportional to the range of possible outcomes, meaning each incremental increase in contribution corresponds to a roughly equal increase in satisfaction.

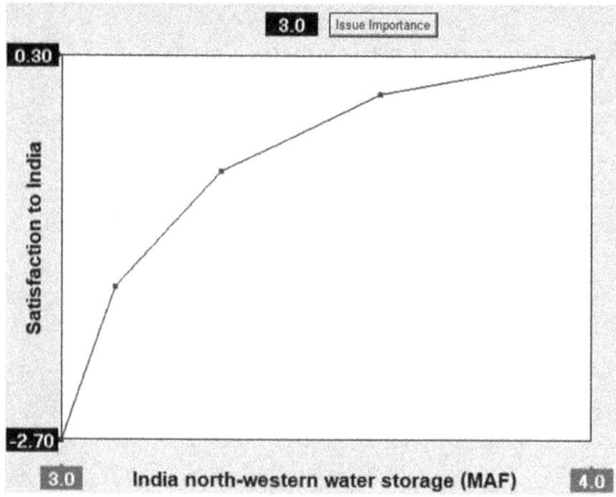

Figure 2.7 India's Satisfaction Graph for Water Storage
Note: MAF = million acre-feet. Elaborated by the authors.

The point on the satisfaction curve at $1 billion corresponds to 10 satisfaction points, meaning each satisfaction point in this range is worth approximately $100 million. Therefore, with the Siachen Glacier issue valued at 6 points, retaining control over the glacier is equivalent to around $600 million in value for India. Since India already controls the Siachen Glacier, maintaining the status quo nearly matches the value India would place on formalizing this control through negotiation.

Figure 2.7 presents India's satisfaction graph for water storage. The curve for water storage satisfaction is concave, reflecting India's current contentment with the existing capacity of 3.6 million acre-feet. This concave shape indicates that any further increase in storage capacity offers diminishing satisfaction returns for India.

Among India's private packages is a Status Quo package, which represents the absolute minimum acceptable outcome for India in this negotiation. India has set the Status Quo rating to zero, providing a baseline for comparison with other packages. This allows India to easily evaluate the relative value of alternative packages generated during the negotiation process.

With the Status Quo package set to zero, India can easily observe that its Target package is valued at 65 points higher, which equates to approximately $6 to $7 billion (see Figure 2.8). India aims to achieve at least this level of added value over the Status Quo in the negotiation process.

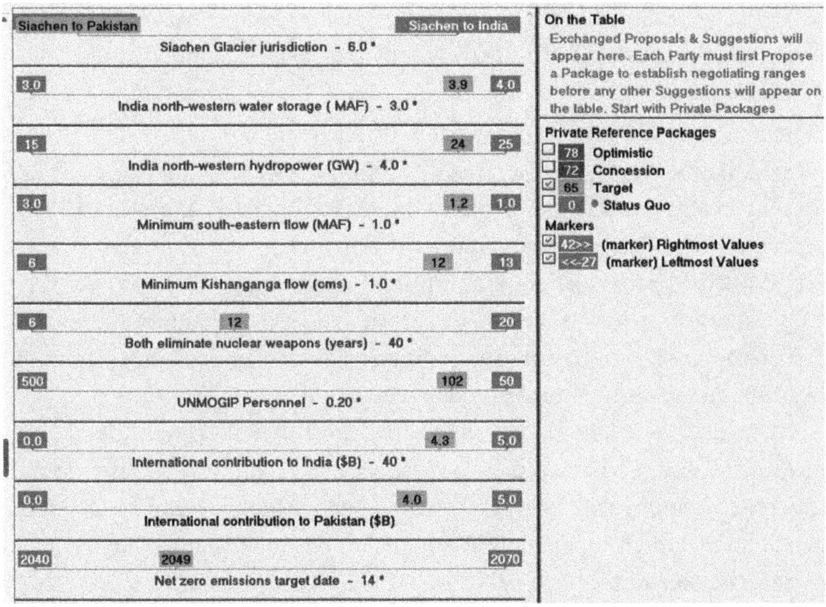

Figure 2.8 India's Target Package

Note: GW = gigawatts; MAF = million acre-feet; UNMOGIP = United Nations Military Observer Group in India and Pakistan. Elaborated by the authors.

Stage 3: Comprehensive Optimistic Proposals

With each party's preferences accurately represented, the bargaining phase begins with the exchange of optimistic proposals. Unlike traditional negotiations that address issues sequentially, Smartsettle Infinity enables parties to consider comprehensive proposal packages. This approach encourages India, Pakistan, and the World Bank to focus on the overall outcome rather than specific issues, helping to avoid impasses on individual points of contention.

The negotiation unfolds across several sessions, with each session building on the progress of the last. Initially, each party submits optimistic proposals that reflect slightly more than it realistically expects to achieve. This strategy leaves room for concessions, which are essential for reaching a mutually agreeable solution.

India initiates the bargaining process by submitting its optimistic proposal. When the other parties do the same, all three proposals appear "on the table." These initial optimistic proposals not only help to narrow the negotiating ranges but also allow space for each party to make concessions. The parties can continue negotiating in this way using complete packages, which is significantly more effective than addressing each issue individually.

Stage 4: Concessions and Dynamic Feedback

As negotiations progress, Smartsettle Infinity's *Multivariate Visual Blind Bidding* feature enables each party to submit visible concessions, complemented by intelligent suggestions from the system that significantly accelerate the process. These semi-optimal suggestions, tailored to the preferences and priorities of each side, act as guideposts, helping the parties explore potential agreements and optimal trade-offs without the distraction of knowing each other's exact preferences.

Through *anonymous suggestions*, parties can also make proposals without directly attributing them, reducing biases and fostering a cooperative atmosphere. This anonymity helps prevent any perception of weakness or undue conciliation, which is particularly important in sensitive negotiations such as those between India and Pakistan.

The goal of Smartsettle-generated suggestions is to guide the negotiation toward the *Pareto efficiency frontier*, where no party can improve its position without diminishing the satisfaction of another. When India privately accepts one of these suggestions, a yellow dot appears to indicate agreement, although it remains invisible to the other parties.

In this way, if all parties were to accept the same package, a consensus would be reached. When Session 1 ends with no agreement, the negotiation resumes in Session 2. In this session, India visibly offers a concession and utilizes a feature to submit an *anonymous proposal*. This proposal, which masquerades as a system-generated suggestion, helps to remove potential biases that could discourage acceptance by other parties.

Stage 5: Reaching a Baseline Agreement

As the parties move closer to consensus, Smartsettle Infinity provides semi-optimal suggestions for consideration. When one or more packages are mutually accepted at the end of a session, Infinity selects the fairest among them to establish a baseline agreement. This baseline serves as a stable foundation that reflects the progress made toward a balanced and mutually acceptable solution. At the conclusion of Session 2, India is pleased to see that its Masquerade proposal has become the Baseline Agreement, indicated by a green dot.

Stage 6: Final Agreement Optimization and Efficiency Frontier

Once a Baseline Agreement was established, Smartsettle Infinity applied its signature Maximize the Minimum Gain algorithm to harvest any remaining hidden value, guiding the parties toward a fair and optimized solution on the efficiency frontier. This final, optimized consensus is designed to be Pareto-optimal, ensuring that no party can improve its position without reducing the satisfaction of another.

As shown in Figure 2.9, the values for each issue in the final agreement differ from those in the Baseline. Some issue values are worth slightly less to India, while others have increased, resulting in an overall improvement of 4 points over the Baseline and 69 points above the Status Quo. Recall that each point is valued at approximately $100 million for India, signifying a considerable benefit. Smartsettle Infinity's algorithms ensure that the final package is both fair and efficient, maximizing the minimum gain for all

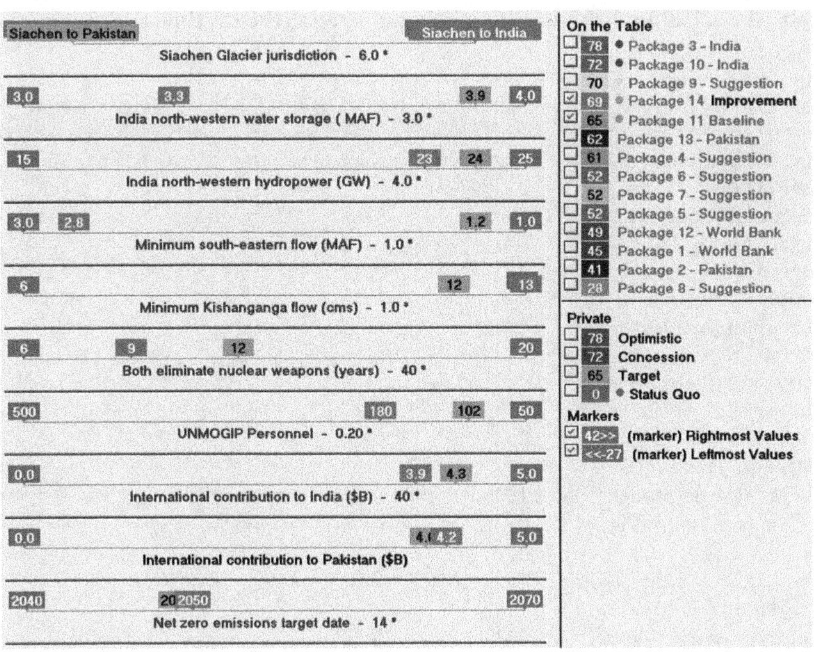

Figure 2.9 Improved Final Agreement Generated by Infinity Compared to the Baseline

Note: GW = gigawatts; MAF = million acre-feet; UNMOGIP = United Nations Military Observer Group in India and Pakistan. Elaborated by the authors.

parties and achieving a balance where further improvements for one party are not possible without reducing another's satisfaction.

Upon mutual acceptance of the improvement, Package 14 officially replaces the Baseline Agreement, becoming the Final Agreement. This efficient and equitable resolution marked the conclusion of the Kashland simulation as India, Pakistan, and the World Bank reached a mutually beneficial consensus on water allocation and related issues. By streamlining the decision-making process and guiding participants to an optimal solution, Smartsettle Infinity showcased its potential to significantly reduce negotiation time while enhancing outcomes.

With a robust framework established as the foundation for an international treaty, finalizing the negotiation involved simply filling in the agreed values, thus completing the process. Table 2.2 summarizes the Improvement compared to both the Baseline and Status Quo.

Table 2.2 Final Improved Agreement Compared to the Baseline and Status Quo

Negotiation issue	Status Quo	Baseline	Improvement
Siachen Glacier jurisdiction	Status Quo	Siachen to Pakistan	Siachen to India
India northwestern water storage (MAF)	3.6	3.9	3.3
India northwestern hydropower (GW)	20	24	23
Minimum southeastern flow (MAF)	2.0	1.2	2.8
Minimum Kishanganga flow (cm)	9	12	13
Both eliminate nuclear weapons (years)	20	12	9
UNMOGIP personnel	100	102	108
International contribution to India ($B)	0	4.3	3.9
International contribution to Pakistan ($B)	0	4.0	4.2
Net zero emissions target date	2070	2049	2050
Satisfaction rating to India	0	65	69

Note: GW = gigawatts; MAF = million acre-feet; UNMOGIP = United Nations Military Observer Group in India and Pakistan. Elaborated by the authors.

Given the earlier estimation of $100 million per point, the Improvement represents an added value of nearly $7 billion to India relative to the Status Quo. The simulation results demonstrate that Smartsettle Infinity not only addresses water-related conflicts but also fosters resolutions on other critical issues, contributing to a comprehensive and cooperative agreement.

This step marks the culmination of the Kashland simulation, where India, Pakistan, and the World Bank reached a fair and balanced agreement on water allocation and associated issues.

2.6 Simulation Review

Next, let us review the simulation by examining how the Smartsettle Multivariate Visual Blind Bidding process operates in satisfaction space. As depicted in Figure 2.10, this view of the negotiation assumes that each party's preferences have already been fully modeled and are known only to the Smartsettle system at the neutral site. This composite information remains strictly confidential and is never disclosed, even after the negotiation concludes. Figure 2.10 illustrates a two-dimensional projection of satisfaction space, showing India's preferences relative to Pakistan's.

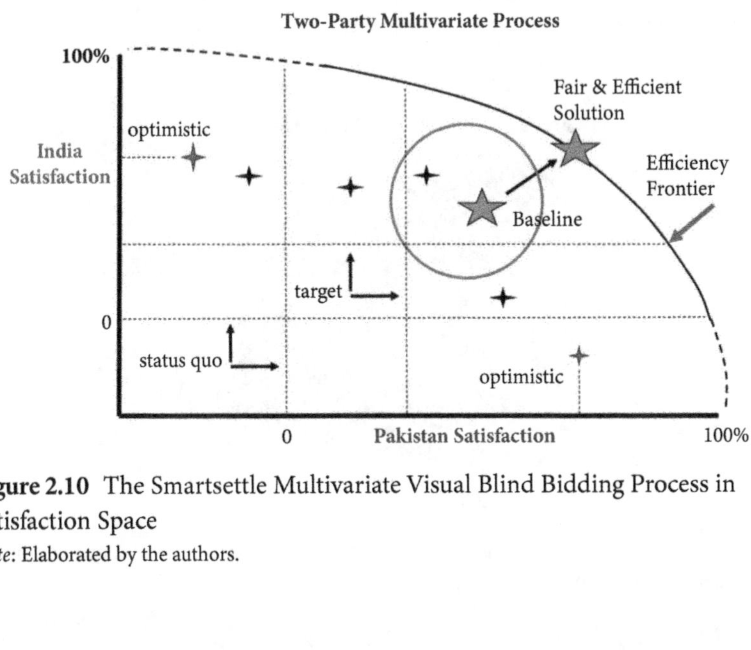

Figure 2.10 The Smartsettle Multivariate Visual Blind Bidding Process in Satisfaction Space

Note: Elaborated by the authors.

Each party has privately specified a minimum acceptable level of satisfaction, which we refer to here as the *Status Quo*. Above these levels is a space known as the *Zone of Possible Agreement* (ZOPA) bounded on the other side by the efficiency frontier, which represents the complete set of optimal outcomes. Smartsettle's objective is to help the parties reach a fair solution on the efficiency frontier.

A smaller area within this space is defined by each party's secret targets, which mark the satisfaction level each party privately hopes to achieve. During the bargaining phase, the Multivariate Visual Blind Bidding process encourages parties to begin with optimistic proposals—slightly more favorable than what they expect to settle for—allowing room for concessions without alienating the other side. In this example, both parties' initial proposals fall outside the ZOPA, meaning they would not be immediately acceptable to one another. However, Smartsettle can generate intelligent suggestions (represented by black stars) between these proposals. Some of these suggestions fall within the ZOPA and may appeal to both parties. Suggestions above the target levels, marked within the circle, are the ones most likely to lead to an agreement.

An agreement is reached at the end of a session if all parties accept the same package. This shared consensus, represented by the orange star, is called the *Baseline*. From this Baseline, Smartsettle then generates an optimized Improvement suggestion, represented by the green star, as the most balanced solution for all parties involved.

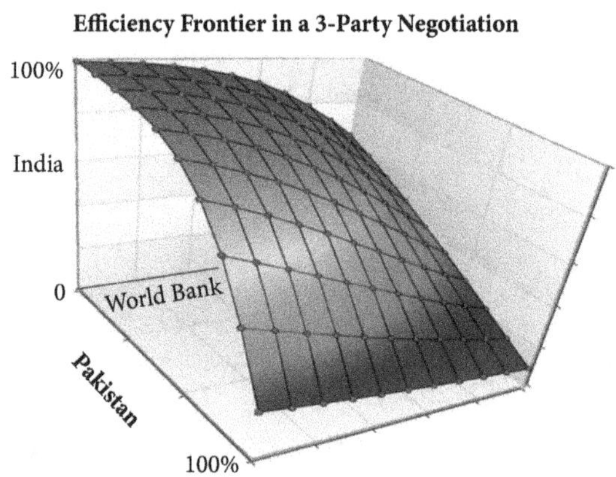

Figure 2.11 Hypothetical Efficiency Frontier in a Three-Party Negotiation
Note: Elaborated by the authors.

This negotiation approach can theoretically support any formal negotiation scenario between any number of stakeholders. In our case, with the addition of the World Bank, the efficiency frontier extends from a curve to a surface, as shown in Figure 2.11. While this three-party setup increases the negotiation's complexity, Smartsettle Infinity's interface maintains consistency for each party, focusing its view solely on its own perspective. This approach enables multi-party negotiations to feel as straightforward as two-party interactions, empowering each party to stay engaged with its individual priorities and the broader negotiation goals.

2.7 Conclusion

The Kashland simulation demonstrates Smartsettle Infinity's transformative potential in managing complex international water negotiations. Through its advanced preference modeling, dynamic feedback mechanisms, and Multivariate Visual Blind Bidding, Smartsettle Infinity enabled India, Pakistan, and the World Bank to move toward a fair, efficient agreement addressing water allocation and related regional challenges. By guiding participants through a structured negotiation process, the system promoted collaborative problem-solving while preserving each party's confidentiality and independence.

Unlike traditional DSMs that offer limited decision support or focus primarily on data analysis, Smartsettle Infinity provided a comprehensive negotiation experience. Its ability to generate semi-optimal suggestions, facilitate concessions, and refine solutions up to the efficiency frontier exemplifies a high level of process support that significantly accelerates reaching consensus.

The success of this simulation underscores the broader applicability of Smartsettle Infinity across various international disputes. Its capacity to handle complex, multi-stakeholder negotiations with sophisticated algorithms opens new avenues for addressing transboundary issues, from water management to environmental treaties and beyond. As global challenges become increasingly interconnected, the need for advanced tools like Smartsettle Infinity will only grow, paving the way for equitable, sustainable solutions in an era defined by resource scarcity and regional tensions.

Smartsettle Infinity stands out as a unique and advanced negotiation tool, offering features that go beyond conventional DSMs:

1. **Comprehensive Framework:** Smartsettle Infinity supports the end-to-end negotiation process, from defining shared objectives to reaching a final agreement, within a structured, collaborative environment.
2. **Advanced Problem-Solving Algorithms:** The system's multivariate preference modeling and optimization capabilities enable solutions tailored to each party's needs while maintaining confidentiality.
3. **Scalability and Flexibility:** Capable of handling any number of parties and issues, Smartsettle Infinity is adaptable to a broad range of formal negotiation contexts.
4. **Consensus Optimization:** The unique Multivariate Visual Blind Bidding feature allows parties to focus on the final resolution, minimizing interpersonal biases and emphasizing the overall outcome.

In summary, Smartsettle Infinity's eNegotiation and Collaboration System represents a significant advancement in conflict resolution, offering an innovative pathway to fair, sustainable agreements. As demonstrated in the Kashland simulation, this system has the capacity not only to resolve disputes but to foster cooperative, lasting relationships among nations and stakeholders worldwide.

References

Bolch, T., Kulkarni, A., Kääb, A., Huggel, C., Paul, F., Cogley, J. G., Frey, H., Kargel, J. S.,Fujita, K., Scheel, M., Bajracharya, S., & Stoffel, M. (2012). The state and fate of Himalayan glaciers. *Science, 336*(6079), 310–314.

Dinar, A., Dinar, S., McCaffrey, S., & McKinney, D. (2013). *Bridges over water: Understanding transboundary water conflicts, negotiation, and cooperation* (2nd ed., case study 3). World Scientific Publishers.

Droogers, P., & Immerzeel, W. (2010). *Preliminary data compilation for the Nile basin decision support system* (FutureWater Report 92). FutureWater. https://www.futurewater.eu/wp-content/uploads/2011/05/NBI_Data_Analysis_v7.pdf

Hipel, K. W., Fang, L., & Kilgour, D. M. (2003). *Conflict analysis: Models and resolutions.* Springer.

Immerzeel, W. W., van Beek, L. P. H., & Bierkens, M. F. P. (2010). Climate change will affect the Asian water towers. *Science, 328*(5984), 1382–1385.

India, Pakistan, and International Bank for Reconstruction and Development. The Indus Waters Treaty (with annexes). Signed at Karachi on 19 September 1960. United Nations—Treaty Series (vol. 419, pp. 125–292). https://treaties.un.org/doc/Publication/UNTs/Volume%20419/volume-419-I-6032-English.pdf

Kittikhoun, A., & Staubli, D. (2018). Water diplomacy and conflict management in the Mekong: From rivalries to cooperation. *Journal of Hydrology, 567*, 107–115. https://www.sciencedirect.com/science/article/abs/pii/S0022169418307534

Mirumachi, N. (2015). *Transboundary water politics in the developing world.* Routledge.
Salman, S. M. A., & Uprety, K. (2002). *Conflict and cooperation on South Asia's international rivers: A legal perspective* (Pt. 2). Law, Justice, and Development Series. World Bank.
World Bank. (2013). *Glaciers of the Himalayas: Climate change, black carbon, and regional resilience.*

3

A Painted Water Theory to Equip International Transboundary Basins Decision Support Models with Future Negotiation Vision

Mohammadreza Shahbazbegian and Ariel Dinar

3.1 Introduction

The evolution of decision support models (DSMs) in international transboundary water negotiations has shown significant progress in recent decades, with numerous scholars developing increasingly sophisticated tools for conflict resolution and cooperative management.[1] Thiessen and Louks's (1992) and Lotov's (1998) efforts to incorporate computer-based negotiation in water resources conflict management demonstrated early attempts to systematize negotiation processes through DSMs. The technical sophistication of DSMs has evolved remarkably, beginning with Palmer et al.'s (1999) basic optimization models and advancing through Cai et al.'s (2002) integration of multi-criteria decision analysis. The research conducted by Nandalal and Hipel (2007) on the graph model for conflict resolution in the Syr Darya River basin demonstrates an effort to suggest a DSM that provides optimal solutions for riparian states. Significant contributions have emerged in various geographical contexts, such as Pinard et al.'s (2009) analysis of the La Plata River basin negotiations and the implementation of the water allocation system in the Jordan River basin (Fisher & Huber-Lee, 2012), showcasing the diverse applications of DSMs

[1] This chapter departs from Shahbazbegian and Dinar (2023).

Mohammadreza Shahbazbegian and Ariel Dinar, *A Painted Water Theory to Equip International Transboundary Basins Decision Support Models with Future Negotiation Vision*. In: *Decision Support Models to Assist International and Transboundary Water Negotiations*. Edited by: Mohammadreza Shahbazbegian and Ariel Dinar, Oxford University Press. © Oxford University Press (2026). DOI: 10.1093/9780197802601.003.0003 in complex transboundary scenarios. A more recent investigation conducted by Comair et al. (2015) in the Orontes River basin integrated hydrological modeling with stakeholder perspectives, emphasizing the significant function of DSMs as tools for promoting negotiation rather than solely proposing optimal solutions. Modern systems have incorporated cutting-edge technologies, including Castelletti et al.'s (2013) pioneering implementation of reinforcement learning and recent innovations in uncertainty analysis through Wheeler et al.'s (2018) probability-based scenario analysis.

The odds are that contemporary advancements in negotiation will increase the potential for further enhanced DSM capabilities through interactive visualization tools (Almajano et al., 2013), digital platforms for multi-stakeholder participation (O'Sullivan et al., 2020), and sophisticated climate change integration models (Madani 2013). Moreover, the emergence of blockchain technology for transparent data sharing (Fasihullah et al., 2023) and advanced AI applications for pattern recognition in negotiation behaviors (Falcão Filho 2024) may represent the frontier of technical innovation that will enhance the applicability of DSMs in the near future for international water negotiation.

However, despite these impressive technical advancements, DSMs face a fundamental conceptual challenge when confronting human uncertainties and the complex reality of water politics. The fundamental limitation of DSMs in international water negotiations becomes evident when examining the critical gap between hydraulic mission and actual water demand. Consider a hypothetical transboundary river system shared by three riparian states—Upper, Middle, and Lower Riparian—with a total annual flow of 30 billion cubic meters (BCM). The DSM receives inputs based on each country's hydraulic mission: Upper Riparian declares 18.5 BCM for its national irrigation scheme, Middle Riparian claims 11 BCM for agricultural development, and Lower Riparian demands 13 BCM citing historical rights. Even the most sophisticated DSM, employing state-of-the-art optimization algorithms, machine learning, and multi-criteria analysis, would process these inputs to generate what appears to be an optimal allocation—perhaps 14, 9, and 7 BCM, respectively.

Nevertheless, this "optimal" solution basically misrepresents reality because it fails to recognize that the declared demands are manifestations of hydraulic missions rather than reflections of actual water needs. A deeper analysis reveals that real water demand, based on genuine consumption patterns and socioeconomic needs, might be significantly lower: approximately

8 BCM for Upper Riparian, 6 BCM for Middle Riparian, and 7 BCM for Lower Riparian. This disparity emerges not from technical limitations or infrastructural constraints but from politically motivated factors. States often include in their hydraulic missions agricultural projects that do not align with market demands or ecological conditions, water-intensive development plans maintained for political prestige rather than economic viability, and historical usage patterns that no longer reflect current societal needs. The DSM's output thus legitimizes and perpetuates unsustainable water capture goals rather than facilitating efficient resource allocation based on actual needs.

This conceptual gap creates a paradoxical situation where increasingly sophisticated technical solutions—whether employing AI, real-time data processing, or advanced uncertainty analysis—actually reinforce suboptimal outcomes by providing scientific legitimacy to politically motivated water capture goals. The challenge lies not in the DSMs' technical capabilities but in their fundamental inability to distinguish between politically driven hydraulic missions and genuine water needs. This suggests that future development in transboundary water negotiation support systems requires not just technical advancement but a paradigm shift in how we conceptualize and model water demand stemming from human behavior. Without such reconceptualization, DSMs face a risk of becoming increasingly sophisticated tools that precisely solve the wrong problem, ultimately contributing to, rather than resolving, the challenges of international water allocation.

The painted water (PW) concept, introduced originally by Shahbazbegian and Dinar (2023), emerges as a promising framework to address this fundamental limitation in DSMs by using a structured approach to decompose water demands into meaningful, reality-based categories. By classifying water into red water (non-negotiable), yellow water (negotiable), and green water (unnegotiable), PW offers DSMs a systematic method to distinguish between politically driven hydraulic missions and genuine water needs. This chapter argues that this categorization enables DSMs to transcend their current role of processing aggregate demands and instead evaluate water claims through multiple lenses of negotiability. The integration of PW into DSMs can transform these models from tools that inadvertently legitimize inflated water capture goals into systems that facilitate more realistic, acceptable, and sustainable water-sharing arrangements.

This chapter is structured to first highlight the key limitations of traditional DSMs and subsequently introduces the concept of PW as a promising alternative. Following this introduction, a detailed analysis of the PW framework is presented, exemplified by its application in the Blue Nile case study. The chapter then delineates seven notable advantages of incorporating PW into DSMs, which encompass flexible treaty development, encouragement of innovative solutions, enhancement of collaboration and conflict resolution, evaluation of environmental impacts, building of trust, scenario analysis, and the alignment of DSMs with hydropolitical factors. Furthermore, the chapter discusses the institutional frameworks essential for establishing water classifications, concluding with a reflection on future implications and strategic recommendations.

3.2 The PW Concept

3.2.1 Framework Overview

According to Shahbazbegian and Dinar (2023), the PW concept categorizes water flowing in a riparian state into three distinct classifications as follows:

Green water represents surplus water that riparian states cannot capture due to limited infrastructure, financial constraints, or geographic conditions. This category provides a foundational volume of water that naturally flows downstream, serving as an initial negotiation point and establishing a baseline for equitable allocation. It captures the water that exists beyond immediate national water-capturing ability, offering a transparent starting point for interstate discussions.

Yellow water introduces a more complex layer of water management, representing water that riparian states can technically control but do not immediately require for consumption. This category enables flexible, adaptive management strategies that can adjust to the dynamic demands of both upstream and downstream users. It allows for periodic reallocation based on current hydrological conditions and socioeconomic needs, creating a negotiable space for cooperative water resource management.

Red water represents the critical water resources fully captured and utilized by riparian states to meet domestic, agricultural, industrial, and environmental needs. This category is considered non-negotiable, highlighting the inherent limits of water sharing when riparian states' demands are high. It underscores the importance of clear communication and careful negotiation to prevent potential conflicts over essential water resources.

The combination of the three colors leads to a classification system showing how transboundary water negotiation can deteriorate from ideal cooperation (Class 1) to severe conflict (Class 7) as follows, largely based on water availability and upstream–downstream power dynamics:

1. DreamWater (Class 1): Ideal scenario where downstream states' water needs are fully met by upstream states' green water. No negotiations needed. Many major water treaties were signed during this phase.
2. Trust or Dare (Class 2): Similar to Class 1, but some downstream needs fall in the yellow water zone, requiring negotiation. Marks the beginning of upstream states' hydraulic development.
3. Give-and-Take (Class 3): Downstream states completely depend on negotiating for yellow water. Optimal for upstream states that gain maximum geographical advantage, though they do not need this water themselves.
4. Purgatory (Class 4): Downstream states must accept reduced water supply and some red water usage. No room for negotiation over green or red water.
5. Fear and Loathing (Class 5): More complex than Class 4. Downstream states must negotiate for yellow water while accepting red water usage, though they still receive some green water.
6. Hope Gap in Twilight (Class 6): No green water available. Downstream states must abandon red water–dependent activities and negotiate seriously for remaining needs.
7. Duel (Class 7): Most severe scenario. Minimal hope for downstream states to meet water needs even with negotiations. Upstream states make negotiations prohibitively costly, risking the entire basin's stability.

3.2.2 Adopting the PW concept in the Blue Nile River

Shahbazbegian and Dinar (2023) incorporated the PW concept into a system dynamics–based DSM to examine PW's applicability in future negotiation on the Blue Nile river basin, a critical water source that originates in Ethiopia's Lake Tana and contributes nearly 80% of the total Nile River's streamflow below Khartoum. The basin's significance is highlighted by its role in providing water and hydropower to multiple nations, particularly Ethiopia, Sudan, and Egypt, with complex historical relationships marked by both cooperation and conflict.

For their analysis, they employed the international futures model, developed at the Pardee Center for International Futures at the University of Denver, and Vensim software as a well-known tool for system dynamics to build a DSM that can map PW combinations for Ethiopia and Sudan as upstream states, while also examining possible PW combinations for Sudan and Egypt as downstream states over the long term until 2100. The DSM incorporates the United Nations Environment Program's Global Environment Outlook series, enabling comprehensive analysis across multiple domains including four main scenarios—"market first," "policy first," "security First," and "sustainability first"—each representing a different governmental priority and approach.

The results of the PW model provide critical insights into the potential future water dynamics in the Blue Nile basin, presenting a transformative perspective on water resource management among Ethiopia, Sudan, and Egypt through comprehensive scenario projections until 2100 (Figures 3.1 and 3.2).

The model demonstrates that Ethiopia will consistently generate a substantial amount of yellow water, positioning the country to potentially establish hydro-hegemony in the basin (Figure 3.1). The most significant finding suggests that Ethiopia could maintain strategic water control, with downstream states potentially remaining dependent on its yellow water allocation. The maximum potential for Ethiopia emerges when downstream states continue to rely on yellow water, primarily maintaining access to both green and yellow water supplies.

Sudan's water dynamics reveal a complex transition trajectory. The model predicts a potential movement from a state of purely green water availability to a combination of green and yellow water, with a brief interlude where

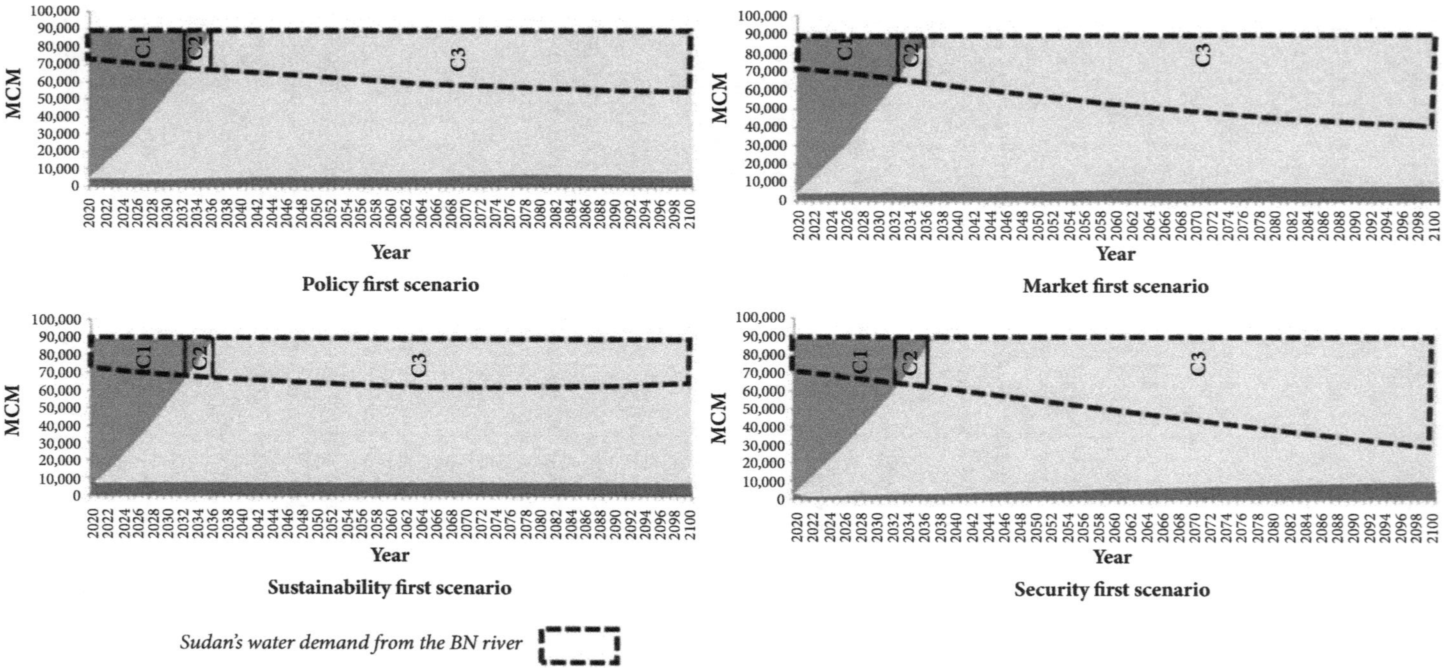

Figure 3.1 Simulated Results for Ethiopia's Available Water From the Blue Nile (BN) Through a Painted Water Lens and Negotiation Classes Before Sudan

Note: MCM = million cubic meters. From Shahbazbegian and Dinar (2023) with permission from the journal *Water*.

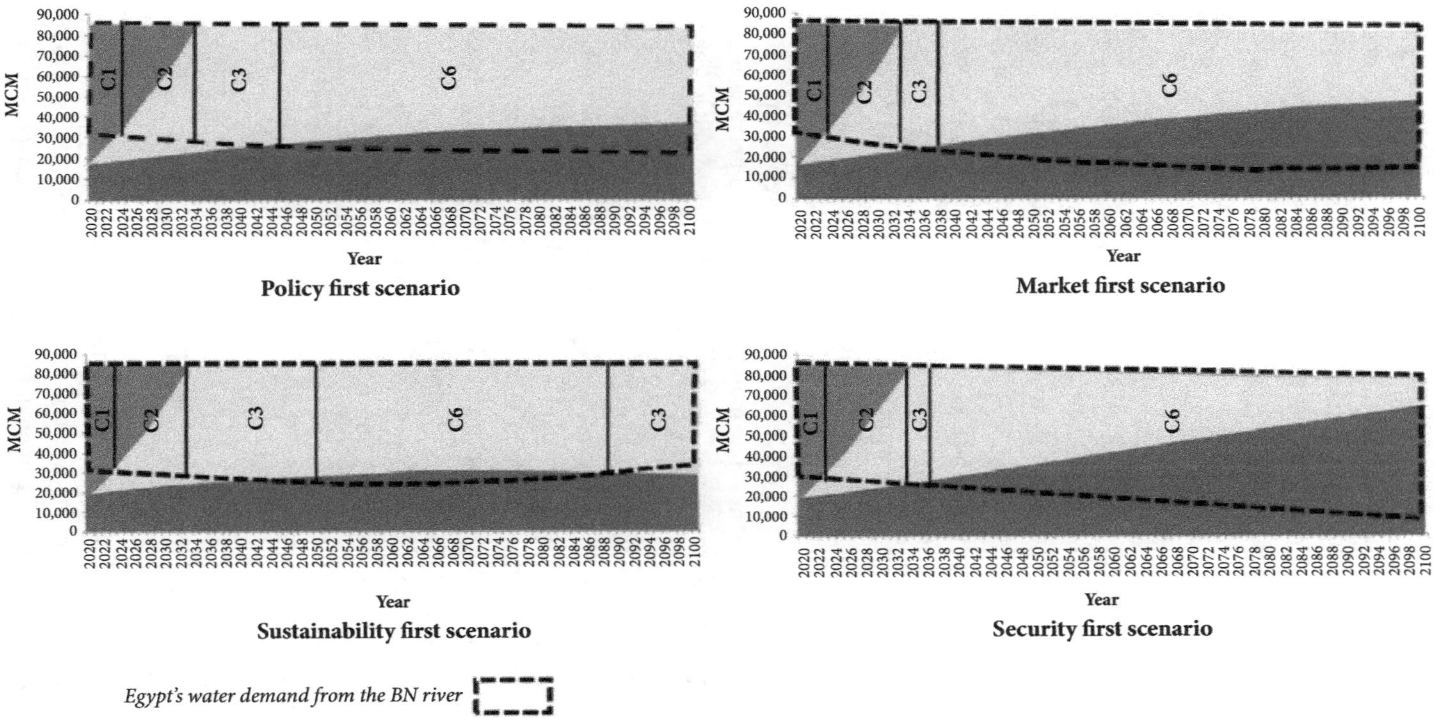

Figure 3.2 Simulated Results for Sudan's Available Water From the Blue Nile (BN) Through a Painted Water Lens and Negotiation Classes Before Egypt

Note: MCM = million cubic meters. From Shahbazbegian and Dinar (2023) with permission from the journal *Water*.

they have access to just yellow water (Figure 3.2). Despite these undesirable changes, the research indicates that Sudan would retain sufficient water resources to meet its demands through negotiation processes with Ethiopia. This suggests that Sudan's primary strategic approach should focus on successful negotiations while maintaining water availability as a key negotiation element.

Egypt faces the most challenging water scenario, with the model indicating a potential long-term situation where they must rely on a combination of yellow and red water under most scenarios, particularly the security-focused projections (Figure 3.2). This water availability pattern seriously jeopardizes Egypt's national security, potentially leaving the country with limited water resources. The model highlights that Sudan's and Egypt's growing water demands are the most significant factors driving Egypt's transition to more complex water availability patterns.

The research provides a critical warning: Reliance on purely green water will become obsolete in the Blue Nile basin, inevitably transitioning to more complex combinations of water types. The completion of Ethiopia's Renaissance Dam accelerates this transition, fundamentally altering the water dynamics for downstream states. The model suggests that to prevent unintended consequences, all riparian states must proactively coordinate their strategies.

For Egypt, the model recommends several critical strategies: decreasing dependency on Blue Nile water, carefully monitoring Sudan's water demand, and supporting Sudan's water management before engaging with Ethiopia. The finding suggests that Egypt can potentially avoid falling into a situation of relying solely on red water or a challenging combination of yellow and red water by changing its transition path, particularly by reducing water dependency in parallel with negotiations. The model indicates that Egypt should aim to maintain access to a combination of green and yellow water, rather than being forced into more constrained water availability patterns that could threaten its water security.

3.3 Added Value of PW for Traditional DSMs

By equipping DSMs with the PW lens, these models become valuable diplomatic instruments that can support the entire negotiation process, from initial technical analysis to final agreement implementation. Given the Blue

Nile case study, some of the prospective advantages of incorporating PW in DSMs will be elaborated in this chapter from several points of view.

3.3.1 Flexible Treaty Design

PW-based systems provide a comprehensive framework for designing adaptive water treaties that respond to changing conditions through water classification. These systems can support treaties that can adjust, based on water classification changes, such as modifying sharing arrangements for yellow water during wet versus dry years while maintaining minimum green water flows for ecosystem sustainability. The Blue Nile case study, particularly regarding Grand Ethiopian Renaissance Dam (GERD) operations, demonstrates how flexible release patterns based on water classifications can better serve the interests of multiple stakeholders.

The PW framework supports practical implementation through a staged approach that evolves with infrastructural and control capabilities. Treaties can include distinct provisions for different phases, such as GERD's filling period (converting green water to yellow water) versus long-term operation, with classification-based triggers marking transitions between stages. This approach extends to future infrastructural development, creating clear pathways for managing and compensating new projects that modify water classifications.

Operational mechanisms within the framework encompass several integrated components. The system enables sophisticated compensation mechanisms by identifying where and when compensation might be needed, such as benefit-sharing arrangements based on flow regulation values. Dispute resolution procedures can be precisely tailored, with different resolution pathways for yellow water management versus green water flow disputes. Monitoring and compliance mechanisms benefit from clear distinctions between water classifications, allowing for targeted oversight and graduated responses to non-compliance.

Environmental and emergency considerations are effectively incorporated through explicit recognition of green water's role in ecosystem services. Treaties can establish minimum flow requirements tied to green water proportions, ensuring environmental sustainability alongside development. During crises, specific provisions can govern temporary classification changes, with clear procedures for returning to normal operations, creating robust emergency response mechanisms that surpass traditional fixed-allocation approaches.

For long-term management, the framework enables data-driven treaty evolution through review and amendment procedures based on tracked changes in water classifications. This creates dynamic agreements that maintain stability while adapting to changing conditions, ensuring that treaties remain relevant and effective over time.

3.3.2 Reconciling DSMs With Hydropolitics

The PW classification system transcends traditional DSMs by explicitly acknowledging the political dimensions of water control, particularly in complex situations such as the Blue Nile basin. Using the GERD as an example, the framework demonstrates how converting green water to yellow water represents both a technical change and a shift in political leverage, making explicit the power dynamics that traditional models often leave implicit.

The framework effectively manages multilayered power relationships through its sophisticated classification system. In upstream–downstream dynamics, it balances growing physical control (through yellow water creation) with historical rights and vulnerabilities, creating nuanced negotiating spaces. This is particularly evident in complex positions like Sudan's dual upstream–downstream status, where water classification by controllability and use enables more dynamic agreements that accommodate evolving development needs and political priorities.

Sovereignty and security considerations are central to the framework's political capabilities. The system acknowledges each state's legitimate control over certain water resources (particularly yellow water) while maintaining shared responsibilities for others (such as green water flows). This balanced approach helps manage water-related security concerns by identifying when classification changes might create risks, enabling preemptive diplomatic interventions. The framework also bridges historical grievances with current realities, helping balance development aspirations with historical water dependencies.

The system strengthens regional cooperation and institutional management through several mechanisms. It identifies opportunities for broader cooperation beyond water management, such as power-trading arrangements based on hydroelectric generation from yellow water. The framework also effectively incorporates third-party interests, including international donors and regional organizations that influence water classifications, creating more comprehensive agreements within broader geopolitical contexts.

Political transitions and public engagement are enhanced through the framework's clear classification system. During periods of institutional reform or changing government priorities, understanding water classification impacts on state power helps maintain stable water relationships. Additionally, the system helps governments effectively communicate water management decisions to their populations, facilitating domestic support for international agreements in ways traditional DSMs cannot achieve.

3.3.3 Trust-Building

The PW framework enhances transparency in water management by making explicit each state's actual control capabilities. This is clearly demonstrated in the GERD case, where Ethiopia's conversion of green water to yellow water becomes visible to all parties, eliminating hidden assumptions about water control. This transparency extends to understanding genuine constraints as the classification system helps validate essential needs through objective criteria—whether identifying Ethiopia's red water requirements or Egypt's critical minimum flow needs.

The PW framework facilitates trust development through structural collaboration mechanisms. At the technical level, the classification system provides water experts from all countries with a common language, fostering professional relationships and cooperation. This technical foundation supports transparent data sharing by clearly defining monitoring requirements for each water classification, creating clear expectations and building confidence in shared information systems.

Trust-building is further strengthened through phased collaboration and joint planning. The framework transparently illustrates potential changes in water classifications over time, such as during GERD's filling phases, enabling nations to develop gradual confidence-building strategies. When countries can clearly see how their management decisions affect each other's water classifications, they engage in more meaningful joint planning discussions, building trust through shared problem-solving experiences.

The system effectively manages expectations and crises through clear delineation of water types. By explicitly identifying negotiable (yellow water) versus non-negotiable (red water) shares of the water flow, the framework prevents misunderstandings that could damage trust. During crises, this clarity helps countries demonstrate good faith through flexible management of yellow water while protecting essential red water needs.

3.3.4 Fostering Innovative Solutions

The PW framework promotes innovation by identifying opportunities in water classification transitions, particularly in infrastructure and operations. Using the GERD case study, innovations can focus on maximizing yellow water flexibility rather than just storage capacity, leading to advanced release patterns that benefit multiple stakeholders. This extends to downstream infrastructure, where smart technologies like automated gates can optimize water capture based on upstream yellow water availability while maintaining environmental flows.

The PW framework drives technological advancement across multiple operational areas. In monitoring and data management, the framework encourages development of sophisticated networks that track water classification changes in real time, potentially utilizing AI-powered systems for predictive management and blockchain-based platforms for transparent cross-border water accounting. These technological innovations support the development of integrated data platforms that provide comprehensive tracking of water classification changes and their implications (Katz, 2024).

Financial and economic innovations emerge through new understandings of water classification values. When converting green water to yellow water through infrastructure like GERD, innovative financing mechanisms can monetize downstream benefits from regulated flow, creating revenue streams for infrastructural improvements or compensation. This extends to risk management through innovative insurance products based on yellow water availability, providing financial protection during drought periods when water transitions to the red classification.

The framework promotes sectoral innovations in agriculture and energy production. Understanding water classification reliability enables development of smart farming solutions with adaptive irrigation systems and cropping patterns. In energy, clear visualization of how classifications affect hydropower potential encourages innovative hydropower-sharing arrangements and regional trading schemes. These sector-specific innovations benefit from targeted technology transfer, such as advanced seepage control and evaporation reduction systems for yellow water management.

Institutional and environmental adaptations complete the innovation set. The PW framework encourages development of new institutional arrangements specifically designed for managing different water classifications, such as joint bodies for yellow water coordination. Environmental innovations focus on nature-based solutions that maintain ecological flow levels while maximizing efficiency, including artificial wetlands for yellow water utilization. Looking forward, the system supports climate adaptation innovation by identifying where water classification changes might occur under different climate scenarios, encouraging development of resilient infrastructural designs for managing varying proportions of green, yellow, and red water.

3.3.5 Enhancing Cooperation and Conflict Prevention

DSMs based on PW provide a clearer framework for understanding each nation's actual capabilities and constraints. For example, in the case of GERD, when Ethiopia claims it cannot release more water during GERD filling, a PW-based DSM can help Sudan and Egypt understand whether this water is truly red (essential for Ethiopia's needs) or yellow (potentially negotiable), creating a more transparent basis for dialogue.

The framework excels at identifying negotiation windows during high-flow seasons, when Ethiopia's yellow water could support downstream needs while maintaining control—opportunities that traditional DSMs focusing solely on total volumes might miss.

PW-based DSMs are particularly effective at highlighting mutual benefits. Consider Sudan's position regarding Ethiopia and Egypt: A PW-based system shows how Sudan could benefit from Ethiopia's conversion of green to yellow water through GERD by having more regulated flow for its agricultural needs, while still maintaining sufficient flow to Egypt.

The framework provides superior capabilities for early warning of potential conflicts. By tracking transitions between water classifications, it can identify when a country might be approaching critical thresholds—for instance, if Egypt's reliance on yellow water from upstream is approaching unsustainable levels or if Ethiopia's conversion of green to yellow water is happening faster than downstream states can adapt to. This allows for preemptive diplomatic interventions before crises develop.

The system enhances trust-building by providing a common language for negotiations. Rather than each country using its own metrics and models, the PW framework offers a shared way of understanding and discussing water availability and control. This has been particularly valuable in the Blue Nile context, where different technical vocabularies and assessment methods have sometimes hindered productive dialogue.

In terms of power dynamics, PW-based DSMs help balance upstream physical control with downstream historical rights, creating a more balanced negotiating environment than traditional approaches.

During drought periods, understanding which water is green, yellow, or red helps countries prioritize their positions and identify where flexibility exists for emergency sharing arrangements, creating more options for crisis resolution than traditional approaches focused solely on fixed allocations.

3.3.6 Environmental Impact Assessment

Regarding dynamic water negotiability, GERD's 79-BCM capacity transforms Ethiopia's green water (naturally flowing downstream) into yellow water (manageable flow). A PW-based DSM can track this transformation's cascading environmental impacts, particularly on sediment transport patterns critical for Sudan's Gezira Scheme agriculture.

The case of Sudan's Roseires Dam demonstrates temporal analysis capabilities. A PW-based DSM analyzes how GERD's upstream conversion of green to yellow water affects Roseires's water management, especially during droughts when it must maintain critical environmental flows for wetlands and fishing communities.

Cross-border impact assessment through PW-based DSMs is illustrated by the High Aswan Dam. The PW framework analyzes how upstream water classification changes affect Egypt's ability to maintain environmental flows, particularly for the Nile delta's ecological functions and saltwater intrusion prevention.

For scenario analysis, PW-based DSMs evaluate how GERD's filling periods affect downstream water classifications. Rapid filling could force Sudan to convert its yellow water to red water to meet critical environmental needs, such as maintaining minimum flows for aquatic ecosystems.

The PW framework excels at assessing cumulative impacts of multiple dams. When GERD and Sudan's dams (Roseires, Merowe, Sennar) modify flows, a PW-based framework tracks how these successive conversions affect groundwater recharge and riverbank vegetation.

For stakeholder engagement, the PW framework helps communicate how operating scenarios affect each country's water security and environmental needs. It illustrates the importance of maintaining green water flow for ecological services, from Sudan's fishing to Nile delta agriculture.

Regarding climate change uncertainty, PW-based DSMs help predict how drought-induced water reclassification might affect environmental conditions throughout the basin, from the Ethiopian highlands to the Egyptian delta.

3.3.7 Scenario Analysis

A PW-based framework enhances scenario modeling by tracking transitions between green, yellow, and red water classifications across different scenarios, providing deeper insights than traditional flow volume analysis. This capability is particularly valuable when modeling complex situations like GERD operations, where understanding the conversion between water classifications directly impacts development and management strategies.

The framework excels at modeling comprehensive system dynamics through several integrated aspects. It can analyze power dynamics by tracking how development scenarios affect political leverage through water classification changes, helping anticipate potential tensions. The system also effectively models cumulative effects, showing how multiple changes throughout a basin might interact to create different futures, particularly valuable when analyzing the combined impact of multiple development projects.

Uncertainty and adaptation are core strengths of this modeling framework. It integrates various uncertainties—including climate change, population growth, and economic development—to show their impacts on water classifications over time. This connects directly to adaptive response modeling, demonstrating how countries might adjust their water management strategies based on classification changes. For crisis scenarios, the system analyzes how different emergencies affect water classifications and management capabilities, supporting more robust contingency planning.

The PW framework supports collaborative decision-making through enhanced stakeholder engagement and benefit-sharing analysis. The clear classification system helps stakeholders understand and contribute to scenario development, while the ability to model different approaches to yellow water management helps identify opportunities for mutual benefits. Additionally, the system can evaluate how different institutional arrangements and technological innovations might affect water classification management, helping identify robust governance structures and strategic investment opportunities.

A practical example of GERD operation during drought demonstrates these integrated capabilities:

1. Tracking drought impacts on green to yellow water conversion
2. Modeling classification changes under different operating rules
3. Analyzing adaptive responses to changing water classifications
4. Identifying cooperation opportunities and political pressure points
5. Evaluating potential benefit-sharing arrangements

3.4 Who Is Responsible for Reckoning PW?

If the PW concept were to be recognized in international water negotiation worldwide, the determination of water colors would require a sophisticated, multilayered approach involving multiple stakeholders and international mechanisms. The process would likely necessitate the establishment of an independent, internationally recognized body with representation from riparian states, scientific experts, and neutral international organizations.

A comprehensive water color classification commission would emerge as the primary mechanism for determining water colors. This commission would comprise experts from hydrology, international law, environmental science, and geopolitical studies, with mandatory representation from each riparian state in a transboundary basin. The classification process would rely on rigorous, transparent methodologies that consider multiple factors: hydrological data, infrastructural capabilities, seasonal variations, ecological requirements, and each state's demonstrated water needs. Scientific working groups would develop standardized protocols for quantifying water volumes, assessing infrastructural capacities, and evaluating critical consumption thresholds that differentiate between green, yellow, and red water categories.

The determination process would incorporate multiple validation mechanisms to ensure objectivity and prevent unilateral classifications. This would involve the following:

1. Mandatory multi-stakeholder consultations
2. Peer review processes involving independent scientific bodies
3. Regular reassessments using advanced monitoring technologies
4. Dispute resolution mechanisms through international water tribunals
5. Periodic reviews accounting for climate change, technological advancements, and evolving socioeconomic conditions

The ultimate governance of water color classification would likely fall under the broader framework of international water law, potentially overseen by bodies like the United Nations International Law Commission or a specially established transboundary water management authority. The goal would be to create a globally recognized system that provides a common language for water negotiations, moving beyond traditional sovereignty-based approaches to a more holistic, interdependent model of resource management.

3.5 Conclusion

The integration of the PW concept into DSMs represents a transformative approach to transboundary water negotiations, addressing fundamental limitations that have historically constrained these tools' effectiveness. By providing a structured framework for distinguishing between politically motivated water capture goals and genuine needs, PW-enhanced DSMs offer a more nuanced and realistic approach to water resource allocation. The framework's demonstrated capabilities in the Blue Nile context—from flexible treaty design to sophisticated scenario analysis—illustrate its potential to bridge the gap between technical optimization and political reality.

The enhanced DSMs show particular promise in several critical areas: They support the development of adaptive treaty mechanisms that can evolve with changing conditions, facilitate innovative technical and institutional solutions, provide more sophisticated environmental impact assessments, and create stronger foundations for trust-building among riparian states. Perhaps most importantly, they offer a practical pathway for reconciling the technical capabilities of modern DSMs with the complex realities of hydropolitics.

Looking forward, the success of PW integration will depend largely on the development of robust institutional frameworks for water classification and the willingness of riparian states to engage with this more transparent approach to water negotiations. While challenges remain in implementing such systems at an international scale, the potential benefits—including more sustainable agreements, reduced conflict potential, and improved environmental outcomes—suggest that this evolution in DSM capability represents a crucial step toward more effective transboundary water management. The PW framework thus offers not just a technical enhancement to existing models but a new paradigm for understanding and negotiating shared water resources in an increasingly water-stressed world.

References

Almajano, P., Trescak, T., Esteva, M., Rodriguez, I., & Lopez-Sanchez, M. (2013). v-mwater: An e-government application for water rights agreements. In S. Ossowski (Ed.), *Agreement Technologies* (pp. 583–595). Springer.

Cai, X., McKinney, D. C., & Lasdon, L. S. (2002). A framework for sustainability analysis in water resources management and application to the Syr Darya basin. *Water Resources Research*, *38*(6), 21-1–21-14.

Castelletti, A., Pianosi, F., & Restelli, M. (2013). A multiobjective reinforcement learning approach to water resources systems operation: Pareto frontier approximation in a single run. *Water Resources Research*, *49*(6), 3476–3486.

Comair, G., Maidment, D., & McKinney, D. (2015). Decision support for improvement of the management and cooperation for the Orontes River. In R. Ballabio, F. G. Comair, M. Scalet, & M. Scoullos (Eds.), *Science diplomacy and transboundary water management: The Orontes River case* (pp. 185–208). UNESCO.

Falcão Filho, H. A. (2024). Making sense of negotiation and AI: The blossoming of a new collaboration. *International Journal of Commerce and Contracting*, *8*(1–2), 44–64.

Fasihullah, A., Awan, B., & Hulio, A. K. (2023). Negotiating in the digital age: Exploring the role of technology in modern negotiations. *Law and Policy Review*, *2*(1), 61–86.

Fisher, F., & Huber-Lee, A. (2012). *Liquid assets: An economic approach for water management and conflict resolution in the Middle East and beyond*. Routledge.

Katz, D. (Ed.). (2024). *World scientific handbook of transboundary water management: Science, economics, policy and politics: Vol. 2. Tapping technologies: The role of technological change in transboundary water management.* World Scientific Publishers.

Lotov, A. V. (1998). Computer-based support for planning and negotiation on environmental rehabilitation of water resource systems. In D. P. Loucks (Ed.), *Restoration of degraded rivers: Challenges, issues and experiences* (pp. 417–445). Springer Science+Business Media.

Madani, K. (2013). Modeling international climate change negotiations more responsibly: Can highly simplified game theory models provide reliable policy insights? *Ecological Economics, 90*, 68–76.

Nandalal, K. D. W., & Hipel, K. W. (2007). Strategic decision support for resolving conflict over water sharing among countries along the Syr Darya River in the Aral Sea basin. *Journal of Water Resources Planning and Management, 133*(4), 289–299.

O'Sullivan, J., Pollino, C., Taylor, P., Sengupta, A., & Parashar, A. (2020). An integrative framework for stakeholder engagement using the basin futures platform. *Water, 12*(9), Article 2398.

Palmer, R. N., Werick, W. J., MacEwan, A., & Woods, A. W. (1999). Modeling water resources opportunities, challenges and trade-offs: The use of shared vision modeling for negotiation and conflict resolution. In E. M. Wilson (Ed.), *WRPMD'99: Preparing for the 21st Century* (pp. 1–13). ASCE Press.

Pinard, M., Kempkey, N., Dinar, A., & Pochat, V. (2009). Negotiations over water and other natural resources in the La Plata River basin: A model for other transboundary basins? *International Negotiation, 14*(2), 253–279.

Shahbazbegian, M., & Dinar, A. (2023). Painted water—A concept to shape water negotiation strategies in shared river basins. *Water, 15*(19), Article 3343.

Thiessen, E. M., & Loucks, D. P. (1992). Computer assisted negotiation of multiobjective water resources conflicts 1. *JAWRA Journal of the American Water Resources Association, 28*(1), 163–177.

Wheeler, K. G., Hall, J. W., Abdo, G. M., Dadson, S. J., Kasprzyk, J. R., Smith, R., & Zagona, E. A. (2018). Exploring cooperative transboundary river management strategies for the eastern Nile basin. *Water Resources Research, 54*(11), 9224–9254.

4
Multi-Criteria Decision Analysis and the Eristic-Dialectical Model for Conflict Resolution in Transboundary Water Resources Management

Jacques Ganoulis and Charalampos Skoulikaris

4.1 Introduction

Barriers can be on different issues, such as natural, cultural, linguistic, administrative, or political, when they separate countries at the international level. Very often, natural barriers, such as significant rivers and mountain chains, have become historically political boundaries for different nations. Examples are the Pyrenean Mountains separating France from Spain, the Alps between Italy and several other European countries, the Rhine River as a political border between France and Germany, and the Danube River as a frontier between 17 European countries. During historical armed conflicts, when technical military tools were limited, armies were stopped in front of significant rivers or mountains that became political borders.

Transboundary water resources (TWRs) can be surface freshwater, like river and lake catchments, or groundwater in the form of transboundary aquifers and groundwater bodies. Most of the world's TWRs are shared by two or more countries. Globally, 310 transboundary river basins have been identified, covering 47% of the globe's land surface and hosting 45% of the world's population (McCracken & Wolf, 2019). About 592 transboundary aquifers and 226 transboundary "groundwater bodies," as defined by the European Union Water Framework Directive, have also been identified (UNESCO, International Groundwater Resources Assessment Centre, & World Meteorological Organization, 2015). These numbers may change

Jacques Ganoulis and Charalampos Skoulikaris, *Multi-Criteria Decision Analysis and the Eristic-Dialectical Model for Conflict Resolution in Transboundary Water Resources Management*. In: *Decision Support Models to Assist International and Transboundary Water Negotiations*. Edited by: Mohammadreza Shahbazbegian and Ariel Dinar, Oxford University Press. © Oxford University Press (2026). DOI: 10.1093/9780197802601.003.0004 if new countries emerge by adding new political borders, and better technology may increase the counting of transboundary aquifers. In the era of climate change and especially in regions of persisting drought and water scarcity, TWRs are a significant part of the available freshwater on Earth and can be a vital water resource for many riparian countries.

The etymology of the word *rival* goes back to the Latin *rivus*, meaning "a stream." It is an example of conflict and cooperation about the river because it describes a person who uses the same river as another and, depending on the context, someone who competes with another for the same objective. Further to rivers as political borders, sharing TWRs through conflict and cooperation is much more complicated when political borders divide the river catchment into upper and downstream areas. The upstream–downstream water geography may produce conflicts because upstream countries dominate available water resources and consider water a domestic natural resource (Zeitoun & Warner, 2006). The way TWR management (TWRM) is implemented creates conflicts and cooperation at different levels. Significant global hotspots for conflicts are the United States–Mexico dispute over the Rio Grande, the Egypt–Ethiopia conflict over the Nile, and the Afghanistan–India disagreement on sharing the Indus River water (Ganoulis & Fried, 2018), to name a few. From a spatial point of view, conflicts on TWRM can occur inside the country at local and regional scales and at the international level. Above all these conflicts, we may also recognize those that are generic between humans and the laws of nature. As we explain in this chapter, if TWRM is implemented without major human interventions in accordance with hydrological, hydraulic, and ecological laws, environmental externalities can be reduced, and a harmonic symbiosis between humans and nature can be achieved.

TWRM's primary goal is to allocate TWRs between riparian countries, considering different parameters, such as population, climate, hydrological and socioeconomic characteristics, and the application of international law (United Nations [UN], 1997). Water-generated conflicts may have different origins, such as socioeconomic, technical, environmental, and political. They can be related to water quantity, water quality, climatic conditions, economic revenues, implementation measures of water resource management (WRM), and political issues of water governance. Tayia (2019) presented a comprehensive review of various approaches for TWR conflict resolution. Engineering studies focus on optimal TWR allocation using a systems formulation. Economic studies use game theory, virtual water, and socioeconomic planning to identify economic benefits for a fair sharing of TWRs among riparian states. Political and institutional studies use alternative dispute resolution and hydropolitics to promote cooperation agreements. In the past, conflict and cooperation were considered in one-dimensional space, starting from conflict with a minimum indicator value to a maximum indicator for cooperation (Yoffe et al., 2003). The Transboundary Waters Interaction NexuS introduced by Mirumachi and Allan (2007) underlines the coexistence of conflict and cooperation, offering a two-dimensional approach for conflict resolution.

TWRM can be formulated on a multi-objective conflict resolution framework involving different general goals with many particular targets described by multiple indicators. In our approach, we aim to identify WRM options acceptable to all parties based on a fair distribution of socioeconomic, technical, and environmental benefits that will lead to a win–win agreement. A multiple-objective formulation aims to identify alternatives that maximize benefits and minimize losses. For example, we can cite the UN Sustainable Development Goal (SDG) 6 on Water and Sanitation (UN, n.d.). The particular target 6.5 on integrated WRM (IWRM), including TWRM, contains two particular indicators, 6.5.1 and 6.5.2, that describe the percentage of IWRM implementation and the proportion of a river's catchment covered by a common agreement.

In this chapter, we focus on modeling TWRM conflict resolution in two ways: (1) as a complex multi-criteria process of conflict and cooperation between riparian countries and (2) as a sociotechnical activity based on an eristic-dialectical model (EDM) showing human behavior against nature. Although conflicts have a negative connotation, in our approach they play a positive role in enhancing cooperation. For example, transboundary water-related conflicts can be the driver for promoting international agreements, and their conflict resolution can be an essential step for efficient cooperation. The background for understanding the origin of transboundary and domestic conflicts on WRM is based, on the one hand, on hydrological simulation and multi-criteria decision analysis (MCDA) models of conflict resolution between stakeholders (Ganoulis et al., 2008) and, on the other, on a dialectical analysis of the interplay of conflicts between humans and the laws of nature (Ganoulis, 2021, 2023, 2024).

A historical analysis indicates that the human–water interaction depends on the balance of power between human societies and nature. It contains the coexistence of an apparent contradiction of *conflict* and *cooperation*. This paradox is *dialectical* because it can be explained by formulating opposite logical arguments. Conflict and cooperation dialectics can be taken as an ontological and as an epistemic principle as well (Ganoulis, 2023, 2024). Depending on the socioeconomic development of human societies and the climate conditions on Earth, the dialectical conflict and cooperation behavior has taken historically three different cluster forms: *naturalistic*, *dualistic*, and *anthropocentric*.

The anthropocentric WRM approach became visible after the Industrial Revolution in the late 18th century, in relation to global climate change. It produced massive environmental externalities, like water pollution, loss of biodiversity, and an increase of natural disasters, such as heat waves, floods, and droughts. The MCDA methodology addresses the resolution of domestic and international conflicts, mainly related to socioeconomic and environmental issues. The EDM is used as a tool for tuning human social activities with the water-related laws of nature. Both approaches are illustrated in the case study of the Mesta/Nestos River, shared between Bulgaria and Greece.

4.2 The Dialectics of Human–Nature Conflicts

In previous studies, the paradox of conflict and cooperation coexistence in TWRM was recognized without a theoretical explanation (Mirumachi & Allan, 2007; Yoffe et al., 2003). Based on a historical review of the human–nature interaction, we argue that this paradox is apparent and therefore dialectical. It can be explained logically by considering the balance of power between humans and nature (Ganoulis, 2021, 2023, 2024).

Considering the IWRM model as the state-of-the-art model of WRM, the integrated TWRM (ITWRM) is the best available TWRM model. However, the ITWRM model is technocratic and human-centered. Consequently, to ensure environmental resilience, a new model of a dialectical behavior of humans to nature is suggested based on tuning human activities to the laws of nature.

4.2.1 Historical Analysis of Human–Nature Interaction

The way humans represent nature and natural resources depends on the degree of socioeconomic and cultural development of human societies. Our modern living conditions are pretty different from those in the past. For example, traveling long distances by airplanes at high altitudes and using

GPS and satellite communications daily have influenced our viewpoint of nature. Our current image of the universe is undoubtedly quite different from what we may have had in the past. The contemporary vision of nature is not due to the progress made in natural philosophy but mainly related to modern developments in science and technology.

Heisenberg (1958), the German physicist and Nobel laureate in 1927, suggested in his paper that the change in the human–nature relationship has its roots in the historical evolution of our scientific representation of nature. The medieval picture of nature with the Earth at the center of the universe was understood as the perfect work of God. In the 17th century, the works of Kepler, Galileo, and Newton created the foundations of a science independent from God. Newtonian mechanics formulated the background for the experimental and mathematical description of the "laws" of nature that are valid throughout the cosmos. The progress in mechanics and the development of thermodynamics in the 18th and early 19th centuries were at the origin of the Industrial Revolution. Technological progress in this context made using natural forces for human interests possible. With atomic physics in the late 19th century and quantum mechanics and the uncertainty principle in the early 20th century, our vision of nature at a scale finer than an atom is not independent of our visioning method. Still, it depends on the means at our disposal.

Operated by NASA, the Hubble space telescope made recently possible observations of the "redshift" phenomenon that used to determine the expansion rate of our universe ("Hubble Space Telescope," 2025). From the so-called Hubble constant the cosmic clock was rewound and the age of the universe estimated to be 13.8 billion years, roughly three times the age of Earth. About six million years ago the first hominids appeared on our planet, and the human–nature interaction has been since then in constant evolution. Although humans are closely related to nature and are part of it, in prehistoric times they felt it necessary to compete with natural forces to survive and improve their living conditions. This was not only for protecting themselves from natural disasters, such as floods, hurricanes, and tsunamis, but also for controlling, appropriating, and even mastering natural resources, such as water, food, and energy. This was obvious when humans struggled to survive in a hostile environment dominated by wild animals, floods, volcanic eruptions, and low temperatures.

During the era between 100,000 and 12,000 years ago, a period scientists call the *Pleistocene*, humans experienced different climatic hazards. As

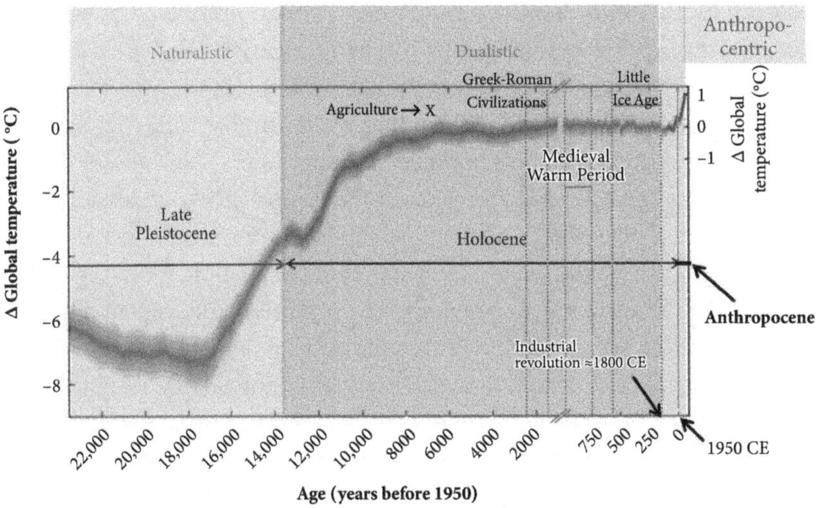

Figure 4.1 Global Temperature–Humans Interplay Over the Past 24,000 Years
Note: From Ganoulis (2023), with automatic permission from the journal *Water*.

shown in Figure 4.1, during the Late Pleistocene, our planet was dominated by temperatures as low as −8°C. During that period, securing life under severe climate conditions was a priority. Scientific developments and technical tools to manage natural resources were almost nonexistent, and humans considered cosmic forces like the sun to be gods controlling human existence. Nature dominated humans during that period, which we can call *naturalistic.*

As we can see in Figure 4.1, after the Late Pleistocene, which had the last glacial period, the global temperature on Earth was steadily increasing to reach a constant mean value. The geological age that started around 11,700 years ago was particularly beneficial to humans and is called the *Holocene* or the *Age of Man* (Muller & MacDonald, 2000). During the Holocene period, humanity started experiencing new ways of living and developing healthy socioeconomic activities, starting with agriculture and trade. Social interaction and cultural progress were facilitated by creating larger human settlements, and the first important cities flourished in places of fertile agricultural land. Extensive agriculture was developed with large quantities of irrigation water from big rivers like the Nile in ancient Egypt, the Tigris and Euphrates in Mesopotamia (Middle East), the Indus River in South Asia, and similar sites in China and South America. Old cities like

Babylon, located in present-day Iraq, were founded more than 4000 years ago, and ancient civilizations like the Minoan on the island of Crete go back more than 3000 years. In island and coastal areas across the Mediterranean nautical powers were developed, leading to the trading of artifacts, pottery, and agricultural products between cultural centers like Knossos on the island of Crete and Mycenae and Pylos in the Peloponnese. Advanced water infrastructure for drinking water supply and sanitation was found in Knossos. Subterranean aqueducts for water supply and irrigation known as *canats* transporting groundwater by gravity were discovered and implemented in ancient Persia, Egypt, and China. At the same time, *norias*, big circular hydraulic pieces of machinery, were invented in the city of Hama, Syria, to elevate water from the Orontes River to a higher elevation for irrigation. There is strong evidence that norias were in operation under the Romans in Syria at least by 350 CE. The rise and fall of the Greek and Roman civilizations in Europe took place roughly from 500 BCE to 400 CE (Whalen, 2020). During that period of significant technical progress, humans gradually moved their relationship with nature from a naturalistic type to a *dualistic* type until the beginning of the second Industrial Revolution in 1800 (Figure 4.1). During that period, although conflict and cooperation coexisted, equilibrium was reached between human respect for nature and fighting against natural forces. Examples of this *dualistic* behavior come from ancient civilizations like the Greek and Chinese where natural resources like rivers were respected as gods and at the same time as enemies producing floods and natural disasters. In ancient Greece, one of the major rivers in central Greece, the Achelous River, although it was considered to be a demigod, at the same time is depicted on pottery as a giant snake producing catastrophic floods fighting with Hercules, the national hero, who finally defeated him (Figure 4.2).

The period starting around 1800 CE introduced new global climatic conditions, with a temperature constantly rising, and a profound change of socioeconomic activities in the Global North (Europe and the United States). The scientific and technical progress in mechanics and thermodynamics accelerated the first industrial revolution (Sharma & Singh 2020), with Otto's steam engine in England as a landmark. Massive production of internal combustion engines like cars and other industrial goods, the railway expansion, and the emergence of electrical inventions modified completely the way of living and working. Agricultural labor has radically changed with the use of tractors, pumps, and other machines. The post-industrial era we experience was dominated by an intensive use of carbon-related fossil

Figure 4.2 Hercules Combating Achelous River (British Museum, London)
Note: https://www.wikiwand.com/en/Achelous (open-access source).

resources and the emission of huge quantities of the so-called greenhouse gases, like CO_2 and methane. As shown in Figure 4.1, after 1800 we observe a systematic temperature rise as an indication of global climate change. During this period, progress in science and technology made humans believe they could domesticate nature and use natural resources to maximize their benefits. We may call this period *anthropocentric*, and according to some scientists we entered a new era, called the *Anthropocene*, which means a period dominated by humans (Figure 4.1).

We may resume our historical analysis as follows:

(1) From prehistorical times, the human–nature relationship has been composed of two opposites: conflict and cooperation.
(2) The coexistence of conflict and cooperation can also be accepted as an ontological and epistemic principle. The following relationship can express it:

$$(\text{Conflict}) \times (\text{Cooperation}) = \text{C} \qquad (1)$$

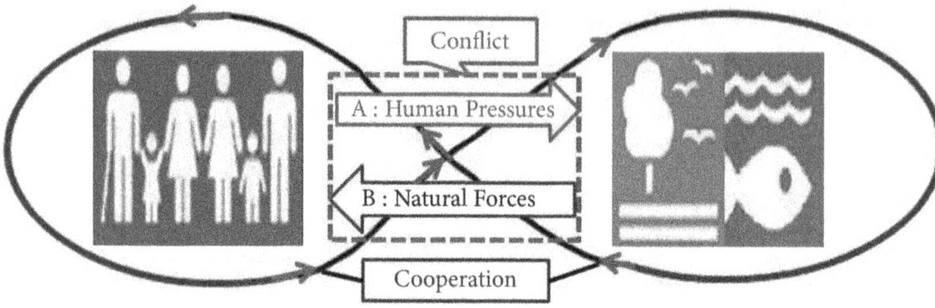

Figure 4.3 The Human–Nature Paradox of Conflict and Cooperation
Note: Elaborated by the authors.

This relation means that increased cooperation reduces conflict and vice versa. C is a constant depending on the degree of conflict or cooperation in any particular watershed.

(3) The conflict–cooperation paradox is dialectical because it can be explained by the balance of power between natural forces on humans and human pressures on nature (Figure 4.3).
(4) Depending on the ratio between human pressures and natural forces, three clusters of human–nature interplay are observed historically: naturalistic, dualistic, and anthropocentric.

4.2.2 The Anthropocentric Human–Nature Interplay

As shown in Figure 4.4, the global temperature has steadily increased since the Industrial Revolution, a phenomenon well known as *global warming* (GW). GW is producing substantial environmental challenges, including risks to water security, floods, and droughts. The change in WRM models following the global temperature rise is shown in Figure 4.4.

Three types of temperature variation and subsequent models of WRM are distinguished:

(1) Early GW, from 1850 to 1945. During this period, an increase of less than 0.5°C in the global mean temperature was observed (Figure 4.4). This is the period with massive CO_2 emissions following the second Industrial Revolution in 1850. During these years, science and technology grew exponentially, especially in the hydraulic/hydrological

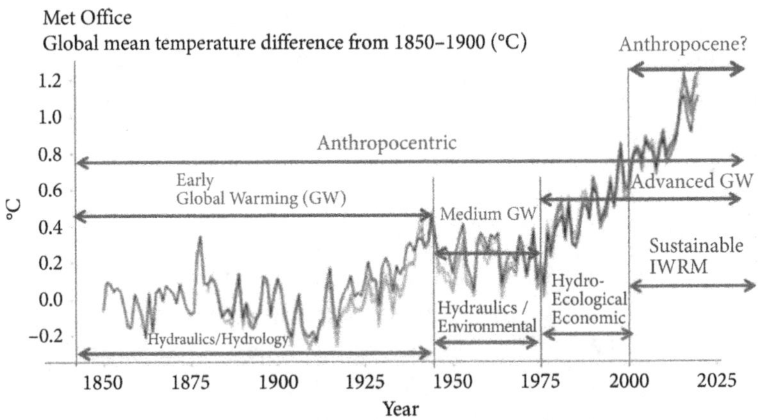

Figure 4.4 Change of water resources management in relation to global warming since the industrial period.

Note: GW = global warming; IWRM = integrated water resources management. From Ganoulis (2024), with automatic permission from the journal *Sustainability*.

engineering domain. In 1935, designing and constructing the giant Hoover Dam, which created Lake Mead in the Colorado River, USA, was a milestone for civil engineering performance. Although it was designed to last more than a millennium, today, less than a century after its construction, persistent drought, water overuse, and climate change have reduced Lake Mead to 35% of its capacity (Rivera-Torres et al., 2021). Since the time of the Industrial Revolution, humans have become confident and have thought of dominating nature by managing big rivers and water resources as human assets. We may call this period anthropocentric, that is, human-dominated (Figure 4.4).

(2) Medium GW, from 1945 to 1975. The global mean temperature during this time seems stable but still exceeds the average 1850–1900 reference temperature. Over these 30 years of implementation of anthropocentric WRM models, signs of adverse environmental impacts started to be visible. Point and diffuse pollution in rivers, lakes, and groundwater mobilized environmentalists and nongovernmental organizations. A milestone of this period was the 1972 UN Stockholm Declaration stating that economic development cannot be effective without environmental protection and emphasizing the necessity of an environmental impact assessment.

(3) Advanced GW, from 1975 to 2025. During this period the exponential increase in CO_2 continued, with the global mean temperature increasing by more than 1.2°C. In terms of change in the WRM model, this anthropocentric period can be divided into two subperiods.

(3.1) 1975–2000, a period of ecological concern. The 1992 UN Rio Summit, in Chapter 18 of Agenda 21, reflects the need for environmental protection. The text defines the need to establish the IWRM model, considering the ecological dimension of water and its economic value. Agenda 21 was the base for formulating the Millennium Development Goals during the 2000 UN Summit in New York.

(3.2) After 2000, a period some scientists call the *Anthropocene*. The UN World Summit on Sustainable Development in Johannesburg in 2002 marked political engagements in adopting multilateral partnerships to promote sustainable economic development. Later on, the Johannesburg Declaration promoted the 17 UN SDGs at the 2015 New York World Summit. However, almost 50 years after the 1972 Stockholm Declaration, the integrated management of natural resources produced severe externalities. The IWRM remained anthropocentric, and one-third more CO_2 accumulated in the atmosphere. At the same time, the global temperature exceeded 1.5°C, causing substantial topsoil degradation and rising seas from glaciers melting. The footprint of recent human activities after 2000 on geological strata is so drastic that many experts suggest the initiation of a new geological epoch, the Anthropocene.

As shown in Figure 4.5, the particular form of the dialectic relationship between humans and nature depends on the ratio of two opposite forces: (1) A: human pressures on nature (externalities) and (2) B: natural forces on humans (natural constraints). The power ratio of B/A is a function of the climate and human societies' scientific and technical development. We can distinguish three clusters: (1) $B > A$, naturalistic, during the Pleistocene epoch; (2) $B \approx A$, dualistic, during the Holocene; and (3) $B < A$, anthropocentric, after the Industrial Revolution.

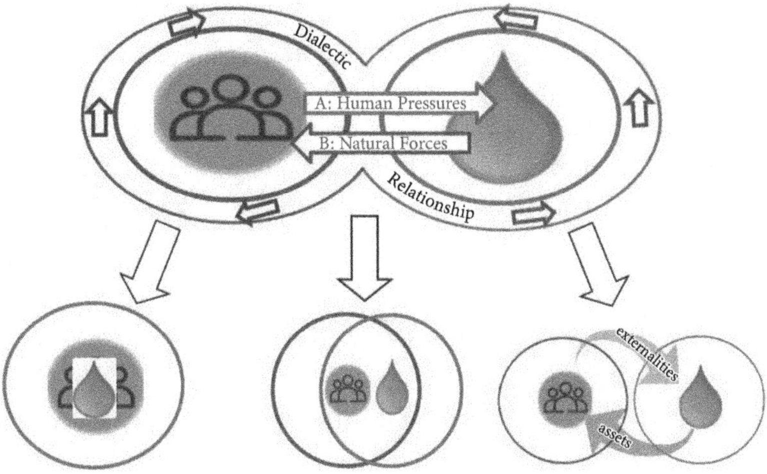

Figure 4.5 Three Clusters of the Human–Nature Relationship
Note: From Ganoulis (2024), with automatic permission from the journal *Sustainability*.

We should notice here that the dialectical nature–human relationship shown in Figure 4.5 as the union of two opposite forces differs from the recently promoted nature-based solutions (NBs). The use of natural materials and the bioengineering approach of NBs are very useful for small-scale restorations of water infrastructural works and ecosystem preservation. However, NBs do not include the conflictual character of nature–human dialectics, and they do not define how human prosperity can be preserved by implementing NBs. The dialectical conflict resolution model we suggest brings a harmonic symbiosis with nature when the opposite dialectical forces come into equilibrium (tuning human pressures to natural forces).

4.3 MCDA for Conflict Resolution

MCDA is a mathematical method for exploring "optimum" alternative solutions in operational research (Goicoechea et al., 1982; Xiujuan & Zhongke, 2004). *Criteria* in the MCDA methodology also means *objectives*. This chapter uses the MCDA tool to resolve TWRM conflicts under climate change conditions. These are between stakeholders across borders or between riparian countries that can lead to international disputes. Alternative solutions refer to maximizing or minimizing multiple criteria or objectives. For example, when designing a new dam, the decision maker aims to maximize the dam's safety while minimizing the costs.

Before applying MCDA for conflict resolution between at least two stakeholders or two countries, we distinguish between *optimization* and *trade-off* subject to various preferences. Mathematically, there is not a single optimal solution for multi-objective problems but a set of solutions representing a trade-off.

4.3.1 Optimization versus Multiple Criteria Trade-off

A multi-criteria programming problem can be represented in a vector notation as:

$$\text{“Satisfy”} \quad \mathbf{f}(\mathbf{x}) = (f_1(\mathbf{x}), f_2(\mathbf{x}), \ldots, f_I(\mathbf{x})) \tag{2}$$

$$\text{Subject to} \quad g_k(\mathbf{x}) \geq = \leq 0, \quad k = 1, 2, \ldots, K \tag{3}$$

$$x_j \geq 0, \quad j = 1, 2, \ldots, J \tag{4}$$

In Expression (2), *satisfy* means maximize or minimize the objectives. $\mathbf{f(x)}$ is the vector representation of I objective functions, each of which is to be "satisfied" subject to the constraint sets (3) and (4). Objectives are functions of $\mathbf{x}$, a J-dimensional geographic position vector in a finite Euclidean space that we call a *decision variable.* For instance, in agriculture, as part of TWRM activities, objectives aim to maximize food production while minimizing water for irrigation and energy use. The constraints (3) can be of different types, such as economical (budget limitation), ecological, or social. They can also describe the effects of climate change conditions. The geographic constraints (4) describe the *feasible region* of the J-dimensional *decision space.*

In MCDA, when dealing with two or more conflicting objectives, one cannot, in general, optimize all of them simultaneously because an increase in one objective usually results in a deterioration of another (or others). In such circumstances, trade-offs between the objectives are made to reach solutions that are still acceptable to the decision maker(s) according to their preferences (Romero & Rehman, 2003). Before applying MCDA for multiple decision makers, the following example illustrates the meaning of acceptable, feasible, non-dominated, or trade-off solutions for one decision maker.

4.3.2 Illustrative Example: Feasible Region and Non-dominated Solutions

In MCDA, instead of one optimum solution, we get a "feasible region" bounded by a set of "non-inferior" or "non-dominated" solutions. It is a region of solutions in which all objectives are feasible and can be improved simultaneously. Along the boundary, no solution can improve one objective without causing degradation to at least another.

To illustrate the terminology, let us consider the example of minimizing two conflicting objectives—Y1, irrigation water, and Y2, risk of food loss—subject to geographic boundaries: Y1 ≥ 0, Y2 ≥ 0, and other additional constraints. Each couple of values Y1 and Y2 that satisfy the constraints lies within the *feasible region* or *feasible space* (Figure 4.6). Every point, like A and B in this domain, represents acceptable or feasible solutions. The main property of this region is that by moving from A to B, we can improve both criteria Y1 and Y2. The feasible region is limited by the curve CDE called the *feasibility frontier*, the set of *non-dominated* solutions. Mathematically, all points outside the feasible region are not acceptable or non-feasible because

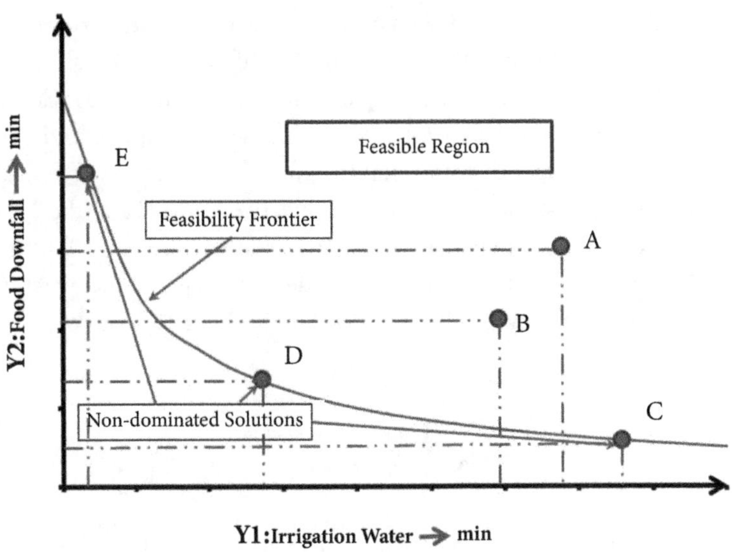

Figure 4.6 Non-dominated Solutions for Two Objectives: Irrigation and Food Downfall

Note: Elaborated by the authors.

of the constraints. The feasibility frontier CDE has the following property: If we move across this boundary to improve one objective, we deteriorate the other. For example, moving from C to D and from D to E, we improve criterion Y1, but criterion Y2 deteriorates. Every point on this curve is *satisfactory, non-inferior, non-dominated,* or a *trade-off* because there can be no increase in one objective without a decrease in the value of the other objective. Selecting one particular between non-inferior solutions depends on the decision maker's preferences. Point E can be the final solution on the feasibility frontier with the maximum preference level.

Classical methods to determine the feasibility frontier include the weighting sum approach, the e-constraint, the global criterion method, goal programming, and the complex method (Goicoechea et al., 1982; Xiujuan & Zhongke, 2004).

4.3.3 Compromise Programming

Determining the feasibility frontier as a continuous curve has the advantage of finding all spectrums of feasible solutions. However, the solution of the mathematical formulation given by Equations (2), (3), and (4) for every particular case is complicated. As an alternative, *composite* or *compromise programming* offers the possibility to compare different discrete alternatives and select those that perform better (Romero & Rehman, 2003). Compromise programming is a distance-based technique. It is simple and can be applied to one or many decision makers. In the previous case (see 4.3.2), of two objectives, first, we identify every objective's "ideal" and the "worst" value. For example, if the irrigation water Y1 varies between Y1, min and Y1, max, then to save water, Y1, min is the ideal project, and the worst is Y1, max. The non-dimensional value of an alternative $Y1$, a is the absolute value of the ratio:

$$\left|\frac{Y1, min - Y1, \mathrm{a}}{Y1, min - Y1, max}\right|$$

It will vary between 0 and 1, where 0 is the ideal point and 1 is the worst.

The next step is to measure alternative a's distance from the ideal point as a vector or as a more general L_p-metric and select alternatives close to the ideal point.

If the aim is to maximize an objective, criterion, or strategy a, the following formula is used for the L_p-metric:

$$L_p(a) = \left[\sum_{j=1}^{J} w_j \left|\frac{f_j{}^* - f_j(a)}{M_j - m_j}\right|^p\right]^{\frac{1}{p}} \tag{5}$$

where

$L_p(a) = L_p$-metric for alternative a
$f_j(a)$ = value of criterion j for alternative a
M_j = maximum (ideal) value of criterion j
m_j = minimum (anti-ideal) value of criterion j
f_j^* = ideal value of indicator j
w_j = weight of indicator j

The exponent p gives different ways of calculating the distance. The most frequently used values for p are 1 for the simple formulation, 2 for the Euclidean distance, and ∞ for the Tchebycheff norm. Different strategies or options are ranked using the minimum composite distance from the ideal solution (Figure 4.7) (Goicoechea et al., 1982).

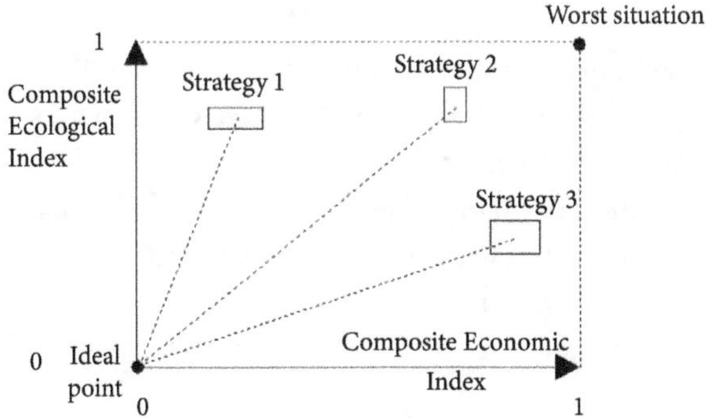

Figure 4.7 Ranking Alternative Options in Terms of Minimizing Economic and Ecological Goals
Note: Elaborated by the authors.

4.4 The Eristic-Dialectical ITWRM Model

We could develop a nature–human conflict resolution model to avoid environmental externalities by analyzing the dialectic character of the water–human interplay. The terms *dialectic* and *dialectical approach* derive from the Greek *dialogos*, a conversation between two persons exchanging contradictory arguments. Instead of two persons, we have humans and nature, as described by nature's laws. By *nature*, we mean all nonhuman entities (i.e., the natural environment, the soil, the atmosphere, the hydrosphere and biosphere, the flora and fauna, and all ecosystems on our planet). Nature does not have a voice, but it has its laws. Natural scientists like hydrologists aim to understand and describe these laws. In a conflict resolution negotiation, scientists and other stakeholders, including lawyers and politicians, should analyze how human strategies comply with the laws of nature. Tuning human activities to natural laws is the eristic-dialogical methodology for conflict resolution.

In our approach, humans are not a homogeneous group of individuals but societies consisting of different categories of stakeholders with particular water-related socioeconomic interests. These social groups are farmers, industrialists, water professionals, environmentalists, and other social entities developing economic activities that interact with water use. They are categorized into four stakeholder groups.

The dialectical conflict resolution model consists of the following main steps:

(1) Defining human–human and nature–human conflicts.
We call this step *eristic* from the Greek *eris*, which means strife. Two kinds of conflicts are distinguished:
  (1a) Conflicts between different social groups (human–human)
  (1b) Conflicts between social groups and the laws of nature (human–nature)

(2) Dialectical resolution

Logical arguments and alternative measures are formulated to attenuate the nature–human conflicts. The best solution is the unification of the opposites, which means respecting the natural laws. The harmonic symbiosis between humans and nature also reduces human–human conflicts.

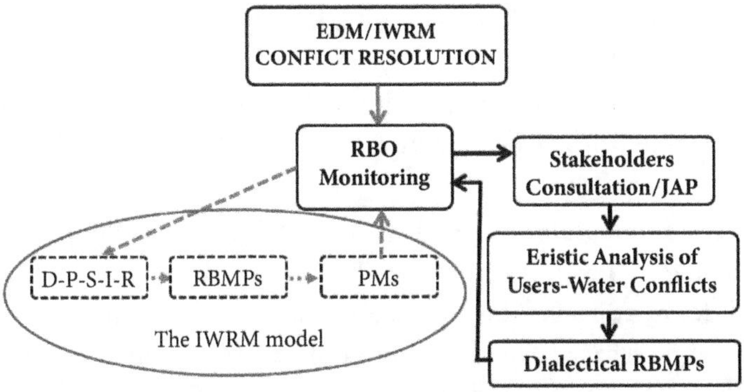

Figure 4.8 The EDM-ITWRM model in comparison with the IWRM model
Note: D-P-S-I-R = driving force–pressure–state–impact–response; EDM = eristic-dialectical model; IWRM = integrated water resources management; JAP = joint action plan; PMs = program of measures; RBMPs = river basin management plans; RBO = river basin organization. From Ganoulis (2024), with automatic permission from the journal *Sustainability*.

The steps to follow in the EDM-ITWRM are shown in Figure 4.8, in which a comparison is illustrated with the state-of-the-art IWRM model.

Step 1: Conflict resolution is undertaken by a river basin organization (RBO) responsible for monitoring at the river catchment scale.
Step 2: The RBO organizes a consultation with all stakeholders to define a joint action plan (JAP).
Step 3: Different human–human and water–human conflicts are identified that correspond to each socioeconomic activity (eristic analysis).
Step 4: Dialectical river basin management plans (D-RBMPs) are formulated dialectically by unifying human interests and natural laws.
Step 5: Monitoring D-RBMPs can initiate a new JAP, followed by a revision of Steps 3 and 4.

Comparing the EDM with the anthropocentric ITWRM model, we can observe in Figure 4.8 that Step 1 is expected to be shared for the two models, followed in IWRM by the driving force–pressure–state–impact–response step, the establishment of river basin management plans (RBMPs), and the program of measures.

The prerequisites for the use of this model are as follows:

(1) A legal definition of the RBO. This agency could have public or private status and is responsible for the IWRM at the basin level.

(2) The rules for the economic evaluation of different water and wastewater uses should be defined by law.
(3) Environmental standards and guidelines for water quantity and quality should also be defined by the country's legislation.

The main advantages of the application of the new dialectical model are the stakeholders' involvement in the ITWRM process and the reduction in externalities by adjusting the stakeholders' activities to natural laws.

Potential drawbacks can result from difficulty in reaching an agreement for establishing the JAP and resolving conflicts between different stakeholder groups, such as farmers and industrialists. However, if all groups adjust their activities to natural laws, it would facilitate potential human–human conflicts.

4.5 The Mesta/Nestos Case Study

4.5.1 Hydrographic Characteristics

The Mesta/Nestos transboundary river basin (Figure 4.9) is one of the three international basins that are shared between Bulgaria, which is the upstream country, and Greece, which is the downstream country in all cases. The Mesta River originates in the Rila and Pirin Mountains in southern Bulgaria at an altitude of 2925 meters. After traversing a valley with granite geology, it reaches the Rhodopi mountain range and crosses the border into Greece, where it changes its name to *Nestos*. From there, it flows southeast through a region characterized by marble rocks before entering a deltaic area of 550 km^2, eventually outflowing into the north Aegean Sea, in northern Greece (Skoulikaris & Ganoulis, 2011).

The basin, as depicted in Table 4.1, is almost equally shared between the two countries, in terms of both area extent and river length (Skoulikaris, 2021). However, the more mountainous nature of the upstream part of the basin, with a mean elevation of 1255 meters compared to a mean elevation of 606 meters in the downstream part, results in higher rainfall amounts of 810 mm in Bulgaria compared to 675 mm in Greece. This leads to larger discharges in the Bulgarian part of the basin. Consequently, as depicted in Table 4.1, the Bulgarian part of the basin contributes approximately 58.3% (958×10^6 m^3) of the mean interannual discharges of 1645×10^6 m^3 recorded

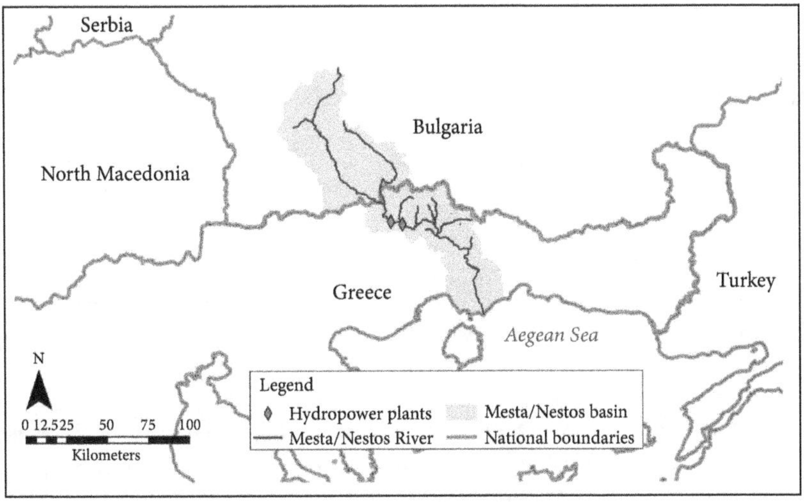

Figure 4.9 The Mesta/Nestos Transboundary River Basin
Note: Elaborated by the authors.

Table 4.1 Topographic and Hydrologic Characteristics of the Mesta/Nestos Basin

River basin	Riparian countries	Area (km^2)	Country's share (%)	Mean elevation (m)	River length (km)	Rainfall (mm)	Discharge ($\times 10^6$ m^3)
Mesta/ Nestos	Bulgaria	2,785	49.5	1,225	125	810	958
	Greece	2,834	50.5	606	130	675	687
	Total	5,619	100%	916	255	743	1,645

at the basin outlet, compared to 687 × 10^6 m^3 drained from the Greek part of the basin.

Based on the implementation process of the Water Framework Directive (WFD) (refer to the next section for more details), the Mesta/Nestos basin is divided into 112 designated river waterbodies (RWBs). Of these, 50 RWBs are located in the Nestos basin, with a total length of 430.4 km (Table 4.2). In contrast, the Mesta basin has 62 designated RWBs with a total length of 927 km. Most of these waterbodies are classified as natural (101 RWBs), with no artificial waterbodies, and 11 are classified as heavily modified waterbodies (European Communities [EC], 2003). Notably, 87.5%, or 98 out of 112 waterbodies, are associated with protected areas. In the Bulgarian part of the

Table 4.2 River Waterbodies in the Mesta/Nestos Basin, Classification Based on the Human Interventions on Them and Association With Protected Area.

Basin	Country	No. of RWBs	RWB length (km)		Type of RWB			Protected area(s)	
			Total	Average	Natural	AWB	HMWB	Yes	No
Mesta	Bulgaria	62	927	14.95	57		5	62	
Nestos	Greece	50	430.4	8.61	44		6	36	14
	Totals	112	1,357.4	23.56	101		11	98	14

Note: AWB = artificial waterbody; HMWB = heavily modified waterbody; RWB = river waterbody.

basin, this percentage reaches 100%. Conversely, in the Greek part, approximately 12.5% of the RWBs are not linked to areas under environmental protection, which is a more typical figure.

4.5.2 Administrative Structure

Administratively, Greece and Bulgaria are both currently member states (MSs) of the European Union (EU), having joined at different times and under varying circumstances. Greece became an EU MS on January 1, 1981, making it one of the earlier members of the then European Economic Community. The country has benefited from EU funding and development programs, which have played a crucial role in modernizing its infrastructure, improving public services, and fostering economic growth. Conversely, Bulgaria joined the European Union much later, on January 1, 2007, as part of the European Union's eastward expansion. Bulgaria's accession marked a major milestone in its transition from a communist state to a democratic, market-oriented society. Since joining the European Union, Bulgaria has made significant strides in economic development, legal reform, and governance, largely due to EU structural funds. As EU MSs, Greece and Bulgaria, in addition to benefiting from participation in various EU institutions and contributing to decision-making processes, are obligated to reform their national legislation to align with EU laws and adopt EU regulations and standards. In the environmental sector, especially regarding water resources, both countries have ratified the WFD as the primary legislative framework for water management and the Floods Directive (FD) to address growing flood risks.

Based on the water-related administrative division of the river basin, the upstream part of the basin belongs to the West Aegean River Basin Management District (RBMD; BG4000), which is one of the four RBMDs of Bulgaria. BG4000 encompasses the southwestern regions of Bulgaria, and it includes all river basins that flow directly into the Aegean Sea, specifically the Struma, Mesta, and Dospat Rivers. The district covers an area of 35,230 km^2, accounting for 10.8% of the country's total territory. The management of the waters at the regional level is conducted by the West Aegean region, with the city of Blagoevgrad being the center of the river basin district (RBD). The Greek part of the basin (i.e., the Nestos River basin) belongs to the Thrace RBD (EL12), which is one of the 14 water districts into which the country was divided by Law 1739/1987 (Government Gazette 201/A/1987). The total continental area of RBD EL12 (i.e., excluding the RBD's islands) is 10,676 km^2 and includes, apart from the Nestos basin, three more basins. Basin governance is conducted at the central administration level by the Ministry of Environment and Energy, while at the regional level the competent authorities are the Water Council of Decentralized Management. and the Water Directorates of Decentralized Management. Finally, within the basin is the settlement of 175,265 people, with 130,183 inhabitants living in the upstream Bulgarian part of the basin and 45,082 inhabitants living in the downstream Greek part of the basin (Skoulikaris, 2024).

4.5.3 Water Quantity Status

As mentioned above, the Mesta/Nestos bilateral agreement stipulated that Greece should receive 29% of the 1.5×10^9 m^3 of water drained in the Bulgarian part of the basin on the basis of historical data collected from 1935 until 1970. This implies that out of the 48.77 m^3/s of water collected in the upstream basin, at least 14.14 m^3/s (i.e., 29%) should flow into Greece on an interannual basis (Ganoulis et al., 2008). However, more recent data indicates that the hydrometeorological regime of the basin has changed. The latest RBMP EL12 reports that upstream water flow now accounts for 27.2 m^3/s, which is almost 45% less than the water volumes considered in the original agreement. Similar findings are presented in the research by Skoulikaris (2024), who used two well-known large-scale hydrological models, E-HYPE and LISFLOOD. The study shows that the simulated discharges at the border between the two countries over a 30-year period (1992 to 2010) are 19.41 m^3/s and 22.08 m^3/s, respectively—an even greater decrease than that shown in the corresponding RBMP. The reduction in upstream water flow directly impacts downstream waters. The RBMP estimates the runoff at the basin's outlet to be 50.04 m^3/s, while the E-HYPE and LISFLOOD models show a greater reduction, with the final runoff reaching the outlet estimated at 34.75 m^3/s and 28.33 m^3/s, respectively (Skoulikaris, 2024). Comparison of the figures between the border and the basin outlet shows that the contribution of the Greek part of the basin to the total streamflow regime has been decreasing over the years.

4.5.4 River Water Quality Status

The implementation process of the WFD designates the quality status of a river waterbody as a combination of two components, the chemical status and the ecological status. Based on data from 103 monitoring stations in the Mesta basin and 29 in the Nestos basin (Skoulikaris & Zafirakou, 2019), the analysis focused on the chemical status reveals that in the Greek part of the basin, only one waterbody failed to achieve good water quality. However, for most river waterbodies in the Bulgarian part of the basin, the water quality status is unknown, making it difficult to draw clear conclusions. Regarding ecological status, the analysis of the gauged data provides a more comprehensive overview of the waterbodies' conditions. Specifically, at the scale of transboundary basins, the ecological status is known for 91.9% of the river waterbodies. In the Mesta basin, 62.9% of the river waterbodies have good or high ecological status, 30.6% have moderate status, and only 3.2% have poor or bad status. In the downstream Nestos basin, 84% of the river waterbodies have good or high ecological status, 6.0% have moderate status, and only 4% have poor or bad status.

However, and despite the limited knowledge about the overall water quality status in Bulgaria, the analysis of the Greek part of the transboundary basin reveals a generally good-quality status for waterbodies near the borders. This suggests that the main courses of the Nestos River downstream of the borders are of good quality, indicating that no significant pollution is being caused by upstream transboundary waters. An exception to this pattern is the Dopsat River, which enters Greece within the Nestos basin and fails to achieve good-quality status (Skoulikaris & Zafirakou, 2019). The fact that the waters of the Mesta River entering Greece are of good quality and have at least moderate ecological status challenges older claims, as noted in the Second Assessment and other literature, that polluted waters were entering Greece from Bulgaria. This improvement highlights the positive impact of the WFD implementation process on the quality of transboundary waters entering Greece in recent years.

4.5.5 Development Perspectives and Land Uses

In Bulgaria, the mountainous landscape and limited plain areas result in a low water demand for agricultural purposes. Conversely, the substantial annual snowfall has shifted the regional economy toward the tertiary sector, leading to the development of relevant infrastructure and services. The region is particularly known for its numerous winter vacation centers, including one of the most famous ski resorts in the Balkans, located in the Pirin Mountains. The excess water volumes that are not utilized within the basin have prompted various development plans aimed at diverting water to neighboring agriculture-dependent basins, as in the case of the Dospat River which was implemented more than half a century ago. However, EU environmental water-related legislation is very cautious about such large-scale alterations, so these development plans remain largely theoretical.

In Greece, hydropower production is the largest water user, with 582 million m^3 (40.2% of the annual water volumes) utilized for energy purposes (Skoulikaris & Ganoulis, 2017). Two large hydropower plants, Thisavros and Platanovrisi, are in operation in the Greek part of the basin, just a few kilometers downstream from the border, relying on upstream waters for their operation. The average power production between 2004 and 2013 was 59.58 MW for the Thisavros dam and 36.1 MW for the Platanovrisi dam. These dams serve not only for power production but also for storing water to meet downstream irrigation needs. Currently, Greece's national decarbonization plan (Koutsandreas et al., 2021) and the emphasis on renewable energy sources have increased the value of the dam cascade, with new dam constructions planned for the near future (Skoulikaris & Ganoulis, 2017). The water released from these dams is also used to irrigate the extensive agricultural plain in the Nestos River delta. This plain is a highly productive area, with the majority of the local population working in the primary sector, producing high-quality agricultural outputs, with most of them being exported, and thus enjoying increased incomes. Additionally, the growing number of designated environmental areas in the basin recognized as Natura 2000 or Ramsar sites has made environmental protection a key consideration in the basin's water management.

4.6 Stakeholders' and Countries' Conflict Resolution

Different degrees of socioeconomic development on each side of the border resulted in different problems and issues with water-related projects, as shown in detail in the previous sections. Synoptically, in the Greek part of the river flow is controlled by two major dams for energy production. Downstream of the dams there is significant agricultural activity, and the river's delta is protected by the Ramsar treaty. Intensive use of fertilizers, overexploitation of groundwater, and the intensive use of drills have created water quantity and quality problems. As irrigated agriculture is the main area of development in the region, it is important to maintain a level of involvement through a long-term program and a level of interference. The water from the river also covers urban needs and provides the opportunity for recreational activities. In the Bulgarian part the lack of wastewater treatment plants (WWTPs) and significant shortcomings in infrastructure have created unfavorable conditions for water use. Tourism is negatively affected by the underdeveloped road infrastructure and agriculture by the limited availability of land for the development of intensive farming.

4.6.1 Projects for TWRM

In a framework of virtual negotiations, different projects or options are supposedly suggested by the two countries. Because of different hydrological characteristics and socioeconomic needs of the two countries, the contents of projects and their ranking differ, each country giving priority to its own needs (Table 4.3).

When projects are to be implemented in the entire river basin area, this may result in a conflicting situation. Projects 1 to 4 below refer to Greek proposals (GR) and 5 to 8 to Bulgarian (BUL). Previous studies together with hydrological and socioeconomic modeling provided insight for assessing the value of different project indicators. The indicator values differ from country to country, and trade-offs by MCDA can highlight acceptable options from both sides. Negotiations and possible agreements are ultimately necessary for the implementation phase of the projects.

Table 4.3 Assessment of Composite Indicators, Targets, and Goals for Various Projects

Indicators	Targets	Goals	
Economic efficiency (0–2)	Economic	Socioeconomic index (0–1)	Sustainability
Benefits, revenue (0–5)			
Increase of farmers' income (0–4)	Social		
Increase of non farmers' income (0–4)			
Increase in jobs (0–5)			
Change of water quantity (0–3)	Technical/ management	(Enviro-Technical) Ecological index (0–1)	
Change of land quantity (0–3)			
Change of water quality (0–3)			
Change of land quality (0–3)			
Effect on ecosystems (0–3)	Environmental		

Project 1 (GR): Strengthening agricultural practices and crop redistribution

Location: Basin-wide
Objectives: Increase agricultural production and productivity
Financing: Government, through external aid

Project 2 (GR): Review and reappraisal of irrigation development projects

Location: Downstream part of the basin (Greek territory)
Objectives: To improve agricultural production and productivity of high-value crops
Financing: Private and public sector

Project 3 (GR): International wildlife tourism development

Location: Delta region, reservoirs, and other wildlife areas in Greece
Objectives: To improve economic gains from wildlife tourism
Financing: Private sector

Project 4 (GR): Inland fisheries resource development project

Location: Delta region, reservoirs, and other wildlife areas in Greece
Objectives: To improve economic gains from wildlife tourism
Financing: European Union, anticipated

Project 5 (BUL): Water supply distribution project

Location: Delta region, reservoirs, and other wildlife areas
Objectives: To improve economic gains from wildlife tourism
Financing: Private and public sector

Project 6 (BUL): Construction of new reservoirs for multiple water uses

Location: Delta region, reservoirs, and other wildlife areas
Objectives: To improve economic gains from wildlife tourism
Financing: Private and public sector

Project 7 (BUL): Construction of WWTPs

Location: Delta region, reservoirs, and other wildlife areas
Objectives: To improve economic gains from wildlife tourism
Financing: Private and public sector

Project 8 (BUL): Development of local tourism and related activities

Location: Delta region, reservoirs, and other wildlife areas
Objectives: To improve economic gains from wildlife tourism
Financing: EU funding

4.6.2 Ranking of Projects Using Each Country's Indicators

Using Formula (5), each country's project indicators are aggregated in two composite indices: a socioeconomic one, which integrates all social and economic indicators, and an ecological one, which integrates environmental, water, and land quality as well as biological indicators. The composite indices range from 0 (worst case) to 1 (ideal case). In a two-dimensional representation the better options are those located nearest to the ideal point. As shown in Figure 4.10, Projects 3, 2, and 4 for Greece and 6, 8, and 5 for

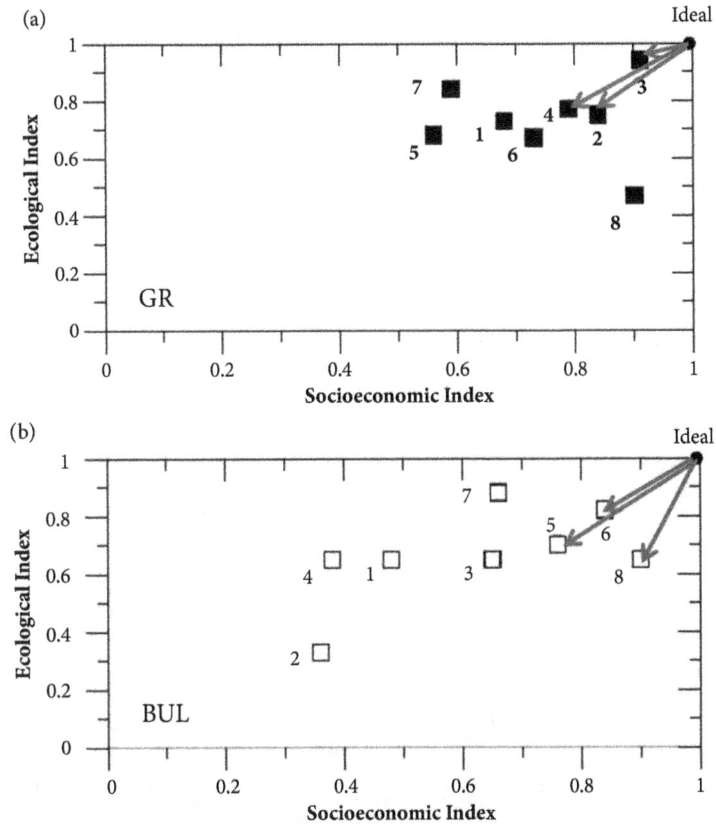

Figure 4.10 Ranking of Projects by Maximizing Composite Indicators of Greece (a) and Bulgaria (b)

Note: BUL = Bulgaria; GR = Greece. Elaborated by the authors.

Bulgaria are preferable as they are closest to the ideal case. They could be suggested as compromise solutions during future negotiations. The budget is included in the socioeconomic index.

4.6.3 Ranking of Projects Using Both Countries' Indicators and Goals

In this case, conflict resolution applies for both countries, supposing a joint WRM planning. The two countries project indicators are aggregated in two composite indices: one socioeconomic and one ecological (Figure 4.11a). In the case of countries' goals, each project may be represented by two indices, one for each country, resulting in the integration of the different indicators,

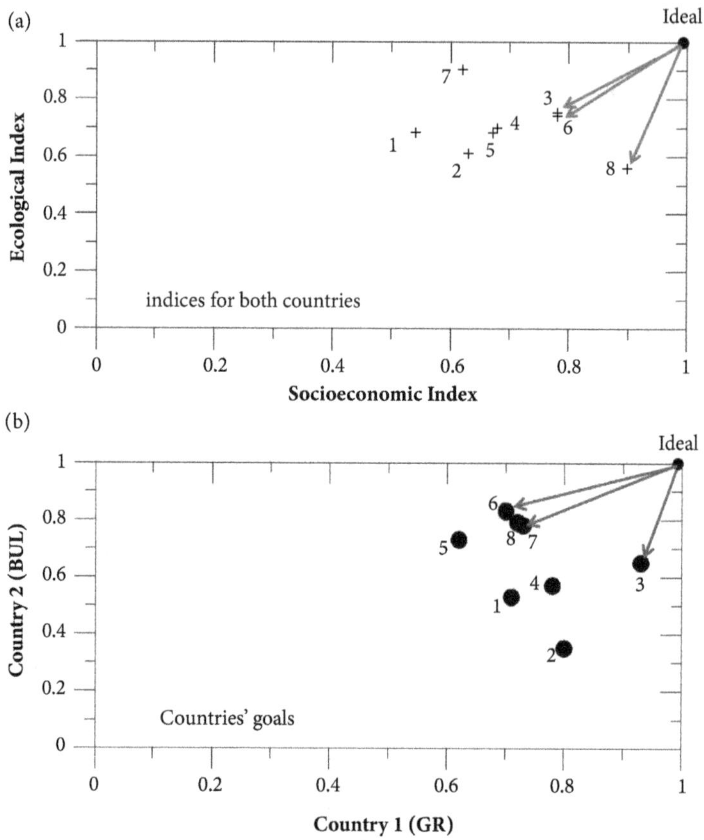

Figure 4.11 Ranking of Projects by Maximizing Composite Indicators of Both Countries (a) and Countries' Goals (b)
Note: Elaborated by the authors.

as shown in Figure 4.11b. It is worth observing that the three better Projects 3, 6, and 8 are the same in both trade-offs at the entire river basin. Taking into account that the Greek economy is better than the Bulgarian one, it is fair to pick up only one project (3) for Greece and two projects (6, 8) for Bulgaria.

4.7 Application of the EDM of Conflict Resolution

The conflict resolution EDM-ITWRM model described in Section 4.4 can be implemented under a joint RBO administrative authority. Establishing an RBO is a prerequisite for developing ITWRM joint plans and reflects the political engagement for cooperation. However, the following brief historical review of past attempts at collaboration reveals that conflicts over sharing water between the two countries still dominate and reduce cooperation activities, meaning that the two countries remain far from being able to design common dialectical RBMPs.

According to the Second Assessment of Transboundary Rivers, Lakes, and Groundwaters (UN Economic Commission for Europe, 2011), hereafter referred to as the *Second Assessment*, as well as relevant literature sources (e.g., Skoulikaris & Zafirakou, 2019), several reported pressures are linked to the Bulgarian part of the Mesta/Nestos basin, with the related impacts being more apparent on the Greek side. In particular, all reported pressures on water resources are primarily associated with water diversions for hydropower production and irrigated agriculture in the Bulgarian territory. A notable example is the water diversion from the Dospat sub-basin, a significant part of the Mesta/Nestos River basin in the southeastern region. Since the construction of a dam-lake in the early 1970s, water from the Dospat sub-basin has been redirected to the neighboring Maritsa basin to meet increased agricultural demands (Zarris et al., 2011). Consequently, the Bulgarian authorities no longer consider the Dospat basin part of the Mesta basin and exclude these water resources from the overall basin water balance. Finally, the Second Assessment notes reduced water inflows in the downstream part of the basin and the issue of polluted water inflows. These concerns have been further substantiated by early 21st-century literature (Darakas, 2002; Papachristou et al., 2000).

Regarding the transboundary cooperation of the Mesta/Nestos basin, Greece and Bulgaria ratified a bilateral agreement in 1995, which has a predefined duration of 35 years and will conclude in 2026 (Kampragou et al., 2007). This agreement entitles Greece to 29% of the total volume of water originating in Bulgarian territories before entering Greece. Additionally, the agreement mandates the establishment of a "hydro-economy committee" to oversee its implementation, including the exchange of information on water status and any development plans that could impact the river's natural flow. However, this agreement has not been fully implemented. The 29% water allocation is based on outdated data that does not reflect current climatic conditions, and the waters of the Dospat basin remained an unresolved issue in the overall water potential of the Mesta/Nestos basin. Because Bulgaria has withheld water for increased agricultural and industrial needs in the past, since 1975 the Mesta/Nestos yearly flow has declined from 1500 million m^3 to 600 million m^3, resulting in repeated Greek protests. Despite negotiations, no new, satisfactory agreement has been reached; failure to resolve the situation has resulted in conflicts between the two countries. Nowadays, noticeable pollution from the Bulgarian part, especially after heavy rainfall, has raised the level of tension in a region of Greece that is highly dependent on irrigated agriculture and hydropower. Since the beginning of 2007, Bulgaria has been a full member of the European Union. There is an urgent need for cooperation and application of EU guidelines for IWRM in the Mesta/Nestos transboundary river basin.

According to the EU WFD 60/2000, each country has to develop a program of measures integral to the RBMPs. The plans are designed to meet environmental objectives by preventing waterbody deterioration, achieving "good" ecological and chemical status, and mitigating pollution from discharges and hazardous substances. Additionally, the program aims to conserve protected areas, enhancing overall WRM and environmental protection. The measures are divided into basic and supplementary types. Greece proposes the continuation of existing measures, such as water monitoring for nitrates or other substances, and the development of 34 basic and 9 supplementary measures. Supplementary measures primarily address "recreation activities and wetland restoration" and "educational activities." In contrast, basic measures are more targeted, focusing on "controlling surface and groundwater abstractions" and "managing point and diffuse sources of pollution." On the other hand, the Bulgarian program of measures proposes 15 measures, which are not categorized, primarily aimed at controlling point and diffuse pollution sources and characterizing waterbodies with unknown chemical or environmental status.

4.8 Discussion/Conclusion/Implications

Sharing transboundary waters is a complex technical–social process combining conflicts and cooperation. According to our historical review and experience in the Mesta/Nestos case, conflict and cooperation coexist as a dialectical relationship between humans and nature. As an ontological principle, this contradictory relationship relates to the balance of power between human activities and the forces of nature. Following the industrial era, by the end of the 18th century, substantial scientific and technical progress made humans believe they could dominate nature and maximize socioeconomic benefits at the expense of natural resources like water and fossil energy resources. Their anthropocentric way of managing natural resources, including freshwater, is the principal reason for the current greenhouse effect and the global climatic crisis. Our eristic-dialectical IWRM is based on resolving conflicts between human activities and the laws of nature, and its application in the Nestos/Mesta River could enhance cooperation.

Although both countries are EU MSs, active cooperation regarding transboundary waters began only in 2010. Specifically, the Hellenic Ministry of Environment, Energy and Climate Change and the Bulgarian Ministry of Environment and Water Resources ratified a joint declaration on the use of water resources in shared river basins, confirming their commitment to collaborate on managing these transboundary basins (European Communities [EC], 2015). The joint declaration introduced new perspectives for coordinating shared waters, leading to the establishment of the Joint Expert Working Group (JEWG) in 2011 to focus on water and environmental issues. The JEWG meets once or twice a year (Skoulikaris & Zafirakou, 2019) and addresses issues related to the WFD and FD implementation processes at the international level, including developing joint basin management plans. However, tangible outcomes from these efforts are still pending, and a strong political will is needed to implement the EDM-ITWRM in the area.

References

Darakas, E. (2002). The transboundary river Nestos and its water quality assessment: Cross-border cooperation between Greece and Bulgaria. *Environmentalist*, *22*, 367–375. https://doi.org/10.1023/A:1020771015365

European Communities. (2003). *Common implementation strategy for the Water Framework Directive (2000/60/EC). Guidance document No 4: Identification and designation of heavily modified and artificial water bodies, Working Group 2.2—HMWB.*

European Communities. (2015). *Report on the implementation of the Water Framework Directive River Basin Management Plans—Member state: Greece. Commission staff working document.* Available from: https://op.europa.eu/en/publication-detail/-/publication/3470c661-c665-11e4-bbe1-01aa75ed71a1/language-en

Ganoulis, J. (2021). The water–man eristic dialectics for sustainable hydro-governance. *Water International*, *46*(7–8), 1135–1157. https://doi.org/10.1080/02508060.2021.2004003

Ganoulis, J. (2023). A new dialectical model of water security under climate change. *Water*, *15*(14), Article 2672. https://doi.org/10.3390/w15142672

Ganoulis, J. (2024). The dialectics of nature–human conflicts for sustainable water security. *Sustainability*, *16*(7), Article 3055. https://doi.org/10.3390/su16073055

Ganoulis, J., & Fried, J. (2018). *Transboundary hydro-governance: From conflict to shared management.* Springer International.

Ganoulis, J., Skoulikaris, H., & Monget, J. M. (2008). Involving stakeholders in transboundary water resources management: The Mesta/Nestos "HELP" basin. *Water SA, 34*(4), 461–467. https://doi.org/10.4314/wsa.v34i4.183657

Goicoechea, A., Hansen, D. R., & Duckstein, L. (1982). *Multiobjective decision analysis with engineering and business applications.* John Wiley & Sons.

Heisenberg, W. (1958). The representation of nature in contemporary physics. *Daedalus, 87*(3), 95–108. https://www.jstor.org/stable/20026454

Hubble Space Telescope. (2025). In *Wikipedia.* Retrieved August 7, 2025, from https://en.wikipedia.org/wiki/Hubble_Space_Telescope#Age_of_the_universe

Kampragou, E., Eleftheriadou, E., & Mylopoulos, Y. (2007). Implementing equitable water allocation in transboundary catchments: The case of river Nestos/Mesta. *Water Resources Management, 21*, 909–918. https://doi.org/10.1007/s11269-006-9108-1

Koutsandreas, D., Spiliotis, E., Doukas, H., & Psarras, J. (2021). What is the macroeconomic impact of higher decarbonization speeds? The case of Greece. *Energies, 14*(8), Article 2235. https://doi.org/10.3390/en14082235

McCracken, M., & Wolf, A. T. (2019). Updating the register of international river basins of the world. *International Journal of Water Resources Development, 35*(5), 732–782. https://doi.org/10.1080/07900627.2019.1590866

Mirumachi, N., & Allan, T. (2007, November 12–15). *Revisiting transboundary water governance: Power, conflict, cooperation and the political economy* [Paper presentation]. CAIWA International Conference on Adaptive and Integrated Water Management: Coping With Scarcity, Basel, Switzerland.

Muller, R., & MacDonald, G. (2000). Brief introduction to the history of climate. In *Ice ages and astronomical causes: Data, spectral analysis and mechanisms* (pp. 1–6). Springer.

Papachristou, E., Ganoulis, J., Bellou, A., Darakas, E., & Ioannidou, D. (2000). The Nestos/Mesta River: A transboundary water quality assessment. In J. Ganoulis, I. L. Murphy, & M. Brilly (Eds.), *NATO science series 2: Environment security: Vol. 74. Transboundary water resources in the Balkans* (pp. 33–40). Springer.

Rivera-Torres, M., Gerlak, A. K., & Jacobs, K. L. (2021). Lesson learning in the Colorado River basin. *Water International, 46*(4), 567–577. https://doi.org/10.1080/02508060.2021.1913782

Romero, C., & Rehman, T. (2003). *Multiple criteria analysis for agricultural decisions* (2nd ed.). Elsevier.

Sharma, A., & Singh, D. (2020). Evolution of industrial revolutions: A review. *International Journal of Innovative Technology and Exploring Engineering, 9*, 66–73. https://doi.org/10.35940/ijitee.I7144.0991120

Skoulikaris, C. (2021). Transboundary cooperation through water-related EU directives' implementation process. The case of shared waters between Bulgaria and Greece. *Water Resources Management, 35*(14), 4977–4993. https://doi.org/10.1007/s11269-021-02983-4

Skoulikaris, C. (2024). Large-scale hydrological models and transboundary river basins. *Water, 16*(6), Article 878. https://doi.org/10.3390/w16060878

Skoulikaris, C., & Ganoulis, J. (2011). Climate change impacts on river catchment hydrology using dynamic downscaling of global climate models. In H. J. S. Fernando, Z. B. Klaic, & J. L. McCulley (Eds.), *National security and human health implications of climate change* (Vol. 125, pp. 281–287). Springer.

Skoulikaris, C., & Ganoulis, J. (2017). Multipurpose hydropower projects economic assessment under climate change conditions. *Fresenius Environmental Bulletin, 26*, 5599–5607.

Skoulikaris, C., & Zafirakou, A. (2019). River basin management plans as a tool for sustainable transboundary river basins' management. *Environmental Science and Pollution Research, 26*, 14835–14848. https://doi.org/10.1007/s11356-019-04668-2

Tayia, A. (2019). Transboundary water conflict resolution mechanisms: Substitutes or complements. *Water, 11*(7), Article 1337. https://doi.org/10.3390/w11071337

UNESCO, International Groundwater Resources Assessment Centre, & World Meteorological Organization. (2015). *Transboundary aquifers of the world, edition 2015*. https://unesdoc.unesco.org/ark:/48223/pf0000264020

United Nations. (1997). *Convention on the law of the non-navigational uses of international watercourses* (UN Doc. A/RES/51/299). https://treaties.un.org/doc/Treaties/1998/09/19980925%2006-30%20PM/Ch_XXVII_12p.pdf

United Nations. (n.d.). *The 17 goals*. Retrieved August 24, 2014, from https://sdgs.un.org/goals

United Nations Economic Commission for Europe. (2011). *Second assessment of transboundary rivers, lakes and groundwaters*.

Whalen, E. (2020, December 1). *Classical wisdom. Roman Greece: Partner in empire*. https://classicalwisdom.com/culture/history/roman-greece-partner-in-empire/

Xiujuan, L., & Zhongke, S. (2004). Overview of multi-objective optimization methods. *Journal of Systems Engineering and Electronics*, *15*(2), 142–146.

Yoffe, S., Wolf, A. T., & Giordano, M. (2003). Conflict and cooperation over international freshwater resources: Indicators of basins at risk. *Journal of the American Water Resources Association*, *39*, Article 1109. https://doi.org/10.1111/j.1752-1688.2003.tb03696.x

Zarris, D., Vlastara, M., & Panagoulia, D. (2011). Sediment delivery assessment for a transboundary Mediterranean catchment: The example of Nestos River catchment. *Water Resources Management*, *25*(14), 3785–3803. https://doi.org/10.1007/s11269-011-9889-8

Zeitoun, M., & Warner, J. (2006). Hydro-hegemony—A framework for analysis of transboundary water conflicts. *Water Policy*, *8*, 435–460. https://doi.org/10.2166/wp.2006.054

5

Conceptualizing Trust Using the Helmand River as an Example

A Cost–Benefit Decision-Making Framework

Najibullah Loodin, Gabriel E. Eckstein, Vijay P. Singh, Rosario Sanchez, and Robert E. Mace

5.1 Introduction

Cost–benefit decision-making is the foundation of economics, public policy, and strategic decisions, providing a systematic approach for evaluating whether the benefits of a proposed action outweigh its costs. Through conversion of both tangible and intangible impacts into monetary terms, cost–benefit analysis (CBA) helps compare diverse options on a common scale (see Mishan & Quah, 2020). This methodology ensures that resources are allocated efficiently, maximizing societal welfare and minimizing waste. Recent developments in CBA have enabled policymakers to use it as a critical tool in making precise decisions, including in water governance and management both at intra-state and inter-state levels.

In transboundary water management, CBA facilitates the assessment of cooperative initiatives by quantifying the economic, social, and environmental impacts of shared water resource utilization, for example, use of the shared Nile River basin (see Klaphake, 2005). Indeed, the United Nations (UN) Economic Commission for Europe emphasizes that transboundary water cooperation can lead to increased energy and food production, enhanced resilience to disasters, and economic integration. By evaluating these benefits against the costs of cooperation, stakeholders can make informed decisions that promote regional stability and development. The application of CBA in water conflicts is exemplified in the context of hydropower development, where the interests of energy production

Najibullah Loodin et al., *Conceptualizing Trust Using the Helmand River as an Example*. In: *Decision Support Models to Assist International and Transboundary Water Negotiations*. Edited by: Mohammadreza Shahbazbegian and Ariel Dinar, Oxford University Press. © Oxford University Press (2026). DOI: 10.1093/9780197802601.003.0005 often clash with environmental preservation and local livelihoods. Modern approaches to CBA in such scenarios incorporate welfare economics to assess the trade-offs involved (Lindberg & Hagman, 2018). For instance, methodologies that integrate behavioral economics provide a more comprehensive understanding of stakeholder preferences and the value of ecosystem services, leading to more balanced decision-making processes.

Moreover, CBA can serve as a framework for analyzing the costs of inaction in water management (Arjoon et al., 2016). A recent analysis by Carbon Disclosure Project an international nonprofit organization helping companies and public authorities disclose their environmental impacts, highlighted that misgovernance of global river basins poses significant financial risks, with $105 billion in business revenue at stake across 10 major river basins (see Calderon, 2024). The report emphasizes the importance of proactive investment in water conservation and sustainable management practices as the costs associated with inaction can far outweigh those of implementing effective water governance strategies (see Loodin et al., 2024a, on joint investment in transboundary water governance). In the landscape of policy development, CBA assists in designing equitable cost-sharing mechanisms among stakeholders. For example, in cases involving pollution of shared rivers, particularly the pollution that comes from upstream states, CBA can inform the allocation of cleaning costs among upstream and downstream users. By considering factors such as pollution levels, economic capabilities, and benefits derived from the water resources (Dunca, 2018; Li & Lu, 2020; Tyler, 2005), CBA helps establish fair and sustainable financial arrangements that encourage collective responsibility and compliance.

One of the significant advancements in CBA is the integration of environmental factors, particularly through the integration of ecosystem services. While the normative cost–benefit frameworks often overlooked the intrinsic value of natural resources and ecosystems, recent scholarship stresses the need for incorporation of ecosystem services in policy evaluations, ensuring that natural capital is adequately valued (see Saarikoski et al., 2016). This approach has proven essential for decisions related to land use, conservation, and climate policy, where the trade-offs between development and environmental preservation are often challenging. By assigning monetary values to ecosystem services like clean air, water filtration, and shared biodiversity, CBA can provide a more comprehensive assessment of environmental costs and benefits.

This research aims to conceptualize trust using the cost–benefit decision-making analysis framework. We want to know how joint investment, both in terms of infrastructure and technically, ensures water equity and environmental justice in the basin leading to the enhancement of trust-building processes between upstream and downstream states. We apply the CBA framework to one of the most water-insecure basins in South Asia, the Helmand River basin. Through our analysis, we conclude that conceptualizing the trust-building processes between upstream Afghanistan and downstream Iran through the lens of CBA could help both Helmand River riparians to maximize shared benefits while reducing the socioeconomic and political costs of conflicts in the basin.

5.2 Conceptual Framework: A CBA Framework

As a methodological approach that stems from economic theories, CBA is used for quantifying and comparing the costs and benefits of proposed decisions, allowing stakeholders to identify actions that maximize net societal value. The development of this framework is the foundation for policy analysis, business strategy, and resource allocation.

The foundation of CBA lies in the utilitarian objective of achieving the greatest good for the greatest number, a principle articulated by Jeremy Bentham (1789/1970) and later refined through neoclassical economic theories (also see Welch, 1989). Its centrality is that rational decision-making needs the systematic comparison of the positive and negative consequences of an action, in our case the use and allocation of the shared transboundary water among the co-riparians, expressed in monetary terms (see Whittington et al., 2005, on the economic value of cooperation on the Nile River). This conversion enables differing effects—ranging from financial profits to social and environmental effects—to be aggregated and weighed within a unified metric of evaluation. By doing so, CBA paves the way for bridging the gap between qualitative outcomes and quantitative decision criteria, enhancing evidence-based decision-making (see Akron et al., 2017).

Central to the application of CBA is the principle of opportunity cost, which recognizes that the resources devoted to one course of action cannot simultaneously be employed elsewhere. It requires the inclusion of undeniable alternatives in the analysis, ensuring that all costs reflect not only direct expenditure but also the value of opportunities sacrificed. Moreover, CBA incorporates the temporality (temporal landscape) through discounting, a process that adjusts future costs and benefits to their present value. This approach acknowledges the time value of money and societal preferences for present consumption over deferred benefits (Arrow, 1983).

The methodology of CBA is inherently systematic, following clearly defined stages. First, it requires the identification and calculation of all relevant costs and benefits associated with a decision. These may include tangible financial impacts, such as capital and operating expenses, as well as intangible effects, such as shifts in farming trends or the shift from rurality to urbanity, environmental degradation, or cultural heritage (Larsen et al., 2004; Sesana et al., 2021). Through advanced economic and mathematical techniques, one can monetize non-market goods and services, thereby ensuring comprehensive inclusion of all impacts (Hanley et al., 2009). For instance, the benefits of reduced air pollution from an urban transportation project might be quantified using the societal cost of carbon or decarbonization (see Wang & Chen, 2017).

Despite its wider applications, CBA is not without challenges. The process of assigning monetary values to intangible or non-market effects can be mixed with subjectivity and ethical concerns. For example, valuing biodiversity raises complex moral questions, even when guided by established methodologies such as the value of a statistical life (Bartkowski et al., 2015). Additionally, the selection of the discount rate, which significantly shapes or co-shapes the valuation of long-term benefits and costs, remains a pressing issue, particularly in areas like climate changes where addressing intergenerational equity is challenging (Mishan & Quah, 2020). Thus, these limitations require a careful balance between quantitative rigor and qualitative judgment, highlighting the importance of transparency and stakeholder engagement in the application of CBA. In practice, CBA has proven indispensable across diverse domains. In public policy, it has guided investments in infrastructure (e.g., water infrastructures and ecosystem revitalization), ensuring that scarce resources are governed such that societal returns are expected at higher scale. In fact, in relation to its application in water and environmental governance, CBA has informed strategies for conservation, pollution control, and climate adaptation, illustrating its versatility and relevance (Newton et al., 2012).

When it comes to the governance of the shared watercourse, CBA is a vital tool in dialogues and negotiations over the use and allocation of the shared water among the co-riparian nations. It can help riparian nations to analyze critically and systematically the economic, social, and environmental trade-offs concerning the management of their shared water resources (Zhang et al., 2023). For example, analyzing water infrastructure cost (e.g., dam construction costs in an upstream state and potential impact in a downstream state) and assessing the benefits (e.g., hydropower generation or agricultural productivity in an upstream state and flood management or cheap and reliable energy supplies in a downstream state) will lead to the establishment of a structured framework that will mutually benefit both the upstream and the downstream riparians in negotiations over the utilization of the shared water.

For example, in the case of the Nile River, which flows through 11 riparian nations, Yihdego et al. (2017) argue that while the construction of the Grand Ethiopian Renaissance Dam (GERD) in upstream Ethiopia will benefit the riparian nations by supplying cheap and reliable hydropower electricity, it might adversely impact water availability and accessibility for the farming communities in downstream Egypt, which have an established temporal and spatial emotional connection to the historical flow of the Nile River. Application of CBA in the negotiations over the GERD could have enabled the parties, including the farming communities, to evaluate the costs and benefits derived from the GERD that are associated with the use and allocation of the basin's shared water resources.

An example where trust and cooperation are amplified by application of CBA is the massive investments of Thailand in the development and construction of dams in Loa People's Democratic Republic (PDR) on the Mekong River upstream of Thailand. Such investment not only enables regional connectivity that mutually benefits both the upstream and the downstream riparians but also strengthens the value of hydro-diplomacy where powerful states play a vital role in shaping or co-shaping the hydropolitical landscape of the Mekong River basin (see Matthews, 2012).

However, application of CBA in negotiations over the allocation of the shared water comes with a number of challenges. This is due to the fact that the complex interplay between political sovereignty of the riparian nations along with socioeconomic differences—triggering inequity—and eco-environmental limits require both qualitative and quantitative judgments. In the Mekong River, the construction of large-scale dams in China, the most powerful hegemon and upper riparian of the Mekong River, while benefiting China through the production of hydropower energy and agricultural productivity, disrupts the ecology of the river transporting sediment flows to the downstream states. As a result, China's conduct deprives the underserved downstream riparian states of water access for their daily use, thereby complicating negotiations and escalating the risk of water conflict among the co-riparian nations (see Grumbine et al., 2012).

5.2.1 Identification of Costs and Benefits

In transboundary water contexts, costs and benefits can be categorized into direct and indirect costs and benefits and externalities (Sadoff & Grey, 2002).

Direct costs/benefits: These include infrastructural costs (e.g., the cost of diversion channels, dam structures, etc.), operational costs (e.g., the cost associated with the operation of the dam), and direct economic benefits from water use (e.g., agricultural production, hydropower generation, flood control, etc.) (see Loodin et al., 2021, and Queen et al., 2021, on the Columbia River basin; Loodin et al., 2024a, on the Helmand River).

Indirect costs/benefits: These can include the impacts of water infrastructure on regional development, changes in land-use patterns, and effects on local communities. The indirect benefit of Thailand's large-scale investment in hydropower dam construction in upstream Lao PDR (Matthews, 2012) will be the economic development of increased electricity, resulting in the enhancement of industrial activities in a shared basin (see Dombrowsky, 2009; Madani, 2014, 2021; Madani & Mahoozi, 2022).

Externalities: These are positive or negative outcomes of a given economic activity that affects a third party not directly involved in that activity. Examples of negative externalities of a project include environmental impacts, ecosystem degradation, and the degradation of water quality in a downstream state (Giordano et al., 2014); examples of positive impacts can include enhancement of commercial fisheries across the shared basin as well as attraction of tourism between the upstream and downstream states due to the joint investment.

5.2.2 Temporal Considerations

Temporal considerations in CBA consist of three factors, namely, the time horizons, discount rates, and intertemporal distribution of costs and benefits. These factors specify how current decisions impact future outcomes and how future impacts are valued in present terms. When it comes to a transboundary or shared watercourse, temporal considerations are particularly complex because of the long-term nature of water infrastructural projects (e.g., the construction of joint hydropower dams such as the Doosti dam jointly built and operated by Iran and Turkmenistan) (see Loodin & Warner, 2022; Nagheeby & Warner, 2018), the evolving effects of climate changes, and the need to balance immediate development goals with long-term environmental sustainability and equitable resource-sharing.

Time horizons: The time horizon of a CBA defines the period over which costs and benefits are evaluated. For transboundary water projects, such as dam construction, irrigation canals, or hydropower generation, the time horizon often spans several decades. A short time horizon may overlook critical long-term impacts, such as sedimentation, ecosystem degradation, or the effects of climate change on water availability. For example, the GERD on the Blue Nile River has escalated tension between the co-riparians, particularly between upper riparian Ethiopia and lower riparian Egypt (see Loodin, 2024; Sehring & Wolf, 2023; Seide & Fantini, 2023). However, a long-term CBA must consider the potential benefits of hydropower generation for Ethiopia and Sudan alongside Egypt's increasing concerns over water misallocation by Ethiopia, resulting in the arousal of negative emotional dynamics of farming, urban, and industrial communities in Egypt (El Deen, 2022).

Discount rates: Discount rates are used in CBA to reflect the present value of future costs and benefits. At the transboundary watercourse scale, the choice of discount rate can significantly influence project evaluations (Gollier, 2010). A high discount rate may undervalue long-term environmental and social impacts, favoring short-term economic gains. In contrast, a low discount rate places greater emphasis on future outcomes, promoting sustainable practices at the expense of more pressing or near-term benefits. For example, when assessing a transboundary groundwater extraction project on the Guarani Aquifer shared by Argentina, Brazil, Paraguay, and Uruguay, a low discount rate could unveil the long-term importance of conserving the aquifer for future generations, rather than prioritizing immediate economic extraction benefits (see Hirata & Foster, 2021).

Intertemporal distribution of costs and benefits: Temporal considerations also involve the equitable distribution of costs and benefits over time. Transboundary water projects often create disparities where costs and benefits are realized (Asheim, 2010). For example, the construction of a dam may generate immediate economic benefits for upstream nations through energy production, whereas downstream nations may face delayed and long-term costs, such as reduced water quality and ecosystem degradation. In the transboundary Mekong River basin, where upstream dam projects in China (hydro-hegemon of the Mekong River) and Lao PDR supply energy and economic benefits locally, the downstream states of Cambodia, Thailand, and Vietnam face significant environmental and socioeconomic impacts (Olson & Morton, 2018).

5.2.3 Spatial Considerations

The temporality of CBA centers on the geographic distribution of costs and benefits across various scales within a transboundary waterway. In fact, these considerations are of high importance as they ensure equitable allocation and utilization of the shared resources, resulting in the de-escalation of conflicts among the co-riparians.

Geographic variability: The impacts of transboundary water projects are often unevenly distributed across the co-riparians. For instance, upstream countries may benefit from hydropower generation or irrigation, while downstream countries face reduced water flow, altered ecosystems, and loss of livelihoods due to the damming of water in an upstream state (see Loodin & Warner, 2022). The Nile River basin exemplifies this dynamic, where Ethiopia's GERD project provides economic benefits for Ethiopians but deprives downstream Sudanese and Egyptian farming communities, particularly during summertime (Ahmed et al., 2024), whose farming lands were irrigated by the freshwater of the Nile for millennia (Seide & Fantini, 2023). The findings of Basheer et al. (2021) and Siddig et al. (2021) highlight the socioeconomic benefits of the GERD operation on the livelihood of Sudanese including the agricultural productivity in Sudan, whereas the recent work of Basheer et al. (2024)—while acknowledging the broader role of the dam in generating hydroelectricity and flood mitigation—unveils how Sudanese infrastructural developments including water infrastructures are vulnerable due to the operationalization of the GERD.

Localized effects: Spatial CBA must take into consideration the localized environmental and social impacts. For example, dam construction may inundate specific areas, displacing communities and degrading the ecosystem and the landscape, particularly of Indigenous communities who possess deep emotional ties to their historical lands (see Dallman et al., 2013). These site-specific costs need to be weighed against broader regional benefits, such as flood control, agricultural productivity, and energy production.

Cross-border coordination: Effective spatial consideration in CBA requires collaboration among riparian states to ensure that benefits and costs are shared equitably. The Senegal River basin provides a positive example where joint management frameworks under the Organization pour la Mise en Valeur du fleuve Sénégal (OMVS) ensure that hydropower and irrigation benefits are allocated equally among the riparians (Bodian et al., 2020).

5.3 Uncertainty and Risk

Uncertainty and risk in CBA for transboundary waters arise from unpredictable factors such as climate change, variable hydrological conditions, and sociopolitical dynamics. These uncertainties can lead to inaccurate cost and benefit estimates, making it complicated to plan long-term projects. For example, climate variability may alter river flows, triggering water scarcity in the shared basin particularly in downstream states, impacting both hydropower generation and agricultural water availability. Similarly, political instability, especially as a result of political chaos in either upstream or downstream states, or possibly both (see Loodin et al., 2023), or a lack of trust among riparian nations can increase the risk of project delays and disputes, disrupting cooperative water management efforts. Effective risk management strategies, such as scenario planning and adaptive management, are essential for addressing these challenges.

5.4 Political and Institutional Factors

Political and institutional factors significantly influence CBA in transboundary water management by influencing the governance structures, negotiation processes, and implementation mechanisms.

Governance frameworks: Effective transboundary water management is highly reliant on comprehensive legal and institutional arrangements. For instance, the Mekong River Commission facilitates cooperation among member states in the Mekong basin, providing a platform for joint decision-making and equitable resource-sharing (Offerdal, 2019). These legal arrangements can be reinforced by the riparian nations by their adherence to the treaty regime (Fischhendler, 2008).

Power asymmetry: Political power imbalances among riparian states can affect negotiations and project outcomes. Upstream nations may wield greater control over shared resources, as seen in the Nile basin, where Ethiopia's GERD project has raised concerns about Egypt's water security. Similarly, due to the power asymmetry in the Mekong River basin, the hydraulic mission of China, the powerful hydro-hegemon of the Mekong River, has threatened water availability for downstream states (see Ogden, 2023).

Institutional capacity: The ability of institutions to manage, monitor, and enforce agreements is vital. Weak institutional capacity can challenge the effective implementation of CBA recommendations, triggering conflicts (Schmeier, 2012). For example, the lack of a binding enforcement mechanism in the Indus Waters Treaty has posed challenges in addressing emerging disputes between India and Pakistan (Condon et al., 2014). This argument is further reinforced by the latest work of Ilyas (2023), who believes that while the Indus Water Treaty resulted in peace and stability between the riparians in the basin, lack of "monitoring and enforcement mechanisms" hinders it from reaching its full potential (p. 56).

5.5 Stakeholder Engagement

Effective stakeholder engagement in CBA for transboundary water refers to the inclusion of diverse perspectives from local communities, government bodies, and civil society organizations. This approach fosters transparency, builds trust, and mitigates conflicts among riparian states (see Lienert et al., 2015; Loodin et al., 2024a). For example, in the Nile River basin, participatory frameworks involving stakeholders from Ethiopia, Sudan, and Egypt are vital in addressing varying national interests while ensuring equitable water resource governance among the co-riparians. The involvement of stakeholders also ensures that social and cultural values are integrated into cost and benefit evaluations, strengthening sustainability of water management decisions. Figure 5.1 highlights the outcomes of the application of CBA in transboundary water negotiations.

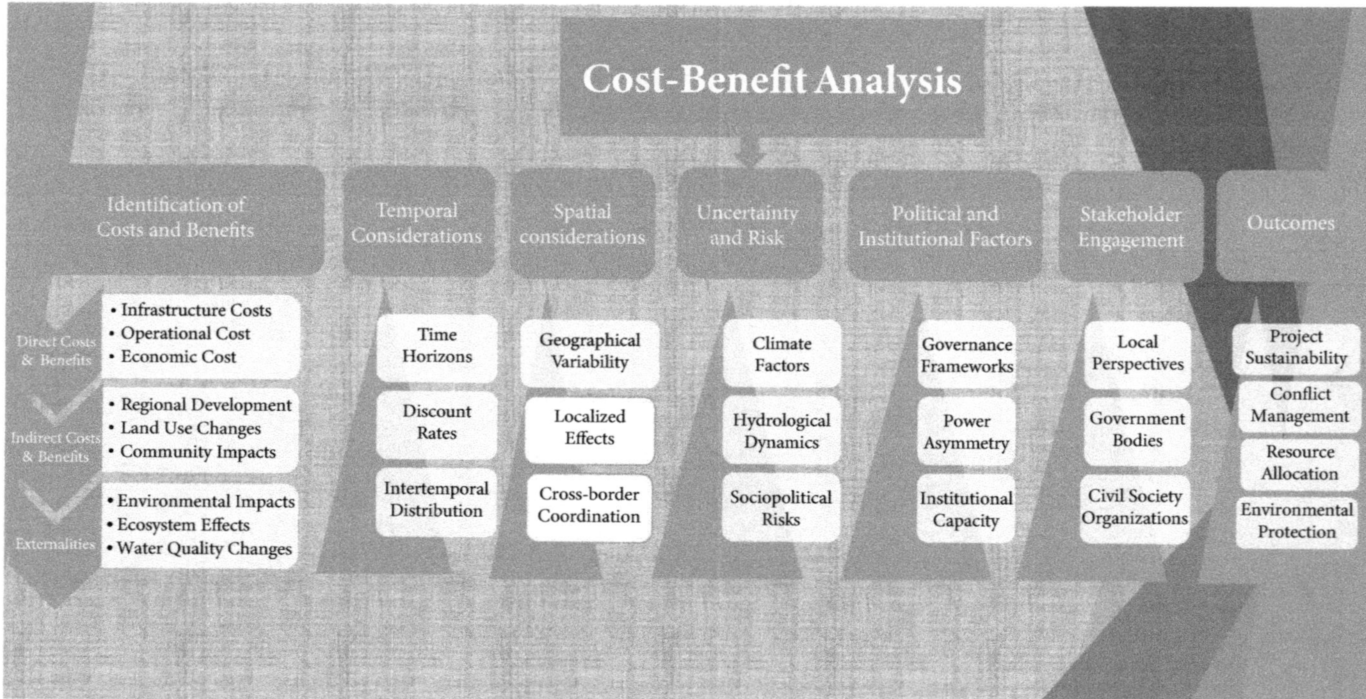

Figure 5.1 Cost–Benefit Analysis in Transboundary Water Negotiations

Note: Elaborated by the authors.

5.6 Empirical Application

Originating in southern Afghanistan, the Helmand River has the largest endorheic and arid basin in the region. The basin has supported various civilizations in the Sistan Valley for over six millennia (Loodin et al., 2024b; Shahbazbegian et al., 2016; Spandyar, 2020; Whitney, 2006). Dominguez et al. (1951) note that agricultural irrigation in the Helmand River delta has been practiced for centuries. The basin spans 400,000 km^2, encompassing approximately 40% of Afghanistan's total area (Loodin, 2021b), with 89% of the basin located in Afghanistan, 9% in Iran, and 2% in Pakistan (see Figure 5.2) (Mianabadi et al., 2020). It is worth noting that Pakistan is not included in this discussion due to its absence from the Helmand River Treaty. The Helmand River is a critical resource, sustaining nearly eight million people in southern Afghanistan and over one million in Iran's Sistan-Baluchistan province (Thomas & Varzi, 2015). Its significance is evident in its irrigation of 97% of southeastern Afghanistan's agricultural lands and 80% of those in Sistan-Baluchistan, Iran (Hanasz, 2012; Loodin, 2021a, 2021b). Daly et al. (2012) emphasize the river's multifaceted importance, noting its role in agriculture, livestock maintenance, hydropower generation, drinking water provision, and ecosystem preservation in both nations.

Water allocation disputes between Afghanistan and Iran have intensified due to climate change, drought, and water misgovernance, threatening diplomatic relations (Loodin & Wolf, 2021; Mayar, 2022, 2023; Ramachandran, 2017). These tensions trace back to the 1870s when British officer Frederick Goldsmid delineated the countries' border along the river. In 1948, the US government mediated ongoing disputes by establishing the Helmand River Delta Commission. This neutral body recommended allocating 22 m^3/s from the river to Iran during normal water years (Dominguez et al., 1951; Loodin, 2021b). Iran initially rejected this allocation, consistently seeking a larger share (Shroder & Ahmadzai, 2016). Afghanistan subsequently offered a "22 plus 4 cubic meters per second" package as a gesture of goodwill, contingent on Iran granting Afghanistan expanded trading access through its Bandar Abbas port (Abidi, 1977; Hearns, 2015; Loodin et al., 2023; Loodin & Wolf, 2022). In March 1973, both nations signed the Helmand River Treaty, committing Afghanistan to provide 26 m^3/s to Iran in normal water years, with provisions for proportional reductions during low-flow periods (International Water Law, 1973; Mianabadi et al., 2020).

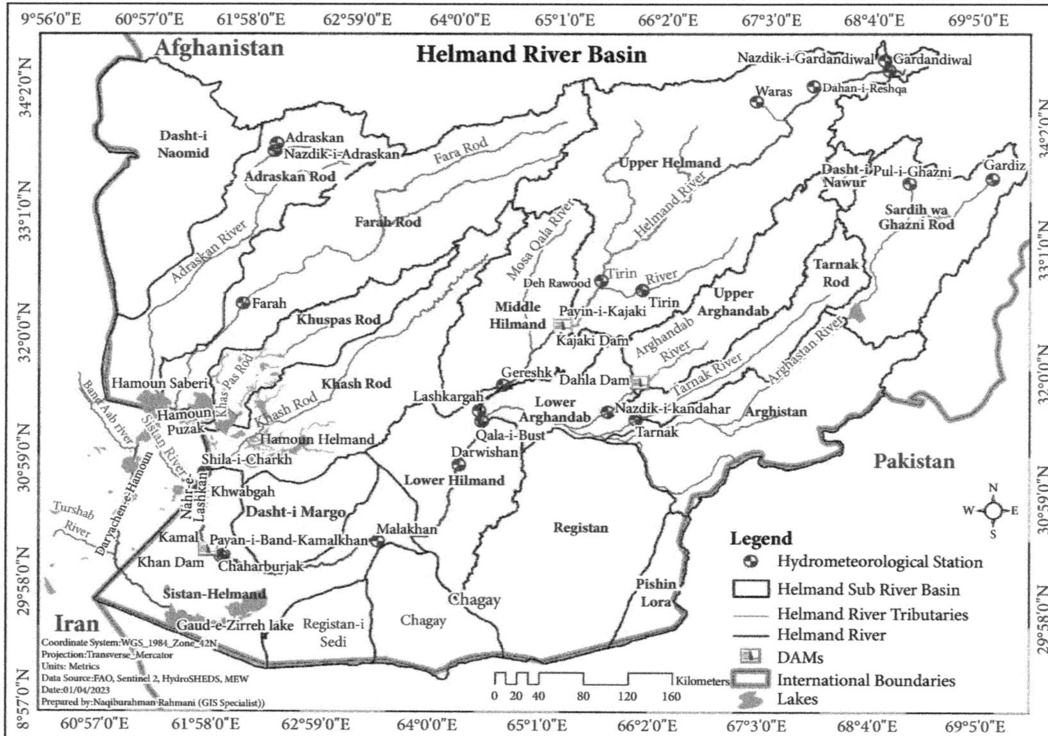

Figure 5.2 The Helmand River Basin Shared Between Afghanistan and Iran

Note: From Ministry of Energy and Water of Afghanistan (2023), with permission.

However, the treaty does not address the impacts of climate change on water availability or mechanisms for assessing drought-induced shortages.

Following the 1973 agreement, Afghanistan experienced social unrest, during which Iran constructed extensive water infrastructure in the lower Helmand basin without prior notification. This included three dams (Zahak, Sistan, and Kahak) for water diversion (Mayar, 2023; Thomas et al., 2016). These reservoirs have the capacity to irrigate over 80,000 hectares, exceeding Iran's rightful share of the Helmand River flow (Bazzi et al., 2021). These developments changed the river's natural flow patterns in the lower basin (Whitney, 2006).

With the fall of the Taliban regime in 2001, Afghanistan resumed its hydraulic development with international support, completing the Kamal Khan Dam in 2021. This project, with a 52 million m^3 capacity, raised concerns in Iran. Former Iranian president Hasan Rouhani expressed environmental apprehensions about Afghan dam construction (Omid, 2017). Afghan analysts argue that the Kamal Khan Dam was designed to facilitate adherence to the 1973 treaty by ensuring controlled water discharge to Iran (Aman, 2016). Nevertheless, operation of Kamal Khan Dam has exacerbated mistrust between the nations, escalating water conflicts, particularly since the Taliban's return to power in Afghanistan in 2021 (Hessami, 2023; Ramachandran, 2022).

5.7 Theoretical Framework: SWOT Analysis in Transboundary Water Governance

The SWOT (strengths, weaknesses, opportunities, threats) analysis framework emerged from research at Stanford Research Institute in the 1960s, initially led by Albert Humphrey. While its exact origins are still debated, the framework has evolved from a strategic planning tool to a comprehensive analytical methodology (Helms & Nixon, 2010). For the case of the drought-stricken Helmand River, we utilize this theoretical framework to examine the strengths, weaknesses, opportunities and threats of joint investment—in terms of infrastructure and technically—on the shared flow of the Helmand River. We first detail the various subcomponents of the framework. Then, we apply the framework to the Helmand River, where we specifically assess how this analytical framework could enable the two riparians to cooperate on the flow of the shared Helmand River.

5.7.1 Strengths of SWOT as a Theoretical Framework?

5.7.1.1 Legal Framework

- Established bilateral/multilateral agreements
- River basin organizations (RBOs)

The foundation for the legal and institutional arrangements of a shared watercourse is the principle of "equitable and reasonable utilization" as outlined in Article 5 of the UN Watercourses Convention (see Salman, 2017). The legal and institutional arrangements outlined in this instrument can help riparians identify and set up the following:

- Conflict resolution mechanisms
- Resource allocation frameworks
- Shared responsibility principles
- Cooperative management structures (Al-Saidi & Hefny, 2018)

5.7.1.2 Technical and Operational Capacity

- Joint monitoring systems
- Shared databases (e.g., hydrological, meteorological, socioeconomic, etc. data; refer to Mukuyu et al. [2023] on exchange of data in transboundary river basins)
- Technical expertise exchange

5.7.2 Weaknesses

5.7.2.1 Institutional Limitations

- Fragmented governance structures (e.g., unrecognized and politically isolated governments)
- Power asymmetries between states
- Weak enforcement mechanisms
- Variable commitment levels

Zeitoun and Warner (2006) developed a hydro-hegemony analytical framework in critical scholarship exploring water conflicts and cooperations among the riparians of politically tense river basins. Hydro-hegemony framework unveils the following:

- Unequal power relations
- Resource capture

- Coercive cooperation
- Limited stakeholder participation among the co-riparians

5.7.2.2 Implementation Challenges

- Insufficient monitoring capacity
- Limitations in data collection and sharing
- Resource disparities
- Technical capability gaps (lack of hydro-cognizant staff)

Mirumachi (2015) emphasizes how implementation weaknesses are often related to the following:

- Limited financial resources
- Technical capacity gaps
- Political unwillingness
- Coordination challenges

5.7.3 Opportunities

5.7.3.1 Cooperation Enhancement

- Joint infrastructural projects
- Technology and knowledge transfer
- Capacity-building initiatives

5.7.3.2 Environmental Innovation

- Green infrastructural development
- Climate change adaptation strategies
- Ecosystem-based management (e.g., nature-based solutions) (Keesstra et al., 2018)
- Sustainable water-use practices

5.7.4 Threats

5.7.4.1 Environmental Challenges

- Climate change impacts
- Water scarcity
- Ecosystem degradation
- Natural disasters

5.7.4.2 Sociopolitical Risks

- Regional conflicts
- Political instability (refer to Figure 5.3)
- Population growth
- Socioeconomic development pressures

Fischhendler (2015) identifies key threats that prevent riparians from engaging in water cooperation over the use of a shared watercourse.

- Security concerns
- Resource nationalism (see Loodin, 2024b; Wheeler & Hussein, 2021)
- Development conflicts (e.g., dam construction in an upstream or downstream state)

Given the differences in the socioeconomic, political, and environmental landscape of the co-riparian nations, the integration of the conceptual framework (CBA) with the SWOT analysis offers a comprehensive approach to understanding the complexity of transboundary water relations as the evolving impacts of climate change and devastating droughts impact the livelihood of communities that directly rely on the shared waters. While CBA offers a structured method to quantify the economic and environmental costs and benefits related to shared water, the SWOT analysis enables us

Strengths	**Weaknesses**
• **Legal Framework** • Binational Agreement • **Cultural Commonality** • Language • Regional Interest • Religion • Historical Ties	• **Institutional Limitations** • Fragmented Governance • Power Asymmetries • **Implementation Challenges** • Insufficient Monitoring • Data Sharing Restrictions
Opportunities	**Threats**
• **Cooperation Enhancement** • Joint Research • River Basin Organization • Joint Infrastructures • **Environmental Innovation** • Green Infrastructures • Climate Adaptation	• **Environmental Challenges** • Climate Change • Water Scarcity • **Socio-Political Risks** • Regional Conflicts • Political Instability

Figure 5.3 A Theoretical Framework for the SWOT Analysis
Note: Elaborated by the authors.

to contextualize the capabilities—both internal and external—of the riparian nations (Sadoff & Grey, 2002). For instance, while the development of dam construction in Lao PDR unveils its upstream economic superiority (generating revenues), its activities impact fishing industries and socioeconomic conditions of the farming and fishing communities in downstream Vietnam, threatening regional and political instability in the region (see Grumbine et al., 2012). Thus, leveraging the factors of CBA and SWOT in transboundary water negotiations will help negotiators and policymakers of the riparian nations to trade off between the costs and benefits of dam construction and its potential impacts on the riparians. This will lead to maximization of the use and allocation of the shared water while ensuring ecosystem sustainability.

5.8 Research Methodology

This research aims to conceptualize trust using a cost–benefit decision analysis framework for the riparians of the Helmand River. Utilizing a combined framework, we have used both document analysis and discourse analysis methodologies to evaluate how a CBA framework helps maximize the benefit of using the shared Helmand River while minimizing distrust between the riparian nations. First, we used discourse analysis to examine language in context, including verbal communication, written texts, and social interactions (see Nikander & Vehviläinen, 2010). This method is of interest particularly for the politically tense and water-stressed basins like that of the Helmand River where water conflict is commonly portrayed not only in academic literature published by inside and outside basin scholars but also in news articles, op-eds, and official and unofficial reports, as well as press releases by the officials of the two riparian nations (see Bowen, 2009, on document analysis). We analyzed the contents of these materials in multiple languages, including English, Persian (called Dari in Afghanistan), and Pashto, to ensure comprehensive coverage of both technical and non-technical sources. In fact, document analysis helps identify the riparian nations' positions, needs, concerns, and interests and their willingness to collaborate on the use of the shared watercourse by examining research articles, technical reports, opinion pieces, and official and unofficial documents and reports. On the other hand, in the case of the Helmand River, discourse analysis reviews language signs and speeches of officials and decision makers in the Helmand River basin in using and allocating the shared waters between the two riparian nations.

The study acknowledges certain limitations, particularly the 1973 Helmand River Treaty. While the treaty serves as the basis for this chapter, the focus remains on exploring ways to enhance trust between the co-riparians through joint investments leading to water equity and justice in the basin rather than an in-depth examination of the terms of the treaty. The research scope primarily covers materials published after the 1973 treaty, with the exception of the Helmand River Delta Commission Report (Dominguez et al., 1951). We decided to explore the documents, reports, news article, and op-eds not only in English but also in local languages (Persian and Pashto) as many authorities from Afghanistan and Iran feel more comfortable expressing their views on Helmand River hydro-politics in their native languages. This diverse view of the hydro-politics of the Helmand River using three different languages strengthens the neutrality of the authors in establishing viable trust-building procedures between the riparian nations.

5.9 Application of CBA to the Helmand River Basin

Shared between upstream Afghanistan and downstream Iran, the Helmand River serves as a significant case study for applying CBA in transboundary water governance and management. Given the evolving impact of climate change, the basin grapples with complex challenges, including water scarcity, competing demands, and sociopolitical tensions (Mayar, 2023; Mianabadi et al., 2020). We believe that through incorporation of the conceptual framework of CBA, which encompasses temporal, spatial, uncertainty and risk, political, and institutional considerations, a comprehensive analysis of the Helmand River basin can be achieved.

5.9.1 Temporal Considerations in the Helmand River Basin

a. *Time horizons*: Long-term time horizons are essential to assess infrastructural projects such as dams or irrigation systems including large-scale diversion channels within the basin. For instance, Afghanistan's Kamal Khan Dam project aims to enhance agricultural productivity and energy generation. A CBA with a long-term perspective must consider not only the immediate economic benefits but also the downstream impacts on Iran's water availability and the ecological health of the transboundary Hamoun wetlands over several decades.

b. *Discount rates*: The selection of discount rates significantly influences the valuation of future benefits and costs. At a lower discount rate, we can prioritize the preservation of the three interconnected Hamoun wetlands that hold significant ecological and cultural benefits for the riparian nations over their short-term development objectives.

c. *Intertemporal distribution of costs and benefits*: Temporal disparities must be addressed to ensure that both Afghanistan and Iran derive equitable benefits. For instance, while Afghanistan may initially benefit from water accumulation in its upstream territory, Iran may face delayed but severe ecological impacts if the wetlands dry up. Equitable mechanisms, such as water-sharing agreements, including adherence to the proper implementation of the 1973 treaty, will balance these temporal trade-offs.

5.9.2 Spatial Considerations in the Helmand River Basin

a. *Geographic variability*: The Helmand River basin's upstream–downstream dynamic highlights the spatial variability in costs and benefits. Afghanistan's development projects predominantly benefit its upstream regions, whereas the construction of Chahnimehs across the border, to supply water for the Sistan-Baluchistan province, will only benefit Iran. However, integrated joint efforts will balance these geographic disparities in the basin.

b. *Localized impacts*: Localized impacts, such as displacement of communities or loss of traditional livelihoods in areas affected by dam construction, must be integrated into the spatial analysis of CBA. The environmental and social consequences of borderland communities relying on the flow of the Helmand River to sustain their life within the Hamoun wetlands should also be considered.

c. *Cross-border coordination*: Effective collaboration between Afghanistan and Iran is important to ensure that spatial benefits and costs are equitably distributed. Joint management frameworks and shared monitoring systems can foster trust and transparency, mitigating the potential for conflict (refer to Articles 2 and 3 of the International Water Law, 1973).

5.9.3 Uncertainty and Risk in the Helmand River Basin

Uncertainties in hydrological conditions due to climatic conditions, such as fluctuation in rainfall patterns and increasing drought frequency, pose significant challenges to the Helmand River basin. Additionally, sociopolitical instability in the region exacerbates challenges in implementing long-term water management projects. Risk assessment and climate-sensitive adaptive management strategies, such as scenario planning, are crucial to address these uncertainties.

5.9.4 Political and Institutional Factors in the Helmand River Basin: Stakeholder Engagement

Engaging local communities (e.g., the underserved Balouch communities at the two sides of the borderline), governmental bodies, and international organizations is critical for the successful application of CBA in the Helmand River basin. Transparent dialogue and inclusive decision-making—despite the fact that riparians have organized over 27 meetings on the flow of the Helmand River since 2004 (see Loodin et al., 2024b)—can help build trust between Afghanistan and Iran, de-escalating tensions in the basin.

5.9.5 Institutional Frameworks

Strengthening institutional frameworks, such as bilateral water-sharing agreements or regional water commissions (committing to the implementation of the 1973 Helmand River Treaty), can provide a foundation for cooperative governance. These frameworks should address both immediate water needs and long-term water allocation among the co-riparian nations while ensuring ecosystem sustainability in the basin.

5.10 Results and Analysis

5.10.1 Investment in Establishment of RBOs

The establishment of an RBO for the Helmand River basin, shared between Afghanistan and Iran, is critically important for sustainable transboundary water management, especially as the 1973 Helmand River Treaty lacks a robust mechanism for enforcement. In contrast to the shared Helmand River basin, the International Commission for the Protection of the Rhine (ICPR) demonstrates how institutional frameworks can transform water disputes into cooperative mechanisms through systematic dialogue, joint monitoring, and shared decision-making processes (Egli, 2002). The absence of a formal RBO on the Helmand River has contributed to recurring disputes over water allocation, especially as the basin is grappling with the adverse effects of climate change, precipitation decline, and glacial retreat in the upstream section of the river (see Azizi et al., 2024; Daly et al., 2012). The establishment of an RBO could serve as a platform for data-sharing, joint research initiatives, and coordinated response to climate change impacts. A good example is the Mekong River Commission where procedures for data-sharing and prior notification (e.g., notification on dam- and water-related projects along the shared Mekong River) have been implemented despite political tensions among its member states (Mekong River Commission, 2023; Plengsaeng et al., 2014).

The potential benefits of establishing a Helmand River RBO—an autonomous and independent organization—extend beyond mere water allocation, encompassing ecosystem protection, flood management, and drought mitigation, as evidenced by the success of the Murray-Darling Basin Authority in Australia, which has effectively balanced competing water needs while maintaining ecological flows (Hart, 2016). It is worth noting that the Helmand River basin faces additional challenges including post-conflict reconstruction in Afghanistan and regional geopolitical tensions requiring a deeper assessment of the establishment of an RBO for the riparian states (Ahmadi et al., 2023). Recent scholarship in transboundary water conflict and cooperation (hydro-politics), for example, studies by Schmeier (2012) and Zeitoun et al. (2019), articulates that RBOs with clear mandates, sustainable funding acquisition, and strong technical capacities are more effective at promoting cooperation and resolving disputes. In the case of the Helmand River where power asymmetry, socioeconomic differences, and disparities in technical and hydro-cognizant expertise are evident (Thomas et al., 2016), we propose that a Helmand River RBO should incorporate these elements while taking into consideration the specific sociopolitical context of Afghan–Iranian relations.

The establishment of an RBO could lead to enhancement of the implementation of the existing 1973 treaty by creating permanent technical committees—although a committee of commissioners from the two riparians periodically meets in person in either Afghanistan or Iran—establishing joint monitoring stations and developing shared databases (for the type of data-sharing, refer to the latest work of the authors: Loodin et al., 2024a). The Orange-Senqu River Commission—shared between Botswana, Namibia, Lesotho, and South Africa—which successfully operationalized cooperation among its member states through technical working groups and joint studies, despite the challenging political dynamics in southern Africa, can serve as the basis for the Helmand River riparians to learn how water cooperation can be maintained and prioritized in a politically tense region. Furthermore, an institutionalized RBO framework would facilitate access to international funding and technical assistance for basin-wide projects, as demonstrated by the Nile Basin Initiative's success in attracting funding support for cooperative projects (Cascão et al., 2020). Moreover, it would also provide mechanisms for addressing pressing challenges such as climate change impacts (see Mayar, 2022, 2023), population growth, and increasing water demand for agricultural expansion in both Afghanistan and Iran (Akbari & Torabi Haghighi, 2022).

Given the increasing water stress in the region—both surface water and illegal withdrawal of groundwater by the farming communities in the Helmand River basin (see Mayar, 2023)—and projections of climate change impacts, the establishment of a Helmand River RBO becomes even more crucial for ensuring water security and preventing potential conflicts, particularly considering that successful RBOs like the International Boundary and Water Commission between the United States and Mexico have proven effective at managing shared water resources, even during periods of political tension, through institutionalized cooperation mechanisms and technical expertise (Mumme, 2005). The proposed RBO should incorporate lessons learned from these successful models while adapting to local conditions, potentially starting with technical cooperation on non-controversial issues such as flood and drought warning systems and water quality monitoring, before gradually expanding to more complex issues of water allocation and joint infrastructural management.

5.10.2 Investment in Joint Water Infrastructures: A Viable Mechanism for Hamoun Wetland Restoration?

The development of joint infrastructural projects in the Helmand River basin presents a significant opportunity for Afghanistan and Iran to address both flooding challenges and the degradation of the Hamoun wetlands, similar to successful cases of transboundary cooperation elsewhere (see Loodin et al., 2024a, and Shahnawaz & Naqvi, 2024, on the Helmand River; Yu et al., 2024, on the Lancang-Mekong River basin; Tafesse, 2009, on the eastern Nile sub-basin). The Senegal River basin's experience with the OMVS demonstrates how joint infrastructure ownership and management can transform transboundary water relations from conflictive to cooperative (Vick, 2006). The OMVS model, where member states jointly own and operate the Manantali and Diama Dams—the two dams built to generate hydroelectricity, irrigate agricultural lands, and regulate the flow of the shared river (see Diessner, 2012)—can serve as a basis for Afghanistan and Iran to consider, as it has successfully balanced flood control, power generation, diversions for agriculture, and environmental flow preservation.

The current infrastructure in the Helmand basin, both upstream and downstream, operates without coordinated management protocols between the riparian states. Drawing from the successful case of the Columbia River Treaty shared between the United States and Canada (Cosens et al., 2018), a joint operational framework for existing and new infrastructures could optimize flood control, particularly during the rainy season (Goes et al., 2016; Sefat & Tsubaki, 2024), while ensuring environmental flows to the Hamoun wetlands—the most vulnerable ecosystem in the region due to climatic changes, drought, and human activities in the Helmand River basin (Ehsani & Shakeryari, 2021). The Columbia River case demonstrates how coordinated dam operations can reduce flood risks while generating shared benefits through hydropower generation and ecosystem services.

In the case of the Helmand River, as the two riparians grapple with the impacts of climate change and devastating flooding during the rainy season, we argue that coordinated infrastructural development will enable them to not only mitigate the adverse effects of climate change on water resources but also revitalize the desiccated Hamoun wetlands in the basin. In fact, the revitalization of the Hamoun wetlands could benefit from lessons learned in the Murray-Darling basin, where environmental flow requirements have been successfully incorporated into infrastructural operations (Settre et al., 2017). We argue that the development of joint storage facilities in the middle reaches of the Helmand River could help regulate flows during flood periods while storing water for release during dry seasons to maintain and revitalize the Hamoun ecosystem. Similar approaches have been undertaken by the riparians of the Rhine basin (Switzerland, France, Germany, and the Netherlands), where the ICPR has jointly coordinated infrastructural operations to reduce flood risks while improving ecological conditions (Mostert, 2009).

In terms of CBA, the investment in joint infrastructures on the Mekong River not only mitigated the adverse effects of flooding in the delta countries, including Vietnam and Cambodia, but also helped the riparians enjoy the shared benefits (e.g., fishery, vital water resources for agriculture, transportation, hydropower generation, and trade) (see Belinskij, 2015). For the Helmand basin, potential benefits include reduced flood damage, improved agricultural production due to water availability, improvement in the Hamoun wetland ecosystem, and possible hydropower generation in the basin. Thus, coordinated infrastructural operation can increase total basin-wide benefits compared to unilateral infrastructural development.

Additionally, a coordinated approach to joint infrastructural development, starting with shared monitoring stations and gradually expanding to larger projects, could help build trust between Afghanistan and Iran. This way Iran's rightful share of water from the Helmand River can be delivered by tracing the outflow of the Helmand River using the hydro-metric stations constructed at the political border of the two countries, which will eventually lead to water cooperation and trust-building processes in the basin. However, a lack of political will hinders the riparians from establishing and specifying these points of water delivery (Loodin et al., 2023; Mianabadi et al., 2020). The successful case of the Chu-Talas Commission between Kazakhstan and Kyrgyzstan demonstrates how joint infrastructural maintenance and operation can foster cooperation even in politically complex regions (Wegerich, 2008).

Moreover, the Helmand River basin suffers from the rapidly evolving effects of climatic changes and recurring droughts. We argue that climate change adaptation policies could be integrated into joint infrastructural planning using the example of the Danube River basin, where the International Commission for the Protection of the Danube River (2018) has successfully implemented climate-adaptive infrastructural strategies. This approach is particularly relevant for the Hamoun wetlands, where climate change impacts compound the challenges of water availability and ecosystem sustainability among the farming communities on both sides of the border in the basin. The restoration of the Hamoun wetlands through joint infrastructural development would require careful consideration of environmental flow requirements. The successful restoration of the Mesopotamian marshlands provides valuable lessons in wetland revival through coordinated water management (Al-Quraishi & Kaplan, 2021).

In the case of the Helmand River, our assertion is that both riparian nations should jointly invest in upgrading and lining the irrigation canals of the Kamal Khan Dam. In fact, Nevermann et al. (2025) calculated the evaporative loss due to unreliable and unsustainable reservoirs built by both Helmand River riparian states and highlighted a shocking loss of 284 million m^3 in 2023 in the basin. Such joint investment will uplift water allocation efficiency, enabling water-use optimization in the basin and de-escalating water conflicts among the farming communities of the shared river. Indeed, upgrading the water channels and investing in the maintenance of the Kamal Khan Dam will not only ensure sufficient flow of water for irrigation in Afghanistan but also supply Iran's rightful share of water from the river (820 million m^3/year in a normal water year).

For instance, an equal investment of \$50 million by both riparians would enhance water storage capacity by 500 million m^3—we assume that a hypothetical million cubic meters (Mm^3) of water will cost \$100 based on the cost of regional dam construction. As a result of this joint investment, Afghanistan's annual economic growth from agricultural productivity will be \$80 million (assuming \$160/Mm^3 in large-scale agriculture due to irrigation efficiency), while Iran would generate \$60 million through the restoration and revitalization of the Hamoun wetlands and expansion of the fishing industry, resulting in a net benefit of \$90 million annually for the two countries (\$140 million – \$50 million investment = \$90 million). The \$140 million is the annual revenue, while the \$50 million is a joint investment by the two riparian nations that will be utilized over 10 years to optimize the waters of the shared Helmand River. It is worth noting that a 10-year investment period is considered here because it will help riparians revisit or re-evaluate their joint investment mechanisms through which required amendments are provided by the two riparians. In our view, this 10-year investment period will also allow the riparians to examine how the cooperative mechanism evolves within this time frame. Indeed, it is expected to support the inclination and commitment of each riparian to the sustainable allocation and utilization of the shared waters, leading to the reinforcement of water cooperation in the shared waterway and amplifying long-term cooperation in the basin.

$$\text{Net Present Value (NPV)} = \sum_{t=0}^{n} \frac{R_t}{(1+\mathrm{i})^t} \tag{1}$$

where

R_t = net cash inflow–outflow
i = discount rate
t = time period

First, a 5% discount rate is considered for this joint investment over the 10 years. This value was chosen for the joint investment on the flow of the Helmand River because a recent study by Migo-Sumagang et al. (2023) recommends the use of a 5%–6% discount rate for developing countries including Afghanistan and Iran. It is particularly applicable to the Helmand River basin, where the riparians, Afghanistan and Iran, suffer from socioeconomic and political strains imposed and exerted by outside-basin players as well as the existence of high inflation rates particularly in Iran. Second, we consider the need for heavy investment by Afghanistan in the first 5 years (1–5 years) and a slightly lighter investment in the second 5 years (6–10 years). This is because the country's agricultural practices are outdated. The country needs to first invest in upgrading its water infrastructures to regulate the flow of water for optimum and sustainable use while ensuring Iran's rightful share of water from the Helmand River. On the other hand, we recommend that Iran invest heavily in the second 5-year period (6–10 years) in the revitalization of the desiccated Hamoun wetlands while investing slightly lighter in the wetlands in the first 5 years. This latter investment will enable farmers in the downstream segment of the river to sustain their livelihood through agriculture, animal husbandry, pastoralism, fishery, and eco-tourism once the Helmand River flow is better governed and managed, leading to socioeconomic improvements in the basin, resulting in trust-building processes between the co-riparians. Thus, such cooperative engagement will lead to regional stability, ensuring water equity and justice in the basin.

Now, using the NPV formula, we can calculate the discounted cash flow of benefit as well as the benefit–cost ratio (see Table 5.1).

Moreover, another joint investment of $10 million (by upstream Afghanistan and downstream Iran) in the revitalization of the transboundary Hamoun wetlands could restore 200 Mm^3 of the flow of the shared river, generating $30 million for both nations through ecological restoration. We

Table 5.1 Cost–Benefit Analysis Calculation on the Joint Investment by the Riparians of the Helmand River Basin

Year	Afghanistan investment (in million USD)	Iran investment (in million USD)	Total investment (in million USD)	Afghanistan benefit (in million USD)	Iran benefit (in million USD)	Afghanistan net cash flow (in million USD)	Iran net cash flow (in million USD)	Discounted factor	Discounted flow of investment	Discounted cash flow of benefit	Benefit–cost ratio (total cost/total benefit)
1	5.0	1.0	6.0	80.0	60.0	75.00	59.00	0.95	5.71	133.33	
2	4.0	1.5	5.5	80.0	60.0	76.00	58.50	0.91	4.99	126.98	
3	3.5	1.5	5.0	80.0	60.0	76.50	58.50	0.86	4.32	120.94	
4	3.0	2.0	5.0	80.0	60.0	77.0	58.00	0.82	4.11	115.18	
5	2.5	2.5	5.0	80.0	60.0	77.50	57.50	0.78	3.92	109.69	
6	2.0	3.0	5.0	80.0	60.0	78.00	57.00	0.75	3.73	104.47	
7	1.5	3.0	4.5	80.0	60.0	78.50	57.00	0.71	3.20	99.50	
8	1.5	3.5	5.0	80.0	60.0	78.50	56.50	0.68	3.38	94.76	
9	1.0	3.5	4.5	80.0	60.0	79.00	56.50	0.64	2.90	90.25	
10	1.0	3.5	4.5	80.0	60.0	79.00	56.50	0.61	2.76	85.95	
Total (in million USD)	25.0	25.0	50.0			775.00	575.00		39.03	1081.04	27.6977648

Note: Discounted cash flow = $1/(1 + r)^t$.

assume a \$150 per Mm^3 valuation of wetland services, while the annual cost including maintenance of the shared wetlands will be \$2 million. It is worth noting that the second investment in the form of upgrading and maintenance of the water infrastructures built along the Helmand River and the three interconnected Hamoun wetlands will take place once the first investment period ends. Thus, the net benefit of the joint effort in wetland restoration is calculated at \$28 million/year. Added to this, the revitalization of the shared Hamoun wetlands in the drought-stricken basin not only will lead to the maintenance of the livelihood of the farming and fishing communities of the Sistan-Baluchistan province of Iran but will also alleviate hunger and mitigate internal displacement and migration of Afghan communities from southern Afghanistan, leading to socioeconomic and political stability in the region.

Therefore, such coordinated and joint efforts for revitalization of the desiccated Hamoun wetlands, which requires the prioritization of transboundary interest over the national interest (see Loodin et al., 2023, 2024b), not only will benefit the farming communities in the basin but will also trigger sustainable and equitable uses of water among the co-riparians. In turn, this will incentivize the trust-building processes between Afghanistan and Iran in the Helmand River basin.

5.11 Conclusion

Establishing trust serves as a critical prerequisite for long-term cooperation among riparian states sharing a river basin. Indeed, transboundary water security is fundamentally threatened by the absence of trust. This chapter employs a cost–benefit decision-making analytical framework to evaluate trust-related challenges in the Helmand River basin, a highly water-stressed system in South Asia, through the application of a SWOT analysis as a conceptual decision support model. Despite the existence of the ratified Helmand River Treaty, its implementation has remained incomplete by both riparian nations, Afghanistan and Iran. The treaty stipulates that both parties would identify three water delivery points along the Afghan–Iranian political border immediately following ratification. However, several factors have impeded this process: social and political instability in Afghanistan, Iranian political transformation, and the initiation of hydraulic mission in the basin—first in Iran during the 1980s and subsequently in Afghanistan in the 2000s. These circumstances have prevented the establishment of designated water delivery points, consequently fostering mutual distrust. Furthermore, the analysis reveals that both nations' prioritization of national interests over transboundary considerations has exacerbated water security challenges within the basin, particularly as the evolving impacts of climate changes are prevailing in the basin. The implementation of a decision support model is essential, given that climatic changes affect water availability and accessibility at the transboundary level. Such models enable riparian states to address water-related vulnerabilities and ecosystem challenges arising from climate change impacts. The chapter's findings emphasize that strengthening trust within the basin requires prioritizing transboundary advantages over national interests in the decision-making processes between riparian states. This shift in priority is crucial for sustainable water resource management in the region.

References

Abidi, A. H. H. (1977). Irano–Afghan dispute over the Helmand waters. *International Studies, 16*(3), 357–378.

Ahmadi, A., Noorali, H., Campana, M., & Barroudi, M. (2023). Analyzing the hydropolitical tensions of the Hirmand/Helmand River through the evaluation of land use changes using the SVM method. *Human Geography Research, 55*(4), 225–243.

Ahmed, M., Abdelrehim, R., Elshalkany, M., & Abdrabou, M. (2024). Impacts of the Grand Ethiopian Renaissance Dam on the Nile River's downstream reservoirs. *Journal of Hydrology, 633*, Article 130952.

Akron, A., Ghermandi, A., Dayan, T., & Hershkovitz, Y. (2017). Interbasin water transfer for the rehabilitation of a transboundary Mediterranean stream: An economic analysis. *Journal of Environmental Management, 202*, 276–286.

Al-Quraishi, A. K., & Kaplan, D. A. (2021). Connecting changes in Euphrates River flow to hydropattern of the western Mesopotamian marshes. *Science of the Total Environment, 768*, Article 144445.

Al-Saidi, M., & Hefny, A. (2018). Institutional arrangements for beneficial regional cooperation on water, energy, and food priority issues in the eastern Nile basin. *Journal of Hydrology, 562*, 821–831.

Aman, F. (2016, August). *Water dispute escalating between Iran and Afghanistan* [Issue brief]. Retrieved January 8, 2024, from https://www.atlanticcouncil.org/wp-content/uploads/2016/09/Water_Dispute_Escalating_between_Iran_and_Afghanistan_web_0830.pdf

Arjoon, D., Tilmant, A., & Herrmann, M. (2016). Sharing water and benefits in transboundary river basins. *Hydrology and Earth System Sciences, 20*(6), 2135–2150.

Arrow, K. J. (1983). *Collected papers of Kenneth J. Arrow: Social choice and justice* (Vol. 1). Harvard University Press.

Asheim, G. B. (2010). Intergenerational equity. *Annual Review of Economics, 2*(1), 197–222.

Azizi, A. H., Akhtar, F., Tischbein, B., Borgemeister, C., & Wang, Q. (2024). Assessing long-term water storage dynamics in Afghanistan: An integrated approach using machine learning, hydrological models, and remote sensing. *Journal of Environmental Management, 370*, Article 122901.

Bartkowski, B., Lienhoop, N., & Hansjürgens, B. (2015). Capturing the complexity of biodiversity: A critical review of economic valuation studies of biological diversity. *Ecological Economics, 113*, 1–14.

Basheer, M., Nechifor, V., Calzadilla, A., Siddig, K., Etichia, M., Whittington, D., Hulme, D.& Harou, J. J. (2021). Collaborative management of the Grand Ethiopian Renaissance Dam increases economic benefits and resilience. *Nature Communications, 12*(1), Article 5622.

Basheer, M., Siddig, K., Elnour, Z., Ahmed, M., & Ringler, C. (2024). Toward integrated dam assessment: Evaluating multi-dimensional impacts of the Grand Ethiopian Renaissance Dam on Sudan. *Environmental Research Letters, 19*(10), Article 104067.

Bazzi, H., Ebrahimi, H., & Aminnejad, B. (2021). A comprehensive statistical analysis of evaporation rates under climate change in southern Iran using WEAP (case study: Chahnimeh reservoirs of Sistan Plain). *Ain Shams Engineering Journal, 12*(2), 1339–1352. https://doi.org/10.1016/j.asej.2020.08.030

Belinskij, A. (2015). Water–energy–food nexus within the framework of international water law. *Water, 7*(10), 5396–5415.

Bentham, J. (1970). *An introduction to the principles of morals and legislation.* J. H. Burns & H. L. A. Hart (Eds.). Oxford University Press. (Original work published 1789)

Bodian, A., Diop, L., Panthou, G., Dacosta, H., Deme, A., Dezetter, A., Ndiaye, P. M., Diouf, I.& Vischel, T. (2020). Recent trend in hydroclimatic conditions in the Senegal River basin. *Water, 12*(2), Article 436.

Bowen, G. A. (2009). Document analysis as a qualitative research method. *Qualitative Research Journal, 9*(2), 27–40.

Calderon, P. (2024, August 27). *Comment: How mismanagement of global river basins is putting $105 billion in business revenue at risk.* Reuters. Retrieved December 29, 2024, from https://www.reuters.com/sustainability/boards-policy-regulation/comment-how-mismanagement-global-river-basins-is-putting-105-billion-business-2024-08-27/?utm_source=chatgpt.com

Cascão, A. E., Fekade, W., Grossmann, M., & Seid, A. (2020). Water diplomacy and conflict transformation in the Nile River basin: The key role of the Nile basin initiative over the past 20 years. In A. Kittikhoun & S. Schmeier (Eds.), *River basin organizations in water diplomacy* (pp. 141–162). Routledge.

Condon, M., Kriens, D., Lohani, A., & Sattar, E. (2014). Challenge and response in the Indus Basin. *Water Policy, 16*(S1), 58–86.

Cosens, B., McKinney, M., Paisley, R., & Wolf, A. T. (2018). Reconciliation of development and ecosystems: The ecology of governance in the International Columbia River basin. *Regional Environmental Change, 18*(6), 1679–1692.

Dallman, S., Ngo, M., Laris, P., & Thien, D. (2013). Political ecology of emotion and sacred space: The Winnemem Wintu struggles with California water policy. *Emotion, Space and Society, 6*, 33–43.

Daly, S. F., Vuyovich, C. M., Deeb, E. J., Newman, S. D., Baldwin, T. B., & Gagnon, J. J. (2012). Assessment of the snow conditions in the major watersheds of Afghanistan using multispectral and passive microwave remote sensing. *Hydrological Processes, 26*(17), 2631–2642. https://doi.org/10.1002/hyp.9367

Diessner, C. (2012). Dam complications in Senegal: How river dams may hurt more than help vulnerable populations in water-stressed regions. *Journal of Environmental & Sustainability Law, 19*, 247–263.

Dombrowsky, I. (2009). Revisiting the potential for benefit sharing in the management of trans-boundary rivers. *Water Policy, 11*(2), 125–140.

Dominguez, F. J., Lowry, B. L., & Webb, C. E. (1951, February 28). *The Helmand River basin dispute*. Retrieved January 2, 2024, from https://aquapedia.waterdiplomacy.org/wiki/index.php?title=The_Helmand_River_Basin_Dispute

Dunca, A. M. (2018). Water pollution and water quality assessment of major transboundary rivers from Banat (Romania). *Journal of Chemistry, 2018*(1), Article 9073763.

Egli, T. (2002). *Non structural flood plain management: Measures and their effectiveness* (K. Wehner, Trans.). International Commission for the Protection of the Rhine.

Ehsani, A. H., & Shakeryari, M. (2021). Monitoring of wetland changes affected by drought using four Landsat satellite data and Fuzzy ARTMAP classification method (case study Hamoun wetland, Iran). *Arabian Journal of Geosciences, 14*(14), Article 1363.

El Deen, S. M. (2022). *Egypt's water policy after the construction of the Grand Ethiopian Renaissance Dam*. Arab Reform Initiative. Retrieved March 19, 2025, from https://www.arab-reform.net/publication/egypts-water-policy-after-the-construction-of-the-grand-ethiopian-renaissance-dam/

Fischhendler, I. (2008). When ambiguity in treaty design becomes destructive: A study of transboundary water. *Global Environmental Politics, 8*(1), 111–136.

Fischhendler, I. (2015). The securitization of water discourse: Theoretical foundations, research gaps and objectives of the special issue. *International Environmental Agreements: Politics, Law and Economics, 15*, 245–255.

Giordano, M., Drieschova, A., Duncan, J. A., Sayama, Y., De Stefano, L., & Wolf, A. T. (2014). A review of the evolution and state of transboundary freshwater treaties. *International Environmental Agreements: Politics, Law and Economics, 14*, 245–264.

Goes, B. J. M., Howarth, S. E., Wardlaw, R. B., Hancock, I. R., & Parajuli, U. N. (2016). Integrated water resources management in an insecure river basin: A case study of Helmand River basin, Afghanistan. *International Journal of Water Resources Development, 32*(1), 3–25.

Gollier, C. (2010). Ecological discounting. *Journal of Economic Theory, 145*(2), 812–829.

Grumbine, R. E., Dore, J., & Xu, J. (2012). Mekong hydropower: Drivers of change and governance challenges. *Frontiers in Ecology and the Environment, 10*(2), 91–98.

Hanasz, P. (2012). *The politics of water security between Afghanistan and Iran* [Strategic Analyses Paper, Future Directions International].

Hanley, N., Barbier, E. B., & Barbier, E. (2009). *Pricing nature: Cost–benefit analysis and environmental policy*. Edward Elgar Publishing.

Hart, B. T. (2016). The Australian Murray-Darling Basin Plan: Factors leading to its successful development. *Ecohydrology & Hydrobiology, 16*(4), 229–241.

Hearns, G. (2015, July 23). The Helmand River and the Afghan–Iranian Treaty of 1973. *International Water Law Project Blog*. Retrieved December 25, 2023, from https://www.internationalwaterlaw.org/blog/2015/07/23/the-helmand-river-and-the-afghan-iranian-treaty-of-1973/

Helms, M. M., & Nixon, J. (2010). Exploring SWOT analysis—Where are we now? A review of academic research from the last decade. *Journal of Strategy and Management, 3*(3), 215–251.

Hessami, E. B. (2023). Avoiding a central Asian water war: Challenges and opportunities for cooperation between the Islamic Republic of Iran and the Islamic Emirate of Afghanistan. *SAIS Review of International Affairs, 43*(2), 21–38.

Hirata, R., & Foster, S. (2021). The Guarani aquifer system—From regional reserves to local use. *Quarterly Journal of Engineering Geology and Hydrogeology, 54*(1), Article qjegh2020-091.

Ilyas, M. (2023). *Pakistan, India and the Indus River basin* [Master's thesis, City University of New York]. https://academicworks.cuny.edu/cgi/viewcontent.cgi?article=2192&context=cc_etds_theses

International Commission for the Protection of the Danube River. (2018). *Danube Watch 1/2018—the ICPDR's climate change adaptation strategy*. https://www.icpdr.org/publications/danube-watch-1-2018-icpdrs-climate-change-adaptation-strategy

International Water Law. (1973). The Afghan Iranian Helmand River Water Treaty. Retrieved October 19, 2024, from https://www.internationalwaterlaw.org/documents/regionaldocs/1973_Helmand_River_Water_Treaty-Afghanistan-Iran.pdf

Keesstra, S., Nunes, J., Novara, A., Finger, D., Avelar, D., Kalantari, Z., & Cerdà, A. (2018). The superior effect of nature-based solutions in land management for enhancing ecosystem services. *Science of the Total Environment, 610*, 997–1009.

Klaphake, A. (2005, March). Economic and political benefits of transboundary water cooperation. In *Proceedings of the IHP-HWRP, The value of water—Different approaches in transboundary water management* (pp. 91–99). International Hydrological Programme/Hydrology and Water Resources Programme. https://waterandchange.org/wp-content/uploads/2017/04/Heft3_en.pdf#page=98

Larsen, M. S. B., Owaygen, M., & Sarraf, M. (2004). *Cost of environmental degradation—The case of Lebanon and Tunisia*. World Bank Environmental Department. Retrieved February 2, 2007, from http://www.moe.gov.lb/NR/rdonlyres/D5075FD1-9B98-4BA1-B5E0-8D4CBA039AE4/123/CostEnvDegLebanonTunisiaJune04EDP97.pdf

Li, H., & Lu, J. (2020). Can regional integration control transboundary water pollution? A test from the Yangtze River economic belt. *Environmental Science and Pollution Research, 27*(22), 28288–28305.

Lienert, J., Scholten, L., Egger, C., & Maurer, M. (2015). Structured decision-making for sustainable water infrastructure planning and four future scenarios. *EURO Journal on Decision Processes, 3*(1–2), 107–140.

Lindberg, J., & Hagman, S. (2018). *CBA of environmental projects within hydropower* [Master's thesis, University of KTH Industrial Engineering and Management]. https://www.diva-portal.org/smash/get/diva2:1267986/FULLTEXT01.pdf

Loodin, N. (2021a). *Is it time to incorporate Islamic water management principles into existing global water governance policies?* Water Science Policy. Retrieved September 19, 2024, from https://www.watersciencepolicy.com/2020/08/10/is-it-time-to-incorporate-islamic-water-management-principles-iwmp-into-existing-global-water-governance-policies/

Loodin, N. (2021b). *The role of Islam in water resources management: Could it be integrated into international water law principles (IWLP) for the Islamic-dominated states?* [Master's thesis, Oregon State University]. Retrieved August 2, 2024, from https://ir.library.oregonstate.edu/concern/graduate_thesis_or_dissertations/zs25xg973

Loodin, N. (2024). Emotionality in transboundary water: A case study of Helmand River. *Environmental Management, 75*(1), 63–79.

Loodin, N., Eckstein, G., Singh, V. P., & Sanchez, R. (2023). Assessment of the trust crisis between upstream and downstream states of the Helmand River basin (1973–2022): A half-century of optimism or cynicism? *ACS ES&T Water, 3*(6), 1654–1668. https://doi.org/10.1021/acsestwater.2c00428

Loodin, N., Eckstein, G., Singh, V. P., & Sanchez, R. (2024a). Reframing a data sharing mechanism for the riparian nations of Helmand River basin: Theory of planned behavior is revisited. *Chinese Journal of Urban and Environmental Studies, 12*(4), Article 2450019.

Loodin, N., Eckstein, G., Singh, V. P., & Sanchez, R. (2024b). The role of data sharing in transboundary waterways: The case of the Helmand River basin. In K. Szálkai & M. Szalai (Eds.), *Theorizing transboundary waters in international relations* (pp. 165–194). Springer. https://doi.org/10.1007/978-3-031-43376-4_10

Loodin, N., Keith, T., Arynova, A., Rosenblum, Z., & Ruzmatova, Z. (2021). A critical analysis of the food–energy–water nexus in the Kootenai River basin. *Sustainable Water Resources Management, 7*, 1–13.

Loodin, N., & Warner, J. (2022). A review of hydro-hegemonic dynamics on the transboundary Harirud River basin: 2001–present. *Water, 14*(21), Article 3442.
Loodin, N., & Wolf, A. (2021). *Comparison and contrast of Islamic water management principles with international water law principles: A case study of Helmand River basin.* Preprints. https://doi.org/10.20944/preprints202104.0624.v1
Loodin, N., & Wolf, A. T. (2022). Will Islamic water management principles be included if the Helmand River Treaty is revisited? *Water, 14,* Article 67. https://doi.org/10.3390/w14010067
Madani, K. (2014). Water management in Iran: What is causing the looming crisis? *Journal of Environmental Studies and Sciences, 4*(4), 315–328. https://doi.org/10.1007/s13412-014-0182-z
Madani, K. (2021, December 5). *Explainer: Iran's "water bankruptcy."* The Iran Primer. Retrieved January 2, 2024, from https://iranprimer.usip.org/blog/2021/dec/05/explainer-irans-water-bankruptcy
Madani, K., & Mahoozi, S. (2022, January 4). *Kaveh Madani.* DAWN. Retrieved April 19, 2023, from https://dawnmena.org/author/kaveh-madani/
Matthews, N. (2012). Water grabbing in the Mekong basin—An analysis of the winners and losers of Thailand's hydropower development in Lao PDR. *Water Alternatives, 5*(2), 392–411.
Mayar, M. A. (2022, June 14). *The Climate Change Crisis in Afghanistan: The catastrophe worsens—What hope for action?* Afghanistan Analysts Network. Retrieved June 17, 2023, from https://www.afghanistan-analysts.org/en/reports/economy-development-environment/the-climate-change-crisis-in-afghanistan-the-catastrophe-worsens-what-hope-for-action/
Mayar, M. A. (2023). *The long winding river: Unravelling the water dispute between Afghanistan and Iran.* Afghanistan Analyst Network. Retrieved October 27, 2024, from https://www.afghanistan-analysts.org/en/reports/economy-development-environment/the-long-winding-river-unravelling-the-water-dispute-between-afghanistan-and-iran/
Mekong River Commission. (2023). *Mekong climate change adaptation strategy and action plan.* Retrieved September 22, 2024, from https://www.mrcmekong.org/wp-content/uploads/2024/09/Mekong-Climate-Change-Adaptation-Strategy-and-Action-Plan-MASAP.pdf
Mianabadi, A., Davary, K., Mianabadi, H., & Karimi, P. (2020). International environmental conflict management in transboundary river basins. *Water Resources Management, 34*(11), 3445–3464. https://doi.org/10.1007/s11269-020-02576-7
Migo-Sumagang, M. V., Tan, R. R., & Aviso, K. B. (2023). A multi-period model for optimizing negative emission technology portfolios with economic and carbon value discount rates. *Energy, 275,* Article 127445.
Mirumachi, N. (2015). *Transboundary water politics in the developing world.* Routledge.
Mishan, E. J., & Quah, E. (2020). *Cost-benefit analysis.* Routledge.
Mostert, E. (2009). International co-operation on Rhine water quality 1945–2008: An example to follow? *Physics and Chemistry of the Earth, Parts A/B/C, 34*(3), 142–149.
Mukuyu, P., Lautze, J., Rieu-Clarke, A., Saruchera, D., & McCartney, M. (2023). Do needs motivate the exchange of data in transboundary waters? Insights from Africa's shared basins. *Water International, 48*(8), 915–941.
Mumme, S. P. (2005). The International Boundary and Water Commission under fire: Policy prospective for the 21st century. *The Journal of Environment & Development, 14*(4), 507–524.
Nagheeby, M., & Warner, J. (2018). The geopolitical overlay of the hydropolitics of the Harirud River basin. *International Environmental Agreements: Politics, Law and Economics, 18*(6), 839–860.

Nevermann, H., Madani, K., Zampieri, M., Hoteit, I., & Shokri, N. (2025). Struggling over water, losing it through evaporation: The case of Afghanistan and Iran. *Journal of Environmental Management, 375*, Article 124319.

Newton, A. C., Hodder, K., Cantarello, E., Perrella, L., Birch, J. C., Robins, J., Douglas, S., Moody, C.,& Cordingley, J. (2012). Cost–benefit analysis of ecological networks assessed through spatial analysis of ecosystem services. *Journal of Applied Ecology, 49*(3), 571–580.

Nikander, P., & Vehviläinen, S. (2010). Discourse analysis. In P. Peterson, E. Baker, & B. McGaw (Eds.), *International encyclopedia of education* (3rd ed., pp. 373–379). Elsevier. https://doi.org/10.1016/b978-0-08-044894-7.01521-9

Offerdal, K. C. (2019). *The effectiveness of the Mekong River Commission: Information sharing and cooperation mechanisms in a regional riparian regime* [Unpublished master's thesis]. University of Oslo.

Ogden, S. (2023). The impact of China's dams on the Mekong River basin: Governance, sustainable development, and the energy–water nexus. *Journal of Contemporary China, 32*(139), 152–169.

Olson, K. R., & Morton, L. W. (2018). Water rights and fights: Lao dams on the Mekong River. *Journal of Soil and Water Conservation, 73*(2), 35A–41A.

Omid, M. H. S. (2017). Afghans react to Iranian president's comments on dam projects. Retrieved September 22, 2024, from https://tolonews.com/afghanistan/afghans-react-iranian-president%E2%80%99s-comments-dam-projects

Plengsaeng, B., Wehn, U., & Van Der Zaag, P. (2014). Data-sharing bottlenecks in transboundary integrated water resources management: A case study of the Mekong River Commission's procedures for data sharing in the Thai context. *Water International, 39*(7), 933–951.

Queen, L. E., Mote, P. W., Rupp, D. E., Chegwidden, O., & Nijssen, B. (2021). Ubiquitous increases in flood magnitude in the Columbia River basin under climate change. *Hydrology and Earth System Sciences, 25*(1), 257–272.

Ramachandran, S. (2017, May 12). Unquiet flows the Helmand. *Asia Times*. Retrieved April 9, 2023, from https://asiatimes.com/2017/05/unquiet-flows-helmand/

Ramachandran, S. (2022, February 15). Afghanistan–Iran disquiet over the Helmand River. *The Diplomat*. Retrieved January 9, 2024, from https://thediplomat.com/2022/02/afghanistan-iran-disquiet-over-the-helmand-river/

Saarikoski, H., Mustajoki, J., Barton, D. N., Geneletti, D., Langemeyer, J., Gomez-Baggethun, E., Marttunen, M., Antunes, P., Keune, H., & Santos, R. (2016). Multi-criteria decision analysis and cost–benefit analysis: Comparing alternative frameworks for integrated valuation of ecosystem services. *Ecosystem Services, 22*, 238–249.

Sadoff, C. W., & Grey, D. (2002). Beyond the river: The benefits of cooperation on international rivers. *Water Policy, 4*(5), 389–403.

Salman, S. M. (2017). Agreement on declaration of principles on the GERD: Levelling the Nile basin playing field. In Z. Yihdego, A. Rieu-Clarke, & A. E. Cascão (Eds.), *The Grand Ethiopian Renaissance Dam and the Nile basin* (pp. 41–60). Routledge.

Schmeier, S. (2012). *Governing international watercourses: River basin organizations and the sustainable governance of internationally shared rivers and lakes*. Routledge.

Sefat, K., & Tsubaki, R. (2024). Flood risk assessment of the middle reach of the Helmand River, Afghanistan. *Journal of Disaster Research, 19*(2), 455–464.

Sehring, J., & Wolf, A. T. (2023). Affective hydropolitics: Introduction to the themed section. *Water Alternatives, 16*(3), 900–911.

Seide, W. M., & Fantini, E. (2023). Emotions in water diplomacy: Negotiations on the Grand Ethiopian Renaissance Dam. *Water Alternatives, 16*(3), 912–929.

Sesana, E., Gagnon, A. S., Ciantelli, C., Cassar, J., & Hughes, J. J. (2021). Climate change impacts on cultural heritage: A literature review. *Wiley Interdisciplinary Reviews: Climate Change, 12*(4), Article e710.

Settre, C., Connor, J., & Wheeler, S. A. (2017). Reviewing the treatment of uncertainty in hydro-economic modeling of the Murray-Darling basin, Australia. *Water Economics and Policy, 3*(3), Article 1650042.

Shahbazbegian, M. R., Turton, A., & Mousavi Shafaee, S. M. (2016). Hydropolitical self-organization theory; system dynamics to analyse hydropolitics of Helmand transboundary river. *Water Policy, 18*(5), 1088–1119.

Shahnawaz, M., & Naqvi, S. F. H. (2024). *Water security: The importance of the Helmand River in alleviating Iran's water scarcity.* Institute of Regional Studies Islamabad, Pakistan. Retrieved September 12, 2024, from https://irs.org.pk/Focus/FJuly24.pdf

Shroder, J., & Ahmadzai, S. J. (2016). *Transboundary water resources in Afghanistan.* Elsevier.

Siddig, K., Basheer, M., & Luckmann, J. (2021). Economy-wide assessment of potential long-term impacts of the Grand Ethiopian Renaissance Dam on Sudan. *Water International, 46*(3), 325–341.

Spandyar, Y. A. (2020). سیستم آبیاری سیستان چگونه تخریب شد؟ [How was the Sistan irrigation system destroyed?]. *8am Newspaper Afghanistan.* Retrieved January 29, 2025, from https://8am.media/fa/how-was-the-sistan-irrigation-system-destroyed/

Tafesse, T. (2009). Benefit-sharing framework in transboundary river basins: The case of the eastern Nile subbasin. In S. B. Awulachew, T. Erkossa, V. Smakhtin, & A. Fernando (Eds.), *Improved water and land management in the Ethiopian Highlands: Its impact on downstream stakeholders dependent on the Blue Nile* (p. 232). IWMI.

Thomas, V., Azizi, M. A., & Behzad, K. (2016). *Developing transboundary water resources: What perspectives for cooperation between Afghanistan, Iran and Pakistan?* (Vol. 6). Afghanistan Research and Evaluation Unit.

Thomas, V., & Varzi, M. M. (2015). A legal license for an ecological disaster: The inadequacies of the 1973 Helmand/Hirmand water treaty for sustainable transboundary water resources development. *International Journal of Water Resources Development, 31*(4), 499–518. https://doi.org/10.1080/07900627.2014.1003346

Tyler, Z. (2005). Transboundary water pollution in China—An analysis of the failure of the legal framework to protect downstream jurisdictions. *Columbia Journal of Asian Law, 19*, 572–613.

Vick, M. J. (2006). Arizona water policy: Management innovations in an urbanizing, arid region, edited by Bonnie G. Colby & Katherine L. Jacobs [Book review]. *Natural Resources Journal, 46*(4), 1081–1086.

Wang, S., & Chen, B. (2017). The societal costs of deep decarbonization in China. *Energy Procedia, 142*, 3115–3121.

Wegerich, K. (2008). Passing over the conflict. The Chu Talas basin agreement as a model for central Asia? In M. M. Rahaman & O. Varis (Eds.), *Central Asian waters: Social, economic, environmental and governance puzzle* (pp. 117–131). Water & Development Publications, Helsinki University of Technology.

Welch, C. (1989). Utilitarianism. In J. Eatwell, M. Milgate, & P. Newman (Eds.), *The invisible hand.* The New Palgrave. Palgrave Macmillan. https://doi.org/10.1007/978-1-349-20313-0_35

Wheeler, K. G., & Hussein, H. (2021). Water research and nationalism in the post-truth era. *Water International, 46*(7–8), 1216–1223.

Whitney, J. W. (2006). *Geology, water, and wind in the lower Helmand basin, southern Afghanistan* (Scientific Investigations Report 2006-5182). US Geological Survey. Retrieved December 12, 2023, from https://pubs.usgs.gov/sir/2006/5182/

Whittington, D., Wu, X., & Sadoff, C. (2005). Water resources management in the Nile basin: The economic value of cooperation. *Water Policy, 7*(3), 227–252.

Yihdego, Z., Rieu-Clarke, A., & Cascão, A. E. (Eds.). (2017). *The Grand Ethiopian Renaissance Dam and the Nile basin: Implications for transboundary water cooperation.* Routledge.

Yu, Y., Bo, Y., Castelletti, A., Dumas, P., Gao, J., Cai, X., Liu, J., Kahil, T.,Wada, Y.,Hu, S.,Liu, B.,Zhou, F.& Zhao, J. (2024). Transboundary cooperation in infrastructure operation generates economic and environmental co-benefits in the Lancang-Mekong River basin. *Nature Water*, *2*(6), 589–601.

Zeitoun, M., Abdallah, C., Dajani, M., Khresat, S. E., Elaydi, H., & Alfarra, A. (2019). The Yarmouk tributary to the Jordan River I: Agreements impeding equitable transboundary water arrangements. *Water Alternatives*, *12*(3), 1064–1094.

Zeitoun, M., & Warner, J. (2006). Hydro-hegemony—A framework for analysis of transboundary water conflicts. *Water Policy*, *8*(5), 435–460.

Zhang, H. Z., He, L. Y., & Zhang, Z. (2023). Can transverse eco-compensation mechanism correct resource misallocation in watershed environmental governance? A cost–benefit analysis of the pilot project of Xin'an River in China. *Environmental and Resource Economics*, *84*(4), 947–973.

6
Decision Support Models Under International Water Law

Raya Marina Stephan

6.1 Introduction

International water law (IWL) was initially developed for navigational uses of international rivers and expanded in the 20th century, with the utilization of water for non-navigational purposes such as irrigated agriculture, domestic, and industrial needs. The focus shifted to include protection of water quality and the adoption of more holistic approaches to water management with greater consideration of water systems such as the ecosystem approach or integrated water resources management. In addition, IWL was developed to include global considerations such as the adoption of the Millennium Development Goals followed by the Sustainable Development Goals.

Various efforts of codification of these emerging rules took place in the 20th century, which resulted mainly in the Helsinki rules prepared and adopted in 1966 by the International Law Association, followed by the work of the United Nations (UN) International Law Commission (ILC) and of the UN Economic Commission for Europe (UNECE). The UN ILC started developing "the law of non-navigational uses of international watercourses" in 1974, and it resulted in the adoption by the UN General Assembly of the Convention on the Law of Non-navigational Uses of International Watercourses in 1997, in force since 2014[1] (hereafter *Watercourses Convention*). Later on, the UN ILC complemented this work by covering transboundary aquifers since they were not fully included under the Watercourses Convention (Yamada, 2003). The Draft Articles on the Law of Transboundary

[1] 40 states parties.

Raya Marina Stephan, *Decision Support Models Under International Water Law*. In: *Decision Support Models to Assist International and Transboundary Water Negotiations*. Edited by: Mohammadreza Shahbazbegian and Ariel Dinar, Oxford University Press. © Oxford University Press (2026). DOI: 10.1093/9780197802601.003.0006

Aquifers were adopted in 2008 and included the same year in a resolution of the UN General Assembly (2008). In parallel, the countries of the UNECE negotiated the Convention on the Protection and Use of Transboundary Watercourses and International Lakes (hereinafter the *Water Convention*) as a regional framework intended for the pan-European region, which was adopted in 1992 and entered into force in 1996 (UNECE, 1992). Following an amendment procedure, the Water Convention turned as of March 2016 from a regional instrument to a global one, and all UN member states can on a voluntary basis accede to it.[2]

These three legal instruments are considered complementary despite their differences. They follow the same objective, which is the efficient and equitable management of shared waterbodies despite some distinctions in their scope: The Watercourses Convention applies to international watercourses, which include surface and groundwater when they are linked together and flow to a "common terminus" (Article 2§a); the Draft Articles cover all transboundary aquifers; and the Water Convention is comprehensive and concerns all waters, surface or ground, as long as they "mark, cross or are located on boundaries between two or more States" (article 1§1). They are different in force: The two conventions are binding for their parties, whereas the Draft Articles are a guidance instrument.[3] However, these instruments include the same substantive norms and rather similar procedural rules.

It is in the frame of the procedural rules that these instruments of IWL include obligations requiring recourse to decision support models (DSMs) for their proper implementation. This chapter demonstrates how IWL through its instruments has established the requirement for DSMs resulting from its rules. It also shows how these DSMs can be useful tools in applying the other requirements of IWL, such as its core principle, equitable and reasonable use, but also more specific rules related to the protection against pollution or the protection of ecosystems and other concerns. The chapter includes specific illustrations and examples from various transboundary waterbodies.

[2] 55 states parties.

[3] In the first UN General Assembly resolution 63/124 of 2008 on the law of transboundary aquifers and in the following one, the Draft Articles were "commended to the attention of Governments." Starting from resolution 68/118 the Draft Articles are commended "as guidance" for agreements on transboundary aquifers.

6.2 Resorting to DSMs

Resorting to DSMs is not mentioned explicitly in the IWL instruments; it is, however, implied by various provisions.

Since they are about cooperation on transboundary water management, the three instruments mentioned above include a related obligation, from which derives the first use of technical tools to build models. These represent the first step for establishing sustainable management, and since it is about a transboundary waterbody, management should preferably be jointly.

6.2.1 Under the Obligation of Cooperation

The three instruments mentioned above include a general obligation to cooperate for the states sharing a transboundary waterbody, very much related to the same general duty already existing in international law (Rieu-Clarke et al., 2012). As mentioned in the ILC's commentary under Article 8 of the Draft Articles (UN ILC, 2008), the first step in cooperation is the exchange of data, and this is reflected in the three instruments. This obligation is the first one related to scientific aspects involving directly the use of technical data-processing tools. This is an essential step, especially for transboundary aquifers, which are by nature invisible and where knowledge becomes more important because of this specificity. The common approach to the three instruments on the exchange of data is that it has to be regular, it concerns the readily available data, and it can be extended to collecting more data that can help to develop the knowledge. According to the Draft Articles, this step can be undertaken "individually or jointly" by the riparian states and with the support of one or more international organizations. The obligation is not only about the exchange of data, but it also adds the requirement that this data be collected and processed in a way that it can be used by all concerned states in the basin, surface or underground. It is then also about the exchange of methodology and metadata, specifically when the data is collected individually by each of the riparian states. In some cases, even if the data is not collected jointly, this additional burden may not be required.

Specificities about the data to be collected are provided such as, and not limited to, the geological, hydrological, hydrogeological, meteorological, and ecological nature of the transboundary waterbody, as well as the water quality. While this data relates to the current condition of the watercourse and of the aquifer, the provision mentions also data about related forecasts concerning "weather patterns and the possible effects thereof upon water levels and flow; the amount of recharge and discharge; foreseeable ice conditions; possible long-term effects of present utilization; and the condition or movement of living resources" (UN ILC, 2008). In times of climate change and other evolutions, this additional requirement is no doubt of valuable importance. In the case of a transboundary aquifer, the requirements concerning the exchange of data apply even when "an aquifer State is not utilizing, or has no plan of utilizing, the transboundary aquifer" (UN ILC, 2008). This request remains understandable as the collected data is useful for the other states to develop their knowledge about the whole aquifer.

6.2.2 The Obligation of Monitoring

In addition to the exchange of data, the Water Convention and the Draft Articles include a provision on monitoring. Monitoring is very important especially regarding groundwater. In the Water Convention the monitoring obligation appears for two different situations. First, it appears as a general obligation to all parties who are required to establish monitoring programs for their transboundary waters. This means that the obligation applies in all cases, whether the parties have entered into an agreement or not with the other riparians. It implies that their national legal framework needs to comply with the provisions of the Water Convention. The obligation also appears under Part II of the convention concerning the provisions relating to riparian parties, which means that they apply when the parties have entered into an agreement. In this case the convention provides more details. The monitoring programs must be organized jointly and concern water quantity and quality (Article 9§b). Article 11 details furthermore with the obligation and specifies that the characteristics for the monitoring, which needs to be jointly established, are to cover the conditions of the transboundary waters, including floods and ice drifts, and transboundary impact (Article 11§1). In addition, the parties need to agree on the "pollution parameters and pollutants whose discharges and concentration in transboundary waters shall be regularly monitored" (Article 11§2). They also need to harmonize the rules for setting up and operating the monitoring programs.

In the Draft Articles, monitoring is also an obligation on the states sharing a transboundary aquifer. The provision details the process. Whenever it exists, monitoring is first conducted individually by each state. At a later stage, if cooperation between the riparian states develops, monitoring can evolve and be undertaken jointly. However, as a first step, and until joint monitoring is established, it is important that states conduct this activity individually and share the data with the other concerned states. The same requirements identified earlier apply here. As for the monitoring, the states are required to use agreed or harmonized standards and methodologies and to identify key parameters to monitor, based on an agreed conceptual model (Article 13 DA). These parameters should cover the condition of the transboundary aquifer as those listed for the regular exchange of data and information. In addition, they should comprehend the utilization of the aquifer.

By fulfilling the data exchange and monitoring obligations states can build tools such as common databases and models of the transboundary waterbody, contributing to developing and achieving a full understanding of the concerned water resource and its functioning. This takes on special importance in the case of transboundary aquifers, where the exchange of data, the monitoring, and the development of knowledge are even more important because of the invisible character.

6.3 The Required Frame

In the conventions and the Draft Articles, collecting and exchanging data and monitoring the joint waterbody are aimed at developing knowledge, with the ultimate objective to adopt the best management decisions based on the hydrologic/hydrogeologic reality, in view of reaching sustainable use. Therefore, these cooperation actions engage within the management frame as defined by the instruments and are handled by established mechanisms or institutions. These two aspects are detailed below, illustrated by specific examples.

6.3.1 Management

The three instruments include a provision on management which appears as an extension of the obligations detailed above (Rieu-Clarke et al., 2012). Indeed, according to the Watercourses Convention, management refers to "planning the sustainable development of an international watercourse" or "promoting . . . (its) . . . rational and optimal utilization, protection and control" (Article 24§2). The Water Convention refers to "rational water management" (Article 2§b) and "sustainable water management" (Article 3§i). The Draft Articles do not specify more than the obligation for each aquifer state to establish its own plan and to consult the other riparian states (Article 14). As it appears from these definitions and references, management needs to be based on the hydrologic or hydrogeologic realities of the transboundary watercourse or aquifer so that it can be planned in a sustainable manner. This implies that management decisions and approaches are based on the data collected and recourse to the eventual tools developed with the information compiled such as a model, predictions, or other. Therefore, IWL through the provisions of these instruments considers that management decisions and plans need to be based on science and knowledge. The elaboration of models built on the data collected helps lead to the adoption of decisions and plans on the water resource based on knowledge and science, complying with IWL requirements and aiming at the sustainable use and development of the resource (Warren, 2024).

6.3.1.1 DSMs in the Case of the North Western Sahara Aquifer System

The North Western Sahara Aquifer System (NWSAS; Algeria, Libya, and Tunisia) is one of the few transboundary aquifers for which cooperation between the riparian countries is established. After engaging jointly in projects (Machard de Gramont et al., 2011), the three countries have entered into a cooperative arrangement in order to sustain the results they had reached and to continue the production of knowledge. The countries have achieved the following:

- Knowledge and data exchange and data standardization
- Development of a common database and information system
- Development of a model, including local sub-models
- Identification and mapping of vulnerable and high-potential abstraction zones in the aquifer system

Based on this produced knowledge and the resulting tools, the countries have adopted development and planning decisions, mainly at the national level. For instance,

- The database and the model are used by countries to estimate water potential and to simulate the expected impact of any possible new drilling or agricultural project.
- The countries refrain from drilling near vulnerable zones such as the chotts areas (UNECE, 2020).

6.3.1.2 DSMs Under the Convention on Cooperation for the Protection and Sustainable Use of the Danube River (1994)

The objective of this convention is to achieve the "sustainable and equitable water management, including the conservation, improvement and the rational use of surface waters and ground water in the catchment" (Article 2§1).[4] For this purpose, the parties are required to cooperate in the monitoring and assessment of the waters, by harmonizing the methodology (Article 9). Under this obligation, tools such as the Joint Danube Surveys have been carried out, which have provided critical information on the biology, chemistry, and hydromorphology of the watercourse. The results of these surveys are included in each cycle of the Danube River Basin Management Plan. This helps the Danube countries, which are all parties to the convention, to select the right measures to solve the problems in the basin (International Commission for the Protection of the Danube River [ICPDR], 2018).

6.3.2 The Establishment of Institutions

As mentioned in the Watercourses Convention and in the Draft Articles, management can be conducted through joint institutions "wherever appropriate" (Article 14, Draft Articles) or as the states decide (Article 24, Watercourses Convention). Under the Water Convention, establishing "joint bodies," which can take any form, joint institutions, commissions, or other, appears as an obligation. According to Article 9§2, "The agreements . . . *shall* provide for the establishment of joint bodies" (emphasis added). The convention mentions some of the tasks that can be assigned to these joint bodies. These include the exchange and compilation of data, the elaboration of joint monitoring programs, setting water quality objectives, and developing concerted action programs for the reduction of pollution loads

[4] Signatories Austria, Bosnia and Herzegovina, Bulgaria, Croatia, Czech Republic, Germany, Hungary, Moldova, Montenegro, Romania, Slovakia, Slovenia, Serbia, Ukraine, and the European Union.

(Article 9§2). All of these tasks are closely related or included in management decisions and plans.

Establishing a joint mechanism for cooperation is therefore necessary for handling the various tools and instruments for all the knowledge development procedures mentioned above and the use of their results in, for example, a model or other tool. In practice, riparian states have established cooperation mechanisms under various forms (commission, organization, etc.) as a platform for cooperation, whether these are limited to consultations and exchanges or in charge of management (UN ILC, 1994).

6.3.2.1 The ICPDR

The ICPDR was established to implement the Danube River Protection Convention (1994). It was also nominated by the parties (14 countries and the European Union) as the platform for the implementation of all transboundary aspects of the EU Water Framework Directive, in addition to taking responsibility for coordinating the implementation of the EU Floods Directive within the Danube River basin. The ICPDR determines the "reasonably available data" to be exchanged by the parties on inter alia the general conditions of the riverine environment; measures taken and planned to be taken to prevent, control, and reduce transboundary impact; or the regulations for wastewater discharges (Article 12). Since its creation in 1998 the ICPDR has promoted policy agreements and the setting of joint priorities and strategies for improving the state of the Danube and its tributaries. This includes improving the tools used to manage environmental issues in the Danube basin, such as the following:

- The Accident Emergency Warning System
- The Trans-National Monitoring Network for water quality
- The Information System for the Danube (Danubis)

With all this, the ICPDR developed the Danube River Basin Management Plan. The plan was updated in 2021, focusing on five main pressures and effects that affect the water status: pollution by organic substances, nutrients, and hazardous substances; hydromorphological alterations and effects of climate change (drought, water scarcity, extreme hydrological phenomena, and other impacts).

6.3.2.2 The Consultation Mechanism on the NWSAS

In the case of the NWSAS mentioned above, the countries have established a Consultation Mechanism representing the framework for exchange and cooperation between the three countries. It aims mainly at outlining the common studies and research, defining the procedures for data exchange, updating and running the models, and identifying risk areas and formulating appropriate proposals (Machard de Gramont et al., 2011).

6.3.2.3 The Mekong River Commission

The Mekong River Commission (MRC) was established by the *Agreement on the Cooperation for the Sustainable Development of the Mekong River Basin* (MRC, 1995) (between Cambodia, Lao, Thailand, and Vietnam[5]), whose objective is cooperation between the four countries in all fields of sustainable development, including the utilization, management, and conservation of the water and related resources of the Mekong River basin extending to irrigation, hydropower, navigation, flood control, fisheries, and other activities (Article 1). Under the agreement, the countries are requested to collect and supply monitoring data, which the secretariat of the commission consolidates and analyzes before preparing reports with recommendations (Articles 24 and 30). To this effect, the MRC established a regional information system called the MRC-IS as a structured communication and information management system, which is managed by the secretariat of the MRC. The New Basin Development Strategy (2021–2030) and MRC Strategic Plan (2021–2025) provides for the modernization of data and information acquisition, processing, and sharing, which involves inter alia the establishment of a core river monitoring network managed by the MRC, as well as the enhancement of the MRC Decision Support Framework and development of compatible decision support system platforms in the region to support implementation of all river basin management functions (MRC, 2021). It calls for a more proactive approach to basin planning and joint action and to coordinated operational basin management in areas that have a transboundary aspect such as river flow management or sediment management. It also provides for a more integrated entire river basin information management system and increasing data sharing and cooperation. It is expected that these developments will lead to higher levels

[5] The other two riparian countries, China and Myanmar, of the Mekong River are not party to the agreement. They joined as dialogue partners.

of transboundary cooperation and regional integration. Through these policies and plans, the MRC is considered to have contributed to promoting development in its member countries and enhanced cooperation among them, at the same time expanding cooperation with the two dialogue partners. Its activities are important for economic and social development and environmental protection of the region (Jia et al., 2024).

6.3.2.4 The Nile Basin Initiative

Under the Nile Basin Initiative (NBI) a decision support system (Nile-DSS) was developed, providing a framework for sharing knowledge, understanding river system behavior, evaluating alternative development and management strategies, and supporting informed decision-making. The tool provides scientifically accepted methods for quantifying the value of water and allows the 10 NBI countries to publish and share data, models, and information among themselves, contributing to building trust among themselves (DHI, n.d.). The Nile-DSS has been applied by several countries to analyze the costs and benefits of different water resource management and development scenarios in relation to projects and policy (World Bank Group, 2015). However, while the tool might be successful regarding some aspects within the NBI, and probably generates enough relevant data to inform water managers and decision makers, it did not prove to be enough to allow the success of the negotiations on the Grand Ethiopian Renaissance Dam between Egypt, Ethiopia, and Sudan as well as the other tool used by Egypt during this phase (RIBASIM) (Helal & Bekhit, 2023). In this case, the failure of the negotiations can be attributed to the strong differences in the agendas of the concerned countries.

It is worth mentioning here that, contrary to the previous examples, the Nile-DSS was not developed under the umbrella of an agreement but within an initiative intended as a "new transitional institutional arrangement" between the riparian countries of the Nile.[6]

An overview of these examples is provided in Table 6.1, including the legal principle(s) underlying resorting to a DSM, the outcome reached through the DSM, followed by the substantive and procedural legal principles reached and applied. While a DSM is certainly important for developing cooperation between riparian countries of a shared water resource, it needs to be supported by an agreement to provide a more tangible effect and result.

[6] Including the riparian countries Burundi, Democratic Republic of Congo, Egypt, Ethiopia, Kenya, Rwanda, South Sudan, Sudan, Tanzania, and Uganda. Eritrea participates as an observer.

Table 6.1 Decision Support Model and International Water Law Principles

Legal principles through the DSM tool	Basin	Outcome of the DSM tool(s)	Substantive legal principles	Procedural legal principles
Regular exchange of data and information, monitoring	North Western Sahara Aquifer System	Adoption of management plans at the national level Protection of vulnerable zones	General obligation of cooperation Equitable and reasonable utilization Obligation not to cause significant harm	Management Prevention from pollution
	Danube River	Joint management plan of surface and groundwater in the basin		
	Mekong River	Basin development strategy, under the coordination of the MRC		
Regular exchange of data and information	Nile basin	Management decisions at the country level	General obligation of cooperation	

Note: DSM = decision support model; MRC = Mekong River Commission.

6.4 Discussion

IWL relies on two core substantial principles: equitable and reasonable use and the obligation not to cause significant harm, or the *no-harm rule*. These two principles are codified in the two conventions as well as in the Draft Articles. They are also considered customary, meaning that they apply to all states, even if they are not party to any convention.

Cooperation on the transboundary water resource, and its management, therefore has to obey to these two principles. The equitable and reasonable use principle is about the right to use the waters in an equitable manner, not necessarily equal. It also includes the duty to protect the resource. This principle relies on the consideration of various factors for its implementation. A non-exhaustive list is provided in the Watercourses Convention and in the Draft Articles (Articles 6 and 5, respectively). These are related inter alia to the natural characteristics of the transboundary watercourse or of the aquifer and its surroundings, the population, and the socioeconomic conditions. According to the Watercourses Convention and to the Draft Articles, to determine what is equitable and reasonable utilization, all factors are to be considered *together*. The conclusion is then reached on the basis of the whole, with priority given to what these instruments have called "vital human needs," which can nowadays be assimilated to the human right to water.

The no-harm rule is a due diligence rule, which means that the harm is caused unintentionally; the harm caused has to be significant, which is determined on a case-by-case basis, and concerns the quantity and the quality.

These principles rely therefore on the knowledge generated for their proper implementation and any DSM developed, resulting in implementation of the procedural rules such as the regular exchange of data or monitoring, based on the data collected, and the monitoring results. This applies mainly for the equitable and reasonable use principle as a DSM can present the various scenarios and choices to apply for management by putting together the identified factors in each specific case and weighing each one in the best manner for reaching sustainable management and the rational and optimal utilization of the transboundary waterbody. Additionally, any DSM can help minimize any possible harm even if caused unintentionally with the possibility of showing differences in predictions. In times of climate change, such tools turn out particularly useful and necessary to prepare adaptation plans at the level of the transboundary waterbody and to increase the resilience of the system. The tool therefore contributes to the proper implementation of IWL in transboundary basins.

References

Danube River Protection Convention. (1994). https://www.icpdr.org/about-icpdr/framework/convention. Retrieved January 31, 2025

DHI. (n.d.). *Equitably sharing the Nile River: Using Nile basin NSS to foster cross boundary water management.* https://www.dhigroup.com/upload/publications/misc/SurfaceAndGroundwater_EY_CaseStory_Fairly%20sharing%20the%20water%20of%20the%20Nile%20River.pdf

Helal, M., & Bekhit, H. M. (2023). So near, yet so far: An Egyptian perspective on the US-facilitated negotiations on the Grand Ethiopian Renaissance Dam. *Water International*,

48(5), 580–614. Retrieved January 31, 2025, from https://doi.org/10.1080/02508060.2023.2230851

International Commission for the Protection of the Danube River. (2018, April). *Lessons from the Danube: A world leader in transboundary river basin management.* Retrieved January 31, 2025, from https://www.icpdr.org/sites/default/files/nodes/documents/lessons-from-the-danube-a-world-leader-in-transboundary-river-basin-management.pdf

Jia, S., Wang, Y., Do, H., Gojenko, B., & Man, C. (2024). Basin governance and international cooperation. In D. Chen, J. Liu, & Q. Tang (Eds.), *Water resources in the Lancang-Mekong River basin: Impact of climate change and human interventions* (pp. 327–375). Springer. Retrieved March 2, 2025, from https://link.springer.com/chapter/10.1007/978-981-97-0759-1_9

Machard de Gramont, H., Noel, C., Oliver, J.-L., Pennequin, D., Rama, M., & Stephan, R. M. (2011). *Toward a joint management of transboundary aquifer systems: Methodological guidebook* (A Savoir 03). Agence France de Développement. Retrieved January 31, 2025, from https://www.afd.fr/en/ressources/toward-joint-management-transboundary-aquifer-systems

Mekong River Commission. (1995). *Agreement on the cooperation for the sustainable development of the Mekong River basin.* Retrieved March 1, 2025, from https://www.mrcmekong.org/wp-content/uploads/2024/08/1995-Mekong-Agreement.pdf

Mekong River Commission. (2021). *The integrated water resources management–based basin development strategy for the lower Mekong basin 2021–2030 and the MRC strategic plan 2021–2025.* MRC Secretariat. Retrieved January 31, 2025, from https://www.mrcmekong.org/wp-content/uploads/2024/08/Basin-Development-Strategy-BDS-2021-2030-and-MRC-Strategic-Plan-SP-2021-2025.pdf

Rieu-Clarke, A., Moynihan, R., & Magsig, B.-O. (2012). *UN Watercourses Convention: User's guide.* IHP-HELP Centre for Water Law, Policy and Science (under the auspices of UNESCO). Retrieved January 31, 2025, from https://discovery.dundee.ac.uk/ws/portalfiles/portal/1477328/UN_Watercourses_Convention_User_s_Guide.pdf

United Nations Economic Commission for Europe. (1992). *Convention on the Protection and Use of Transboundary Watercourses and International Lakes.* Retrieved January 31, 2025, from https://unece.org/DAM/env/water/pdf/watercon.pdf

United Nations Economic Commission for Europe. (2020). *Policy brief highlights the benefits of strengthening transboundary cooperation in the North Western Sahara Aquifer System shared by Algeria, Libya and Tunisia* (Policy brief). Retrieved March 1, 2025, from https://unece.org/environment/press/policy-brief-highlights-benefits-strengthening-transboundary-water-cooperation

United Nations General Assembly. (1997). *Convention on the Law of the Non-navigational Uses of International Watercourses.* Retrieved January 31, 2025, from https://legal.un.org/ilc/texts/instruments/english/conventions/8_3_1997.pdf

United Nations General Assembly. (2008, December 11). *Draft articles on the law of transboundary aquifers* (Resolution 63/124). Retrieved January 31, 2025, from https://documents.un.org/doc/undoc/gen/n08/478/23/pdf/n0847823.pdf

United Nations International Law Commission. (1994). *Report of the International Law Commission on the work of its forty-sixth session, 2 May–22 July 1994, official records of the General Assembly, forty-ninth session* (Supplement No. 10, Document No. A/49/10). Retrieved January 31, 2025, from https://legal.un.org/ilc/documentation/english/reports/a_49_10.pdf

United Nations International Law Commission. (2008). *Annual report. Shared natural resources* (Chapter IV). Retrieved January 31, 2025, from https://legal.un.org/ilc/reports/2008/english/chp4.pdf

Warren, L. K. (2024). The role of science in international water law. *Water International, 49*(6), 721–737. Retrieved January 31, 2025, from https://doi.org/10.1080/02508060.2024.2380141

World Bank Group. (2015). *Cooperation in the Nile basin: Sharing and using knowledge to improve water resource management* (Briefing note 6). Retrieved March 2, 2025, from https://openknowledge.worldbank.org/entities/publication/4c816c31-3f13-516a-8f59-bd0c5f24ada0

Yamada, C. (2003). *Shared natural resources: First report on shared natural resources outlines* (Document A/CN.4/533). Retrieved January 31, 2025, from https://legal.un.org/ilc/documentation/english/a_cn4_533.pdf

7

An Interdisciplinary Decision Support Model Based on System Dynamics to Reach Consensus-Building in the Helmand/Hirmand Transboundary River

Mohammadreza Shahbazbegian, Anthony Turton, and Ismail Najafi

7.1 Introduction

The management of international transboundary water (ITW) has become one of the most complex and pressing challenges in international relations as these shared water resources, accounting for an estimated 60% of global freshwater, flow and support the livelihoods of more than 3 billion people (Gökçekuş & Bolouri, 2023). As population growth and agricultural demands increase, disputes over the division of water have intensified, often leading to tensions between riparian countries (Falkenmark & Widstrand, 1992; Swain, 2004; Wolf et al., 2003; Zeitoun & Warner, 2006). The indispensable part of the conflict-management process over ITW has been the negotiation between riparian countries. However, this process can be hindered by the inherent complexities and multifaceted nature of these water resource systems. Decision support models (DSMs) have emerged as powerful tools to address this challenge, providing a structured framework for analyzing and evaluating the potential outcomes of different policy or management strategies (Simonovic, 2009). The DSMs' ability to test "what-if" scenarios enables negotiators to explore the impacts of changes in water supply, demand, infrastructure, or policies on critical factors such as water availability, agricultural productivity, hydropower generation, and environmental flows (Meadows et al., 1972; Sterman, 2000; Vennix, 1996; Winz

Mohammadreza Shahbazbegian et al., *An Interdisciplinary Decision Support Model Based on System Dynamics to Reach Consensus-Building in the Helmand/Hirmand Transboundary River*. In: *Decision Support Models to Assist International and Transboundary Water Negotiations*. Edited by: Mohammadreza Shahbazbegian and Ariel Dinar, Oxford University Press. © Oxford University Press (2026). DOI: 10.1093/9780197802601.003.0007 et al., 2009). This allows them to make more informed decisions that balance the diverse interests of all stakeholders involved.

Among the various modeling approaches maintaining the potential to serve as DSMs for negotiation, system dynamics (SD) has proven to be particularly well-suited for analyzing and managing complex ITW systems (Duran-Encalada et al., 2017; Kotir et al., 2016; Sehlke & Jacobson, 2005; Shao et al., 2020). A core contribution of SD which makes it a relevant candidate to do so is its ability to capture the inherent complexity and interdependencies that characterize these interactive processes. The literature demonstrates SD's significant value in negotiation processes accordingly.

Richardson and Andersen (2010) and Eden and Ackermann (2021) established how system-thinking helps parties develop shared mental models and translate theoretical frameworks into practical decision-making tools. Further research has expanded SD's applications in negotiation contexts: Sánchez-García and López-Hernández (2020) used SD to analyze stakeholder interactions and identify negotiation leverage points, while Zomorodian et al. (2017) combined SD with game theory to model complex water resource management scenarios. Piya et al. (2016) integrated SD into a negotiation-based DSM for scenario simulation, complementing Druckman's (2007) identification of SD as crucial for capturing negotiation dynamics. Elliott and Kaufman (2016) demonstrated SD's effectiveness in modeling environmental negotiations through feedback loops and stakeholder interactions. These collective findings highlight SD's key benefits in negotiations: developing shared mental models, simulating various scenarios and strategies, informing negotiation support system design, and addressing complex multi-stakeholder environmental negotiations.

Correspondingly, in the field of ITW negotiation, SD operates as a bridge that connects different forms of knowledge (Madani & Mariño, 2009). Using this method, hydrologists, economists, sociologists, and policymakers can find a common language to understand complex issues (Winz et al., 2009). In this regard, studies have produced valuable insights that can enhance negotiation processes in the ITW terrain. For instance, the hydropolitical self-organization theory developed by Shahbazbegian et al. (2016) in the Helmand/Hirmand River basin provides negotiators with frameworks to understand power dynamics and political interactions in water governance. Similarly, the comprehensive approach by Bazrkar et al. (2013) in the Hirmand basin, which integrated political, social, and environmental factors, offers negotiators a holistic perspective for addressing complex water-sharing challenges. Shahbazbegian and Dinar (2023) specifically built on these foundations to develop the "painted water" concept, demonstrating how SD can directly inform diplomatic approaches to water management negotiations across shared river basins. The system archetype analysis conducted by Shahbazbegian and Nabavi (2023) in the Euphrates, Nile, Zambezi, and Lake Kivu basins provides negotiators with valuable tools for scenario exploration and trade-off analysis. In the US–Mexican transborder region, the climate change impact analysis by Duran-Encalada et al. (2017) offers critical insights that can inform long-term planning discussions and policy negotiations. As water management challenges intensify due to scarcity and climate uncertainty, these types of SD analyses become increasingly valuable for negotiation support. Looking forward, Palmate et al. (2022) suggest that incorporating more sophisticated climate change scenarios, developing user-friendly interfaces for stakeholder engagement, and exploring hybrid modeling approaches could further enhance SD's utility in supporting water management negotiations. In the Zhanghe River basin (China), Yuan et al. (2023) developed an SD model that combined evolutionary game theory to analyze water-sharing problems, revealing how different strategies and cooperation levels affect allocation and system stability. This approach informs negotiation strategies by illustrating long-term consequences of policy options. Similarly, in the Volta River basin (Ghana), Kotir et al. (2016) used SD to support sustainable water resources management and agricultural development, providing insights for negotiations on water use across sectors.

By leveraging these advanced techniques, policymakers and negotiators can better navigate the complexities of ITW management, fostering cooperation and sustainable water governance across shared river basins (Shahbazbegian & Noori, 2022; Yuan et al., 2020). This chapter aims to demonstrate the application of an interdisciplinary DSM based on SD to facilitate negotiation and consensus-building in the case of the Helmand/Hirmand transboundary river, the most important shared water resource between Iran and Afghanistan.

This chapter is organized into four primary sections. The "Methods and Materials" section is divided into two subsections: one addressing the specific negotiation issues of the Helmand/Hirmand transboundary river and another detailing the SD model used in the study. This methodological explanation is followed by a section ("7.3 Building a Decision Support Dashboard for Facilitating the Negotiation") which presents the outcomes of applying the SD model to the Helmand/Hirmand River case. The "Discussion" section then interprets these results, exploring their implications and contextualizing them within the broader field of transboundary water management. Finally, the chapter concludes with a summary of key findings and their significance, potentially offering recommendations for future research or policy applications.

7.2 Methods and Materials

7.2.1 Helmand/Hirmand Transboundary River Negotiation Issue

The Helmand/Hirmand River is a vital ITW in central Asia, flowing from Afghanistan's Hindu Kush Mountains into Iran's Hamoun wetland across 800 miles. While covering 40% of Afghanistan's land area, it contributes only 11% of the country's total water flow (Hayat & Elçi, 2017). The river serves as a critical source of irrigation, drinking water, and hydropower in Afghanistan (Bidabadi & Afshari, 2020), while supporting the ecosystem and economy of Iran's Sistan region through fishing, hunting, and farming (Nagheeby & Warner, 2022; United Nations Environment Programme [UNEP], 2006).

Water-sharing negotiations between Iran and Afghanistan culminated in the 1973 Helmand/Hirmand River Water Treaty, allocating Iran 26 m^3 per second of annual flow (Aman, 2016; Nagheeby & Warner 2022). Implementation has been complicated by climate change impacts, including global warming and severe droughts (Sharifikia, 2013; UNEP, 2006), population growth, agricultural expansion (King & Sturtewagen, 2010), and political instability in Afghanistan (Hanasz, 2017).

Post-2001 cooperation efforts, including the 2004 Helmand/Hirmand River Commission, have shown limited progress due to disputes over water allocation and infrastructure development. Afghanistan's construction of new dams, like the Kamal Khan Dam, has raised concerns in Iran about reduced water flow, while Afghanistan views water control as a strategic development asset (Faizee & Schmeier, 2023; Nagheeby & Rieu-Clarke, 2020). The basin continues to face challenges including flow fluctuations, droughts, and increasing water demand, despite the existing 1973 treaty (Nagheeby & Warner, 2022; Whitney, 2006).

7.2.2.1 Constructing an SD-Oriented DSM for Negotiation in the Helmand/Hirmand Transboundary River

The SD modeling process follows a structured approach that begins with defining the problem in a precise way (Sterman, 2002). From this foundation, experts collaborate to develop diagrams depicting cause-and-effect relationships between various factors, which then evolve into mathematical models capable of simulating system behavior over time (Ford, 2000). These models serve as virtual laboratories where different scenarios can be tested while bearing no risks and costs in the real world (Sterman, 2002). At its core, SD utilizes casual loop diagrams (CLDs), delays, and stock flow diagrams (SFDs) as flow-accumulation structures (Forrester, 1961). While CLDs focus on identifying and analyzing cause-and-effect cycles within the system (Meadows, 2008), delays account for the time intervals between actions and their consequences (Forrester, 1971). SFDs are instrumental in modeling changes in key system variables over time (Sterman, 2000). This comprehensive approach reveals that predicting river water flow pattern, for example, requires consideration of multiple factors beyond rainfall patterns, including climate change, water consumption patterns, and neighboring countries' water policies (Simonovic, 2009).

To create an SD-oriented DSM for negotiation in the Helmand/Hirmand transboundary river, the following steps have to be taken:

1. Variable Identification: The model begins by comprehensively identifying key variables affecting the Helmand/Hirmand River, including hydrological, climatic, demographic, agricultural, industrial, and ecological factors that influence water resource dynamics.
2. Relationship Mapping: Researchers analyze the intricate relationships between these variables, creating CLDs that visualize complex interactions, feedback mechanisms, and system dependencies.
3. Mathematical Modeling: Qualitative relationships are transformed into precise mathematical equations and computational models, enabling simulation of water resource behaviors and interactions across different system components through SFDs.
4. Model Validation: The developed model undergoes rigorous validation by comparing its predictions with historical data, consulting

domain experts, and conducting comprehensive statistical analyses to ensure accuracy and reliability.

5. Designing a Decision Support Dashboard: The validated model is used to explore potential water management scenarios, evaluate policy interventions, and provide decision makers with insights into complex system behaviors and potential future outcomes through a user-friendly decision support dashboard.

Among the aforementioned steps, mapping CLDs and SFDs will be further elaborated in the following.

7.2.2.2 CLDs Governing the Helmand/Hirmand Transboundary River

In the context of negotiation, CLDs can be employed to map out the dynamic interactions between stakeholders, their objectives, and the factors influencing the negotiation process. By identifying the reinforcing and balancing loops, negotiating parties can gain insights into the system's behavior and potential leverage points for intervention (Shahbazbegian et al., 2016). Following is the CLD developed from Shahbazbegian et al. (2016) to explore the system mechanism governing the hydropolitical situation in the Helmand/Hirmand transboundary river.

The development of CLDs can be significantly enhanced through a participatory approach, which involves directly engaging stakeholders in the mapping process. This methodology allows for a more comprehensive and nuanced understanding of complex systems by incorporating diverse perspectives and local knowledge. However, in this study, we faced challenges in data collection due to the geopolitical complexities of the region. Consequently, the CLD is primarily based on data from the Iranian side of the transboundary river as the research team could not establish a partnership with stakeholders from Afghanistan to provide a complete bilateral perspective. In the subsequent analysis, we only focused on the part of the CLD whose variables are written in black in Figure 7.1, which represents the key dynamics captured from the available Iranian-side data.

7.2.2.3 Turning the CLDs Into SFDs and Subsystems

Built on CLDs, SFDs provide a more detailed and quantitative representation of the system. These diagrams distinguish between stocks (accumulations) and flows (rates of change) within the system, allowing for the modeling of material, information, and financial stocks and the associated inflows and outflows. In the water negotiation domain, SFDs can be used to model

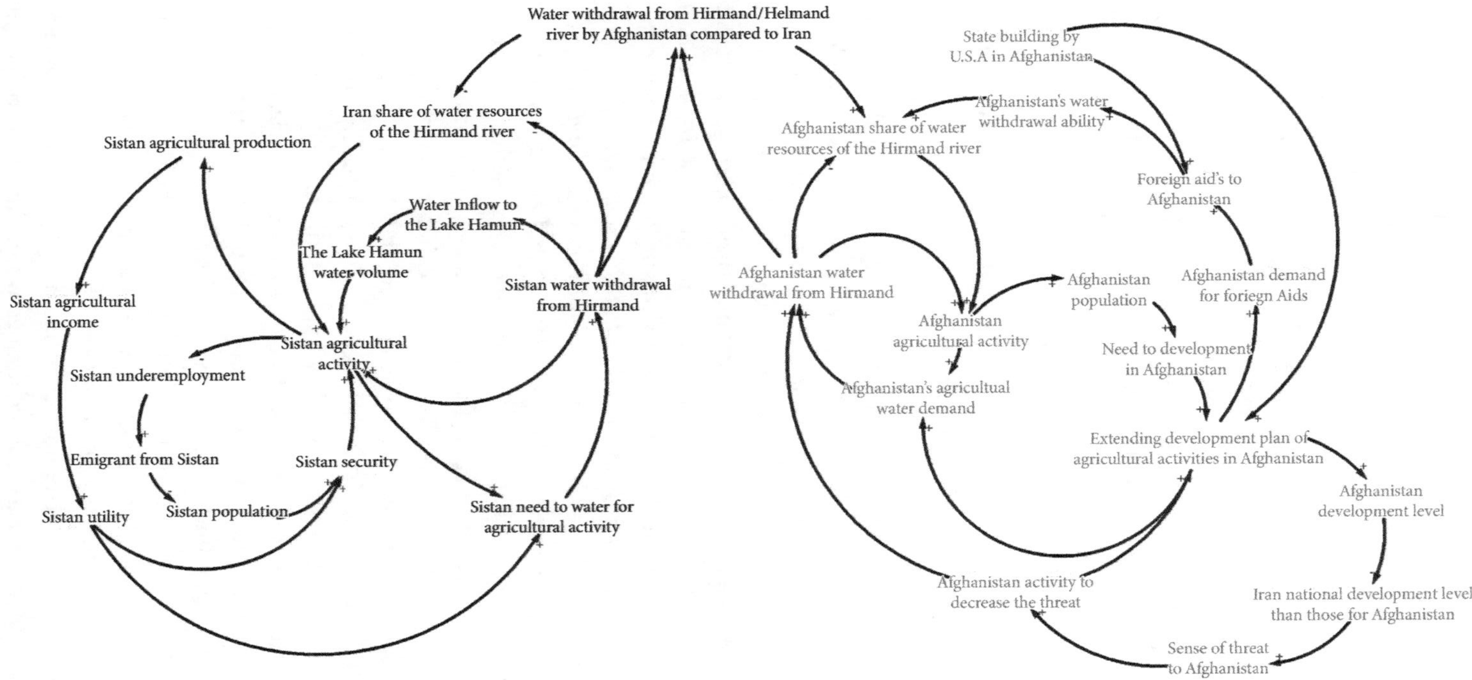

Figure 7.1 Casual Loop Diagrams Governing the Hydropolitical Situation in the Helmand/Hirmand Transboundary River

Note: GDP = gross domestic product. Adapted from Shahbazbegian et al. (2016).

the accumulation of negotiation resources, such as lakes, dams, groundwater resources, population, agricultural area, or political capital, as well as the flows that govern their dynamics such as river discharges, evaporation, spills from dams, birth and death rates, and agricultural development. By explicitly representing these stocks and flows, negotiating parties can better understand the system's behavior over time and the impacts of their actions on the negotiation outcomes. Accordingly, six interconnected subsystems consisting of SFDs have been mapped and formulated to serve as the engine behind the intended DSM and decision support dashboard for negotiators (7.A1).

7.3 Building a Decision Support Dashboard for Facilitating the Negotiation

After calibration and verification of the model (Figure 7.5), the decision support dashboard on the Iranian side is designed. It includes six monitors as dependent variables, including *regional gross domestic product (GDP) per capita on the Iran side, Lake Hamun volume, total living population, total water supply for economic sectors, GDP per non-consumptive water*, and *total water supply certainty*. Hence, six slider keys including the *capacity of the water desalination site, agricultural water demand per hectare, percent of Iran water right from the Helmand/Hirmand River, percent of decreasing evaporation from the Lake Hamun surface based on shade balls technology, GDP per consumptive water*, and *total water demand* as independent variables (Figure 7.2). It serves as a user-friendly and constructive platform for dialogue and joint decision-making between Iran and Afghanistan.

The designed dashboard works like a shared digital brain that helps both countries make informed decisions based on facts rather than perceptions. Instead of Iran and Afghanistan having separate, potentially conflicting assessments of the water situation, they have a unified, trusted source of information and projected impacts. It takes what has historically been a source of tension and turns it into an opportunity for cooperation based on a shared understanding of the river system's realities.

By capturing the complex interrelationships within the river system, the model enables both countries to explore water allocation strategies that balance agricultural productivity, economic development, and environmental sustainability. It can simulate how changes in water rights, desalination capacity, and water management techniques would impact variables like

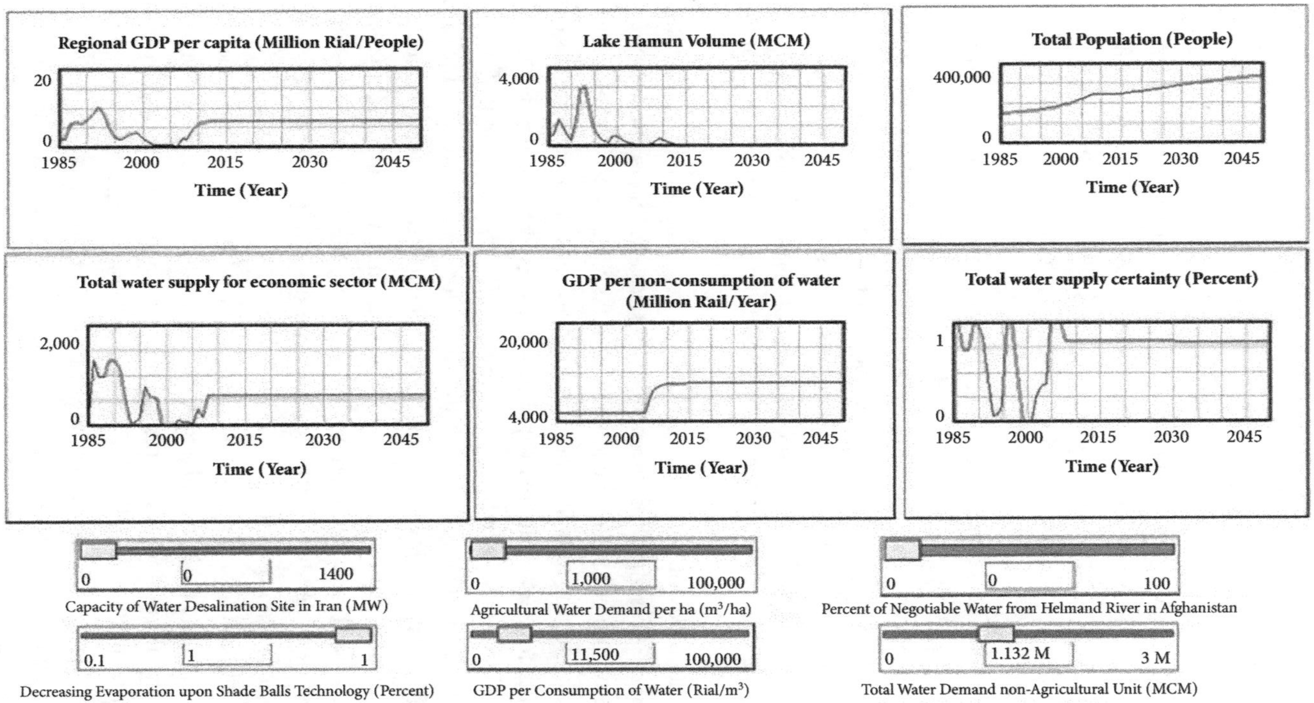

Figure 7.2 The Decision Support Dashboard Available for Decision Makers

Note: GDP = gross domestic product; MCM = million cubic meters. Elaborated by the authors.

agricultural value added, regional GDP, and the ecological health of Lake Hamun on the Iranian side.

A key strength of the model is its ability to simulate long-term trends and scenarios, extending projections up to 2050. This allows negotiators to stress-test proposed agreements, identify potential unintended consequences, and develop contingency plans. By demonstrating the interconnected impacts of water management decisions—such as how changes in Lake Hamun's volume might affect regional economic and population dynamics—the model provides a holistic view of potential outcomes until 2050.

Beyond its technical capabilities, the SD model can create a shared understanding between Iran and Afghanistan. By shifting discussions from specific numerical targets to cause-and-effect relationships, the model helps reduce tensions and foster more constructive cooperation. It serves as a platform for collaborative learning, enabling both parties to gain deeper insights into the river system's complexities and each other's needs, ultimately supporting the development of mutually beneficial and sustainable water management agreements.

Having attributes of concern variables on the Afghanistan side within the dashboard is essential for independently stress-testing proposed agreements, identifying potential impacts on its water security and development goals, and developing informed negotiating positions. Acknowledged as the study's limitation, without this capability, both riparian states would be unable to effectively evaluate long-term consequences of proposed water management decisions or advocate for their interests based on objective data in Afghanistan. However, the model demonstrates interconnected impacts—such as how changes in Lake Hamun's volume might affect regional economic and population dynamics on the Iran side—allowing both parties to understand and address some parts of potential outcomes until 2050 from their own national perspective.

As an applicable example, the analysis of five different policy packages implemented in the DSM reveals significant variations in their effectiveness for addressing the water–environment–society nexus in southeastern Iran through the year 2050, which can shed light on a part of the course of negotiation between the two riparian states (Table 7.1). These policy packages were evaluated based on their impacts on three key variables as the highest attribute of concern in the Sistan region located in Iran: the Hamun Lake water volume, per capita value added in Iran, and the resident population in the region (Figure 7.3).

Table 7.1 Policy Packages Examined Through the Designed Decision Support Model

Name of policy	Explanation
Policy 0	Business as usual
Policy 1	Engage in negotiations to secure the entirety of the negotiable water[a] from the Helmand/Hirmand River in Afghanistan, estimated at 3 billion m^3/year, putting the value of the "Percent of Iran water right from the Helmand/Hirmand River" slider key on 100%.
Policy 2	Reduce reliance on the flow of the Helmand/Hirmand River by strategically planning to depend on 820 million m^3, which aligns with Iran's water rights as stipulated in the 1972 Helmand/Hirmand Water Treaty, increasing the value of the "GDP per consumptive water" slider key to the maximum amount.
Policy 3	Combine the objectives of Policies 1 and 2 by optimizing the requirements of each, aiming for a total reliance on 1820 million m^3, which includes the acquisition of 1000 million m^3 from Helmand/Hirmand's negotiable water in Afghanistan, ranging values of the "GDP per consumptive water" and "Percent of Iran water right from the Helmand/Hirmand river" slider keys.
Policy 4	Establish a nuclear-powered desalination (1400 MW) facility in the Oman Sea to produce approximately 230 million m^3 of freshwater annually, increasing the value of the "Capacity of the desalination site" slider key to its maximum amount.

[a] Negotiable water, defined by Shahbazbegian et al. (2016), also referred to as *yellow water* defined by Shahbazbegian and Dinar (2023) in relation to negotiations over international transboundary rivers, refers to the quantity of natural discharge that upstream states are able to harness without the necessity of utilizing it for their own consumption.

The baseline scenario (business as usual or Policy 0) demonstrates the unsustainability of current practices, while four alternative policy packages were tested: water negotiation with Afghanistan (Policy 1), improving water economic productivity and resilience (Policy 2), a combination of Policies 1 and 2 (Policy 3), and the construction of a nuclear desalination plant in the Oman Sea (Policy 4).

The simulation results indicate a clear hierarchy in terms of sustainability and effectiveness among these options (Figure 7.3).

According to the results, Policy 3, which combines diplomatic efforts to secure water rights with improvements in water productivity, emerged as the most sustainable option, showing the highest positive impact across all three variables. Notably, Policy 2 (focusing on water productivity and resilience) demonstrated greater sustainability than Policy 4 (nuclear desalination) in

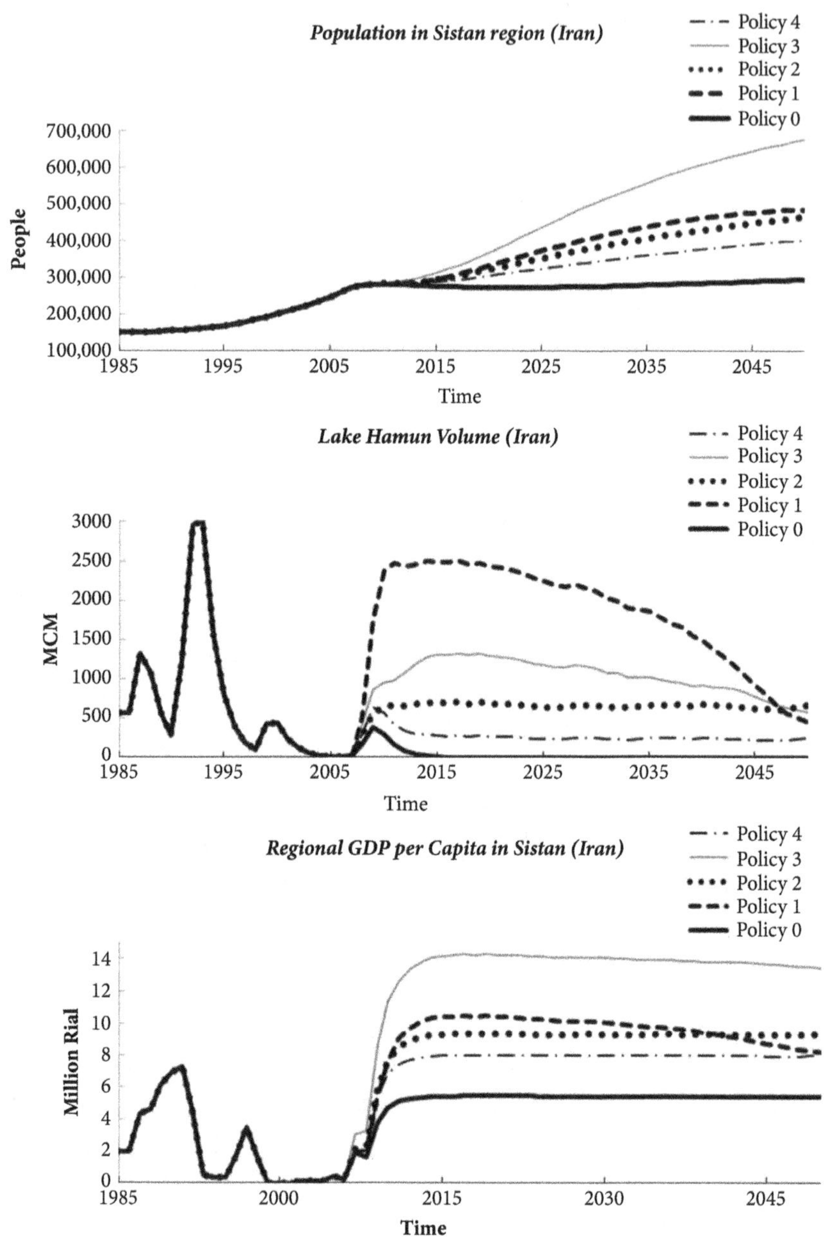

Figure 7.3 The Simulation Results for Attributes of Concern in the Sistan Region Located in Iran

Note: GDP = gross domestic product; MCM = million cubic meters. Elaborated by the authors.

terms of keeping Lake Hamun volume, which in turn proved more sustainable than Policy 1 (purely diplomatic approach). The nuclear desalination option (Policy 4) showed the least effectiveness in restoring Hamun Lake, despite its potential contributions to water security through alternative supply.

A critical finding from the model simulations is that while Iran may be able to keep the living population in the region and even improve welfare levels through various policy interventions, the restoration of Hamun Lake is impossible without cooperation with Afghanistan. This highlights the transboundary nature of the challenge and emphasizes the importance of bilateral cooperation. The model serves as a valuable tool for both countries to quantify the water volumes needed for lake restoration and to understand the associated benefits. It demonstrates that the desiccation of Hamun Lake would have adverse effects for both nations, underlining the necessity of collaborative solutions.

These findings suggest that while technological solutions like desalination plants may contribute to water security, they cannot substitute for transboundary cooperation in managing shared water resources. This finding is similar to the set of findings in Katz (2025). The superior performance of Policy 3 indicates that a comprehensive approach combining diplomatic efforts with domestic efficiency improvements offers the most promising path forward for sustainable regional development and ecological restoration.

Notwithstanding the dashboard asymmetry in including Afghanistan's attributes of concern, the designed DSM can facilitate these specific negotiation scenarios between Iran and Afghanistan, focusing on mutual benefits around Lake Hamun and agricultural development as follows.

7.3.1 Potential Application of the DSM for the Lake Hamun Rehabilitation Exchange Strategy

The model can be developed to demonstrate how controlled water releases from Afghanistan could help rehabilitate Lake Hamun while creating benefits for both countries. Also, it has the potential to be expanded to investigate the effect of released water from Afghanistan on local fisheries, dust storms, tourism initiatives, and wetland habitats. For instance, if Afghanistan releases an additional *X*% of water flow during specific months, the model could show how this would result in the following:

- Restore Lake Hamun's water levels to support local fisheries
- Reduce dust storms that affect both countries (particularly Afghan provinces like Nimroz and Farah) (It has the potential to expand in the model.)
- Create tourism opportunities beneficial to both sides
- Improve the local microclimate, benefiting agriculture in both countries
- Create wetland habitats that support migratory birds and biodiversity

The DSM could also be extended to calculate specific trade-offs. For example, if Afghanistan releases X million m^3 of water during non-peak agricultural months, it could still maintain its essential needs while helping restore Lake Hamun. In return, Afghanistan could benefit from the following:

- Reduced dust storm impacts on its southern provinces
- Access to fish resources in the restored lake
- Joint ecotourism ventures
- Improved regional climate conditions for its own agriculture

7.3.2 Potential Application of the DSM in an Agricultural Cooperation Strategy

The DSM can illustrate how strategic water releases to support Iranian agriculture could create a win–win situation:

- Cross-border agricultural markets: Afghanistan could secure preferential access to Iranian agricultural markets
- Technology transfer: Iran could share advanced irrigation and farming techniques
- Joint processing facilities: Establishment of food processing plants near the border serving both countries
- Shared agricultural research: Collaborative research on drought-resistant crops

The key is that the model provides concrete numbers and projections that both sides can trust, helping move negotiations from abstract discussions to specific, actionable agreements based on mutual benefits.

7.4 Discussion

The proposed SD-based DSM provides a comprehensive analytical framework. It transcends traditional negotiation approaches, offering a sophisticated platform for understanding the intricate interactions within water resource systems. The model's strength lies in its ability to build a common understanding between Iran and Afghanistan, transforming potential conflict into an opportunity for collaborative problem-solving by creating a shared language and perspective on water resource management.

The DSM's innovative approach enables data-driven decision-making by simulating long-term scenarios and potential consequences of water allocation strategies. Unlike conventional negotiation methods that often rely on assumptions and political posturing, this model allows stakeholders to explore quantitative analyses of complex systemic interactions. Through scenario simulation, negotiators can identify win–win solutions that balance agricultural productivity, economic development, and environmental sustainability. This can be institutionalized, thereby creating sufficient consensus on which to build trust between the parties (Turton, 2004). The model's capacity to facilitate dialogue and reduce misunderstandings by providing a transparent, comprehensive view of the water system represents a crucial breakthrough in transboundary water management.

However, use of the SD is not always simple. One of the main challenges is the need for accurate and up-to-date data. In the case of transboundary rivers, it can be difficult to collect reliable data from all riparian countries (Mirchi et al., 2012). In addition, the complexity of the models sometimes makes it difficult for non-experts to understand and interpret the results (Voinov & Bousquet, 2010). To overcome these challenges, SD professionals have moved toward collaborative approaches. In these methods, stakeholders with different expertise are involved from the beginning of the modeling process. This partnership not only helps to increase trust in the model but also provides an opportunity for dialogue and mutual understanding between different parties (Voinov & Bousquet, 2010).

However, the current model confronts several significant limitations that must be critically addressed. The model's complexity poses challenges for stakeholder comprehension, while the quality of outputs remains dependent on data accuracy. Long-term forecasts inherently carry uncertainty, and the model struggles to fully capture nuanced political, social, and cultural factors that influence water negotiations. Most critically, the current DSM was developed primarily using Iran-side data, creating a fundamental imbalance by excluding the perspective of Afghanistan, the upstream country from which the Helmand/Hirmand River originates.

By establishing a permanent joint committee to oversee model development and training experts from both countries, the project could transform the DSM from a technical tool into a diplomatic bridge, fostering more constructive negotiations and sustainable water management agreements (Turton, 2003).

The proposed collaborative model exemplifies how advanced technological approaches can convert historical water-related tensions into opportunities for regional cooperation. By creating a transparent, data-driven platform for understanding complex systemic interactions, this chapter offers a transformative methodology for resolving transboundary water conflicts. The approach demonstrates that innovative DSMs can serve not merely as analytical tools but as catalysts for dialogue, mutual understanding, and shared environmental stewardship.

7.5 Conclusion

The Helmand/Hirmand River, a crucial transboundary water resource between Afghanistan and Iran, exemplifies the complex challenges of managing shared water resources in the 21st century. Traditional negotiation approaches have proven inadequate for addressing current needs, necessitating the implementation of SD-based DSMs. This model provides a comprehensive analysis of the region's water system by incorporating variables like wetland volume, population, GDP, and sectoral water demands, enabling decision makers to simulate scenarios and understand long-term impacts while fostering constructive dialogue between parties.

The current model faces limitations, including complexity, data accuracy requirements, and challenges in modeling human and political factors. Most critically, the current DSM lacks Afghan participation in its development. To address these constraints, a joint Iran–Afghanistan research project is proposed to improve the model through collaborative data collection, shared priority setting, and expert training. This approach could enhance both model accuracy and interstate cooperation, potentially leading to sustainable water management solutions. Success depends on mutual cooperation, data transparency, and balancing national interests with regional sustainability goals.

7.6 Supporting Figures

Figures 7.4 and 7.5 provide additional insight into the system of relationships in the basin.

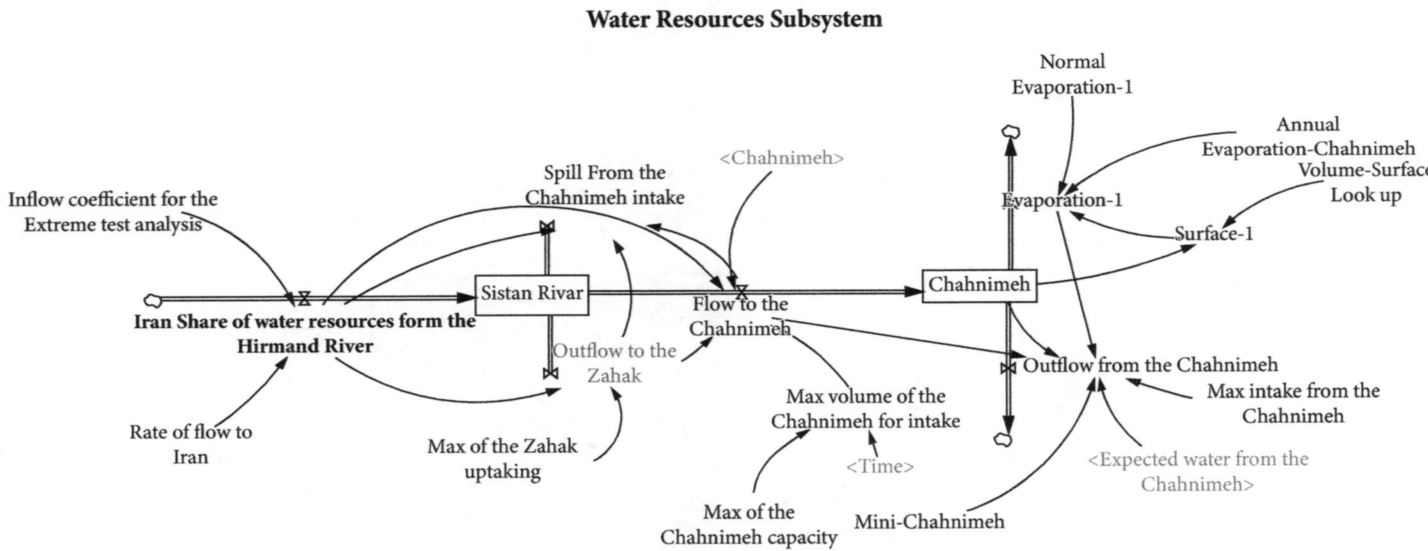

Figure 7.4 Stock-Flow Diagrams Based on the Casual Loop Diagrams Mapped in Vensim Software

Note: AG = agricultural; FCJ = fixed cost of jobs; FLJ = fixed labor in jobs; GDP = gross domestic product; MCM = million cubic meters; PCJ = per capita job availability; PHRJ = population in high-risk jobs; PLI = population leaving jobs; T = time (years or iterations). Elaborated by the authors.

Socio-Economic Subsystem

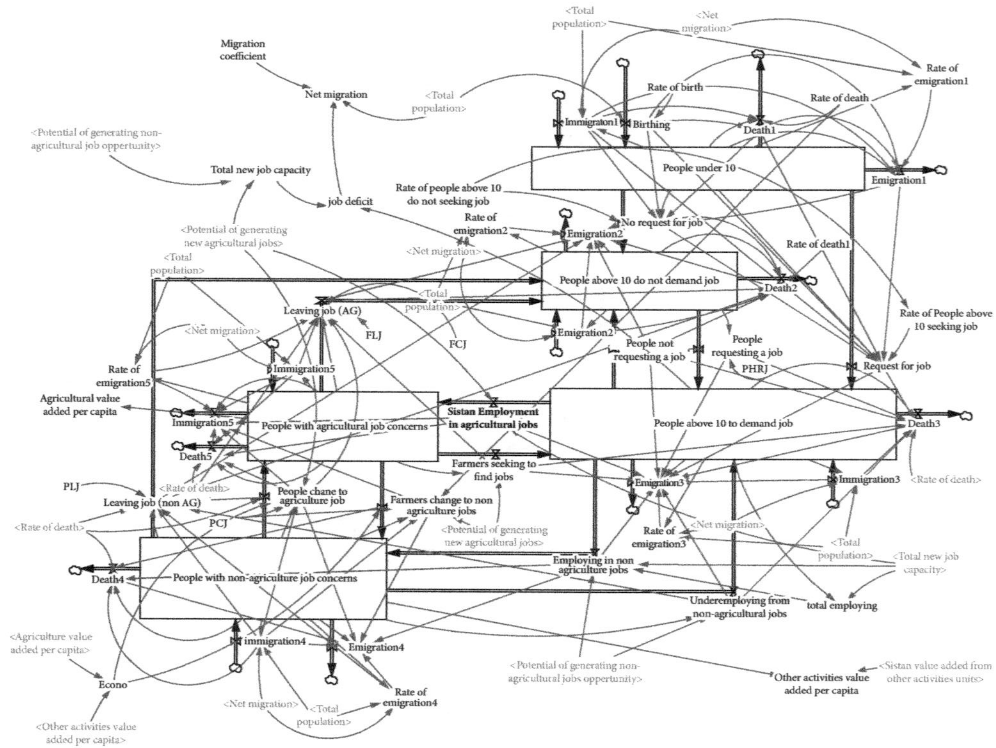

Figure 7.4 continued

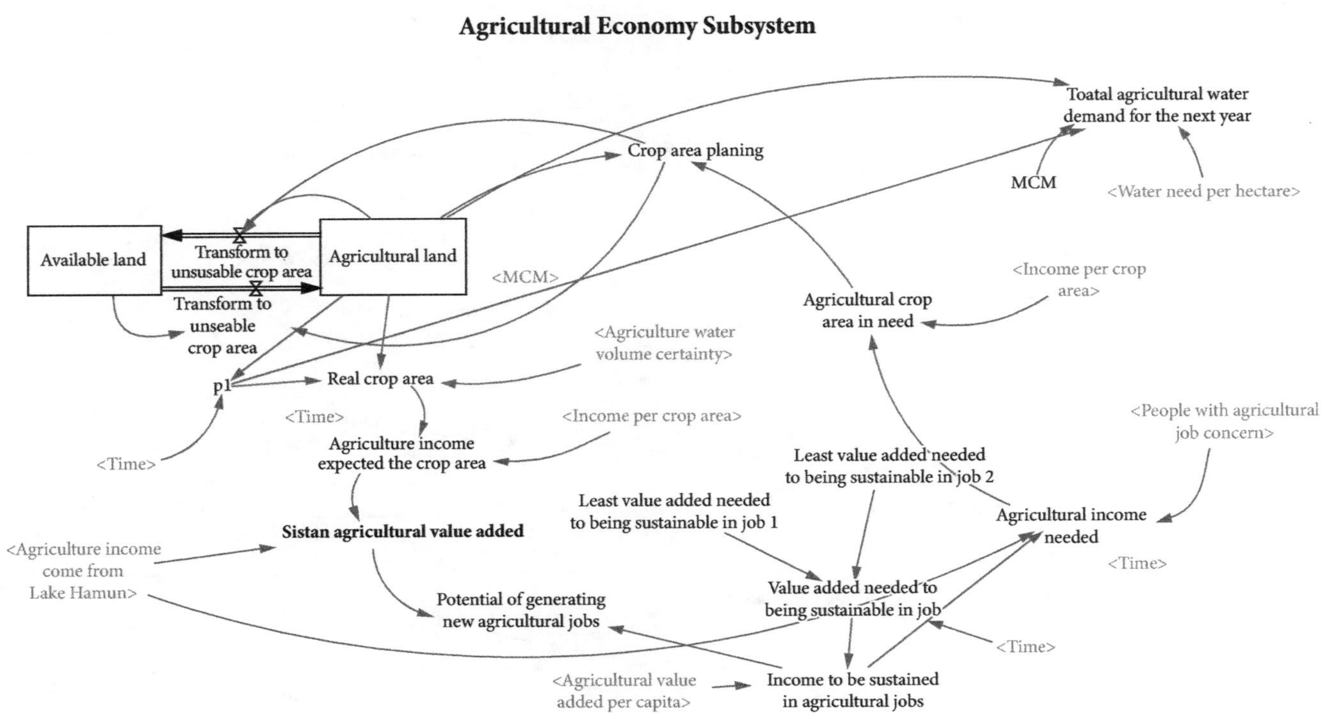

Figure 7.4 continued

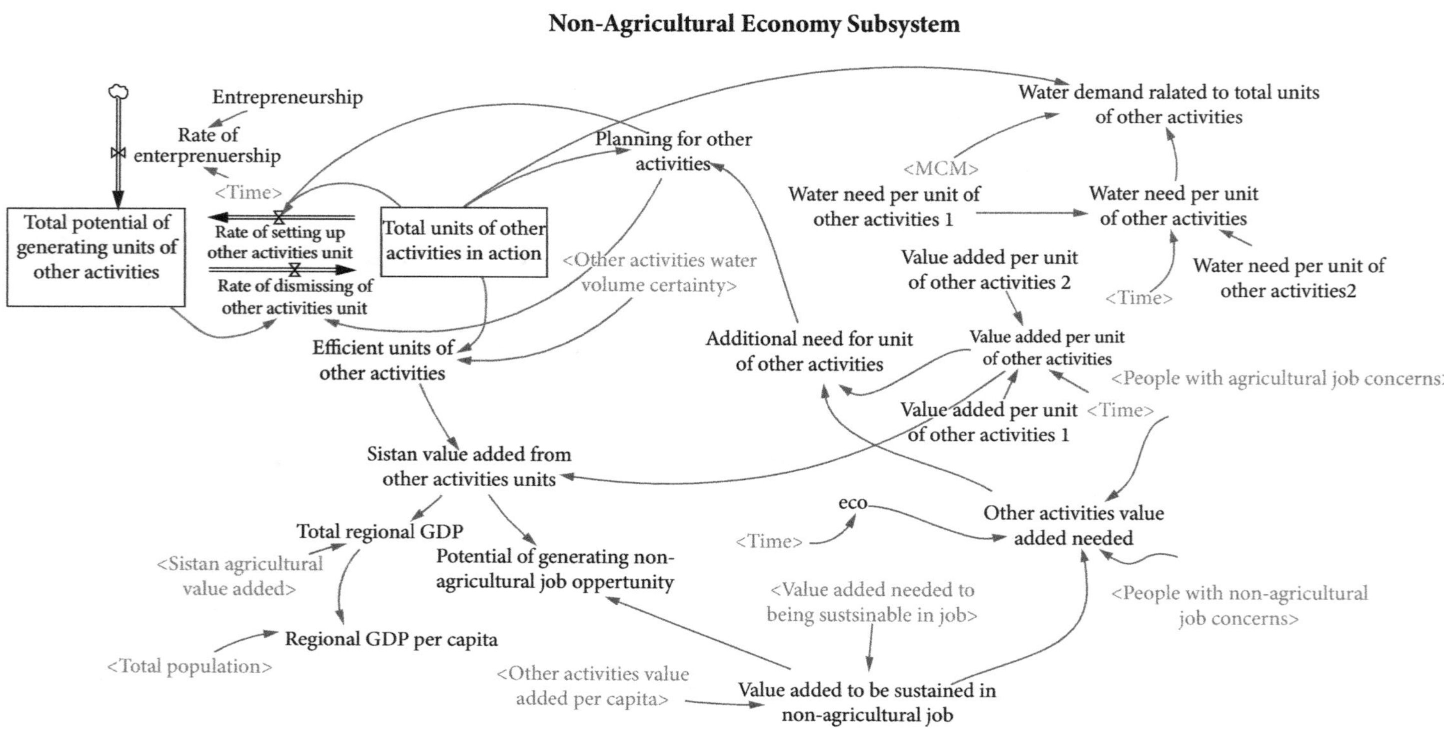

Figure 7.4 continued

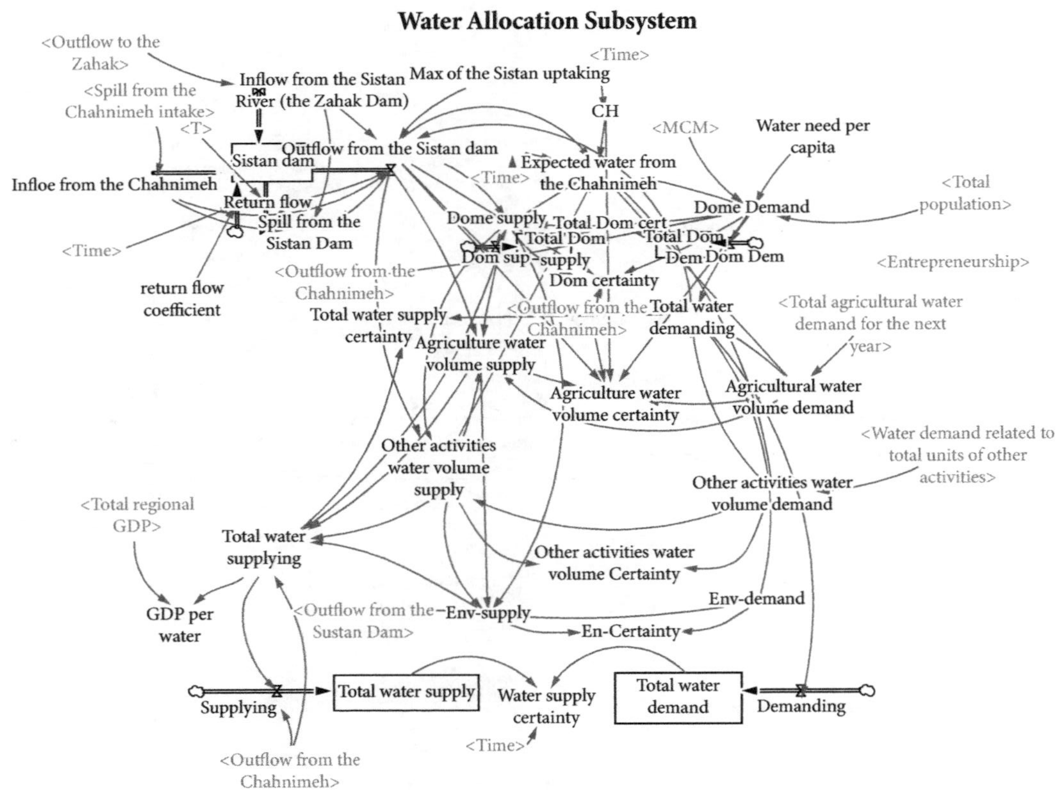

Figure 7.4 continued

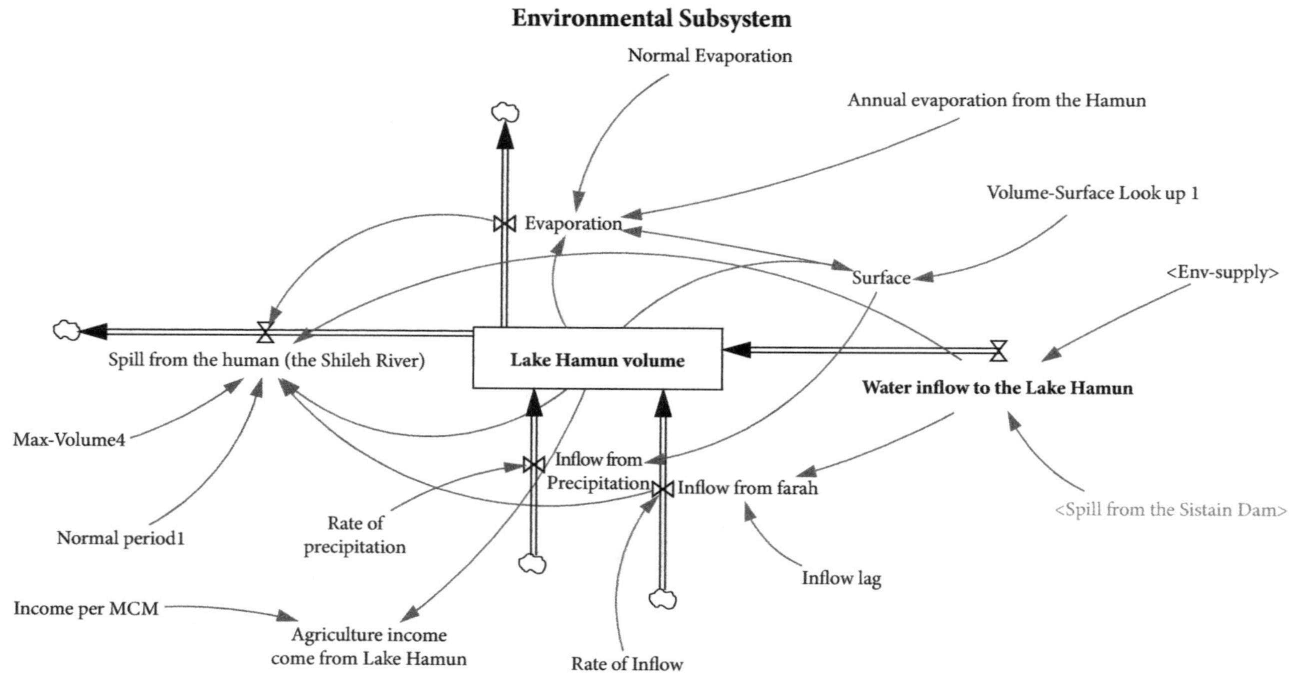

Figure 7.4 continued

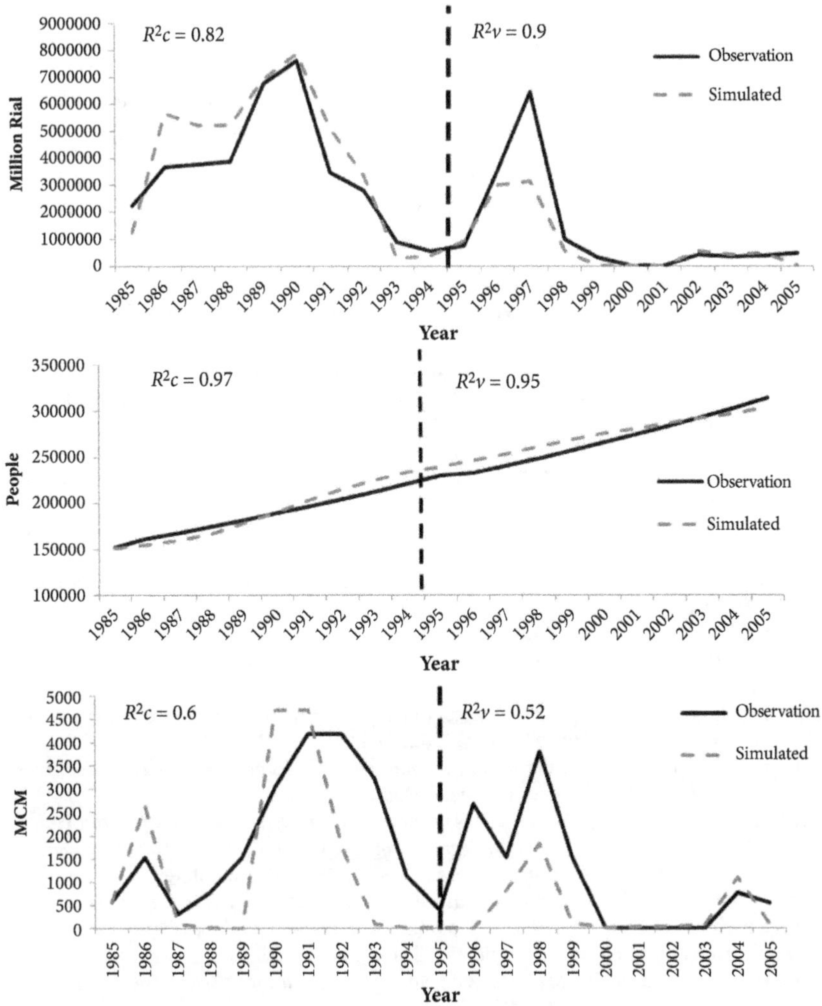

Figure 7.5 The Calibration (1985–1995) and Verification (1995–2005) Results for Three Variables: Agricultural Gross Domestic Product, Population in the Region, and Volume of Water in Lake Hamun

Note: MCM = million cubic meters. Adapted from Shahbazbegian and Sadeghi (2018), with permission from the journal.

References

Aman, F. (2016). *Water dispute escalating between Iran and Afghanistan*. Atlantic Council, South Asia Center.

Bazrkar, M. H., Tavakoli-Nabavi, E., Zamani, N., & Eslamian, S. (2013). System dynamic approach to hydro-politics in Hirmand transboundary river basin from sustainability perspective. *International Journal of Hydrology Science and Technology*, *3*(4), 378–398.

Bidabadi, F. S., & Afshari, L. (2020). Human right to water in the Helmand basin: Setting a path for the conflict settlement between Afghanistan and Iran. *Utrecht Law Review, 16*(2), 150–162. https://doi.org/10.36633/ulr.566

Druckman, D. (2007). Negotiation models and applications. In R. Avenhaus & I. W. Zartman (Eds.), *Diplomacy games: Formal models and international negotiations* (pp. 83–96). Springer.

Duran-Encalada, J. A., Paucar-Caceres, A., Bandala, E. R., & Wright, G. H. (2017). The impact of global climate change on water quantity and quality: A system dynamics approach to the US–Mexican transborder region. *European Journal of Operational Research, 256*(2), 567–581.

Eden, C., & Ackermann, F. (2021). Modelling stakeholder dynamics for supporting group decision and negotiation: Theory to practice. *Group Decision and Negotiation, 30*(5), 1001–1025.

Elliott, M. L., & Kaufman, S. (2016). Enhancing environmental quality and sustainability through negotiation and conflict management: Research into systems, dynamics, and practices. *Negotiation and Conflict Management Research, 9*(3), 199–219.

Faizee, M., & Schmeier, S. (2023, August). *Navigating water (in)security in Taliban's Afghanistan: Insights into local, national, and regional water security challenges.* Water Peace and Security. https://waterpeacesecurity.org/files/380

Falkenmark,M., & Widstrand, C. (1992). Population and water resources: A delicate balance. *Population Bulletin, 47*(3), 1–36.

Ford, A. (2000). *Modeling the environment: An introduction to system dynamics models of environmental systems.* Island Press.

Forrester, J. W. (1961). *Industrial dynamics.* MIT Press.

Forrester, J. W. (1971). Counterintuitive behavior of social systems. *Theory and Decision, 2*(2), 109–140.

Gökçekuş, H., & Bolouri, F. (2023). Transboundary waters and their status in today's water-scarce world. *Sustainability, 15*(5), Article 4234.

Hanasz, P. (2017). *Transboundary water governance in the Helmand River basin: Identifying obstacles and opportunities.* Global Water Forum.

Hayat, E., & Elçi, Ġ. (2017, March 22–24). *Adopting a strategic framework for transboundary water resources management in Afghanistan* [Paper presentation]. *IWA 2nd Regional Symposium on Water, Wastewater and Environment*, Çesme-Izmir, Turkey.

Katz, D. (Ed.) (2025). *World scientific handbook of transboundary water management: Science, economics, policy and politics: Vol. 2. Tapping technologies: The role of technological change in transboundary water management.* World Scientific Publishers.

King, M., & Sturtewagen, B. (2010). *Making the most of Afghanistan's river basins: Opportunities for regional cooperation.* EastWest Institute.

Kotir, J. H., Smith, C., Brown, G., Marshall, N., & Johnstone, R. (2016). A system dynamics simulation model for sustainable water resources management and agricultural development in the Volta River basin, Ghana. *Science of the Total Environment, 573*, 444–457.

Madani, K., & Mariño, M. A. (2009). System dynamics analysis for managing Iran's Zayandeh-Rud River basin. *Water Resources Management, 23*(11), 2163–2187.

Meadows, D. H. (2008). *Thinking in systems: A primer.* Chelsea Green Publishing.

Meadows, D. H., Meadows, D. L., Randers, J., & Behrens, W. W. (1972). *The limits to growth.* Universe Books.

Mirchi, A., Madani, K., Watkins D., Jr., & Ahmad, S. (2012). Synthesis of system dynamics tools for holistic conceptualization of water resources problems. *Water Resources Management, 26*(9), 2421–2442.

Nagheeby, M., & Rieu-Clarke, A. (2020). Water diplomacy in the Helmand River basin: Exploring the obstacles to cooperation within the shadow of anarchy. In A. Kittikhoun & S. Schmeier (Eds.), *River basin organizations in water diplomacy* (pp. 201–221). Routledge.

Nagheeby, M., & Warner, J. (2022). The 150-year itch: Afghanistan–Iran hydropolitics over the Helmand/Hirmand River. *Water Alternatives, 15*(3), 551–573.

Palmate, S. S., Kumar, S., Talchabhadel, R., & Mokari, E. (2022, August 7). *A system dynamic approach for managing transboundary water systems* [Paper presentation]. 11th iEMSs Conference, East Lansing, MI, United States.

Piya, S., Khadem, M. M. R. K., & Shamsuzzoha, A. (2016). Negotiation based decision support system for order acceptance. *Journal of Manufacturing Technology Management, 27*(3), 443–468.

Richardson, G. P., & Andersen, D. F. (2010). Systems thinking, mapping, and modeling in group decision and negotiation. In D. M. Kilgour & C. Eden (Eds.), *Handbook of group decision and negotiation* (pp. 313–324). Springer.

Sánchez-García, J. Y., & López-Hernández, C. (2020). Applying system dynamics to a negotiation diagram. In S. García-Álvarez & C. Atristain-Suárez (Eds.), *Strategy, power and CSR: Practices and challenges in organizational management* (pp. 85–99). Emerald Publishing.

Sehlke, G., & Jacobson, J. (2005). System dynamics modeling of transboundary systems: The Bear River basin model. *Groundwater, 43*(5), 722–730.

Shahbazbegian, M., Bagheri, A., & Mousavi Shafaiee, S. M. (2016). Analysis of mechanisms governing water withdrawal from Helmand transboundary river originated from Afghanistan, emphasizing on the role of state building project in the country. *Geopolitics Quarterly, 12*(43), 168–190.

Shahbazbegian, M., & Dinar, A. (2023). Painted water—A concept to shape water negotiation strategies in shared river basins. *Water, 15*(19), Article 3343.

Shahbazbegian, M., & Nabavi, E. (2023). How to incorporate system archetypes into water conflicts analysis: Application in Euphrates, Nile, Zambezi, and Lake Kivu transboundary basins. *Water, 15*(7), Article 1270.

Shahbazbegian, M., & Noori, R. (2022). Hydropolitical system archetypes: Feedback structures, physical environments, unintended behaviors, and a diagnostic checklist. *Hydrology, 9*(12), Article 207.

Shahbazbegian, M., & Sadeghi, M. (2018). تحلیل سیستمی الزامات، هزینه ها و اثربخشی بسته سیاستی احداث آب شیرین کن اتمی در سواحل دریای عمان برای انتقال آب به دشت سیستان [Systematic analysis of the requirements, costs and effectiveness of setting up nuclear water desalination at Oman Sea coasts for water transferring to Sistan Plain]. *Geopolitics Quarterly, 14*(50), 197–223.

Shahbazbegian, M. R., Turton, A., & Mousavi Shafaee, S. M. (2016). Hydropolitical self-organization theory; system dynamics to analyse hydropolitics of Helmand transboundary river. *Water Policy, 18*(5), 1088–1119.

Shao, Z., Wu, F., Li, F., Zhao, Y., & Xu, X. (2020). System dynamics model for evaluating socio-economic impacts of different water diversion quantity from transboundary river basins—A case study of Xinjiang. *International Journal of Environmental Research and Public Health, 17*(23), Article 9091.

Sharifikia, M. (2013). Environmental challenges and drought hazard assessment of Hamoun Desert Lake in Sistan region, Iran, based on the time series of satellite imagery. *Natural Hazards, 65*(1), 201–217.

Simonovic, S. P. (2009). *Managing water resources: Methods and tools for a systems approach.* UNESCO Publishing.

Sterman, J. D. (2000). *Business dynamics: Systems thinking and modeling for a complex world.* McGraw-Hill Education.

Sterman, J. (2002). *System dynamics: systems thinking and modeling for a complex world* [Working Paper Series ESD-WP-2003-01.13]. Massachusetts Institute of Technology.

Swain, A. (2004). *Managing water conflict: Asia, Africa and the Middle East.* Routledge.

Turton, A. R. (2003). *The political aspects of institutional development in the water sector: South Africa and its international river basins* [Unpublished draft of a doctoral dissertation]. University of Pretoria.
Turton, A. R. (2004). The evolution of water management institutions in select southern African international river basins. In C. Tortajada, O. Unver, & A. K. Biswas (Eds.), *Water as a focus for regional development* (pp. 251–289). Oxford University Press.
United Nations Environment Programme. (2006). *History of environmental change in the Sistan basin: Based on satellite image analysis: 1976–2005.*https://wedocs.unep.org/handle/20.500.11822/7690
Vennix, J. A. (1996). *Group model building: Facilitating team learning using system dynamics.* John Wiley & Sons.
Voinov, A., & Bousquet, F. (2010). Modelling with stakeholders. *Environmental Modelling & Software, 25*(11), 1268–1281.
Whitney, J. W. (2006). *Geology, water, and wind in the lower Helmand basin, southern Afghanistan* (Scientific Investigations Report 2006-5182). US Geological Survey.
Winz, I., Brierley, G., & Trowsdale, S. (2009). The use of system dynamics simulation in water resources management. *Water Resources Management, 23*(7), 1301–1323.
Wolf, A. T., Yoffe, S. B., & Giordano, M. (2003). International waters: Identifying basins at risk. *Water Policy, 5*(1), 29–60.
Yuan, L., He, W., Degefu, D. M., Liao, Z., Wu, X., An, M., Zhang, Z., & Ramsey, T. S. (2020). Transboundary water sharing problem; a theoretical analysis using evolutionary game and system dynamics. *Journal of Hydrology, 582*, Article 124521.
Yuan, L., He, W., Degefu, D. M., Wan, Z., Ramsey, T. S., & Wu, X. (2023). A system dynamics simulation model for water conflicts in the Zhanghe River basin, China. *International Journal of Water Resources Development, 39*(6), 1039–1055.
Zeitoun, M., & Warner, J. (2006). Hydro-hegemony—A framework for analysis of transboundary water conflicts. *Water Policy, 8*(5), 435–460.
Zomorodian, M., Lai, S. H., Homayounfar, M., Ibrahim, S., & Pender, G. (2017). Development and application of coupled system dynamics and game theory: A dynamic water conflict resolution method. *PLoS ONE, 12*(12), Article e0188489.

8

Developing a Decision Support Model to Assess the Value of Cooperation Benefits Under Climate Change

Case of the Colorado River Basin in the United States

Daniel Crespo, Mehdi Nemati, Ariel Dinar, Zachary Frankel, and Nickolas Halberg

8.1 Introduction

Cooperative arrangements have long been central to the public interest, especially regarding the mechanisms communities use to share and manage water resources. Basin water allocation arrangements and institutions are water policy instruments based on cooperation that seek to reduce water conflicts between the stakeholders that share the basin water among countries, regions/states, and various sectors. Compared with unilateral strategies of the riparian stakeholders, cooperative water management approaches reduce conflicts in the long run and contribute to creating benefits in the water systems (Cao et al., 2023).

Efficiency is a fundamental principle of water management that can lead to stable solutions and reduce conflicts in the basin. Information and knowledge are essential to achieve efficient water use due to the cumulative effects and interactions of water use. The willingness to come together to a common ground of consensus solutions is the basis of water arrangements and the development of basin institutions. Addressing the present and future challenges of water management requires recognition that partnerships and cooperation are essential for the success of water negotiations, leading to

Daniel Crespo et al., *Developing a Decision Support Model to Assess the Value of Cooperation Benefits Under Climate Change*. In: *Decision Support Models to Assist International and Transboundary Water Negotiations*. Edited by: Mohammadreza Shahbazbegian and Ariel Dinar, Oxford University Press. © Oxford University Press (2026).
DOI: 10.1093/9780197802601.003.0008

efficient and stable water-use arrangements in the basin. Unilateral solutions based on non-cooperative initiatives could be inefficient and produce inferior levels of benefits, as well as high costs and losses (Wolf, 2007).

Water scarcity, water quality degradation, infrastructure development, and ecosystem protection are examples that lead to conflicts among riparians that require coordinated solutions at the basin level. The basin's physical and political characteristics, the degree of development of economic activities and institutions, and upstream–downstream relationships determine the success of water policy based on basin-wide cooperation (Britz et al., 2013; Madani, 2010; Wolf, 2007).

The Colorado River basin (CRB) is one of the most important basins in the southwestern United States, supporting economic activities and a rich ecosystem (US Bureau of Reclamation [USBR], 2012). However, the basin faces significant pressure, raising concerns about the sustainability of its water management system. These concerns are prompting adjustments in water policy. Given the basin's importance and the attention it receives, analyzing the cooperation schemes between water users is interesting and relevant. In this chapter, a cooperative game solution is applied to the water allocation problem of the CRB.

Under water scarcity induced by climate change, benefits from water use in urban centers and irrigation districts in the seven US states that are part of the CRB are subject to negotiation and possible reallocation following an agreed-upon water exchange in the form of water trade.[1] Other sectors and water users, such as hydropower and environmental users, are excluded due to their relatively smaller share of water consumption than the agricultural and urban sectors (Crespo et al., 2025).

The analysis in this chapter includes non-cooperative solutions and cooperative ones. The cooperative game theory allocations include the Shapley value (Shapley, 1953), the nucleolus (Schmeidler, 1969), and the Nash-Harsanyi solution (Harsanyi, 1959). We use stability, power, and disruption indexes to explain possible negotiation results and provide insights into the acceptability and stability of the possible arrangement. Such comparison allows the stakeholders in the basin to rank options that result in different shared benefits that they receive if they cooperate. The analysis is performed at the sectorial and state levels. In the first step, cooperation

[1] This chapter focuses on the seven US states, excluding important stakeholders such as Indian tribes and Mexico, as the states are currently negotiating the distribution of water drawdowns in case of scarcity. The deadline to reach an agreement between the seven states is the end of 2025.

between irrigation districts and urban centers is allowed within each state only to determine the value of cooperation between sectors. In the second step, cooperation is allowed between any sectors in all states, which helps identify cooperation's value at the basin level.

The rest of this chapter is organized as follows: Section 8.2 describes the main characteristics of the CRB, the existing rules of water allocation in the basin, and the challenges the basin faces due to the rigidity of these rules. Section 8.3 explains the decision support model's (DSM's) capacity as a tool for negotiation and cooperation. Section 8.4 describes the background of game theory that supports the share of benefits and the DSM, a reduced version of a larger hydro-economic model of the CRB (Crespo et al., 2025).[2] Section 8.5 describes the data sources, the game theory concepts applied, and the water allocation scenarios under two climate change–induced water scarcity possible values. Results are presented in Section 8.6. Conclusions, policy implications, and future work are given in Section 8.7.

8.2 The CRB and the Institutions That Regulate Water Allocations

The CRB covers an area of over 246,000 square miles[3] across the United States and Mexico. It supplies drinking water to 40 million people in the United States, including Arizona, California, Nevada (lower basin), Colorado, New Mexico, Utah, Wyoming (upper basin), and Mexico. The water extracted for agriculture irrigates nearly 2.2 million acres[4] and supports livestock production. The CRB's hydropower capacity is 4600 megawatts, and aquatic ecosystems provide recreational and environmental benefits to society (Crespo et al., 2023, 2025). Figure 8.1 illustrates the CRB's main river stems and lakes, the upper and lower basins, the states within the basin, the major cities the Colorado River water serves, the primary hydropower facilities, and the irrigated areas.

[2] The hydro-economic model includes several sectors: irrigation, urban, hydropower, Indian tribes, and the environment. However, for the purpose of this chapter, and without loss of generality, only two sectors (that consume nearly 90% of the available water) are considered—irrigated agriculture districts and urban centers.

[3] 1 square mile = 2.59 square kilometers.

[4] 1 acre = 0.405 hectares.

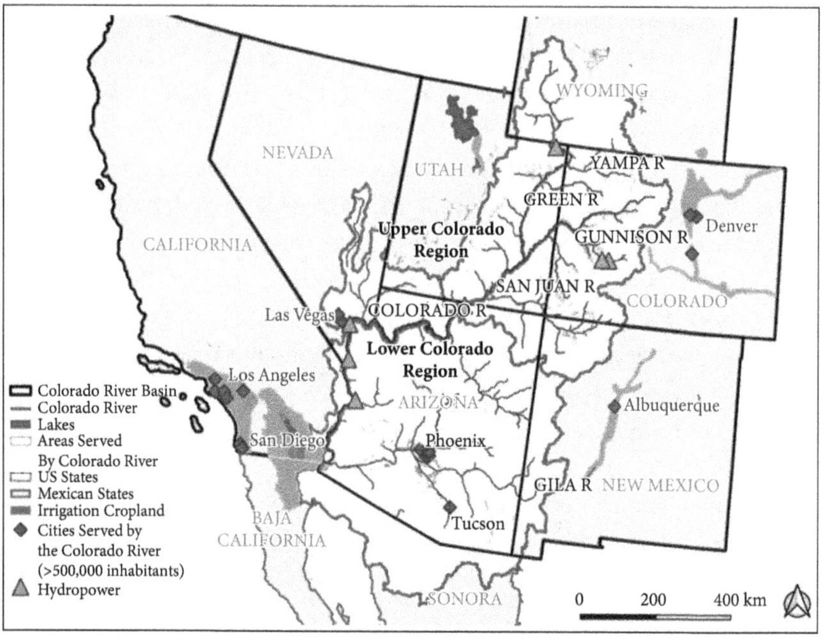

Figure 8.1 Colorado River Basin, Water Users, and Administrative Division
Note: Elaborated by the authors.

Natural water resources in the basin, measured at Lees Ferry in Arizona between 1906 and 2007, were estimated at 15 million acre-feet (maf)[5] per year. According to the USBR, the average flow of the Colorado River in the 21st century is currently about 18% lower than the average flow in the 20th century (12.4 vs. 15.2 maf).

Increasing temperature is the main factor contributing to the decrease in water inflows and alteration of the snowmelt period observed in the basin (Clow et al., 2016; Sexstone et al., 2016, 2018). Climate change is expected to increase temperatures and evaporation, reducing water availability in the basin by up to 30% compared to the 20th century (Udall & Overpeck, 2017; Whitney et al., 2023).

The CRB relies on institutions and agreements to alleviate water conflicts resulting from water scarcity. Two main agreements set the water allocation in the basin: the 1944 treaty between the United States and Mexico and the 1922 Compact (the Compact) between the seven US states that share the

[5] 1 acre-foot ≈ 1233 m^3.

river basin (Treaty between the United States of America and Mexico, 1944; USBR, 1922). One instrument of water management is the 2007 Interim Guidelines, which define the water allocation under shortage conditions. The 2007 Interim Guidelines expire at the end of 2025, and the states need to develop and negotiate the guidelines post-2026. For more information on the institutions of the CRB, see Crespo et al. (2025) and Frankel et al. (2024).

Agricultural users usually hold senior water rights in the CRB, while urban centers typically have junior water rights. As a result, urban centers seek long-term water lease contracts with irrigators to increase the reliability of their water supply. Also, there is asymmetry between states.

8.3 A DSM Based on the Hydro-economic Model and Game Theory: An Effective Tool Enhances Negotiations Toward Cooperation in the CRB

This section explains the capacity of the DSM presented in the chapter and the power of combining hydro-economic modeling and game theory as tools for negotiation on water shortage allocation in the basin. The section first describes the differing roles and interests of the federal government and the states. It then outlines the conditions necessary for cooperation, negotiation, and consensus. Next, it details the elements of the DSM that provide capacity as a decision support tool. Finally, it discusses the effectiveness of the tool in aiding negotiations.

The federal government and the seven US states in the CRB are the main actors in the negotiations. However, the role of the federal government differs from that of the states. The federal government promotes negotiations and establishes the framework and conditions for their success. The states actively participate in the negotiation process to achieve agreements. Initially, states will reach a consensus on water shortage allocation at the sub-basin level. Subsequently, representatives of the upper and lower basins confront the proposals for the allocations. This process is repeated to close the gap between proposals. If consensus is not achieved by the states, the federal government unilaterally determines shortage allocations to the basin states.

The negotiation process seeks solutions (under established roles such as water rights and treaties) that meet the needs of as many stakeholders as possible. Giving concessions to receive something in return is the principle that underpins collaborative negotiations. Two main conditions are necessary for cooperation and negotiation: the cost imposed on one state must be offset by benefits, and the states must be compensated for the additional cost. In other words, the participating states can share the incremental benefits resulting from cooperation. To achieve incremental benefits, the water distribution must enhance water-use efficiency, implying that initial conditions were not optimal. The capacity to compensate for water exchange results from improvements in water efficiency but requires a mechanism for compensation to materialize. A consensus in negotiations requires compensation for water that satisfies the benefit losses of the states that transfer water. Additionally, achieving consensus may require considering aspects such as justice and equity.

The DSM supports decision-making activities using analytical models and effectively aids in designing and evaluating management instruments. The DSM presented in this chapter results from two methods: hydro-economic modeling and cooperative game theory. The DSM in this chapter is founded on both prescriptive and descriptive modeling. Prescriptive models recommend actions based on optimization problems, while descriptive models inform possible outcomes given certain conditions. Simulation and optimization enable the DSM to handle various climate change scenarios and institutional restrictions. Any policy change must improve efficiency. Solutions provided by the economic model are optimal, ensuring incremental benefits and room for negotiation, thus satisfying the first condition for negotiation, the efficiency condition. Cooperative game theory offers a set of benefit allocation solutions where allocation of incremental benefits satisfies the second condition for negotiation: compensation incentivizes participation as all water users achieve a better outcome.

Efficient bargaining requires decisions based on consensus. The results of DSMs highlight critical points within the range of values where negotiation is possible. Firstly, they show the retirement value, which is the minimum benefit a state accepts in order to participate in the cooperative arrangement. They also indicate the maximum benefit obtainable by states when they cooperate. Additionally, DSMs present a set of solutions that could be accepted by the states according to game theory, meeting various criteria. Other key information includes the states' power index and the agreements' stability. Depending on their political preferences, states may prefer different solutions, selecting optimal ones according to policy priorities. For example, states may favor a solution that provides an equal distribution of benefits or allocates the marginal benefit to each state. Alternatively, the states may prefer stable solutions that will last for a long time. The federal government also prefers stable solutions that will eliminate the need for a unilateral action on the part of the government (Congressional Research Service, 2024).

The results presented by our suggested DSM address economic and distributional criteria while recognizing the interrelationship between sectors and states. Moreover, the DSM anticipates the possible effects of climate change, allowing for the reduction of negative impacts from decisions based on partial information. The DSM provides a common framework for evaluating alternatives to share the negative impacts of climate change and water scarcity where all stakeholders can compare the outcome of the negotiation.

8.4 Methodology: Game Theory Allocations and the DSM of the CRB

This section presents the theory that supports the benefit allocations and the economic model of water in the agricultural and urban sectors of the CRB, which is the DSM used to inform negotiations over water allocations.

8.4.1 Allocation Solutions With Game Theory and Stability of the Game

Under game theory specifications, voluntary collective action and independence in regional water management underpin water allocation problems. In this chapter, cooperation requires that water users are willing to contribute water to the common pool, where it is used to maximize the basin-wide welfare and share its incremental benefits. The set of rules to allocate the benefits resulting from cooperation, proposed by cooperative game theory, aims to distribute the social planner's overall basin benefits, obtained by maximizing water allocations without considering political borders or prior water rights. In other words, the social planner's solution allocates all available water of all water users by maximizing the joint benefit of the activities in the basin as if the basin is one decision unit. The social planner maximization provides a *first best* solution that serves as a benchmark to all other allocations. The limitation of the social planner's solution is that it does not specify how to distribute benefits among all water users. The nucleolus, the

Shapley value, and the Nash-Harsanyi allocation are cooperative game theory solutions that address this limitation and suggest schemes to share the benefits resulting from the social planner's overall solution.

8.4.1.1 Cooperative Games

A cooperative game with transferable utility is defined as a pair (N, v), where N is the set of players, $N = 1, 2, \ldots, n$, and v is the characteristic function of the game, $v : 2^N \to R$, with $v(\emptyset) = 0$. A characteristic function is the best value that such a set of players can obtain. For each coalition $S \subseteq N$, there is a value $v(S)$ that represents the benefit (or payoff) that the players in the coalition secure, independently of the behavior of the players outside the coalition. The benefit of a coalition is the minimum benefit that the coalition can obtain if the players in the coalition cooperate. The game is about allocating the joint benefits in a certain way that will make every participant (player) better off compared to non-cooperation, thus leading to stable agreement.

Players in the game are the states, and their benefits in non-cooperation are the sum of the benefits of irrigation districts and urban centers working unilaterally. Sectorial, state, and regional benefits result from the sum of benefits from irrigation districts and urban centers belonging to a certain sector, state, or region and are represented by the following:

$$\Pi_{state,\,sector} = \sum_{u \in g} \Pi_u \tag{1}$$

$$\Pi_{state} = \sum_{sector} \Pi_{state,sector} \tag{2}$$

$$\Pi_{basin} = \sum_{state} \Pi_{state} \tag{3}$$

Here $g = \{u \mid u \in \{state\} \wedge u \in \{sector\}\}$. The set g represents water users u from the agricultural and urban sectors of a state. Equation (1) states that the benefits of a sector in a state equal the sum of benefits of water users in the state and in the sector. Equation (2) states that the benefit of the state is the sum of all benefits in the state, and the benefits of the basin equal the sum of the benefits from the states, Equation (3).

We now introduce concepts from cooperative game theory that will be used as a basis for the allocation of the social planner benefits and then subjected to further comparative stability measures.

8.4.1.2 The Core

The core of an n-players cooperative game is the set of solutions for benefit allocations not dominated by any other set of solutions. That implies that the core provides a bound for the maximum benefit each player can obtain. The core satisfies individual and group rationality and joint efficiency. Individual rationality requires that the benefits allocated to the player l, Ω_l, must be greater than or equal to the benefit obtained without cooperation, $v(l)$. Group rationality requires that the benefit allocated to the member of a coalition be equal to or greater than the benefits the coalition members obtain if they do not cooperate. And efficiency requires that the benefits obtained by the grand coalition are fully shared between all water users, with no unallocated slack. Individual and group rationality and efficiency are presented in the following equations:

$$\Omega_l \geq v(l) \tag{4}$$

$$\sum_s \Omega_s \geq v(s) \tag{5}$$

$$\sum_N \Omega_N \geq v(N) \tag{6}$$

Equations (4)–(6) define the core.

The cooperative game theory solutions we employ satisfy the conditions of the core. The solution of the system that defines the core is a space that allows multiple solutions.

8.4.1.3 The Nucleolus

The nucleolus (Schmeidler, 1969) is a single-point solution that always exists (if the core is not empty). The nucleolus minimizes the dissatisfaction of the most dissatisfied coalition from the allocation of the game benefits. The nucleolus is calculated by defining the δ-core of the game v to be the set of allocations that would be in the core if each coalition were given a subsidy at the level of δ to join. By changing δ we can find the smallest non-empty δ-core (coined the *least core*). The least core is the intersection of all δ-cores. The least core for a benefit allocation game satisfies the following:

$$\text{Min } \delta \tag{7}$$

subject to (s.t.)

$$\sum_{s} \Omega_s - \delta \geq v(s) \ \forall \{ s \in S \setminus \{N\}\} \tag{8}$$

$$\sum_{N} \Omega_N = v(N) \tag{9}$$

8.4.1.4 The Shapley Value

The Shapley value (Shapley, 1953) assigns the benefits to each player by its incremental contribution to the grand coalition. The Shapley value assigns a value $\phi_i(v)$ to a player i, $i = 1, \ldots n$ in a cooperative game $\{v(S), S \subseteq N\}$, where N is the set of players, S is a subset of N that results from the 2^n sub-coalitions of N, $v(S)$ is the characteristic function that is a measure of the best performance of each coalition, s is the number of players in S, and n is the total number of players; $s = |S|$ and $n = |N|$. The Shapley value is presented in Equation (10).

$$\phi_i(v, N) = \sum_{\substack{S \supseteq N \\ S \ni i}} \frac{(s-1)!(n-s)!}{n!} (v(S) - v(S \setminus \{i\})) \tag{10}$$

The incremental contribution of player i to coalition S, $v(S) - v(S \setminus \{i\})$, is multiplied by the number of coalitions where the player is included, $(s - 1)!$, and the number of coalitions where player i is not included, $(n - s)!$, and divided by the $n!$ different permutations of all players in the grand coalition. The Shapley value is the sum of all weighted marginal contributions. It is a unique solution and is included in the core if it is not empty.

8.4.1.5 Nash-Harsanyi Solution

The Nash-Harsanyi solution maximizes the multiplication of all incremental benefits for each player resulting from participating in the grand coalition. The utility of the players participating in the grand coalition is the product of the incremental benefits. The solutions avoid significant differences in the additional benefit that the player receives for participating in the grand coalition. The benefits allocated by the Nash-Harsanyi solution are represented by the solution of the following maximization problem:

$$max: \prod_{l \in N} (\Omega_l - v(l)) \tag{11}$$

These are subject to the core conditions, Equations (7)–(9). The Nash-Harsanyi solution is unique and is in the core if the core is not empty.

8.4.1.6 Measures of Stability and Acceptability in the Coalitions

Fulfilling the core conditions is necessary for the players to participate in the cooperative game allocation. However, the core solution does not guarantee the game's stability. Some players can threaten the coalition if they challenge the fairness of the allocation solution. Game theory provides methods to measure the stability of the coalitions. The power index for a player, α_i, proposed by Loehman et al. (1979), is the ratio of the incremental benefit allocated to the player and the sum of incremental benefits of the members of the grand coalition:

$$\alpha_i = \frac{x_i - v(i)}{\sum_i (x_i - v(i))}; i \in N; \sum_i \alpha_i \tag{12}$$

The power index can be used to measure the stability of each solution. The stability index is the coefficient of variation of the power indexes over all players:

$$S_\alpha = \frac{\sigma_\alpha}{\bar{\alpha}} \tag{13}$$

The importance of a player in the grand coalition could be critical in producing a large impact on the coalitional outcome in case that player leaves the coalition. This is measured by the propensity to disrupt, which measures the marginal contribution of player *i* in the grand coalition over the benefit allocated to the player and is presented by the following expression:

$$G_i = \frac{V(N) - V(N - I)}{x_i}; i = \{1, 2, .., N\} \tag{14}$$

8.5 The Economic Model of Agricultural Water Use in the CRB

The hydro-economic model of the CRB assumes that irrigation districts maximize crop production's benefits, given water availability restrictions. The decision variables are cropland distribution, the irrigation technologies used, and the amount of water applied per unit of cropped land, with water being a constrained resource. The model assumes that crop yield per unit of land is linearly dependent on water evapotranspiration (Raes et al., 2024). The model also assumes that crop yields and input prices are fixed (Crespo et al., 2025). Equation (15) presents the objective function of irrigated agriculture at the irrigation district level. The benefits Π_u resulting from the income of crop production I_u minus water cost WC_u and production cost PC_u are collectively maximized by the farmers in the irrigation district u. The indexes j and k mean crop type and irrigation technology, respectively.

$$Max\,(\Pi_u) = I_u - PC_u - WC_u \tag{15}$$

In Equation (16), income at the irrigation district level, I_u, is given by the sum of crop production revenue. P_j is the price of crop j; $Y_{u,j,k}\left(\widetilde{w_{u,j,k}}\right)$ is the yield of crop j under irrigation technology k. $L_{u,j,k}$ is the acreage, and $\widetilde{w_{u,j,k}}$ corresponds to the relative evapotranspiration of the crop over the maximum evapotranspiration of the crop, $et^{max}_{u,j,k}$.

$$I_u = \sum_{j,k} P_j Y_{u,j,k}\left(\widetilde{w_{u,j,k}}\right) L_{u,j,k} \tag{16}$$

Yield function is presented in Equation (17), and it depends linearly on evaporation, $w_{u,j,k}$. Water productivity, $WP_{u,j,k}$, is the biomass produced per unit of land and unit of water.

$$Y_{u,j,k}\left(\widetilde{w_{u,j,k}}\right) = Ks\left(\widetilde{w_{u,j,k}}\right) w_{u,j,k} WP_{u,j,k} \tag{17}$$

The current water evapotranspiration of the crop is a proportion of the maximum evapotranspiration, Equation (18). Equation (19) represents the impacts of water stress produced by water deficit. Water stress, $Sr\left(\widetilde{w_{u,j,k}}\right)$, is 0 when the crop is fully irrigated, and the value of the coefficient $Ks\left(\widetilde{w_{u,j,k}}\right)$ is 1. Crop yield is 0 when the water deficit reaches the wilting point, and the value of water stress value is 1 since coefficient $Ks\left(\widetilde{w_{u,j,k}}\right)$ takes the value 0.

$$w_{u,j,k} = et^{max}_{u,j,k}\,\widetilde{w_{u,j,k}} \tag{18}$$

$$Ks\left(\widetilde{w_{u,j,k}}\right) = 1 - Sr\left(\widetilde{w_{u,j,k}}\right) \tag{19}$$

Equation (20) presents water stress, which depends on the relative water evapotranspiration of the crop, $\widetilde{w_{u,j,k}}$. The parameters β_0 and β_1 characterize the response of the crop to the water stress.

$$Sr\left(\widetilde{w_{u,j,k}}\right) = \frac{1}{1 + exp\left(\beta_1\, \widetilde{w_{u,j,k}} - \beta_0\right)} \tag{20}$$

Equation (21) represents the production cost per unit of land (excluding water) in irrigation district u. The production costs depend linearly on the acreage of land, $L_{u,j,k}$. Consequently, the production cost responds quadratically to variations of land. The parameters $\alpha^{pc}_{u,j,k;0}$ and $\alpha^{pc}_{u,j,k;1}$ define the production cost (excluding water).

$$PC_u = \sum_{j,k}\left(\alpha^{pc}_{u,j,k;0} L_{u,j,k} + \alpha^{pc}_{u,j,k;1} L^2_{u,j,k}\right) \tag{21}$$

In Equation (22), the cost of water, WC_u, for irrigation district u is calculated based on the cost of water per unit of water, $\alpha^{wc}_{u,j,k}$, for crop j and irrigation technology k, along with the amount of water applied, $\frac{w_{u,j,k}}{ie_k}$, where ie_k represents the irrigation efficiency of the irrigation technology k.

$$WC_u = \sum_{j,k}\left(\alpha^{wc}_{u,j,k} \frac{w_{u,j,k}}{ie_k} L_{u,j,k}\right) \tag{22}$$

Equations (23) and (24) represent the non-negativity restrictions of cropland acreage and crop evapotranspiration. Equation (25) establishes the domain for the relative water evapotranspiration, $\widetilde{w_{u,j,k}}$, of crop j in irrigation district u with irrigation technology k, which ranges between 0 and 1.

$$L_{u,j,k} \geq 0 \tag{23}$$

$$w_{u,jk} \geq 0 \tag{24}$$

$$0 \leq \widetilde{w_{u,j,k}} \leq 1 \tag{25}$$

The water availability restriction is represented as follows:

$$\sum_{j,k} \frac{w_{u,j,k}}{ie_k} L_{u,j,k} \leq WA_u \tag{26}$$

Here WA_u is the total water availability for the irrigation district. The agricultural model encompasses 40 irrigation districts that cultivate 39 crops using three different irrigation technologies (furrow, sprinkler, drip).

8.6 The Economic Model of Urban Water Use

The economic surplus from water use is maximized in urban centers. This economic surplus is the combined total consumer and producer surpluses across all demand and supply functions of the urban centers. Equations (27–29) outline the optimization problem for urban users, which is stated and represented as follows:

$$Max\Pi_u = \left(\beta_{0,du}X_{du} - \tfrac{1}{2}\beta_{1,du}X_{du}^2 - \beta_{0,su}X_{su} + \tfrac{1}{2}\beta_{1,su}X_{su}^2\right) \quad (27)$$

s.t.

$$X_{du} - X_{su} \leq 0 \quad (28)$$

$$X_{du};\ X_{su} \geq 0 \quad (29)$$

Here Π_u^{URB} is the consumer and producer surplus in urban center u. The variables X_{su} and X_{du} are water supply and demand in u, respectively. The intercept and slope of the inverse demand function are the parameters $\beta_{0,du}$ and $\beta_{1,du}$, and the parameters $\beta_{0,su}$ and $\beta_{1,su}$ are the intercept and slope of the inverse water supply function. Equation (28) indicates that the supply must equal or exceed the water demand. Water demand depends on population growth and the per-capita demand for water. Equation (30) represents water demand:

$$X_{du} = X_{pc}P_{urb} \quad (30)$$

Here X_{pc} is the per-capita demand, and P_{urb} is the population in the urban center u. Equation (31) states that the water supply in the urban center u is inferior to the water availability for the urban center u.

$$X_{su} \leq WA_u \quad (31)$$

The urban models gathered 397 cities in 20 urban centers.

Under water scarcity, water curtails are proportionally shared among water users. The water right holds by water user u, WR_u, u is a proportion τ of the water right hold under normal conditions, $\widetilde{WR}_u$. Under a non-cooperative scheme, the water availability for the water user u equals the water right the user holds.

$$WA_u = WR_u = \tau \widetilde{WR_u} \tag{32}$$

In cooperative schemes, water users unite by contributing their water rights to a shared pool. Coalitions formed by the participating members manage this pool. Formally, let us denote the set of all possible coalitions of water users as S (where s represents a specific coalition within S). For a given water user u, their water availability WA_u should not exceed the sum of the water rights WR_u of all users in coalition s, which can be expressed as follows:

$$WA_u \leq \sum_{(u \in s)} WR_u = WR_s \tag{33}$$

In addition, the effective water used, W_u, by all member of the coalition should not exceed the sum of the water rights of all water users in the coalition, and it is expressed as follows:

$$\sum_{(u \in s)} W_u \leq WR_s \tag{34}$$

The benefit of coalition, $v(s)$, is the sum of the individual benefits of the members that conform to coalitions s, and it is expressed as follows:

$$v(s) = \sum_{state \in s} \Pi_{state} \tag{35}$$

Cooperation between states is analyzed through 128 potential coalition scenarios. Special attention is given to the scenarios where states do not cooperate, where the states of the upper basin cooperate, where the states of the lower basin cooperate, and the grand coalition scenario where all states cooperate. In the context of the CRB, the benefits of a coalition are the sum of the individual benefits of the states presented in Equation (2).

8.7 Scenarios of Cooperation and Climate Change

Regional welfare results from the sum of benefits from the region's urban and agricultural water users. The set of scenarios analyzed in this chapter is the welfare at the state and basin levels under different schemes of cooperation and water scarcity conditions. The value of cooperation is determined by comparing water exchanges between (1) irrigation districts and urban centers and (2) states under conditions of water scarcity, which is simulated by reducing water allocations by 10% and 30% compared to baseline conditions. These reductions in water allocation are intended to represent water scarcity conditions aligned with optimistic and worst projections of climate change models (Lukas & Payton, 2020).

In the non-cooperation scenario, water users are not allowed to exchange water, and water reduction is applied at the irrigation district and urban center levels. This implies that farmers within irrigation districts and cities in the same urban center exchange water. In the scenario of intra-sectorial cooperation at the state level, irrigation districts belonging to the same state exchange water. In the same way, urban centers in the same state can exchange water. Cooperation at the state level implies that water users within the same state interchange water to maximize the combined benefit of water use at the state level. Lastly, cooperation at the basin level involves water exchange among all water users. The value of cooperation between irrigation districts and urban centers is determined by comparing the outcomes of the non-cooperation and cooperation scenarios at the state level.

8.8 Data Source and Calibration

The data required for modeling and calibrating the agricultural sector includes crop acreage distribution, irrigation system technology use, water requirements for crops, crop prices, crop yields, and production costs. The distribution of cropland under irrigation and the technologies used for irrigation are taken from several datasets (US Department of Agriculture [USDA], 2019; USDA, National Agricultural Statistics Service 2023; Xie & Lark, 2021). The water requirements for irrigation are obtained from various studies and specialized software designed to calculate crops' water needs (California Department of Water Resources, 2023; Colorado State University, 2019; New Mexico University, 2023; University of California Davis, 2023). The irrigation technology efficiency for flood, sprinkle, and drip is assumed to be 0.6, 0.8, and 0.9, respectively (Brouwer et al., 1989; Wang, 2019). Economic data is collected from studies of the University of California Davis (2023), New Mexico University (2023), Colorado State University (2019), and the Economic Research Service of the USDA, National Agricultural Statistics Service (2023).

The parameters of the water stress function presented in Equation (20) are determined with the parameters provided in the Aquacrop model developed by the FAO (2024). Positive mathematical programming (PMP) is a procedure of calibration developed by Howitt (1995) that replicates the observed yield, income, crop distribution, and water use in the baseline solution. The calibration of the cost function relies on PMP (Howitt, 1995). The data required for the implementation of the urban model includes water demand function parameters, water price, and water price elasticities, which are gathered from several studies (Chini & Stillwell, 2018; Colby & Hansen, 2022; Crespo et al., 2025; Eden et al., 2014; Luby et al., 2018). Further details on the location of the irrigation districts, as well as the data processing methods and assumptions, can be found in Crespo et al. (2025).

8.9 Results

This section presents the results of the baseline, non-cooperation, and cooperation schemes under climate change conditions. For simplicity, the results display the sectors and states by summing the benefits of urban sectors and irrigation districts. First, the results describe the benefits in the baseline conditions; second, the three cooperative schemes are compared among themselves and with the non-cooperative results. Lastly, the section presents the outcome of full cooperation schemes and compares the benefit allocations proposed by the game theory methods employed.

8.9.1 Base Conditions of Climate Change and Water Sharing

Under normal climate conditions, water use in the basin totals 1.2 maf per year, generating $19.733 million.[6] The urban sector provides 93% of the total benefits, amounting to $18.328 million. California and Arizona are the largest contributors of benefits, accounting for 85% of the total benefit in basin. Urban centers in California and Arizona are the largest contributors, providing $15.760 million, which is 80% of the total benefit in the basin (Figure 8.2).

[6] Benefits are expressed in 2023 constant dollars.

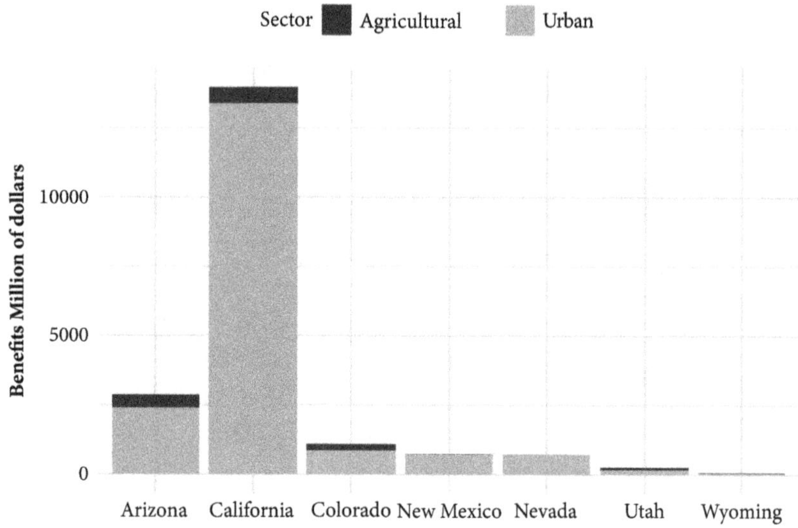

Figure 8.2 Benefits by State and Sector in the Base Conditions
Note: Elaborated by the authors.

In all states, urban centers provide the majority of the total benefits from water use. The agricultural sector is particularly important in Colorado, Utah, and Wyoming, contributing between 21% and 32% of the total benefits. On the other hand, the agricultural sector's relative importance in California, New Mexico, and Nevada is smaller, contributing less than 4% of the total benefits within these states.[7]

8.9.2 Scenario of Non-cooperation and Intra-sector Cooperation Under Climate Change Conditions

Under climate change conditions, water availability is reduced by 10% (moderate) to 30% (severe) compared to base climate conditions. The water

[7] The benefits of the agricultural sector include the benefits of crop production, which exclude important activities such as ranching. Consequently, this represents only a portion of the total benefits produced. The benefits of CRB water use for agriculture, as reported in this chapter, are conservative estimates. We only account for irrigated areas within the CRB's physical boundaries and those irrigated by the All-American Canal. Consequently, this analysis excludes portions of Utah, Wyoming, New Mexico, and Nevada outside the CRB irrigated with CRB water. Water use from the CRB in these areas, regarded as interbasin transfers, is not included in our study. See Crespo et al. (2025).

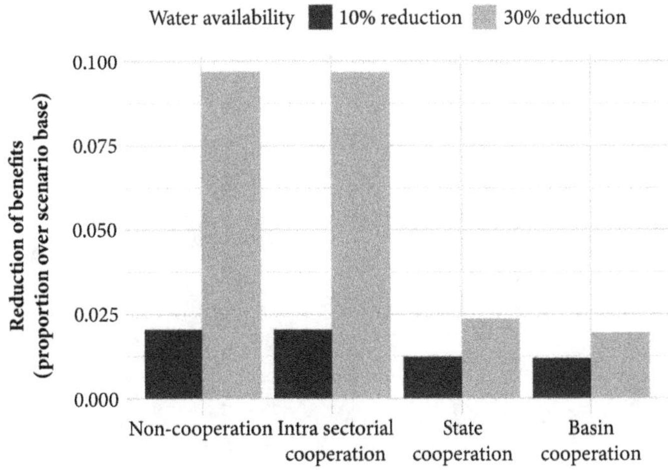

Figure 8.3 Benefits at the Basin Level Under Climate and Cooperation Scheme Scenarios
Note: Elaborated by the authors.

deficit with respect to the water available in the base condition is proportionally shared among water users (urban centers and agricultural water users), and reductions are applied equally. In the non-cooperation scenario, under moderate water scarcity conditions, benefit losses in the basin represent a reduction of less than 1% of the benefits under base climate conditions (around $20 million). Under severe water scarcity, benefit losses reach 9% of the benefits under base conditions ($1740 million) (Figure 8.3). Urban centers face a more significant benefit loss than agricultural water users, especially in Arizona and California, which reaches $1459 million under severe water scarcity. The agricultural sector losses reach $173 million under severe water scarcity (Figure 8.4). The agricultural sector in Arizona, California, and Colorado is responsible for 44%, 22%, and 20% of the total reduction in the basin benefits under severe water reductions. The results indicate that the effects of water scarcity are non-proportional, and worse water scarcity conditions result in large incremental losses (Figures 8.3–8.9).

Under intra-sectorial cooperation at the state level, irrigation districts exchange water among other irrigation districts in the same state to maximize the joint benefits of the state-level agricultural sector. Also, seeking to maximize the joint benefits, urban centers in the same state exchange water. Intra-sectorial water exchange at the state level shows little capacity to reduce benefit losses since the water exchange value is less than $3 million in severe

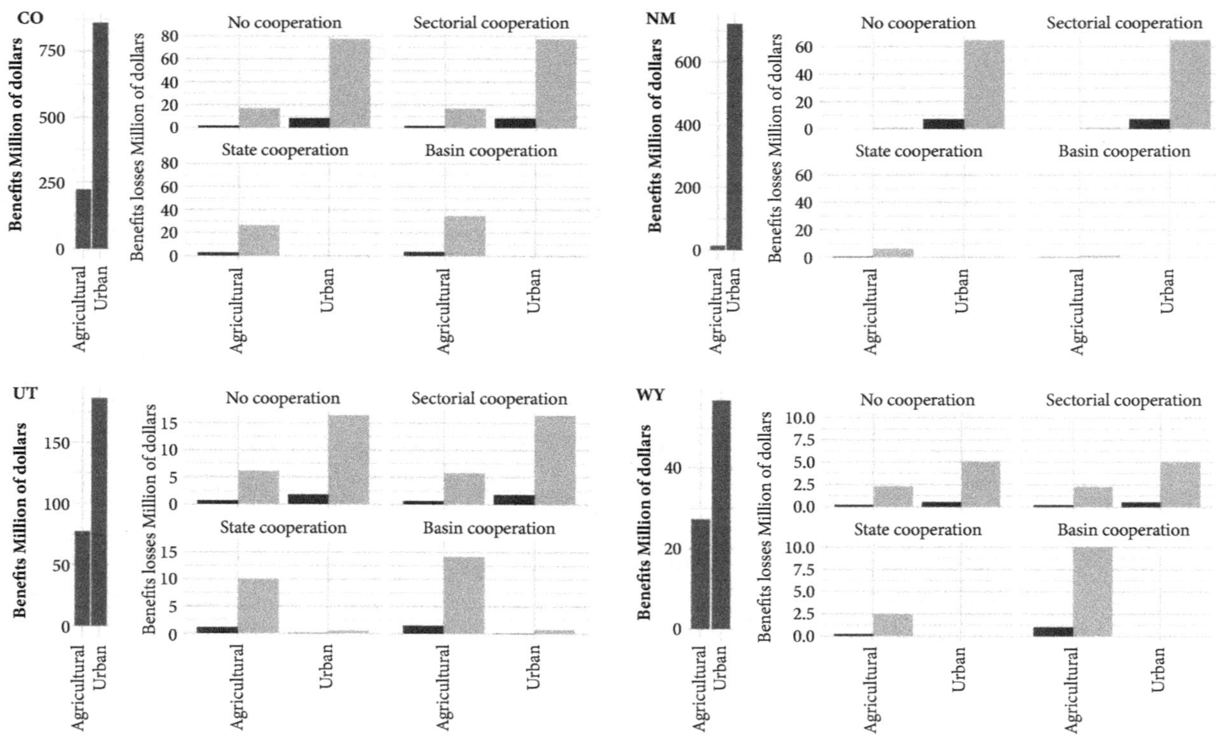

Figure 8.4 Benefits Under Water Scarcity Conditions by State, Climate Change Scenarios, and Scheme of Water Cooperation

Note: Elaborated by the authors.

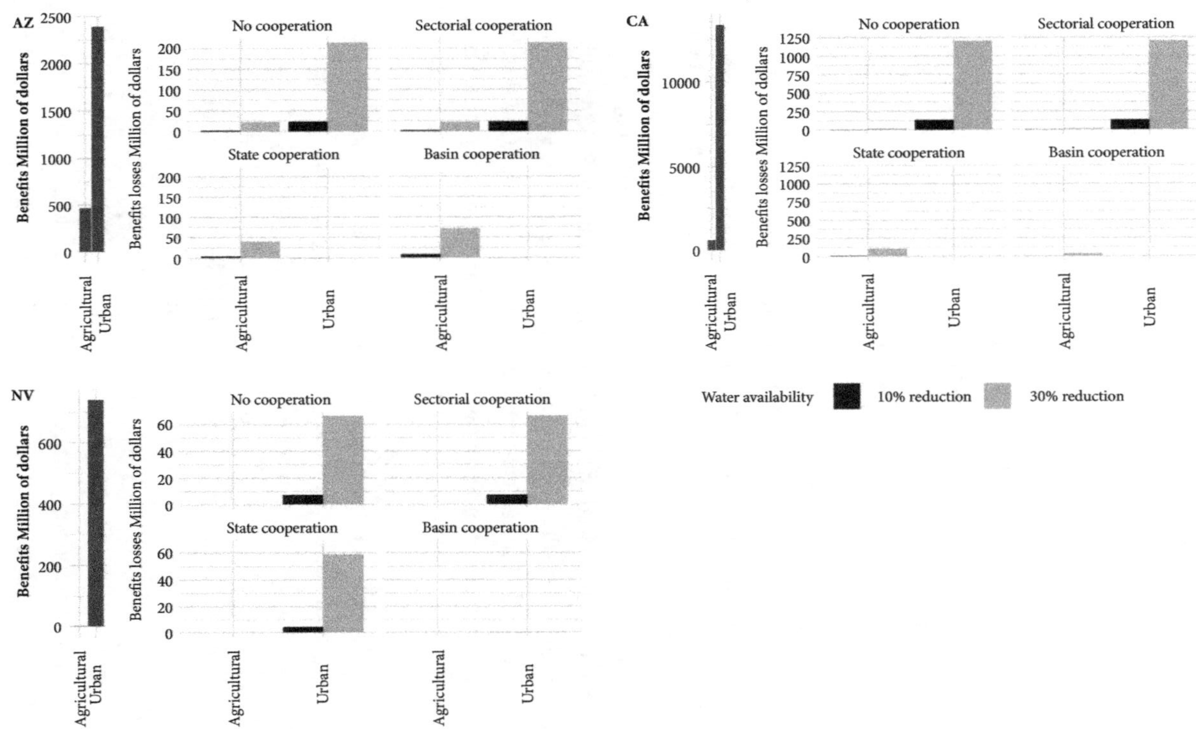

Figure 8.5 Benefits Under Current Conditions and Benefit Reduction by State, Climate Change, and Scenarios of Cooperation

Note: Elaborated by the authors.

drought conditions. The homogeneity at the state level of urban centers and irrigation districts implies that water scarcity equally affects the water users.

8.9.3 State Cooperation Under Water Scarcity Conditions

Under cooperation at the state level, water users in the same state exchange water to maximize the joint benefit at the state level. With severe scarcity conditions and cooperation at the state level, benefit losses represent less than 2% of the benefits of the base scenario. Water exchange between water users at the state level reduces losses substantially as urban centers recover almost all the benefits compared to the baseline scenario. At the same time, irrigation districts face only a small reduction in benefits. To achieve this enhancement, irrigation districts reduce water consumption and thus benefit from crop production to satisfy the water demand in urban centers. Urban centers must compensate for water exchange, as irrigators will participate in the water exchange if urban centers compensate for their incremental benefits for additional water reductions in the agricultural sector. With severe conditions of water scarcity, the difference in benefits for urban centers between non-cooperation and cooperation scenarios sums to $1584 million, which is larger than benefits from the agricultural sector under base conditions. This indicates that urban centers could compensate irrigation districts in any condition of water scarcity However, in Utah, improvements in benefits for urban centers are insufficient to compensate for all the irrigation districts' losses.

Urban districts enhance benefits at the expense of reductions in benefits of the irrigation districts. Accounting for the net effect at the state level of benefits and losses, cooperation at the state level reduces benefit losses with respect to the non-cooperation scenario by $164 million in the case of moderate water scarcity conditions and $1462 million under severe water scarcity conditions—showing that the value of cooperation increases non-linearly when water scarcity worsens (Figures 8.4 and 8.5).

Under severe water scarcity conditions, 8.7 maf is the total water available in the basin. With non-cooperation, 5.3 maf of water is allocated to irrigators, and 3.4 maf is allocated to urban centers. Allowing exchanges within states promotes transfers of 1.3 maf from irrigators to urban centers.

The 1.3 maf has a value of $106 million for irrigators and $1600 million for urban centers. The Metropolitan Water District of Southern California and

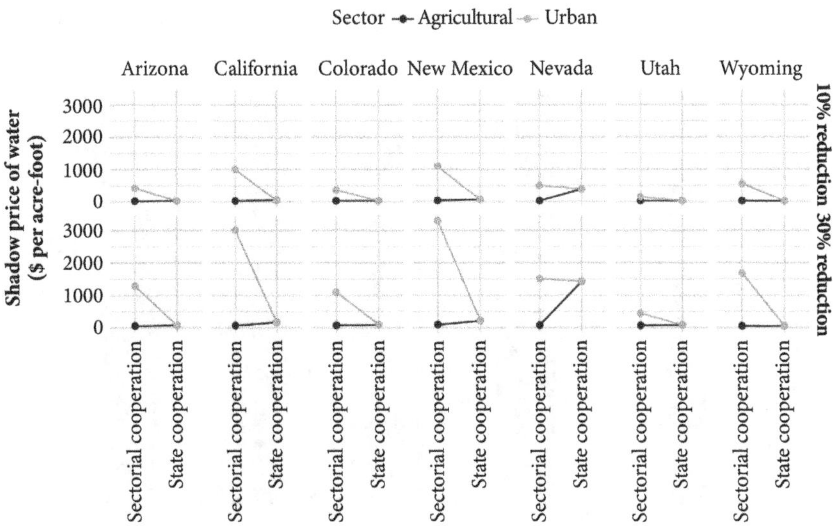

Figure 8.6 Benefits and Benefit Losses Under Climate Change Scenarios in the Upper Basin States and Sectors

Note: Elaborated by the authors.

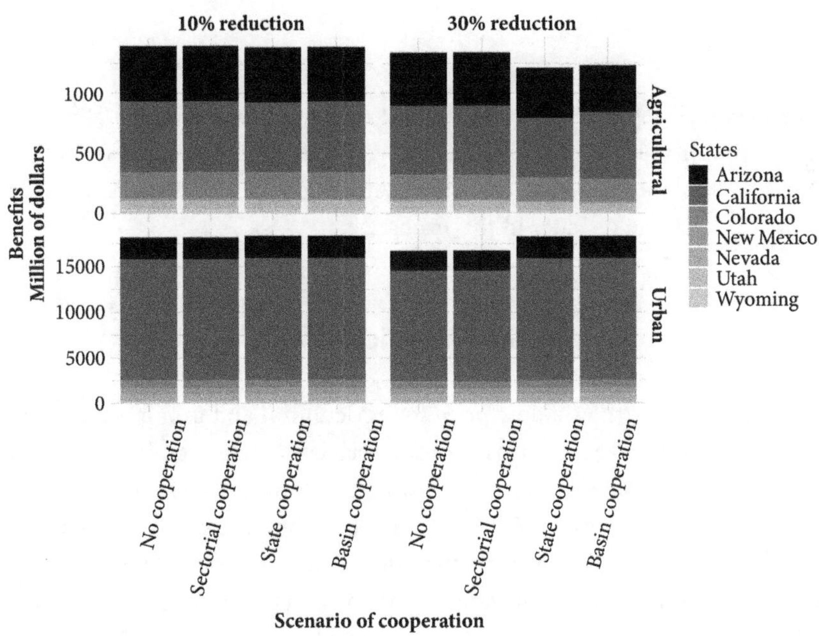

Figure 8.7 Benefits and Benefit Losses Under Climate Change Scenarios in the Lower Basin States and Sectors

Note: Elaborated by the authors.

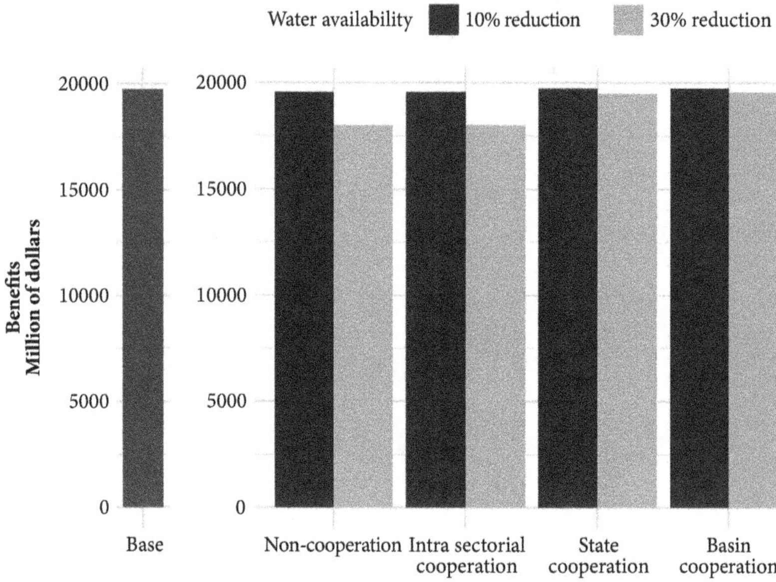

Figure 8.8 Benefits and Benefit Losses Under Climate Change Scenarios in the Upper Basin States and Sectors
Note: Elaborated by the authors.

urban centers dependent on the Central Arizona Project receive 58% and 22% of the 1.3 maf water, respectively. Irrigators from the Imperial Irrigation District, who are the sellers of Central Arizona Project irrigators, provide 60% of the 1.3 maf of water in this exchange.

8.9.4 Shadow Price of Water

Figure 8.10 shows the shadow price for agricultural and urban water users under climate change scenarios with sectorial cooperation and cooperation at the state level. Water scarcity increases the shadow price of water, ranging from $26 per acre-foot to $3000 per acre-foot—the shadow price of water is significantly larger in urban areas than in irrigation districts. The difference between the shadow price of water in urban centers and irrigation districts determines the willingness to pay for and accept the water exchanged. Urban centers in California and New Mexico have the largest shadow price of water. The differences between the shadow price in urban areas and agricultural

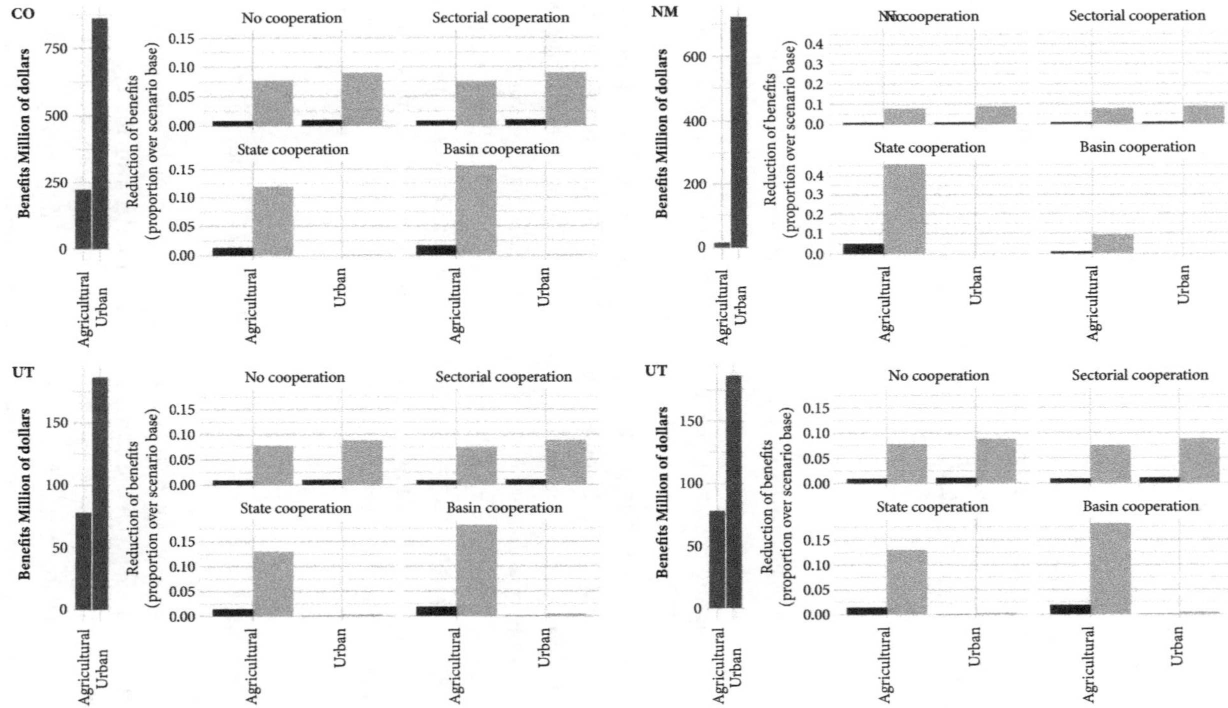

Figure 8.9 Benefits and Benefit Losses Under Climate Change Scenarios in the Lower Basin States and Sectors

Note: Elaborated by the authors.

areas are relatively small in Utah compared with the rest of the states, showing the state's relatively low economic value of water. When water exchanges are allowed, urban centers increase water use, which drops the shadow price of water in urban centers dramatically, except in Nevada, where the contribution of water by the agricultural sector is insufficient to mitigate the intense water scarcity in the urban sector because of the relatively low importance of the agricultural sector in the state. In addition, Nevada shows the largest shadow price because of the current water per capita and the price of water in urban centers. Urban centers in Utah have the same water scarcity conditions as in Nevada. However, the water use per capita in Nevada is lower than in Utah, and Nevada has a higher water price in urban centers than Utah.

8.9.5 Basin Cooperation Under Water Scarcity Conditions

The basin-wide grand coalition increases the total benefits of the basin by \$8 million and \$172 million, under moderate and severe climate change conditions, respectively, compared to the scenario where states do not exchange water, and by \$172 million and \$1544 million compared to the non-cooperation scenario, respectively, under moderate and severe climate change conditions. California, New Mexico, Nevada, and Utah must compensate Arizona, Colorado, and Wyoming with at least \$5 million and \$44 million, under moderate and severe climate change conditions, respectively, to incentivize their participation in the grand coalition, which is the value of losses in crop production in those states.

8.9.6 Game Theory Solutions With Full Cooperation

The social planner solution results from the joint maximization of benefits for all water users, given the constraint of total water availability; and it is equivalent to the characteristic function of the grand coalition solution. However, the social planner solution does not establish the compensations between the players who win and those who lose with the water allocation scheme.

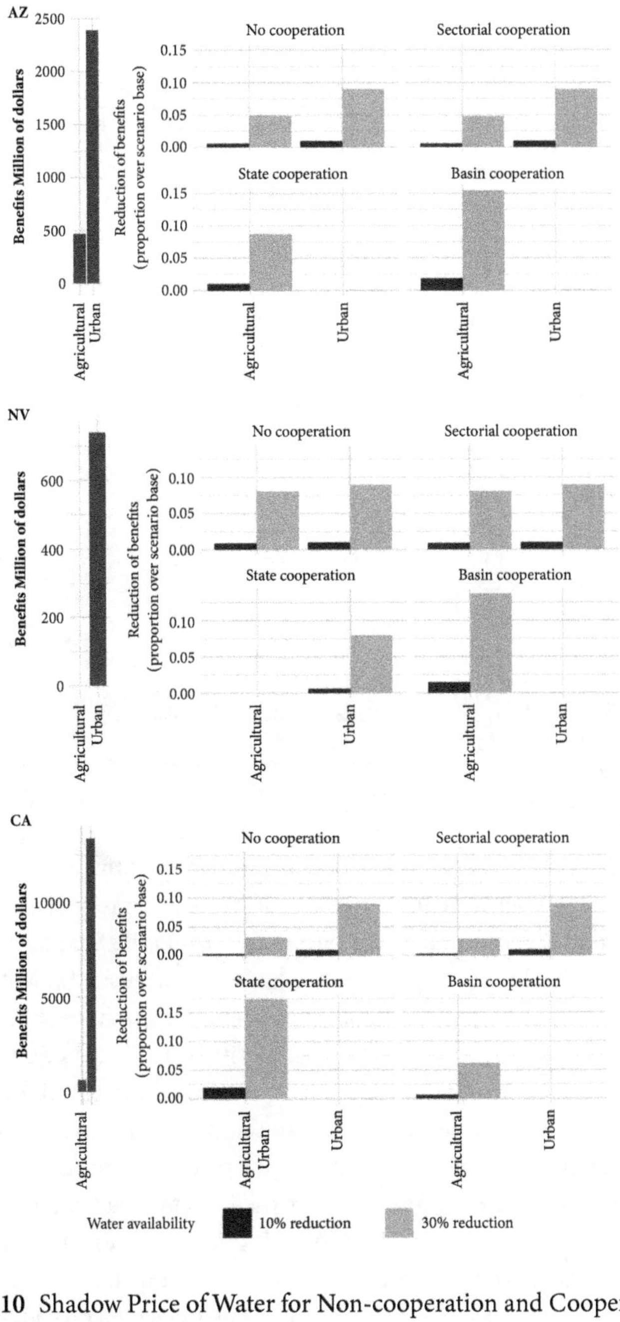

Figure 8.10 Shadow Price of Water for Non-cooperation and Cooperation at the State Level and Sector

Note: Elaborated by the authors.

Table 8.1 Benefits Allocation With Game Theory Solutions and Stability Index of the Solutions

	State	Non-cooperation	Full cooperation		
			Shapley	Nash-Harsanyi	Nucleolus
10% reduction	Arizona	2853	2853	2854	2853
	California	13,951	13,953	13,952	13,951
	Colorado	1082	1082	1083	1082
	New Mexico	737	738	739	737
	Nevada	736	740	737	736
	Utah	263	263	264	263
	Wyoming	84	84	85	84
	Stability index		1.12	0.00	1.39
30% reduction	Arizona	2816	2824	2828	2816
	California	13,856	13,873	13,868	13,856
	Colorado	1057	1061	1069	1057
	New Mexico	731	734	743	731
	Nevada	681	725	693	681
	Utah	254	256	265	254
	Wyoming	82	86	93	82
	Stability index		1.19	0.00	1.47

Table 8.1 shows the benefits of allocating non-cooperative and full cooperation scenarios under climate change scenarios for water reduction availability. Benefits under full cooperation are shared using the Shapley value, the Nash-Harsanyi solution, and the nucleolus solution. Also, Table 8.1 shows the stability indexes of the benefit allocations under game theory solutions.

Full cooperation provides $7.6 million with a 10% reduction in water availability and $81.9 million under severe water scarcity conditions (30%). The Shapley value can be interpreted as the power or interest to participate in the grand coalition. The Shapley value recognizes the contribution of Nevada and California, assigning 50% of the incremental benefit to Nevada and 20% to California. The Nash-Harsanyi solution shares and allocates the incremental benefits equally between states, indicating that the utility of the incremental benefits is equal among states. The nucleolus provides Nevada additional importance, assigning it 63% of the incremental benefit under severe water scarcity conditions.

The benefits to Arizona, Colorado, and Wyoming under the grand coalition are inferior to the solution of non-cooperation between states. States will be willing to participate in the grand coalition if the compensation for participation equals or exceeds the benefit under the non-cooperative solution. Nevada, California, and New Mexico compensate the rest of the states by $70 million, particularly Arizona, which receives $40 million for the contribution of its water.

The stability index ranks the Nash-Harsanyi allocation solution as the most stable solution because the standard deviation of the benefits allocated equals 0. The Shapley value is the second most stable solution, and the nucleolus solution is the least stable allocation. Stability decreases with climate change and worsens water scarcity conditions (Table 8.1).

Table 8.2 shows the incremental benefit of the states in the grand coalition, the propensity to disrupt a coalition, and the index of power. The nucleolus benefit allocations give Nevada the largest power index, indicating that the state has the largest minimum dissatisfaction among states. This solution is similar to the Shapley value and fair, according to the incremental contribution of the states to the coalition; the Nash-Harsanyi solution equally shares the power between the states, and the criteria are fair in terms of sharing the incremental benefits resulting from cooperation. The Nash-Harsanyi solution may be unsatisfactory for Nevada because it has a large propensity to disrupt the coalition.

8.10 Conclusions and Policy Implications

This chapter presents an economic model of urban and agricultural water use in the CRB. The model serves as a DSM framework for evaluating cooperation under water scarcity conditions within the basin and supporting policy interventions and negotiations. Cooperation is achieved in this chapter through water exchanges among the agricultural and urban sectors and states within the basin. Shapley values, the nucleolus, and Nash-Harsanyi solutions are used to allocate benefits from cooperation to the different states, allowing compensations (side payments).

Cooperation between agricultural and urban sectors strongly reduces the effects of water scarcity under various climate change scenarios. The compensation between sectors is essential to incentivize the agricultural sector to participate in the coalition. With cooperation, irrigation districts can recover

Table 8.2 Propensity of Disrupting a Coalition and Power Index

	State	V(*n*)–V(*n* – *j*)	Propensity to disrupt a coalition			Power index		
			Shapley	Nash-Harsanyi	Nucleolus	Shapley	Nash-Harsanyi	Nucleolus
10% reduction	Arizona	2854	0.00	0.00	0.00	0.12	0.14	0.12
	California	13,953	0.00	0.00	0.00	0.22	0.14	0.21
	Colorado	1082	0.00	0.00	0.00	0.04	0.14	0.00
	New Mexico	738	0.00	0.00	0.00	0.04	0.14	0.03
	Nevada	741	0.00	0.00	0.00	0.50	0.14	0.60
	Utah	263	0.00	0.00	0.00	0.03	0.14	0.00
	Wyoming	84	0.00	−0.01	0.00	0.05	0.14	0.03
30% reduction	Arizona		0.00	0.00	0.00	0.11	0.14	0.10
	California	2826	0.00	0.00	0.00	0.20	0.14	0.20
	Colorado	13,880	0.00	−0.01	0.00	0.04	0.14	0.01
	New Mexico	1058	0.00	−0.01	0.00	0.03	0.14	0.03
	Nevada	733	0.01	0.06	0.00	0.53	0.14	0.63
	Utah	733	−0.01	−0.04	0.00	0.03	0.14	0.00
	Wyoming	84	−0.02	−0.10	0.00	0.05	0.14	0.03

the benefits under non-scarcity conditions by water interchanges, and urban centers can recover water use under non-scarcity conditions. In that case, the urban centers support the direct economic impact of water scarcity. However, indirect economic impacts, such as the reduction in labor demand, are not included in the analysis.

Water interchanges between states enhance the benefits of cooperation, specifically for Nevada, where the agricultural sector is not big enough to compensate for water flow reductions to Nevada's urban centers. Also, California has incentives to participate in coalitions with other states since the urban center of California provides a substantial part of the benefits in the basin. On the other hand, Colorado is neutral about participating in the grand coalition since its contribution to the coalition is smaller.

Cooperation can achieve water management goals. However, the initial configuration of water allocation, such as the asymmetry of water users' power or inequality of water use between users and regions, determines the efforts to achieve the goals of efficiency and equity. Rules and treaties that once served to prevent water conflicts are nowadays sources of conflict and stability. Without flexibility in water management, policies are condemned to fail in the long run.

The seven states of the CRB are negotiating water allocations for the post-2026 guidelines, recognizing a present and future with less water available. From a zero-sum game perspective, each state seeks to maximize its share of water while minimizing reductions as much as possible. To balance reductions in water availability among states, proportional reductions ensure that the share of water is equally distributed. However, proportional reductions of water allocations in the CRB produce different impacts on benefit losses among sectors and states, promoting inefficient water use. Differences in the value of water serve as an indicator of this inefficiency, suggesting that water exchanges can resolve the imbalance of impacts produced by proportional reduction allocations. Cooperation based on voluntary and compensated arrangements of water exchange serves as an instrument to achieve incremental benefits through efficiency enhancements, producing a set of benefits that all water users gain. Negotiating compensations requires identifying the differences in the value of water between sectors and regions. Agricultural sectors can maintain their benefits and avoid the effects of climate change through compensated water exchanges with urban centers, which maintain their current water use. The value of cooperation is higher in absolute terms for urban centers than for agricultural sectors as water scarcity is especially harmful in urban areas. However, in relative terms, the value of cooperation is higher in the agricultural sector since it completely avoids the benefit losses associated with water scarcity. The benefits of cooperation increase when states participate in water exchanges, with irrigation districts and urban centers in California and Nevada purchasing water from irrigation districts in Utah and Wyoming. Consequently, achieving the best possible outcome requires cooperation between the states of the upper and lower parts of the basin.

The DSM, along with the results and findings presented in this chapter, contributes valuable information to the current debate on water allocation and can serve as a useful tool for ongoing negotiations among basin states. In particular, the set of solutions produced by game theory represents the possible arrangements between states and how benefits can be shared.

One of the limitations of this analysis is the number of players involved in the cooperation game. The analysis could be improved by extending the game theory analysis by including individual irrigation districts and urban centers as single players. However, the complexity of applying game theory increases exponentially with the number of players. For example, the number of coalitions with 78 players (29 urban centers and 39 irrigation districts) is 2^{78}, which is an extremely large number. If we were able to run one million scenarios per second, the expected time to complete the task would be more than 9583 million years. Future applications of the DSM and game theory analysis will include 14 players (a combination of two sectors and seven states). Along with the game theory instruments presented in this chapter, future analysis will examine the value of cooperation between states resulting from the formation of sub-coalitions.

Another limitation of this analysis is that it does not account for water rights differences between sectors and states. The results presented in this chapter represent an idealized solution, underestimating the actual impacts. This is because currently irrigation districts and urban centers allocate water cutoffs based on water-use priority, and holders of junior water rights are the first to support water cutoffs. Since the agricultural sector holds senior water rights, the impacts on urban centers could be significant. Additionally, states and regions have varying levels of power, and reductions are not applied proportionally among states.

Acknowledgment

The authors of this chapter are grateful for the support from the University of California Riverside OASIS Internal Funding Award, from the W4190 Multistate National Institute of Food and Agriculture–US Department of Agriculture project Management and Policy Challenges in a Water-Scarce World, and from the Giannini Foundation of Agricultural Economics.

References

Britz, W., Ferris, M., & Kuhn, A. (2013). Modeling water allocating institutions based on multiple optimization problems with equilibrium constraints. *Environmental Modelling & Software*, *46*, 196–207. https://doi.org/10.1016/j.envsoft.2013.03.010

Brouwer, C., Prins, K., & Heibloem, M. (1989). *Irrigation water management: Irrigation scheduling* (Training Manual No. 4). Food and Agriculture Organization. https://www.fao.org/4/t7202e/t7202e00.htm

California Department of Water Resources. (2023). *Agricultural water use models*. Consumptive Use Program PLUS (CUP+). https://water.ca.gov/Programs/Water-Use-And-Efficiency/Land-And-Water-Use/Agricultural-Water-Use-Models01/06/2023, https://water.ca.gov/-/media/DWR-Website/Web-Pages/Programs/Water-Use-And-Efficiency/Land-And-Water-Use/Agricultural-water-use-models/Files/Data/CUPM-Version-69.zip

Cao, Z., Zhu, T., & Cai, X. (2023). Hydro-agro-economic optimization for irrigated farming in an arid region: The Hetao Irrigation District, Inner Mongolia. *Agricultural Water Management*, *277*, Article 108095. https://doi.org/10.1016/j.agwat.2022.108095

Chini, C. M., & Stillwell, A. S. (2018). The state of U.S. urban water: Data and the energy–water nexus. *Water Resources Research*, *54*, 1796–1811. https://doi.org/10.1002/2017WR022265

Clow, D. W., Williams, M. W., & Schuster, P. F. (2016). Increasing aeolian dust deposition to snowpacks in the Rocky Mountains inferred from snowpack, wet deposition, and aerosol chemistry. *Atmospheric Environment*, *146*, 183–194. https://doi.org/10.1016/j.atmosenv.2016.06.076

Colby, B. G., & Hansen, H. (2022). Colorado basin incentive-based urban water policies: Review and evaluation. *JAWRA: Journal of the American Water Resources Association*, *58*(6), 1098–1115. https://doi.org/10.1111/1752-1688.13041

Colorado State University. (2019). *Extension: Agriculture and Business Management. Enterprise budgets–crop*. https://abm.extension.colostate.edu/enterprise-budgets-crop/

Congressional Research Service. (2024). *Management of the Colorado River: Water allocations, drought, and the federal role* (Report R45546).

Crespo, D., Nemati, M., Dinar, A., Frankel, Z., & Halberg, N. (2023). Dams and hydropower production in the Colorado River basin. In *The water report* (Issue 238). Sky Island Insights. https://www.thewaterreport.com/

Crespo, D., Nemati, M., Dinar, A., Frankel, Z., & Halberg, N. (2025). Assessing the economic value of water in the Colorado River Basin: A hydroeconomic analysis. Water Resources and Economics 52, 100266. https://doi.org/10.1016/j.wre.2025.100266

Eden, S., Efrein, M., & Radonic, L. (2014). What is the value of water? A complex question. In *Arroyo*. University of Arizona Water Resources Research Center. https://wrrc.arizona.edu/sites/wrrc.arizona.edu/files/attachment/Arroyo-2014-Value-of-Water.pdf

Frankel, Z., Halberg, N., Nemati, M., Dinar, A., & Crespo, D. (2024). Climate crisis is straining the Colorado River's complex policy architecture. *Choices*. https://www.choicesmagazine.

org/choices-magazine/theme-articles/colorado-river-basin/climate-crisis-is-straining-the-colorado-rivers-complex-policy-architecture

Harsanyi, J. C. (1959). A bargaining model for the cooperative n-person game. In A. W. Tucker & D. R. Luce (Eds.), *Contributions to the theory of games* (Vol. 4, pp. 324–356). Princeton University Press.

Howitt, R. (1995). Positive mathematical programming. *American Journal of Agricultural Economics, 77*, 329–342. https://doi.org/10.2307/1243543

Loehman, E., Orlando, J., Tschirhart, J., & Whinston, A. (1979). Cost allocation for a regional wastewater treatment system. *Water Resources Research, 15*, 193–202. https://doi.org/10.1029/WR015i002p00193

Luby, I. H., Polasky, S., & Swackhamer, D. L. (2018). U.S. urban water prices: Cheaper when drier. *Water Resources Research, 54*, 6126–6132. https://doi.org/10.1029/2018WR023258

Lukas, J., & Payton, E. (2020). *Colorado River basin climate and hydrology: State of the science.* University of Colorado. https://doi.org/10.25810/3HCV-W477

Madani, K. (2010). Game theory and water resources. *Journal of Hydrology, 381*, 225–238. https://doi.org/10.1016/j.jhydrol.2009.11.045

New Mexico University. (2023). *Cost and return estimates (CARE) for farms and ranches 2013–2022.* Retrieved June 1, 2023, from https://costsandreturns.nmsu.edu/

Raes, D., Steduto, P., Hsiao, T. C., & Fereres, E. (2023). *AquaCrop version 7.1: Reference manual.* Food and Agriculture Organization of the United Nations. https://openknowledge.fao.org/server/api/core/bitstreams/23621a46-1512-41a7-ad28-5a3d8141b6dc/content

Schmeidler, D. (1969). The nucleolus of a characteristic function game. *SIAM Journal on Applied Mathematics, 17*, 1163–1170.

Sexstone, G. A., Clow, D. W., Fassnacht, S. R., Liston, G. E., Hiemstra, C. A., Knowles, J. F., & Penn, C. A. (2018). Snow sublimation in mountain environments and its sensitivity to forest disturbance and climate warming. *Water Resources Research, 54*, 1191–1211. https://doi.org/10.1002/2017WR021172

Sexstone, G. A., Clow, D. W., Stannard, D. I., & Fassnacht, S. R. (2016). Comparison of methods for quantifying surface sublimation over seasonally snow-covered terrain. *Hydrological Processes, 30*, 3373–3389. https://doi.org/10.1002/hyp.10864

Shapley, L. S. (1953). A value for n-person games. In H. W. Kuhn & A. W. Tucker (Eds.), *Contributions to the theory of games* (Vol. 2, pp. 307–318). Princeton University Press. https://doi.org/10.1515/9781400881970-018

Treaty between the United States of America and Mexico: Utilization of waters of the Colorado and Tijuana Rivers and of the Rio Grande, February 3, 1944, https://www.ibwc.gov/wp-content/uploads/2022/11/1944Treaty.pdf

Udall, B., & Overpeck, J. (2017). The twenty-first century Colorado River hot drought and implications for the future. *Water Resources Research, 53*, 2404–2418. https://doi.org/10.1002/2016WR019638

University of California Davis. (2023). *Sample of cost. Current cost and return studies.* https://coststudies.ucdavis.edu/en/current/

US Bureau of Reclamation. (1922). *The Colorado River Compact.* US Government Printing Office. https://www.usbr.gov/lc/region/g1000/pdfiles/crcompct.pdf

US Bureau of Reclamation. (2012). *Colorado River basin water supply and demand study: Study Report.* US Department of the Interior. https://www.usbr.gov/lc/region/programs/crbstudy/finalreport/Study%20Report/CRBS_Study_Report_FINAL.pdf

US Department of Agriculture. (2019). *2018 Irrigation and water management survey* (Vol. 3, Special Studies, Part 1). https://www.nass.usda.gov/Publications/AgCensus/2017/Online_Resources/Farm_and_Ranch_Irrigation_Survey/fris.pdf

US Department of Agriculture, National Agricultural Statistics Service. (2023). *Research and science–cropland data layer releases.* https://www.nass.usda.gov/Research_and_Science/Cropland/Release/index.php

Wang, H. (2019). Irrigation efficiency and water withdrawal in US agriculture. *Water Policy, 21*, 768–786. https://doi.org/10.2166/wp.2019.175

Whitney, K. M., Vivoni, E. R., Bohn, T. J., Mascaro, G., Wang, Z., Xiao, M., Mahmoud, M. I., Cullom, C., & White, D. D. (2023). Spatial attribution of declining Colorado River streamflow under future warming. *Journal of Hydrology, 617*, Article 129125. https://doi.org/10.1016/j.jhydrol.2023.129125

Wolf, A. T. (2007). Shared waters: Conflict and cooperation. *Annual Review of Environment and Resources, 32*, 241–269. https://doi.org/10.1146/annurev.energy.32.041006.101434

Xie, Y., & Lark, T. J. (2021). Mapping annual irrigation from Landsat imagery and environmental variables across the conterminous United States. *Remote Sensing of Environment, 260*, Article 112445. https://doi.org/10.1016/j.rse.2021.112445

9

Enhancing Transboundary Water Security via a Participatory Negotiation Support Framework

Spotlight on the Congo Basin

Mahmoud Radwan, Nidhi Nagabhatla, and Padmi Ranasinghe

9.1 Introduction

The global water crisis is a pressing issue marked by alarming statistics. Although access to safe drinking water and sanitation has improved, nearly half of the world's population still lacks adequate access, and the situation is particularly severe in Africa, where over a quarter of the population does not have safely managed drinking water (World Health Organization [WHO] & UNICEF, 2017). Sustainable Development Goal (SDG) 6, which aims to "Ensure availability and sustainable management of water and sanitation for all," emphasizes the interconnectedness of water, sanitation, and hygiene (WASH). While the United Nations (UN) *World Water Development Report* (UN-Water, 2022) indicated some progress, the rate of improvement is insufficient to meet the 2030 target; and access disparities remains vast, especially among rural populations, women, and children (UNICEF, 2022). Challenges to achieving SDG 6 are compounded by increasing water scarcity driven by climate change, population growth, and unsustainable water management practices. Inadequate sanitation facilities further contribute to water pollution and public health risks, particularly in developing countries (WHO, 2022). Addressing these gaps requires substantial investment; Hutton and Varughese (2016) estimate a threefold upsurge in the current basic water and sanitation services, translating it to a financial commitment of around $114 billion to meet essential needs.

Mahmoud Radwan, Nidhi Nagabhatla, and Padmi Ranasinghe, *Enhancing Transboundary Water Security via a Participatory Negotiation Support Framework*. In: *Decision Support Models to Assist International and Transboundary Water Negotiations*. Edited by: Mohammadreza Shahbazbegian and Ariel Dinar, Oxford University Press. © Oxford University Press (2026). DOI: 10.1093/9780197802601.003.0009

The complex relationship between water security and conflict underscores the need for comprehensive solutions (Grey et al., 2013). Water security involves the ability to sustainably manage and supply water resources to ensure access to safe and affordable water for livelihoods and socioeconomic development (Hoekstra & Mekonnen, 2012). However, population growth, urbanization, industrialization, and climate change intensify pressures on water resources, creating scarcity and competition, especially in regions vulnerable to social unrest (Damkjaer & Taylor, 2017; Wilkenfeld, 2004). Shared water resources, such as rivers, lakes, and aquifers, often exacerbate tensions, leading to diplomatic disputes and, in extreme cases, armed conflicts (Wolf, 2007). Climate change further intensifies these challenges by disrupting precipitation patterns and increasing droughts and floods, thereby aggravating water-related inequalities (Intergovernmental Panel on Climate Change, 2021).

Shared waterbodies are often a source of contention between countries with divergent interests, making collaborative management and equitable water-sharing agreements essential for preventing disputes and promoting cooperation (Wilkenfeld, 2004). Water negotiation offers an opportunity for parties to forge transboundary water agreements, with or without external support, as illustrated by initiatives like the Blue Peace Initiative (2024). Molle (2004) defines water negotiation as a process to establish flexible allocation rules through a gradual and continuous negotiation. One of the core challenges in water negotiation is managing the trade-offs among competing water uses—agriculture, industry, domestic, and environmental—within the constraints of limited resources. These competing demands require careful analysis and negotiation to find mutually beneficial solutions (Giordano, 2007). Transboundary water resources add complexity, necessitating diplomatic engagement among state and non-state actors. The Clingendael Institute (2014) describes water diplomacy, inclusive of negotiations, as interactions involving both state and non-state actors, as well as at least one international governmental organization, over shared freshwater resources including lakes, rivers, and aquifers.

A negotiation-based approach is critical for addressing these challenges and ensuring equitable water allocation. The UN-Water (2013) water security agenda complement to the integrated water resources management (IWRM) approach by incorporating multidisciplinary aspects such as *water and conflicts*, *water and peace*, *political stability*, *transboundary cooperation*, and *improved governance and capacity development* into conventional water management frameworks to address issues like the water–conflict nexus and enhanced collaboration in transboundary water management (Soto Rois et al., 2018). Transboundary water negotiation requires balancing hydrological, environmental, social, economic, and political factors. Effective negotiations aim to achieve equitable and sustainable water allocation while building trust and cooperation among stakeholders (Wolf, 2007).

This chapter responds to a research gap at the intersection of water security, decision support mechanisms, and transboundary water negotiations. Existing frameworks for addressing water security often lack the integration of localized, multidimensional data into broader negotiation strategies (Tayia, 2019; Zeitoun & Mirumachi, 2008). The Operationalizing Water Security by Indicator Cluster Matrix (WOSCIM) addresses this gap by bridging national water security assessments and international negotiation processes, offering a structured, evidence-based approach to facilitate collaboration among riparian states (Smith & Winterman, 2022). The research questions guiding this chapter are as follows: How can participatory, indicator-based frameworks enhance international water negotiations? Specifically, in what ways do they transform localized water security data into actionable strategies for fostering trust, mitigating conflicts, and promoting equitable resource sharing? By situating WOSCIM within contemporary water diplomacy literature, this chapter contributes theoretically to our understanding of decision support mechanisms that incorporate human security, sociopolitical dimensions, and ecological resilience. Practically, it offers a replicable model for policymakers and stakeholders engaged in transboundary water governance. In highlighting the utility of WOSCIM for the Congo basin, a region characterized by complex sociopolitical dynamics and shared water challenges, this chapter demonstrates how evidence-based tools can turn water conflicts into opportunities for cooperation, providing a scalable framework with global applicability.

9.2 Background and Context

The Congo basin, the world's second-largest tropical rainforest region, is of immense geographic and hydrological importance. It spans nine countries, including the Democratic Republic of Congo (DRC), the Republic of Congo, and the Central African Republic, encompassing over 4 million km^2

of critical ecosystems and hosting the Congo River, the second-largest river by discharge globally (Karam et al., 2023). This basin holds approximately 30% of Africa's freshwater resources, providing a lifeline for over 75 million people (Tshimanga et al., 2021). Socioeconomically, the riparian countries depend on the basin's water for agriculture, fishing, and hydroelectric power, which support regional livelihoods and economic activities. However, governance remains fragmented, with disparities in institutional capacity and regulatory frameworks between countries. Political instability, varying national policies, and weak enforcement mechanisms exacerbate challenges in managing shared water resources (Zeitoun & Mirumachi, 2008). Water security in the Congo basin faces several critical challenges. Hydroclimatic variability results in unpredictable rainfall patterns, seasonal flooding, and prolonged droughts, disrupting water availability and exacerbating resource competition (Tshimanga et al., 2021). Resource mismanagement has led to deforestation, land degradation, and contamination of waterbodies, while infrastructural deficiencies hinder equitable access to clean water and sanitation (Karam et al., 2023). Governance gaps, including the lack of effective transboundary water agreements, further complicate resource management. Although initiatives like the International Commission of the Congo–Oubangui–Sangha Basin aim to foster cooperation, implementation is limited by inadequate funding and coordination (Tshimanga et al., 2021).

The DRC, home to most of the Congo basin, exemplifies the region's water security challenges. Despite vast freshwater resources, including substantial rainfall and rivers such as the Congo River, nearly 65% of the population lacks access to safe drinking water, and about 84% lacks basic sanitation, contributing to high rates of waterborne diseases (UNICEF, 2022; WHO & UNICEF-JMP, 2024b). The DRC faces severe water insecurity challenges due to its underdeveloped infrastructure, inefficient water management and distribution, and institutional inefficiencies (Borja-Vega et al., 2022; Hoekstra & Mekonnen, 2012). The DRC's political instability and armed conflicts have worsened water insecurity. The destruction of water infrastructure and the displacement of populations have heightened the challenges of providing adequate water services (World Bank, 2022a). The country's rapid urbanization has strained water resources, resulting in water scarcity in urban areas (Dadzie et al., 2016). Climate change further exacerbates water security challenges in the region as altered rainfall patterns, increased flooding, and prolonged droughts disrupt water availability (Partow, 2011).

These effects disproportionately affect vulnerable communities, including women and children, who rely on subsistence agriculture and fishing for livelihoods (Giordano, 2007).

In 2023, the DRC ranked among the five poorest nations globally. In 2022, it was home to the second-highest number of extremely poor people in sub-Saharan Africa, with the third-highest poverty rate worldwide (World Bank, 2017, 2023, 2024c). The Joint Monitoring Program (JMP) for water supply reported that, despite the DRC having vast water resources, they remain inadequately managed. This is reflected in the country's low coverage of basic drinking water services and sanitation facilities, which stood at 24% and 3%, respectively, in 2022 (WHO & UNICEF-JMP, 2024b). Additionally, sociocultural conflicts and political instability aggravate water and climate crises, leading to increased water and food insecurity. Unequal distribution, infrastructural deficiencies, and population growth intensify water scarcity, leading to competition and conflict over access to water for agriculture, domestic use, and livestock, which in turn fosters social tensions (Hoekstra & Mekonnen, 2012; Wilkenfeld, 2004). The healthcare system in the DRC has been severely impacted by the COVID-19 pandemic and recurrent disease outbreaks like cholera, measles, and Ebola (World Bank, 2024b). The country has one of the highest stunting rates in sub-Saharan Africa, with 42% of children under 5 affected; and malnutrition is identified as the underlying cause of nearly half of child fatalities (Luzingu et al., 2022; World Bank, 2024).

The sociopolitical landscape complicates water management as ethnic divisions and armed groups leverage control over water resources for power and influence. This dynamic has led to significant population displacement, destruction of infrastructure, and the spread of waterborne diseases, intensifying the humanitarian crisis. The healthcare system has been further burdened by recurrent disease outbreaks such as cholera, measles, and Ebola, coupled with the COVID-19 pandemic, leaving the DRC with one of the highest child stunting rates in sub-Saharan Africa at 42% (Luzingu et al., 2022; World Bank, 2024d). Despite these challenges, the DRC represents an opportunity for transformative change through IWRM and negotiation-based governance frameworks. The WOSCIM framework offers a pathway to addressing these multidimensional issues by combining localized assessments with scalable solutions, fostering collaboration among national and regional stakeholders to advance water security across the Congo basin (Gheuens et al., 2019; Villiers, 2011).

9.3 Theoretical and Analytical Framework

9.3.1 Contemporary Water Negotiation Theories

Water security in transboundary river basins is a deeply complex issue, requiring frameworks that can capture the interplay of sociopolitical, economic, and biophysical factors. Several well-established literatures underpin the discourse on water negotiations, including water diplomacy, cooperative game theory, and negotiation theory. However, these theories often fall short of integrating localized data and multidimensional perspectives into actionable strategies. Moreover, these traditional theories often emphasize legal frameworks or technical solutions without adequately addressing the sociopolitical dynamics that influence negotiations (Gaffal & Gálvez, 2023; Kıbrıs, 2021; Schmeier, 2021). In contrast, the WOSCIM framework is proposed as a decision support model (DSM) that bridges these conceptual gaps, addressing challenges of governance, resource allocation, and stakeholder collaboration. Water diplomacy focuses on fostering cooperation and conflict resolution among riparian states through dialogue and negotiation. It emphasizes water's dual role as both a source of tension and a vehicle for peace-building (Schmeier, 2021; Zeitoun & Mirumachi, 2008). While water diplomacy offers valuable insights into stakeholder dynamics, its operationalization often lacks the quantitative rigor necessary for evidence-based decision-making (Zareie et al., 2020). WOSCIM complements this by providing structured, indicator-based assessments that offer concrete evidence to inform diplomatic discussions, thereby strengthening the trust and transparency essential for successful negotiations.

In addition, cooperative game theory provides a framework for understanding how riparian states can collaborate to achieve mutual benefits. By modeling negotiation as a collaborative game, it highlights the role of incentives, trade-offs, and benefit-sharing mechanisms in achieving equitable outcomes (Kıbrıs, 2010). However, this approach often relies on abstract modeling that may not fully account for the contextual realities of specific basins. WOSCIM addresses this limitation by grounding its assessments in localized data, enabling stakeholders to align their objectives with on-the-ground realities. Negotiation theory, which examines the dynamics of bargaining and decision-making, underscores the importance of framing, power asymmetries, and the availability of robust evidence in shaping outcomes. While negotiation theory is instrumental in understanding the processes of conflict resolution, it often overlooks the need for systematic tools that can integrate diverse dimensions of water security (Carraro et al., 2005). WOSCIM also fills this gap by serving as a practical tool that consolidates biophysical, socioeconomic, and governance indicators into a cohesive framework, thereby enhancing the capacity of stakeholders to negotiate effectively.

9.3.2 WOSCIM Framework Versus Existing DSMs

The WOSCIM framework is designed to support evidence-based decision-making in transboundary water governance. Its core elements are structured around the eight dimensions of water security outlined in the UN-Water framework, including environmental sustainability, human well-being, and institutional governance. The framework employs an indicator-based approach to assess and address water security challenges, emphasizing flexibility, adaptability, and participatory processes. Central to WOSCIM's methodology is the selection of indicators that reflect the specific characteristics of the region under study. For example, in the context of the Congo basin, indicators may include water quality metrics, biodiversity indices, access to drinking water, and institutional capacity for governance. These indicators are chosen based on their relevance, data availability, and potential to inform decision-making. The application of these indicators involves a multistep process, beginning with baseline assessments to identify vulnerabilities and progressing to iterative monitoring that captures changes over time. This approach ensures that the framework remains responsive to evolving challenges, such as climate change and population growth. A distinctive feature of WOSCIM is its integration of participatory mechanisms that involve stakeholders at all levels. This participatory focus enhances the legitimacy and acceptability of decisions, fostering collaboration among riparian states. By combining quantitative assessments with qualitative insights, WOSCIM provides a comprehensive toolkit for addressing the sociopolitical and biophysical complexities of transboundary water management.

Existing DSMs in transboundary water governance, such as the Water Evaluation and Planning System (WEAP) and IWRM approaches, offer valuable tools for resource management. However, these mechanisms often lack the flexibility and context-specific focus necessary for addressing the unique challenges of basins like the Congo. WEAP, for instance, is renowned for its scenario-based modeling capabilities, which allow stakeholders to explore the implications of different management strategies. While effective at simulating water allocation scenarios, WEAP does not prioritize stakeholder engagement or the integration of sociopolitical dimensions. Similarly, IWRM emphasizes holistic resource management but has been critiqued for not being applied sufficiently in conflict-prone regions and its tendency to prioritize technical solutions over participatory approaches (Bhave et al., 2020; Bonzi et al., 2016). WOSCIM complements these frameworks through its adaptability and focus on resilience-building. Its indicator-driven methodology enables stakeholders to tailor assessments to the specific needs of their basin, incorporating localized data and stakeholder inputs to create actionable insights. Furthermore, WOSCIM's emphasis on participatory processes ensures that decisions are evidence-based and aligned with the priorities of affected communities. This dual focus on technical rigor and social inclusivity positions WOSCIM as an operationalized tool for transboundary water governance.

9.4 Methodology

The chapter employs a qualitative research design rooted in an indicator-based framework for evaluating water security in the Congo basin, with a particular focus on the DRC. The design was chosen for its capacity to analyze multidimensional issues, integrating socioeconomic, sociopolitical, and environmental complexities that characterize water security in transboundary settings. The WOSCIM framework methodology provides a structured approach to assess and address water security challenges, serving as a DSM for negotiation processes. This methodology builds on empirical data from the project titled "Addressing Climate and Water-Driven Migration and Conflict Interlinkages to Build Community Resilience in the Congo Basin" (2018–2022), which informed the development and refinement of the WOSCIM framework. The findings with the participatory process, allow the research design to ensure that the framework is not only theoretical but also practically applicable to the governance needs of the Congo basin. Figure 9.1 illustrates the methodological steps undertaken, from defining the problem to monitoring and evaluation, providing a visual representation of the framework's application.

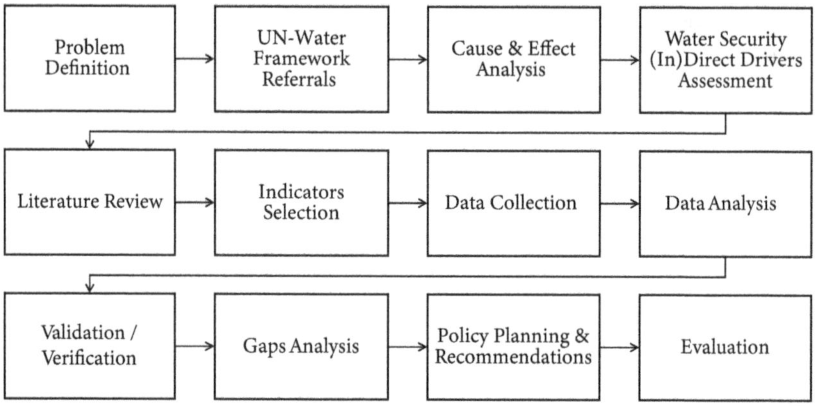

Figure 9.1 Overview of the Steps to Design the WOSCIM Framework Where Indicator-Based Approach Methodology Is Adopted
Note: Elaborated by the authors.

9.4.1 Indicator Selection and Data Collection

The selection of indicators is a critical component of the WOSCIM framework, grounded in relevance, data availability, and applicability to the eight dimensions of the water security framework outlined by UN-Water (2013). These dimensions include ecosystem health, human well-being, and governance, among others. Indicators were prioritized through the analytical hierarchy process, a multicriteria decision-making tool that ranks elements based on their importance to stakeholders and governance objectives (Macharis et al., 2004; Zhang, 2008).

UN-Water defines water security as "The capacity of a population to safeguard sustainable access to adequate quantities of acceptable quality water for sustaining livelihoods, human well-being, and socio-economic development, for ensuring protection against water-borne pollution and water-related disasters, and for preserving ecosystems in a climate of peace and political stability." Using the water security framework proposed by UN-Water, we outlined 26 indicators that were classified based on the eight dimensions of the water security framework (UN-Water, 2013). As depicted in Figure 9.2, the methodology employs an indicator-based approach to evaluate water security in the DRC among the Congo basin riparian region. The indicators were designed to reflect the specific characteristics of the region, leading to the formation of indicator clusters that align with the

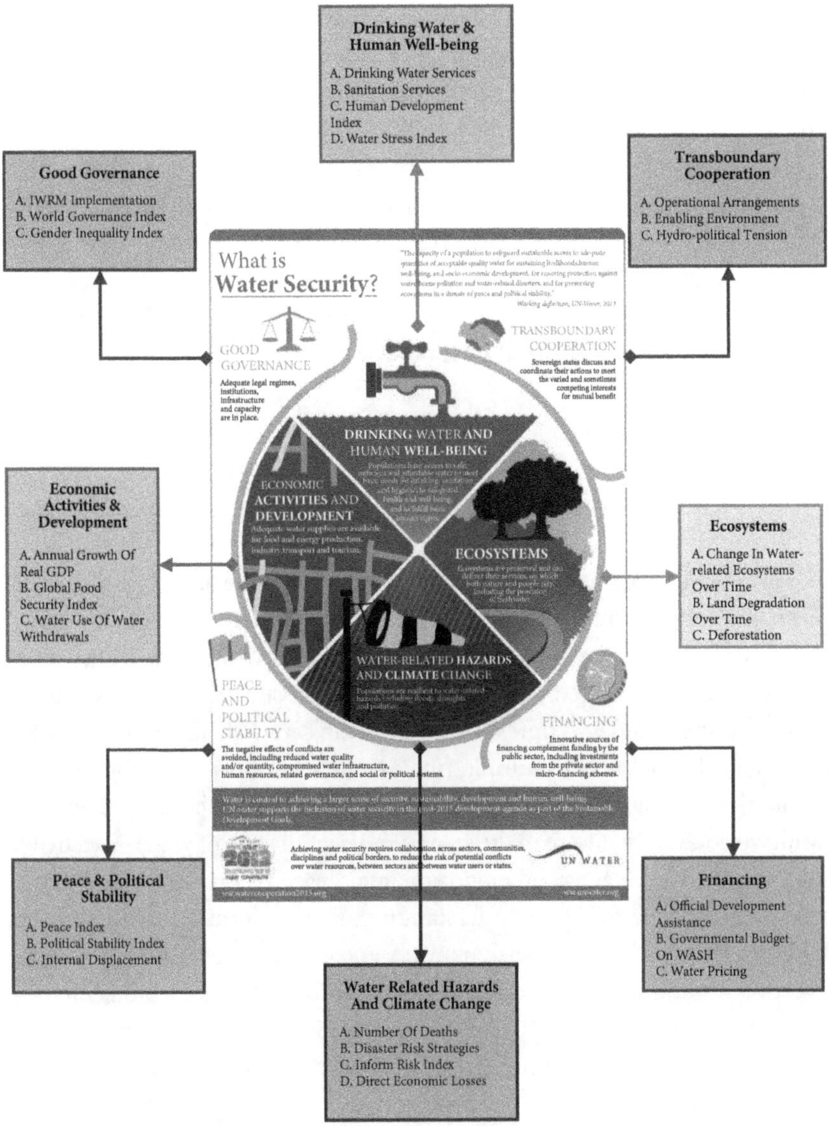

Figure 9.2 WOSCIM Was Designed with Eight Key Elements of Water Security and 26 Selected Indicators to Populate the Framework for the Democratic Republic of Congo and the Region

Note: GDP = gross domestic product; IWRM = integrated water resources management; WASH = water, sanitation, and hygiene. Adapted from United Nations Water (2013) using Automatic Permission to use and cite.

dimensions of the water security conceptual framework (Seaford, 2013). These clusters are intended to facilitate discussion (negotiation) and the implementation of IWRM strategies to support regional water management policies.

Data availability and reliability posed significant challenges, particularly in the DRC, where institutional inefficiencies limit comprehensive data collection. The gap analysis categorized indicators into four levels—high, high-medium, medium-low, and low—based on their importance and urgency for action. For instance, while the DRC's abundant rainfall renders the water scarcity index a low priority, the lack of wastewater treatment emerged as a critical gap.

9.4.2 Step-by-Step Guide to Implementing WOSCIM

The WOSCIM framework operationalizes water security assessments through a series of interlinked steps, integrating these into negotiation processes among riparian states. The process begins with identifying water security challenges specific to the region. These issues are framed within a broader transboundary context, acknowledging how shared resources like the Congo River impact multiple riparian states. This step establishes the foundation for aligning negotiation priorities among stakeholders. Then, the framework is applied to map direct and indirect drivers of water insecurity, such as governance gaps and environmental degradation. Cause-and-effect analysis further refines this understanding, linking local challenges in the DRC to broader basin-wide dynamics. For example, upstream activities affecting water quality can be highlighted to initiate discussions on collaborative water management. Relevant literature is reviewed to contextualize the selected indicators within the sociopolitical and environmental realities of the Congo basin. The indicators are then grouped into clusters that align with the dimensions of water security, ensuring a comprehensive assessment.

Baseline data is collected to establish starting points for assessment. Quantitative and qualitative data is collected to assess the selected indicators. In the DRC, this included metrics on wastewater management, institutional governance, and ecosystem health; these findings are analyzed to identify critical gaps. A gap analysis categorizes indicators into levels of priority, identifying areas requiring immediate action versus those with longer-term implications. For instance, while water scarcity is a low-priority issue for the DRC, governance reforms are critical for addressing systemic challenges. The validation process involves stakeholder consultations to ensure the findings are accurate and actionable. The WOSCIM framework is integrated into negotiation processes by providing a shared evidence base for discussions among riparian states. For example, the prioritization of wastewater treatment in the DRC can serve as a case study to highlight shared governance challenges and foster collaborative solutions. The framework's indicator-driven approach allows stakeholders to move beyond anecdotal arguments, facilitating constructive dialogue. Finally, continuous monitoring of indicators ensures that the framework remains responsive to evolving challenges. Feedback loops enable stakeholders to adapt their strategies, enhancing the effectiveness of negotiated agreements.

9.4.3 Developing the WOSCIM Bundle Matrix: Indicators and Methodology

The WOSCIM framework, encompasses two critical aspects in developing the bundle matrix for water security indicators (detailed in Figure 9.1). First, it identifies indicators that either are currently in use or hold potential for application in the Congo basin and the DRC. These indicators can be customized to suit specific countries or regions, ensuring relevance and adaptability. Second, the framework employs a qualitative assessment technique inspired by Zhang (2008), which incorporates expert judgment to categorize the importance of each indicator. This method provided the analytical foundation for WOSCIM, emphasizing the use of expert judgment and contextual analysis in evaluating complex systems. This methodology was adapted to prioritize indicators, ensuring that the framework reflects both the local realities of the DRC and the broader dynamics of the Congo basin. For instance, this approach informed the weighting of indicators, categorizing them into levels of importance. This prioritization facilitated the gap analysis, enabling stakeholders to focus on high-priority areas such as governance and infrastructure development. This technique aligns technical assessments with stakeholder priorities and allows the framework to bridge the gap between evidence-based analysis and collaborative decision-making, fostering trust and transparency among riparian states.

This study's gap analysis aims to provide actionable recommendations to address deficiencies in water security indicators, classified as high, high-medium, medium-low, and low, per the West Java Water Sustainability Index classification process. Notably, the level of importance assigned to each indicator does not necessarily dictate the priority of actions; instead, each action is tailored to the specific context of the basin, region, or state. However, the relevance of this indicator can vary significantly when weighted against the criteria of "priority" concerning a specific setting. For instance, in the DRC, the water scarcity index is deemed a low priority for action due to the country's abundant water resources and rainfall. Conversely, the indicator for treated wastewater emerges as a critical factor (Level 3) with a high priority for action as the DRC needs more comprehensive information regarding wastewater management. This approach not only ensures that the selected indicators have been utilized by riparian states in the Congo basin over the past two decades but also facilitates a comparative analysis among the countries bordering the Congo River. This framework supports negotiation systems among stakeholders by systematically assessing and prioritizing indicators based on local contexts. Such negotiations can be enhanced by understanding each country's critical water security challenges, fostering collaboration, and promoting informed decision-making. The tailored recommendations derived from the gap analysis can serve as a foundation for dialogue, enabling riparian states to address shared water resources more effectively and equitably. This collaborative approach is key for building resilience and ensuring sustainable water management across the region.

9.4.3.1 Overview of Indicators Applied in the WOSCIM Model

9.4.3.1.1 Drinking Water and Human Well-being

A. **Drinking water services:** The proportion of the *population using safely managed drinking water services* is referred to in SDG indicator 6.1.1.
B. **Sanitation services:** The proportion of the *population using safely managed sanitation services*, aligned to SDG indicator 6.2.1, reflects the availability of sufficient water resources and access to safe sanitation services.
C. **Human Development Index (HDI):** The HDI evaluates a country's well-being based on three dimensions: health (life expectancy at birth), education (mean years of schooling and expected years of

schooling), and standard of living (gross national income per capita) (Klugman et al., 2011; WHO, n.d.).

D. **Water Stress Index (WSI):** The WSI is "the proportion of water withdrawal by all sectors relative to available water resources (Food and Agriculture Organization [FAO], 2018b). In line with SDG indicator 6.4.2, it emphasizes the efficient use of water resources within the country and across all sectors. According to a recent Aqueduct Water Risk Atlas (2019), a quarter of the global population faces severe water stress annually, and at least 50% of the world's population experiences high water stress for at least one month each year. By 2050, water demand in sub-Saharan Africa is projected to increase by 163% (Kuzma et al., 2023; World Resources Institute, 2024).

9.4.3.1.2 Transboundary Cooperation Analysis

Shared water basins hold over half of the world's freshwater supply and are significant for their cultural, spiritual, and economic importance in various communities. SDG indicator 6.5.2 underscores the need to monitor and assess cooperation arrangements within these basins. The Register of the Transboundary Freshwater Dispute Database–supported *Transboundary River Basin* report included 310 international river basins, covering 47.1% of the planet's land surface, most below 10,000 km^2 and inhabited by more than half of the global population (McCracken & Wolf, 2019; Oregon State University, n.d.). These basins are shared by 150 countries, and disputed areas show changes in political boundaries and data quality enhancement (McCracken & Wolf, 2019).

A. **Transboundary Water Operational Arrangements:** The indicator measures the proportion of transboundary basin areas within a country covered by an operational arrangement, including the area of river and lake basins and aquifers (Transboundary Waters Assessment Programme [TWAP], 2024). *Operational arrangements* is defined as "A treaty, convention, agreement or another formal arrangement that meets the following criteria: there is a joint body for transboundary cooperation in place; the countries involved meet at least once per year; there is a joint or coordinated water management plan, or joint objectives have been set, and there is at least an annual exchange of data and information" (UN Statistics Division, 2024).

B. **Enabling Environment:** The enabling environment includes basin-level policies, the presence of institutional frameworks, legal plans, and the management instruments for vital transboundary water resources management (TWAP, 2024). This indicator focuses on stakeholder involvement at all levels in water management and the use of quantitative analysis. *Enabling environment* is defined as "Application of integrated approaches to the development, management, and use of water resources" (UN Environment Programme [UNEP], 2012). This indicator is based on the UN-Water Status Report survey, which states that transboundary basins are categorized on a scale of 1 to 6. A score below 2.7 indicates poor environmental and management systems; 6 represents the optimum score (UNEP, 2012).

C. **Hydro-political Tension:** This indicator introduces a unique method for assessing the formal management institutions that govern transboundary river basins, encompassing critical components such as water allocation, variability management, and conflict resolution (UNEP & DHI, 2010). The indicator's scoring system is based on the tension related to building new dams or water diverts within a country and involves five components of formal transboundary cooperation. To determine the suitability of a particular arrangement, it is essential to consider the availability of treaties, allocation mechanisms, variability management, and conflict resolution mechanisms and the presence of at least one river basin organization, whether bilateral or multilateral, with officials capable of representing participating governments. The political tension indicator ranges from 0 to 5, with 0 indicating very high vulnerability and 5 indicating least vulnerability. This can be reorganized to indicate its hazard level on a scale from 1 to 3, with 3 representing the most hazardous situation. Mapping the vulnerability and hazard levels is reflected in scores from 0 to 9, where 9 indicates a high degree of hydro-political tension.

9.4.3.1.3 Water-Related Ecosystems

This aspect reflects on the water needs for nature and ecological landscapes since ecosystem degradation has led to dire consequences of environmental and climate change, loss of habitat and biodiversity, and impacts on the hydrology/water cycle and ecosystem services, as well as nature's contributions to human well-being. To explain the water–ecosystems nexus, we selected three indicators: change in water-related ecosystems over time, the proportion of lands and forests degraded over time, the public expenditure on conservation and sustainable use of natural resources, and the amount of wastewater being treated to reflect on the ecosystem degradation.

A. **Temporal Changes in Water-Related Ecosystems:** Water-related ecosystem services are provided through various rivers, lakes, and natural wetlands in the region. These services provide nature with various benefits and services that help maintain biodiversity and life, regulate the flows or protect against extreme conditions, water purification, and restock groundwater. They help recreation and tourism (UNEP, 2016). SDG 6.6 proposes the necessity of restoring and protecting all water-related ecosystems by stopping their degradation and demolition or by helping recover or even creating more ecosystems (Bernhardt et al., 2018). SDG indicator 6.6.1 discusses tracking the extent of change in water services and identifying the optimum methodology by monitoring changes through advanced technologies such as Satellite-Based Earth Observation data.
B. **Proportion of Land Degraded Over Time:** Land-use competition has resulted in significant land degradation, especially in agricultural areas. Approximately 23% of the world's land is unproductive, and 75% has been altered (UN Convention to Combat Desertification [UNCCD], 2018). Degradation directly affects the water and food security of different regions seeking development (FAO & UNCCD, 2020). Moreover, to monitor land transformation, it is vital to track land productivity, mainly reporting degradation (Giuliani et al., 2020; Intergovernmental Science-Policy Platform on Biodiversity and Ecosystem Services, 2018).
C. **Deforestation:** Forests have been major protection from runoff and decreasing the frequency and magnitude of the river base flow events over the years, and the loss of natural forests is a threat to surface water quality (FAO, 2010). In Africa, numerous deforestation events have occurred, with the cleared land being replaced by agricultural fields. This can result in runoff and flooding, increased erosion, sedimentation of rivers, and significant pesticide contamination (Mati et al., 2008). In many water-scarce countries, proper management of water catchment areas is essential to ensure maximum water supply capacity with high quality (Masese et al., 2012).

9.4.3.1.4 Financing Water Security

Insufficient investments and poor governance cause a deficiency of access to water services, primarily for vulnerable populations (UNESCO, 2019). Failure to govern water resources efficiently amplifies stress on these resources, escalating competition between different services and conflicts.

A. **Official Development Assistance:** The allocation of official development assistance (ODA) toward water and sanitation is a quantifiable measure of international cooperation and capacity development support in financial terms (UN-Water, 2024c). SDG indicator 6.a.1 monitors the quantity of ODA integrated into a government spending plan. ODA is official financing from donor government agencies to promote economic development and welfare in developing countries, and a government-coordinated spending plan is a financing plan/budget at the national or subnational level, assessing available financial resources and strategies for financing future requirements (UN-Water, 2024b).
B. **Governmental Budget for Water and Sanitation Sector:** Substantial investment in water and sanitation is needed to achieve Sustainable Development Goal 6 by 2030. National WASH plans commonly need more funding (UN-Water, 2024c). Most countries have established WASH policies as part of their national plans. Nevertheless, many countries need more adequate financial resources to execute these plans. Basic WASH services cost just $0.6 per person yearly in the least developed countries, or 6% of current annual least developed government health spending (WHO & UNICEF, 2023).
C. **Water Pricing:** Water charges are calculated based on each country's micro and macro affordability. The International Benchmarking Network for Water and Sanitation Utilities provides an annually updated platform to give the current tariffs for most countries.

9.4.3.1.5 Water-Related Hazards and Climate Change

Water-related disasters are considered key threats to economies and infrastructure, whether in developed or developing countries. Understanding water disasters is significant in building and developing water security planning. Four indicators were selected to comment on water security: the number of deaths from water disasters, the adoption of disaster risk reduction (DRR) strategies, the INFORM Risk Index, and economic loss due to water-related hazards.

A. **Number of Deaths Attributed to Water-Related Disasters:** Water-related hazards were mentioned twice in the SDG indicators, in SDG 11.5.1 and SDG 13.1.1, which relate to the number of deaths, missing persons, and directly affected persons attributed to disasters per 100,000 of the population. These indicators also align with indicators A-1 and B-1 of the Sendai Framework. The EM-DAT database provides up-to-date information on the number of deaths and missing persons and the total affected by each type of disaster. EM-DAT's glossary addresses the indicator as total affected, which is the sum of people who are injured, homeless, and requiring immediate assistance during a period of emergency (Centre for Research on the Epidemiology of Disasters, 2024). The Sendai Framework defines affected persons as injured or ill, whose dwelling is destroyed or damaged, and who are working on assets or facilities (such as industrial, commercial, services, etc.) that have been damaged or destroyed due to disasters.
B. **DRR Strategies:** The SDGs are calibrated to track the countries willing to implement DRR strategies in accordance with the Sendai Framework. The goals and targets also steer the agenda to increase the number of countries implementing DRR strategies at all levels.
C. **INFORM Risk Index:** The Index for Risk Management (INFORM) is a composite indicator developed by the Joint Research Centre, combining 53 indicators into three dimensions of risk: hazards (events that could occur) and exposure to them, vulnerability (the susceptibility of communities to those hazards), and the lack of coping capacity (i.e., lack of resources that can alleviate the impact) (UN Development Programme [UNDP], n.d.). The INFORM Risk Index encompasses all categories of natural disasters, making it challenging to exclusively delineate the risk associated with water-related hazards (UNDP, n.d.). *Hazard & Exposure* is one of the sub-indicators of disasters, and water-related hazards, such as tsunamis, droughts, floods, and tropical cyclones, are also embedded. The indicators *Hazard & Exposure*, *Coping Capacity*, and *Vulnerability* are used to assess the water-related risk.

D. **Direct Economic Losses Due to Water Disasters on Gross Domestic Product:** SDG 1.5.2 aligns with the Sendai Framework indicator C-1, and the UN Statistics Division stores this data for each country. Not every country has a disaster loss database consistent with Open-Ended Intergovernmental Expert Working Group guidelines, but current coverage exceeds 89 countries.

9.4.3.1.6 Peace and Political Stability

Water can be a source of conflict due to water scarcity (dry conditions or drought) or disputes in water-sharing arrangements (Nagabhatla et al., 2021). Peace and political stability within the water security framework are crucial for negotiation support systems (NSSs) and achieving water-related SDGs.

A. **Peace Index:** According to the Passy-Dunant Index, which is calculated based on the average of three sub-indicators—negative peace, positive security, and the culture of peace (Irenees, 2014)—175 countries were measured from 2011 to 2014, with a ranking set from 0 to 1 (most peaceful country).
B. **Political Stability Index:** Political stability is a major determinant of a country's water security (Institute for Economics & Peace, 2018). The Political Stability Index measures violent demonstrations, terrorism, ethnic or religious conflicts, and the frequency of violent protests. The index score scales from −2.5 to 2.5 (a state with solid political stability).
C. **Internal Displacement:** This indicator helps measure the extent of stability in a country, whether against conflicts, violence, or disasters, primarily the number of internally displaced people within a country.

9.4.3.1.7 Economic Activities and Development

Water is critical for economic activities such as agriculture, industries, and energy production. There is a growing focus on developing inclusive and integrated water security strategies at academic and decision-making levels. These strategies must consider equitable shares for various aspects of human development, including food, industrial applications, transportation, and tourism.

A. **Annual Growth Rate of Real Gross Domestic Product:** When exploring any country's economic situation, gross domestic product (GDP) per capita is a standard measure, if not the only one. All countries' GDP per capita data is available through the FAO AQUASTAT database for comparative analysis. The temporal trends of GDP per capita for the DRC in 1997–2017 show a slight increase every 5 years; however, according to the FAO ranking, the DRC is ranked 186 out of 192 countries in its GDP listing (UN-Water, 2018).

B. **Global Food Security Index:** The approach gained traction after the 2011 Bonn Nexus Conference on Water–Energy–Food, which presented an integrated method for addressing complex issues using natural and human-made solutions (Hoff et al., 2019). Food security is an important factor to consider when dealing with water security. Food security is when individuals consistently have physical, social, and economic access to a sufficient and nutritious food supply that caters to their dietary requirements, facilitating a healthy and active lifestyle (FAO, 2023).

   The Economist Intelligence Unit developed a new index, the Global Food Security Index (GFSI), composed of three pillars: affordability, availability, and quality and safety of the food within any country. The GFSI was evaluated for countries by exploring 28 indicators within the mentioned pillars. The GFSI model with a scoring system of 100 (maximum) and 0 (minimum) tackles qualitative and quantitative benchmarking and creates a working framework for addressing food security (Economist Impact, 2022).

C. **Water Use:** Water use is a major indicator designed by water planners in any specific country to assess the gaps between water supply and demand. Water use can be categorized as either *water withdrawn*, which refers to water removed from a lake or river, with a portion of this water often returned to the source and available for reuse (renewable water source), or *water consumed*, which is water removed for use and not returned to its source (Worldometers, n.d.).

   Water use and stress by Our World in Data (FAO/World Bank) provides freshwater usage by country (Ritchie & Roser, 2018). Water stress occurs when the total freshwater withdrawal represents a significant portion of available renewable freshwater resources (Ritchie & Roser, 2018). UN-Water defines water stress categories based on this percentage (of withdrawals to renewable resources) as follows: <25% = no stress, 25%–50% = low stress, 50%–75% = medium stress, 75%–100% = high stress, >100% = critical stress (FAO & UN-Water, 2021).

9.4.3.1.8 Water Governance

Water governance pertains to the comprehensive framework and processes for decision-making and implementation of policies concerning the utilization and management of water resources.

A. **IWRM Degree of Implementation:** SDG indicator 6.5.1 aims to monitor the level of implementation of the IWRM approach in a country to evaluate its effectiveness. The UNEP provides a criterion to measure the IWRM degree of implementation based on four central pillars: enabling environments, institutions and participation, management instruments, and financing mechanisms. The agency created an online platform where updates of dynamic charts for each country's score among 172 countries are provided every 2 years (UNEP, 2018). This indicator helps to establish a baseline and ensures informed decision-making for better management of water resources (Watson et al., 2019).
B. **World Governance Index:** The World Bank created the World Governance Index in 2008 to measure the governance performance of each country in its capacity to develop and enforce integrated social and economic policies effectively (Devarajan, 2007). The index has 30 indicators covering six governance dimensions, using data from 1996, and is updated annually (Devarajan, 2007). Those six dimensions are voice and accountability, political stability and absence of violence, government effectiveness, regulatory quality, the rule of law, and control of corruption. The World Bank has an interactive platform to navigate between countries and provide updates on worldwide governance indicators for each year, scoring dimensions independently (World Bank, 2024a).
C. **Gender Inequality Index:** Gender Inequality Index data shows inequality in 160 countries, and values from 0 to 1 mean the highest gender disparity.

9.5 Results and Discussion

The assessment is structured around critical indicators that reflect eight core elements essential to water security, particularly in the context of developing countries facing significant challenges in managing shared water resources. The WOSCIM model's design (see Section 9.8.2) emphasizes adaptability, allowing it to be tailored to fit diverse contexts and settings within riparian systems. This flexibility is crucial for addressing the unique challenges faced by different countries and regions, ensuring that the model can be effectively implemented where it is needed most. We show the strategic application of the WOSCIM model, underpinned by a robust set of indicators for enhancing water security, in the Congo basin and provide a structured framework for assessing and improving cooperation (showcasing WOSCIM as an NSS) in managing shared water resources, thereby contributing to SDGs and fostering resilience in communities vulnerable to water-related conflicts.

9.5.1 WOSCIM's Role as a DSM in Transboundary Water Negotiations

As Africa faces escalating water-related conflicts amid complex socioeconomic settings, there is a growing need for effective governance frameworks that prioritize transparency and collaboration. WOSCIM emerges as an operational DSM, facilitating cross-border dialogue and supporting evidence-based strategies. The model enables stakeholders to prioritize key water security challenges, identify actionable solutions, and align their interests for equitable water-sharing. For instance, in the context of the Congo basin, WOSCIM has been instrumental in assessing the lack of wastewater management as a high-priority issue. By emphasizing governance reforms and promoting infrastructural development, it serves as a platform for initiating discussions among riparian states. This aligns with broader global efforts, such as UNESCO's FRIEND/Nile flagship initiative, which works to strengthen research cooperation among Nile basin countries, enabling a better understanding of the hydrological regimes of the Nile basin. Similarly, application of WOSCIM in the DRC can provide actionable insights into how transboundary water governance frameworks can evolve to address shared challenges across the Congo River basin. The integration of WOSCIM into negotiation processes fosters trust-building and mutual understanding among stakeholders. For example, prioritizing wastewater treatment not only addresses an immediate need in the DRC but also sets a precedent for collaborative governance that can be scaled to other riparian contexts.

9.5.2 Applications Beyond the Congo Basin

While WOSCIM has been demonstrated in the Congo basin, its adaptability positions it as a valuable tool for transboundary water negotiations in other regions. Shared basins such as the Nile, Mekong, and Indus Rivers face similar challenges, including competing water uses, governance gaps, and sociopolitical tensions. WOSCIM's flexible framework can be tailored to the unique dynamics of these basins, facilitating dialogue and fostering cooperative solutions. In the Nile basin, where disputes over the Grand Ethiopian Renaissance Dam continue to strain relationships between Ethiopia, Egypt, and Sudan, WOSCIM's indicator-based approach could provide a neutral platform for assessing water security challenges and aligning stakeholder priorities. WOSCIM can help identify common ground, such as the shared benefits of sustainable hydropower development and equitable water-sharing, through integrating scientific data with participatory processes. Similarly, in the Mekong River basin, where upstream infrastructural projects have disrupted downstream water availability, WOSCIM can assist in balancing competing demands while promoting inclusive governance. Policymakers could leverage the framework to develop basin-wide strategies that address both environmental and socioeconomic dimensions of water security. For policymakers, the implementation of WOSCIM offers several key recommendations, such as strengthening data collection and management systems to improve the reliability of water security assessments, in addition to fostering regional platforms for sharing data and best practices, ensuring transparency and collaboration, and prioritizing capacity-building initiatives that empower local communities and stakeholders to actively participate in transboundary negotiations.

Another example is Lake Chad, shared by five countries, which has long struggled with water scarcity driven by droughts, climate change, mismanagement, and inefficient governance. Dams constructed on the Komadugu Yobe River between 1960 and 1985, such as Tiga and Challawa, have contributed to the significant shrinking of Lake Chad's surface area. This situation has prompted both regional and global efforts to revive the lake to promote geopolitical stability and resolve water-related conflicts. One notable proposal, the Trans Aqua Project, initiated by the Bonifica Company in the 1970s, aimed to transfer water from the Congo basin through a 2400-km canal into Lake Chad. This ambitious initiative sought not only to restore water supply but also to address energy needs via hydropower, boost industrial and agricultural development, and create employment opportunities for underserved communities. However, the Congo basin represents a complex system due to the interplay of customary practices, cultural norms, state regulations, and environmental consideration. The complexities pose challenges for inter-regional water transfer as they require transparent and inclusive dialogue among multi-stakeholders. While projects like Trans Aqua may hold potential for redefining hydrological relationships between complex water basins in Africa, their success has been limited by a lack of transparent communication and collaboration among authorities and stakeholders, which are crucial for implementation (Sayan et al., 2020).

9.5.3 Strengthening Governance and Collaboration

At its core, WOSCIM emphasizes the importance of inclusive governance, resilience-building, and equitable water-sharing. Through engaging diverse stakeholders, ranging from local communities to national governments, the framework promotes a participatory approach that enhances decision-making and fosters trust among riparian states. This inclusivity is particularly critical in addressing the interconnected challenges of water security and climate change, which disproportionately impact vulnerable populations. WOSCIM's contribution to resilience-building is evident in its focus on evidence-based decision-making and adaptive management. The framework allows stakeholders to monitor and evaluate water security indicators continuously, ensuring that strategies remain responsive to evolving challenges. For example, by identifying gaps in wastewater management infrastructure, WOSCIM provides actionable recommendations that enhance both environmental sustainability and public health outcomes. Moreover, WOSCIM supports the development of robust governance structures that integrate climate risk management into water negotiations. The framework contributes to regional stability and conflict prevention by addressing both immediate needs and long-term sustainability goals. This aligns with global efforts to achieve SDG 6, emphasizing the critical role of water governance in fostering resilience and sustainability across diverse riparian environments.

While the model utilizes a bundle of indicators to assess water security and cooperation in managing shared water resources, WOSCIM effectively identifies existing barriers and develops basin-specific narratives. Its adaptability makes it a valuable tool for stakeholders and decision makers navigating the complexities of water management in different settings. Although WOSCIM's primary objective is to evaluate water security and cooperation, its indicator-based approach extends beyond mere assessment. It allows for the examination of the impact of development aid in the water sector and identifies critical gaps that necessitate context-specific NSSs at the basin scale. By employing a cluster format, WOSCIM facilitates local and national assessments as well as enhances the capacity of governing authorities to monitor and evaluate water security effectively.

9.6 Limitations and Future Research Avenues

While WOSCIM offers a promising framework for enhancing water security and facilitating transboundary water negotiations, it is not without limitations. One of the most significant challenges lies in data availability and reliability, particularly in regions like the Congo basin, where institutional inefficiencies and lack of infrastructure impede comprehensive data collection and validation. The effectiveness of WOSCIM heavily depends on the quality and breadth of the indicators, and gaps in data limit its ability to provide a fully accurate and holistic assessment of water security. For instance, several of the selected indicators in this study lacked consistent datasets, which hindered the evaluation of certain dimensions of water security. Another limitation pertains to the sociopolitical adaptability of the framework. Given the diversity of governance structures, cultural norms, and stakeholder priorities across riparian states, tailoring WOSCIM to fit different sociopolitical contexts can be challenging. The DRC's unique governance and institutional challenges, for example, limit the scalability of findings to other regions without significant adaptation. Additionally, the framework relies heavily on stakeholder participation for both indicator selection and negotiation processes. While participatory approaches enhance inclusivity and trust, they also require significant time, resources, and coordination, which may not always be feasible in conflict-prone or resource-scarce settings.

To address these limitations and enhance the applicability of WOSCIM, several future research directions are proposed. Future studies should explore applying WOSCIM to other regions with limited governance capacity, such as the Sahel, Mekong, and Indus basins. Investigating how WOSCIM adapts to diverse sociopolitical and environmental contexts can provide valuable insights into its scalability. Comparative studies between basins with varying levels of governance maturity would highlight the framework's flexibility and limitations, offering lessons for tailoring its implementation. Longitudinal studies are needed to assess how WOSCIM contributes to conflict prevention and sustainable governance over time. For instance, examining the outcomes of agreements negotiated using WOSCIM versus traditional frameworks could shed light on its effectiveness in fostering durable collaborations. Additionally, future research should explore the ripple effects of WOSCIM on local and national policies, such as the incorporation of shared indicators into regional water management plans or the establishment of joint monitoring mechanisms among riparian states.

In addition, other studies could focus on developing training programs for stakeholders on effectively using WOSCIM. Such initiatives would enhance the framework's adoption and foster regional partnerships and knowledge-sharing. Research could also explore how joint action plans based on WOSCIM indicators encourage cross-border collaborations, ultimately contributing to more cohesive and sustainable water governance structures. Another final research avenue involves examining how WOSCIM complements or enhances existing frameworks like IWRM and WEAP, in addition to identifying pathways for harmonizing these tools to maximize their collective impact on water security and conflict prevention.

9.7 Conclusion

Water security is increasingly recognized as a critical gap, particularly in regions like the Congo basin, where the intertwining of water resources and economic growth presents unique challenges. Achieving water security and addressing water-related SDGs necessitate robust data exchange and knowledge-sharing among stakeholders, including basin countries, local communities, and various agencies. In such a context, the WOSCIM framework can serve as a practical tool for facilitating negotiations as it reflects diverse human security and social justice perspectives, enhancing both disciplinary and operational effectiveness. This approach is particularly relevant in the Congo basin, where ongoing conflicts, poor security levels, and complex sociopolitical dynamics hinder the integration of water resource management bodies.

Water governance negotiations are crucial at all levels, from international to local, to achieve "water security for all" and ensure that "no one is left behind." Initiatives like the UN Economic Commission for Africa and the African Development Bank's 50-year plan aim to promote peace and prosperity in the region. At the local level, efforts such as the USAID-led investment plan for the DRC focus on empowering communities to manage their resources effectively. While progress has been made at the national level in water governance and adoption of IWRM, local-level challenges persist. Studies reveal that the IWRM process often needs to be more inclusive and to fully engage local and community representatives, hindering water use efficiency and service provision. The water security framework underscores the significance of participation, cooperation, inclusive governance, peace, conflict resolution, and political stability. Advancing water management in shared basins requires a strategic NSS that addresses broader issues beyond demand–supply dynamics. To maximize these efforts, it is essential to prioritize inclusive governance practices, ensuring active engagement of local communities, especially marginalized groups, in water management processes to foster resilience and equity.

Overall, the chapter highlights the need for an up-to-date assessment of water security indicators in the Congo basin to identify gaps in sustainable water management. We highlight the importance of addressing poor infrastructure, insufficient water provisioning systems, and competing water uses in designing an NSS at the basin level. These issues underline water security problems, especially for underserved populations and vulnerable communities. Representative indicators, including those from the Sendai Framework, illustrate the complexities of water security negotiations. The study also discusses limitations in data availability, consistency, and reliability, impacting discussions on water quality. A dual-language approach (English and French) was used for data procurement to enhance the depth of some discussions. The study offers valuable insights on negotiating and scaling approaches to assessing factors that support or hinder water security. Integrating the negotiation-based outcomes approach, particularly through the WOSCIM framework, is expected to encourage collaboration and fair water resource management across borders. However, strengthening data collection and management practices is crucial to fully operationalize the WOSCIM framework and ensure effective, data-driven decision-making. Addressing these data gaps will enhance the ability of governing authorities to monitor and evaluate water security comprehensively.

We reiterate that negotiation is crucial for cross-border water governance, fostering dialogue and collaboration among riparian states and local stakeholders. This process helps bridge gaps between governance frameworks and cultural practices, promoting equitable management of shared water resources. It also contributes to political stability and conflict resolution in transboundary contexts. Our model holds the potential to address shared water challenges in the Congo basin and beyond, thereby contributing to a more sustainable and secure water future for all. Future research should focus on adapting the WOSCIM framework to other complex water basins, incorporating lessons learned to refine its indicators and methodologies. This will ultimately broaden its applicability and effectiveness, helping to build resilient and cooperative water management practices across diverse regional contexts.

9.8 Additional Analyses and Data

9.8.1 The UNICEF-JMP Global Monitoring Ladder for Drinking Water Services and Sanitation Services (Urban, Rural)

Values presented in this section are based on WHO & UNICEF-JMP (2024b), with general permission to use with proper citation. Values are expressed in percentages for the period 2015–2022.

A. Drinking-Water Services

- *Safely managed*: In 2015, 27% of urban dwellers and 0.55% of rural residents in the DRC used safely managed drinking water services: improved sources located on-premises, available when needed, and free from microbiological and priority chemical contamination. By 2022, coverage had fallen slightly to 24% in urban areas and 0.51% in rural areas.
- *Basic*: Basic services, an improved source within a 30-minute round-trip collection time, reached 37% of urban and 15.5% of rural populations in 2015. By 2022, these figures were 35% (urban) and 13% (rural).

- *Limited*: Improved sources requiring more than 30-minute round-trip collection served 23% of urban and 14% of rural inhabitants in 2015; by 2022, these figures had climbed to 30% (urban) and 18% (rural).
- *Unimproved*: Unimproved drinking water sources that do not protect against contamination accounted for 12% of urban and 53% of rural use in 2015, rising by 2022 to 9% (urban) and 54% (rural).
- *No service*: In 2015, 2% of urban and 17% of rural Congolese relied on surface water; by 2022, those proportions were 1% (urban) and 14% (rural).

B. Sanitation Services

- *Safely managed*: Safely managed sanitation—private improved facilities where excreta are safely disposed on-site or transported off-site, plus a handwashing station with soap and water—was available to 17% of urban and 14% of rural populations in 2015. By 2022, coverage had declined to 15% (urban) and 11% (rural).
- *Basic*: Basic sanitation—private improved facilities separating excreta from human contact—served 6% of urban and 7% of rural residents in 2015; data for 2022 is not available.
- *Limited*: Improved facilities shared with other households reached 30% of urban and 11% of rural dwellers in 2015; by 2022, these figures were 27% (urban) and 9% (rural).
- *Unimproved*: Unimproved facilities that do not separate excreta from human contact accounted for 44% of urban and 57% of rural use in 2015, increasing to 47% (urban) and 61% (rural) by 2022.
- *No service*: Open defecation was practiced by 4% of urban and 18% of rural dwellers in 2015, improving slightly to 4% (urban) and 19% (rural) in 2022.

9.8.2 Overview of Main Observations from the WOSCIM Model for the DRC

9.8.2.1 Drinking Water and Human Well-being

A. Drinking Water Services

Despite significant surface water resources in the region (Congo basin), water service delivery is below the global average. Over half of the population, approximately 23.4 million, lack access to improved drinking water sources and rely on unprotected wells or springs. Despite the UNEP guidelines, the springs are being exploited without proper development and protection measures. The degradation of water ecosystems and watersheds in urban zones like Lukunga and N'djili catchments in the DRC's Kinshasa affects drinking water supply due to poor standards and inadequate infrastructural maintenance. Basic drinking water services are found in 70% of urban areas. Still, this figure is lower in rural areas. Insufficient water delivery is due to aging and overloaded supply systems. According to JMP data (WHO & UNICEF-JMP, 2024a), nearly 65% of DRC's population lacks basic access to water.

B. Sanitation Services

Sanitation services in the DRC lag significantly behind drinking water access. In 2015, over 40% of the urban population and more than 50% of the rural population had inadequate sanitation facilities. Poor sanitation contributes to water quality and health issues, including the spread of waterborne diseases, which account for 80% of disease outbreaks and one-third of deaths in the country. Rapid population growth in the Congo basin further strains water and sanitation services due to aging infrastructure and poor maintenance. In rural areas, 18% of the population practices open defecation, compared to 4% in urban communities. Sanitation services in rural DRC rank among the lowest, with unimproved facilities reported at 51% in rural areas and 41% in urban areas. According to JMP data (WHO & UNICEF-JMP, 2024a), 84% of the population lacks basic sanitation, and nearly 18% still rely on open defecation. World Bank indicators highlight the DRC's ongoing struggle with inadequate water and sanitation infrastructure across the Congo basin states.

C. HDI

In 2018, the UNDP ranked the DRC 176 out of 189 countries with an HDI score of 0.457, which indicates one of the highest rates of extreme poverty in the world. The DRC ranks 164 out of 174 countries on the 2020 Human Capital Index, reflecting how decades of conflict and fragility have constrained development. The DRC is 0.37, which is below the average of 0.4 (World Bank, 2024d). This low HDI value indicates significant challenges for the country, particularly in achieving the human right to water and sanitation.

D. Water Stress Index

In the past decades, the country did not report many instances of water stress and water withdrawal from available water resources, with statistics remaining optimistic (World Bank, 2017). Level of water stress remained at 0.23 in 2020 (World Bank, 2020). The DRC is 147 out of 163 top water-stressed countries with a total score of 0.01 (World Resources Institute, 2024a). Only 52% have access to improved water sources and 29% to improved sanitation facilities (UNICEF, 2024). The DRC has over 50% of Africa's water reserves, creating a paradox due to its abundant water resources. However rich in natural wealth, access to drinking water in the Congo is gravely limited due to inadequate infrastructure (World Bank, 2023b).

9.8.2.2 Transboundary Cooperation

A. Transboundary Water Operational Arrangements

At the end of 2018, the initial phase of the monitoring process for SDG 6.5.2 was released. Among 19 sub-Saharan African countries, only 12 reported that at least 50% of their transboundary basins had operational arrangements. As for the transboundary rivers and lakes, 18 of the 27 sub-Saharan countries reported at least 75% coverage; for transboundary aquifers, only 5 out of 18 meet this threshold. As of 2023, the global status of indicator 6.5.2 for the DRC, which measures the proportion of transboundary basin area with an operational arrangement for water cooperation, stood at 66%. Specifically, the figure is 99.86% regarding transboundary rivers and lakes, while for transboundary aquafers it remains at 0% (UN-Water, 2023).

B. Enabling Environment

Assessing the risk category reveals a score of 5, indicating the highest level of risk. This reflects poor environmental management and a need for transboundary cooperation mechanisms. For the Congo basin, the DRC has a score of 2.29, ranking fifth from the bottom in terms of enabling the environment (UNEP & DHI, 2016).

C. Hydro-political Tension

The assessment maps vulnerability and hazard levels on a scale from 0 to 9, where a score of 9 indicates a high degree of hydro-political *tension*. For the DRC, using aggregate measures (UNEP & DHI, 2016) results in a score of 3 out of 9, which normalizes to 0.25 on scale of

1. This score indicates a medium level of risk in the transboundary context.

9.8.2.3 Water-Related Ecosystems

A. Temporal Changes in Water-Related Ecosystems

Addressing data and information gaps is essential for improving decision-making, ecosystem planning, and achieving SDG target 6.6. According to a UN Environment report (UN-Water, 2018), satellite data from 2001 to 2015 was used to assess the extent of water-related ecosystems in the DRC, revealing significant changes. Notably, the DRC lost approximately 400 km^2 of these ecosystems due to poor management and planning strategies, as shown in Figure 9.3a (Anderson, 2011).

B. Proportion of Land Degraded over Time

Data on agricultural productivity in the DRC is limited, but a UNCCD report (2022) highlights the link between land productivity, food security, and vulnerability in regions with weak ecosystem management. The DRC experienced a significant drop in land productivity during the 1990s, from which it has not recovered, indicating vulnerabilities in the water–food nexus. Between 1991 and 2005, 24% of the agro-ecological zones in the Congo basin experienced land degradation. However, the region remains one of the least degraded due to its humid climate. In 2016, the DRC committed to restoring 8 out of 100 targeted hectares as part of the African Forest Landscape Restoration Initiative, demonstrating efforts to rehabilitate degraded land by 2030.

C. Deforestation

From 1990 to 2015, the DRC monitored its forest cover using remote sensing to assess land and canopy density. Data showed a decrease in forest cover, from 70% in 1990 to 67.3% in 2015, reflecting ongoing deforestation and its implications for water-related challenges, such as floods and runoff water insecurity (FAO, 2018a).

9.8.2.4 Financing Water Security

A. ODA

Records from 2015 provide a comparative view of spending on WASH across Congo basin countries, aligning with data on SDG indicator

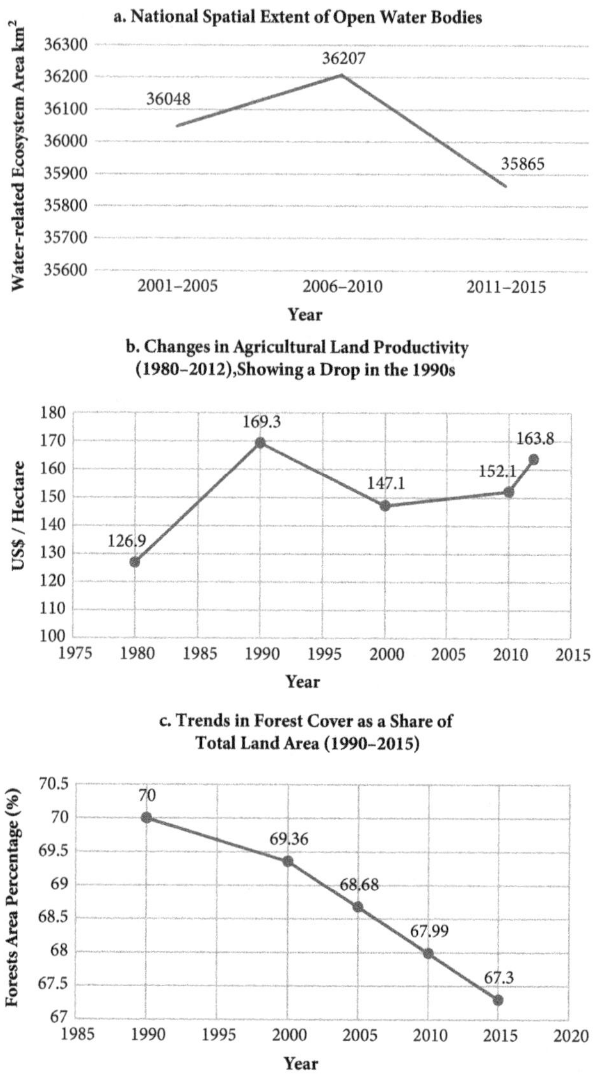

Figure 9.3 Ecosystem Water-Related Activities Through Time in Democratic Republic of Congo

Note: Elaborated by the authors, using own data.

6.4.1 related to IWRM implementation. In 2013, the DRC led the region in WASH spending, with a budget of approximately $215.3 million. However, this amount declined to $76.44 million in 2021 (Our World in Data, 2023). According to the World Bank, the DRC

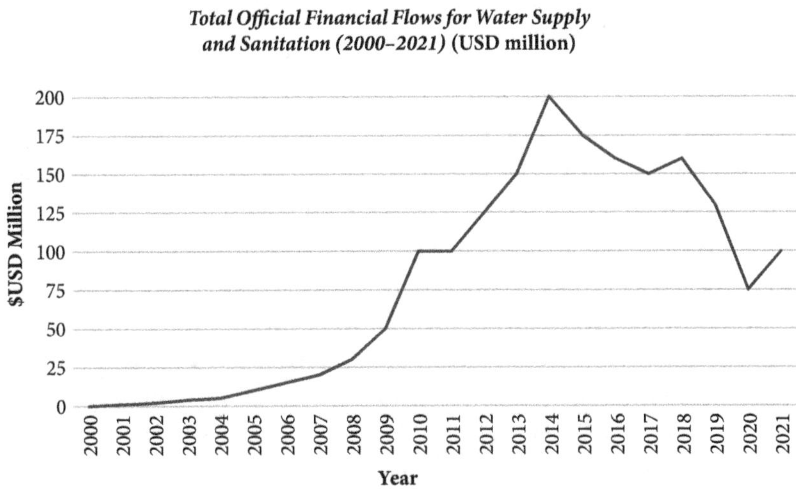

Figure 9.4 Total Official Financial Flows for Water Supply and Sanitation (2000–2021)

Note: Elaborated by the authors *based on Organisation for Economic Co-operation and Development data via the United Nations Sustainable Development Goal Indicators Database* https://archive.ourworldindata.org/20250624-125417/grapher/total-oda-for-water-supply-and-sanitation-by-recipient.html

requires at least $260 million for water services and $190 million for sanitation to meet its needs. The currently available budget for this sector is only $162 million, highlighting a significant financial shortfall (Figure 9.4).

B. Governmental Budget for Water and Sanitation Sector

In the 2007–2008 period, the DRC's public expenditure on WASH, excluding external funding, was around $65 million, accounting for 0.6% of the country's GDP (Komives et al., 2005). Due to limited domestic capacity, 95% of the sector's funding came from external sources (World Bank, 2023a). The current disbursement rate for allocated funds, including external flows, is 49%. Despite this, domestic capital investments remain low, at just $1.7 million annually, aimed at serving 58 million people who still lack basic water access (World Bank & Global Water Security & Sanitation Partnership, 2024). The DRC's reliance on over 90% external funding makes it the largest recipient of global WASH-related assistance, yet this is still insufficient to meet projected needs and infrastructure goals for SDG 6 targets.

C. Water Pricing

In the DRC, the water tariff for a 15-m^3 monthly consumption category is \$0.66 per m^3, which is considerably lower compared to cities like Cape Town (\$1.43), Ottawa (\$1.69), and Washington, DC (\$2). This reflects how some developing countries, including the DRC, use subsidized water pricing mechanisms to improve water security (Soto Rois et al., 2018).

9.8.2.5 Water-Related Hazards and Climate Change

A. Number of Deaths Attributed to Water-Related Disasters

EM-DAT provides information for 1990–2018; the number of deaths and people affected by natural water-related disasters per 100,000 people in the DRC was 5.89, which accounts for 39% of the total population affected plus the deaths from natural disasters. This database also monitors people requiring immediate assistance during an emergency (Centre for Research on the Epidemiology of Disasters & UN Office for Disaster Risk Reduction [CRED & UNDRR], 2015), as well as people affected directly by natural disasters as identified by the Sendai Framework definition (Figure 9.5).

B. DRR Strategies

Table 9.1 summarizes the legislative and regulatory provisions for disaster risk management among six Congo basin countries, in line with the Sendai Framework for Disaster Risk Reduction 2015–2030,

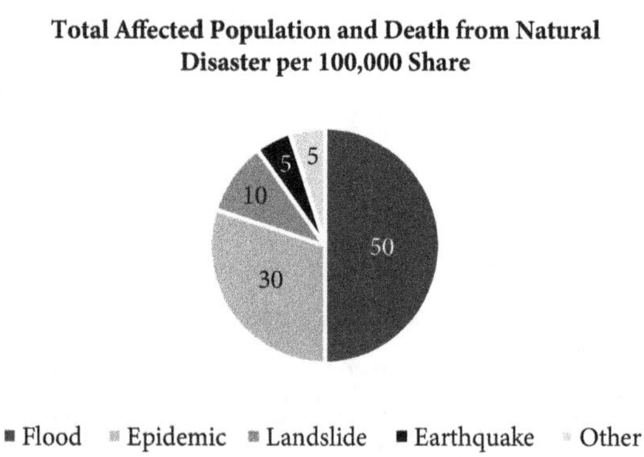

Figure 9.5 Total Affected Population and Death From Natural Disaster Per 100,000 (Percentage)

Note: Elaborated by the authors using data from Centre for Research on the Epidemiology of Disasters (2024).

Table 9.1 Sustainable Development Goal Indicator 11.b.2 Data (Yes/No) and National Budget for Risk Reduction/Prevention of the Congo Basin's Six Countries (2021)

Congo basin countries	Legislative and/or regulatory provision for managing disaster risk	National budget for risk reduction/prevention
Cameroon	Yes	No data
Central African Republic	No data	
Democratic Republic of the Congo	Yes	Nothing to report
Republic of the Congo	No data	
Equatorial Guinea	Yes	<2% (2013) and >12% dedicated to Ebola epidemic (2014)
Gabon	Yes	2.9%

as well as the percentage of national budgets allocated to risk reduction (UN Department of Economic and Social Affairs, 2017). The government of the DRC, in collaboration with the UNDP, is developing its first dedicated DRR policy. Although the country's poverty reduction strategy includes climate adaptation and disaster risk management as core pillars, there is currently no specific budget allocation for DRR (International Monetary Fund, 2013).

C. **INFORM Risk Index**

This indicator illustrates water-related disaster risk scores across six Congo basin countries, showing that most of the region faces high risks related to water hazards and climate adaptation. In the DRC, these challenges are exacerbated by issues such as poor governance, inadequate infrastructure, and high levels of poverty and displacement. Limited financial resources further constrain the state's ability to plan and implement comprehensive DRR strategies, as reflected in poor infrastructural indicators like road density, access to clean water, and sanitation. The deteriorating water infrastructure, coupled with rapid population growth, has led to persistent water supply challenges (Partow, 2011) The Multidimensional Poverty Index score of 0.88 in the DRC highlights significant social vulnerabilities, particularly

Table 9.2 Water-Related Disaster Risk Indicators in Congo Basin Countries: Central African Republic (CAF), Cameroon (CMR), Democratic Republic of the Congo (COD), Republic of the Congo (COG), Gabon (GAB), and Equatorial Guinea (GNQ)

Component	Indicator	CAF	CMR	COD	COG	GAB	GNQ
Coping capacity	Access to healthcare	9.9	7.9	7.8	7.3	7.4	9.3
	Communication	9.1	5.9	7.7	5.5	3.7	8.2
	Disaster risk reduction	0	2.6	7.5	0	6.7	5
	Governance	8.1	7	8	7.6	6.7	7.2
	Physical infrastructure	8.1	6.7	8.9	8	5.9	7.4
Hazards and exposure	Cyclones	0	0	0	0	0	0
	Droughts	0.5	3.1	2	0.5	1.5	0.8
	Floods	5.8	6	3.3	8.6	4.8	5.2
	Tsunamis	0	0	0	0	0	5.2
Vulnerability	Aid dependency	7.7	1.4	2.6	0.6	0.7	2.8
	Development and deprivation	9.5	8	8.8	7.3	5.6	9.1
	Inequality	8.2	6.5	6.6	7	5.8	2.2
	Other vulnerable groups	7.5	3.9	6.6	5.1	3.7	4.4
	Uprooted people	9.8	8.2	9.4	7.4	1.3	2.4

Note: The shading intensity in the table represents the relative magnitude of each indicator value, with darker shades indicating higher risk or greater magnitude for that specific indicator. Elaborated by the authors, using data from the United Nations Development Programme (2024), INFORM Risk Index.

concerning refugees, returned refugees, and internally displaced persons (Table 9.2) (UNDP, 2019).

D. **Direct Economic Losses Due to Water Disasters**

Between 1995 and 2015, floods accounted for 43% of all recorded natural disasters, causing economic damage of $662 billion globally (Centre for Research on the Epidemiology of Disasters, 2024). Direct economic loss, as defined by the Sendai Framework, includes six categories of loss (C1–C6), as shown in Section 9.4, reflecting the substantial impact of water-related disasters on global GDP (CRED & UNDRR, 2015).

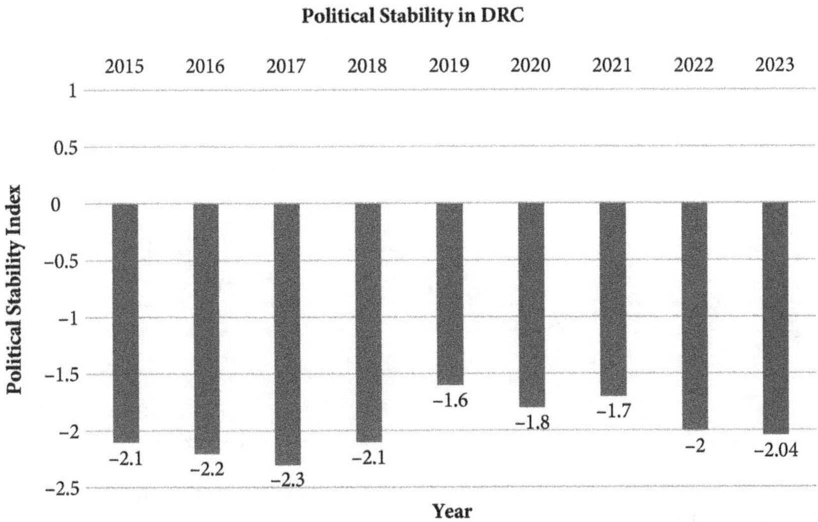

Figure 9.6 Political Stability in Democratic Republic of Congo (DRC)
Note: Elaborated by the authors using data from World Bank (2024a).

9.8.2.6 Peace and Political Stability

A. Peace Index

In 2011, the DRC had a Peace Index score of 0.495, ranking 170th out of 175 countries, while the global average was 0.676. By 2014, the DRC's score slightly improved to 0.476 but remained well below the average. Recent analyses by Nagabhatla et al. (2021) indicate that the DRC continues to face multiple conflict scenarios, with water and climate crises adding a significant burden.

B. Political Stability Index

In 2023, the DRC scored −2.04 on the Political Stability Index, ranking among the lowest out of 193 countries, highlighting weak political stability and regional vulnerability. The World Bank's index, which ranges from −2.5 (weak stability) to 2.5 (strong stability), reflects the persistent instability observed across the region. Temporal data comparisons, illustrated in Figure 9.6, suggest ongoing volatility in political stability across the DRC and other Congo basin states (World Bank, 2017, 2023a).

C. Internal Displacement

In 2018, the DRC ranked second globally for new displacements due to conflicts and violence, with 1.84 million people affected.

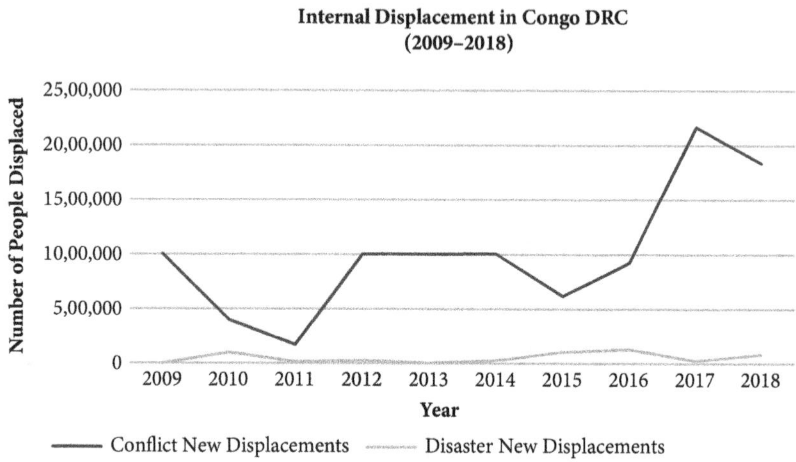

Figure 9.7 Internal Displacement in Congo Democratic Republic of Congo (2009–2018)

Note: Elaborated by the authors using data from Internal Displacement Monitoring Centre (2018).

Since 2009, the Internal Displacement Monitoring Centre (IDMC) has consistently tracked displacements caused by both violence and natural disasters. That year, the DRC also ranked third worldwide in total internally displaced persons, with three million affected (IDMC, 2018). The trend from 2008 to 2018, shown in Figure 9.7, reveals a dramatic rise in displacement linked to escalating violence, conflict, and climate-related disasters. Nagabhatla and Fioret (2020) critically reviewed these issues, highlighting the common misattribution of local conflicts and migration solely to prolonged droughts or flooding, overlooking the broader socioenvironmental impacts. They stress the importance of robust disaster risk management policies across the Congo basin to better address these complex challenges.

9.8.2.7 Economic Activities and Development

A. Annual Growth Rate of Real GDP

The GDP per capita trends for the DRC from 1997 to 2017 show a gradual increase approximately every 5 years. However, according to FAO rankings, the DRC remains low on the GDP list, ranking 186th out of 192 countries (FAO, 2018a). In 2023, the DRC's annual GDP growth rate was 1.9% (World Bank, 2024c).

B. Global Food Security Index

In the 2022 Global Food Security Index, the DRC was ranked 104th out of 113 countries, with scores of 46.9% for Availability, 40.6% for Accessibility, 43.5% for Quality and Safety, and 40.1% for Sustainability and Adaptation. The index also highlighted key issues, including a 39.8% prevalence of undernourishment, 40.8% stunting among children, 23.1% underweight children, and a 5.6% prevalence of obesity (Economist Impact, 2022). The data indicates significant challenges, primarily in agricultural infrastructure, poverty, and the absence of food safety net programs. These challenges intersect with broader economic activities and development issues related to the conceptual water security framework.

C. Water Use and Water Withdrawal

The most recent FAO and World Bank data on water use in the Congo basin, particularly concerning per capita withdrawals, has not been updated since 2000 (Ritchie & Roser, 2018). Water-use efficiency, especially in agriculture, forestry, and fishing, is measured by the gross value added from irrigated activities as these involve water withdrawal unlike rain-fed practices. According to the FAO (2023), water withdrawal rates are distributed across sectors as follows: 11% for agriculture, forestry, and fishing; 21% for industry; and 68% for services (UN-Water, 2024a).

9.8.2.8 Water Governance

A. IWRM Degree of Implementation

The DRC scored 32 in the 2020–2021 SDG 6.5.1 data collection round, indicating a medium-low level of IWRM implementation (Integrated Water Resources Management Action Hub, 2024) (Figure 9.8). The country similarly has medium-low scores for the Enabling Environment and Institutional Arrangements and Participation components, while Management Instruments and Finance are rated as low. This reflects overall weak implementation of IWRM strategies in the DRC.

At the regional level, the DRC's 2017 IWRM score was 31 out of 100, relatively low compared to neighboring countries such as Tanzania, which scored 50. Figure 9.9 provides a comparative overview, showing that all Congo basin states have scores ranging from low to medium, underscoring weak implementation of IWRM strategies and limited

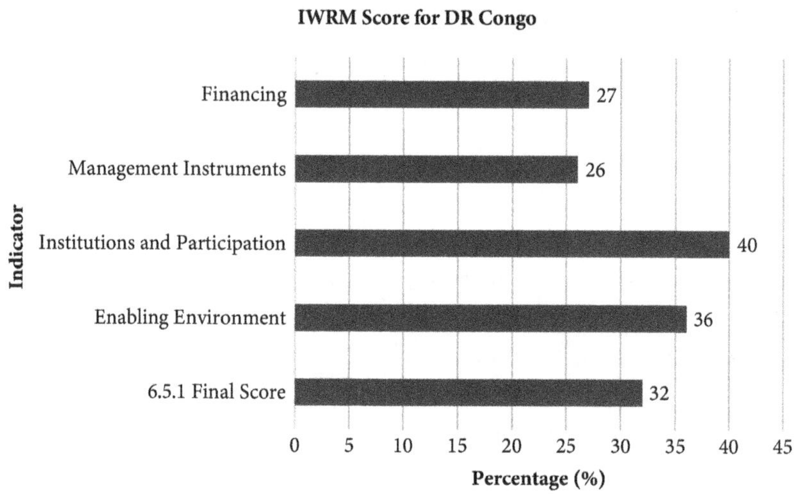

Figure 9.8 Integrated water resources management score for Democratic Republic of Congo

Note: Elaborated by the authors using data from World Health Organization & UNICEF-JMP (2024a).

progress across key pillars, including Financing and the establishment of Enabling Environments, as noted in Figure 9.9.

B. **World Governance Index**

According to the 2022 World Bank Worldwide Governance Indicators, the DRC scored poorly across all six elements: Voice and Accountability (−1.18), Political Stability and Absence of Violence/Terrorism (−2.0), Government Effectiveness (−1.74), Regulatory Quality (−1.48), Rule of Law (−1.67), and Control of Corruption (−1.54) (World Bank, 2024b). This pattern is consistent across the Congo basin region, which has the lowest scores particularly in areas related to violence, corruption control, and political instability, highlighting persistent governance challenges.

C. **Gender Inequality Index**

In the 2021 Gender Inequality Index, the DRC ranked 151st out of 179 countries, reflecting significant gender disparities across reproductive health, empowerment, and labor market participation. Only 14.3% of parliamentary seats are occupied by women (World Bank, 2022a). Additionally, the 2014 Demographic and Health Survey reported that around 50% of women have experienced physical or sexual violence,

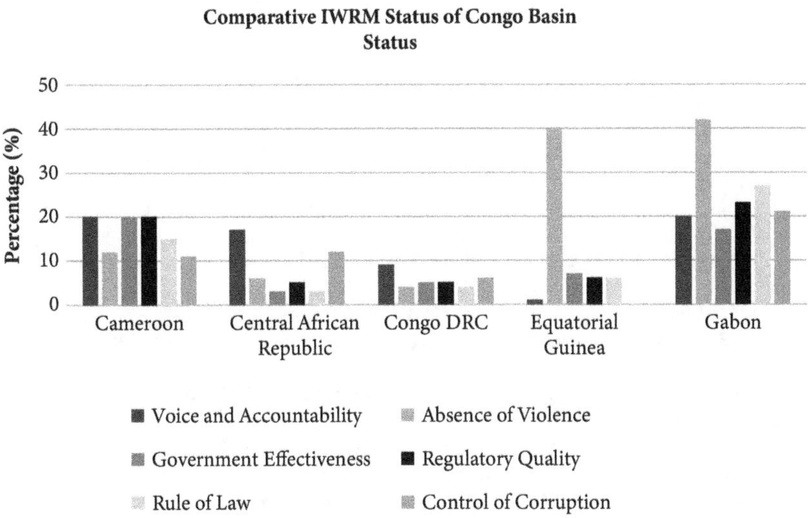

Figure 9.9 Comparative Integrated Water Resources Management Status of Congo Basin States

Note: Elaborated by the authors using data from World Health Organization & UNICEF-JMP (2024b).

and nearly 75% of women, along with 60% of men, accept domestic violence as justified. Acceptance of intimate partner violence is prevalent, particularly among younger age groups, impacting various sectors, including water governance. Given that 84% of the agricultural workforce comprises women, gender inequality could further hinder effective water management and governance in the DRC (USAID, 2024).

References

Anderson, R. L. (2011). Synergism: A rotation effect of improved growth efficiency. In D. L. Sparks (Ed.), *Advances in agronomy* (Vol. 112, pp. 205–226). Academic Press. https://doi.org/10.1016/B978-0-12-385538-1.00005-6

Bernhardt, L., Harlin, J., Tchadie, A., & Midha, N. (2018). *Progress on water-related ecosystems—Piloting the monitoring methodology and initial findings for SDG indicator 6.6.1*. UN-Water.

Bhave, A. G., Bulcock, L., Dessai, S., Conway, D., Jewitt, G., Dougill, A. J., Kolusu, S. R., & Mkwambisi, D. (2020). Lake Malawi's threshold behaviour: A stakeholder-informed model to simulate sensitivity to climate change. *Journal of Hydrology*, *584*, Article 124671. https://doi.org/10.1016/j.jhydrol.2020.124671

Blue Peace Initiative. (2024). *Water diplomacy and mediation.* https://www.thebluepeaceinitiative.org/water-diplomacy.html

Bonzi, C., Onigkeit, J., Hoff, H., Joyce, B., & Tielbörger, K. (2016). Analysing stakeholder driven senarios with a transboundary water planning tool for IWRM in the Jordan River basin. In D. Borchardt, J. Bogardi, & R. Ibisch (Eds.), *Integrated water resources management: Concept, research and implementation* (pp. 413–433). Springer. https://doi.org/10.1007/978-3-319-25071-7_16

Borja-Vega, C., Grabinsky, J., & Kløve, E. (2022). Introducing a framework for analyzing weaknesses in institutional service delivery and the human rights to water and sanitation: Case studies from the Democratic Republic of Congo, Haiti, Mozambique, and Niger. *Water, 14*(20), Article 3209. https://doi.org/10.3390/w14203209

Carraro, C., Marchiori, C., & Sgobbi, A. (2005). *Applications of negotiation theory to water issues* [Policy research working paper]. World Bank. https://doi.org/10.1596/1813-9450-3641

Centre for Research on the Epidemiology of Disasters. (2024). EM-DAT: The International Disaster Database.

Centre for Research on the Epidemiology of Disasters & United Nations Office for Disaster Risk Reduction. (2015). *The human cost of weather-related disasters 1995–2015.*

Clingendael Institute. (2014). *Water negotiations: Sharing a resource without borders.* https://www.clingendael.org/publication/water-negotiations-sharing-resource-without-borders

Dadzie, S. S., Al-Momani, M. A., & Al-Ghando, M. A. (2016). Water security and climate change: A review. *Water Resources Management, 30*(12), 3837–3855.

Damkjaer, S., & Taylor, R. (2017). The measurement of water scarcity: Defining a meaningful indicator. *Ambio, 46*(5), 513–531. https://doi.org/10.1007/s13280-017-0912-z

Devarajan, S. (2007). Two comments on "Governance indicators: Where are we, where should we be going? *The World Bank Research Observer, 23*(1), 31–36. https://doi.org/10.1093/wbro/lkn001

Economist Impact. (2022). *Global Food Security Index 2022.* https://impact.economist.com/sustainability/project/food-security-index/

Food and Agriculture Organization. (2010). *Global forest resources assessment.*

Food and Agriculture Organization. (2018a). *Progress on level of water stress: Global baseline for SDG indicator 6.4.2.*

Food and Agriculture Organization. (2018b). *The state of the world's forests: Forest pathways to sustainable development.*

Food and Agriculture Organization. (2023). *The state of food security and nutrition in the world 2023.* https://openknowledge.fao.org/server/api/core/bitstreams/f1ee0c49-04e7-43df-9b83-6820f4f37ca9/content/state-food-security-and-nutrition-2023/annexes11.html

Food and Agriculture Organization & United Nations Convention to Combat Desertification. (2020). *Land degradation neutrality for water security and combatting drought.*

Food and Agriculture Organization & United Nations Water. (2021). *Progress on the level of water stress: Global status and acceleration need for SDG indicator 6.4.2.* https://doi.org/10.4060/cb6241en

Gaffal, M., & Gálvez, J. P. (2023). Negotiation, game theory and language games. In *Dynamics of rational negotiation* (pp. 11–40). Springer. https://doi.org/10.1007/978-3-031-49051-4_2

Gheuens, J., Nagabhatla, N., & Perera, E. D. P. (2019). Disaster-risk, water security challenges and strategies in small island developing states (SIDS). *Water, 11*(4), Article 637. https://doi.org/10.3390/w11040637

Giordano, G. (2007). Transboundary cooperation on water: A review of concepts, methods, and tools. *Water Resources Management, 21*(10), 1405–1423.

Giuliani, G., Chatenoux, B., Benvenuti, A., Lacroix, P., Santoro, M., & Mazzetti, P. (2020). Monitoring land degradation at the national level using satellite Earth Observation time-series data to support SDG15—Exploring the potential of the data cube. *Big Earth Data*, *4*(1), 3–22. https://doi.org/10.1080/20964471.2020.1711633

Grey, D., Garrick, D., Blackmore, D., Kelman, J., Muller, M., & Sadoff, C. (2013). Water security in one blue planet: Twenty-first century policy challenges for science. *Philosophical Transactions of the Royal Society A: Mathematical Physical and Engineering Sciences*, *371*(2002), Article 20120406. https://doi.org/10.1098/rsta.2012.0406

Hoekstra, A. Y., & Mekonnen, M. M. (2012). The water footprint of humanity. *Proceedings of the National Academy of Sciences of the United States of America*, *109*(9), 3232–3237. https://doi.org/10.1073/pnas.1109936109

Hoff, H., Alrahaife, S., El Hajj, R., Lohr, K., Mengoub, F., Farajalla, N., Fritzsche, K., Jobbins, G.,Özerol, G., Schultz, R., & Ulrich, A. (2019). A nexus approach for the MENA Region—From concept to knowledge to action. *Frontiers in Environmental Science*, 7, Article 48. https://doi.org/10.3389/fenvs.2019.00048

Hutton, G., & Varughese, M. (2016). *The costs of meeting the 2030 Sustainable Development Goal targets on drinking water, sanitation, and hygiene.* World Bank.

Institute for Economics & Peace. (2018). *Global Peace Index 2018: Measuring peace in a complex world.* https://www.economicsandpeace.org/wp-content/uploads/2020/08/Global-Peace-Index-2018-2-1.pdf

Integrated Water Resources Management Action Hub. (2024, September). *Democratic Republic of the Congo (the).* https://iwrmactionhub.org/country-info/CD

Intergovernmental Panel on Climate Change. (2021). *The physical science basis. Contribution of Working Group 1 to the Sixth Assessment Report of the Intergovernmental Panel on Climate Change.* Cambridge University Press.

Intergovernmental Science-Policy Platform on Biodiversity and Ecosystem Services. (2018). *Summary for policymakers of the thematic assessment of land degradation and restoration.* https://www.ipbes.net

Internal Displacement Monitoring Centre. (2018). *Global report on internal displacement by conflict and disasters 2017.*

International Monetary Fund. (2013). *Poverty reduction strategy: Democratic Republic of the Congo.*

Irenees. (2014). *Peace Index.* https://www.irenees.net/rubrique14_en.html

Karam, S., Zango, B., Seidou, O., Perera, D., Nagabhatla, N., & Tshimanga, R. M. (2023). Impacts of climate change on hydrological regimes in the Congo River basin. *Sustainability*, *15*(7), Article 6066. https://doi.org/10.3390/su15076066

Kıbrıs, Ö. (2010). Cooperative game theory approaches to negotiation. In D. Kilgour & C. Eden (Eds.), *Handbook of group decision and negotiation: Vol. 4. Advances in group decision and negotiation* (pp. 151–166). Springer. https://doi.org/10.1007/978-90-481-9097-3_10

Kıbrıs, Ö. (2021). Negotiation as a cooperative game. In D. Kilgour & C. Eden (Eds.), *Handbook of group decision and negotiation* (2nd ed., pp. 545–568). Springer. https://doi.org/10.1007/978-3-030-49629-6_10

Klugman, J., Rodríguez, F., & Choi, H. J. (2011). *The HDI 2010: New controversies, old critiques* [Human Development Research Paper 2011/01]. United Nations Development Programme. http://hdr.undp.org/en/content/hdi-2010-new-controversies-old-critiques

Komives, K., Foster, V., Halpern, J., & Wodon, Q. A. (2005). *Water, electricity, and the poor: Who benefits from utility subsidies?* World Bank.

Kuzma, S., Saccoccia, L., & Chertock, C. M. (2023, August 16). *25 countries, housing one-quarter of the population, face extremely high-water stress.* World Resources Institution. https://www.wri.org/insights/highest-water-stressed-countries

Luzingu, J. K., Stroupe, N., Alaofe, H., Jacobs, E., & Ernst, K. (2022). Risk factors associated with under-five stunting, wasting, and underweight in four provinces of the Democratic Republic of Congo: Analysis of the ASSP project baseline data. *BMC Public Health*, *22*, Article 2422. https://doi.org/10.1186/s12889-022-14842-x

Macharis, C., Springael, J., Brucker, K. D., & Verbeke, A. (2004). PROMETHEE and AHP: The design of operational synergies in multicriteria analysis. Strengthening PROMETHEE with ideas of AHP. *European Journal of Operational Research, 153*, 307–317. https://doi.org/10.1016/S0377-2217(03)00153-X

Masese, F. O., Raburu, P. O., Mwasi, B. N., & Etiégni, L. (2012). Effects of deforestation on water resources: Integrating science and community perspectives in the Sondu-Miriu River basin, Kenya. In A. A. Oteng-Amoako (Ed.), *New advances and contributions to forestry research* (pp. 1–18). IntechOpen. https://doi.org/10.5772/34373

Mati, B. M., Mutie, S., Gadain, H., Home, P., & Mtalo, F. (2008). Impacts of land-use/cover changes on the hydrology of the transboundary Mara River, Kenya/Tanzania. *Lakes and Reservoirs, 13*, 169–177. https://doi.org/10.1111/j.1440-1770.2008.00367.x

McCracken, M., & Wolf, A. T. (2019). Updating the register of international river basins of the world. *International Journal of Water Resource Development, 30*(5), 732–782. https://doi.org/10.1080/07900627.2019.1572497

Molle, F. (2004). Defining water rights: By prescription or negotiation? *Water Policy, 6*(2), 207–227.

Nagabhatla, N., Cassidy-Neumiller, M., Francine, N. N., & Maatta, N. (2021). Water, conflicts and migration and the role of regional diplomacy: Lake Chad, Congo basin, and the Mbororo pastoralist. *Environmental Science & Policy, 122*, 35–48. https://doi.org/10.1016/j.envsci.2021.03.019

Nagabhatla, N., & Fioret, C. (2020). The water–migration nexus—An analysis of causalities and response mechanisms with a focus on the Global South. In G. Rayp, I. Ruyssen, & K. Marchand (Eds.), *Regional integration and migration governance in the Global South* (pp. 85–115). United Nations University Series on Regionalism. Springer. https://doi.org/10.1007/978-3-030-43942-2

Oregon State University. (n.d.). *Program in water conflict management and transformation. International River Basin Register.* Retrieved August 2024, from https://transboundarywaters.ceoas.oregonstate.edu/international-river-basin-register

Our World in Data. (2023). *Total official financial flows for water supply and sanitation, by recipient.* https://ourworldindata.org/grapher/total-oda-for-water-supply-and-sanitation-by-recipient?tab=chart&country=~COD

Partow, H. (2011). *Problématique de l'eau en République Démocratique du Congo: Défis et opportunités* (Technical report). United Nations Environment Programme. https://www.pseau.org/outils/ouvrages/pnue_problematique_de_l_eau_en_republique_democratique_du_congo_2011.pdf

Ritchie, H., & Roser, M. (2018). *Water use and stress.* https://ourworldindata.org/water-use-stress

Sayan, R. C., Nagabhatla, N., & Ekwuribe, M. (2020). Soft power, discourse coalitions, and the proposed inter-basin water transfer between Lake Chad and the Congo River. *Water Alternatives, 13*(3), 752–778. https://doaj.org/article/5f61177cbdc54cc187a06793c6099605

Schmeier, S. (2021). International water law principles in negotiations and water diplomacy. *AJIL Unbound, 115*, 173–177. https://doi.org/10.1017/aju.2021.21

Seaford, C. (2013). The multiple uses of subjective well-being indicators. *Social Indicators Research, 114*(1), 29–43.

Smith, D., & Winterman, K. (2022). Models and mandates in transboundary waters: Institutional mechanisms in water diplomacy. *Water, 14*(17), Article 2662. https://doi.org/10.3390/w14172662

Soto Rois, P. C., Deen, T. A., Nagabhatla, N., & Ayala, G. (2018). Explaining water pricing through a water security lens. *Water, 10*, Article 1173. https://doi.org/10.3390/w10091173

Tayia, A. (2019). Transboundary water conflict resolution mechanisms: Substitutes or complements. *Water, 11*(7), Article 1337. https://doi.org/10.3390/w11071337

Transboundary Waters Assessment Programme. (2024, August). *Transboundary river basins: Status and trends.* Retrieved August 2024, from http://geftwap.org/water-systems/river-basins

Tshimanga, R. M., Lutonadio, G. K., Kabujenda, N. K., Sondi, C. M., Mihaha, E. N., Ngandu, J. K., Nkaba, L. N., Sankiana, G. M., Beya, J. T., Kombayi, A. M., Bonso, L. M., Likenge, A. L., Nsambi, N. M., Sumbu, P. Z., Yuma, Y. B., Bisa, M. K., & Lututala, B. M. (2021). An integrated information system of climate–water–migrations–conflicts nexus in the Congo basin. *Sustainability, 13*(16), Article 9323. https://doi.org/10.3390/su13169323

UNESCO. (2019). *The United Nations world water development report 2019: Leaving no one behind.*

UNICEF. (2022). *Progress on drinking water, sanitation and hygiene in schools: 2000–2021 data update.* Retrieved August 2024, from https://data.unicef.org/resources/jmp-wash-in-schools-2022/

UNICEF. (2024). *Water, sanitation and hygiene.* https://www.unicef.org/drcongo/en/what-we-do/water-sanitation-and-hygiene

United Nations Convention to Combat Desertification. (2018). *Data and facts about recent assessments of land degradation.*

United Nations Convention to Combat Desertification. (2022). *Global land outlook* (2nd ed.). https://www.unccd.int/resources/global-land-outlook/global-land-outlook-2nd-edition

United Nations Department of Economic and Social Affairs. (2017). Classifications. In *Disaster-Related Statistics Framework (DRSF) version 1.0.* (Chapter 3).

United Nations Development Programme. (2019). *Unstacking global poverty: UNDP human development indicators: Congo Democratic Republic.* https://hdr.undp.org/sites/default/files/Country-Profiles/MPI/COD.pdf

United Nations Development Programme. (n.d.). *INFORM (Index for Risk Management).* Retrieved August 2024, from https://www.undp.org/geneva/inform-index-risk-management

United Nations Environment Programme. (2012). *Status report on the application of integrated approaches to water resources management.* https://www.unwater.org/sites/default/files/app/uploads/2017/05/UNW_status_report_Rio2012.pdf

United Nations Environment Programme. (2016). *River partners: Applying ecosystem-based disaster risk reduction (Eco-DRR) in integrated water resource management (IWRM) in the Lukaya basin, Democratic Republic of Congo.*

UN Environment Programme. (2018). *Progress on integrated water resources management. Global baseline for SDG 6 Indicator 6.5.1: Degree of IWRM implementation.* file:///C:/Users/m_radwan/Downloads/IWRM_EN.pdf

United Nations Environment Programme & DHI. (2010). *Climate change adaptation: The pivotal role of water.* https://unepdhi.org/climate-change-adaptation-the-pivotal-role-of-water/

United Nations Environment Programme & DHI. (2016). *Transboundary river basins: Status and trends. Summary for policy makers.*

United Nations Statistics Division. (2024). *Addressing climate and water-driven migration and conflict interlinkages to build community resilience in the Congo basin.*

United Nations-Water. (2013). *Water security & the global water agenda.* https://collections.unu.edu/eserv/UNU:2651/Water-Security-and-the-Global-Water-Agenda.pdf

United Nations-Water. (2022). *UN world water development report.* https://www.unwater.org/publications/un-world-water-development-report-2022

United Nations-Water. (2023). *Progress on transboundary water cooperation (SDG target 6.5).* https://sdg6data.org/en/indicator/6.5.2

United Nations-Water. (n.d.a). *Democratic Republic of the Congo.* Retrieved August 2024, from https://www.sdg6data.org/en/country-or-area/Democratic%20Republic%20of%20the%20Congo

United Nations-Water. (n.d.b). Indicator 6.a.1 "Amount of water- and sanitation-related official development assistance that is part of a government-coordinated spending plan." Retrieved August 2024, from https://www.unwater.org/our-work/integrated-monitoring-initiative-sdg-6/indicator-6a1-amount-water-and-sanitation-related

United Nations-Water. (n.d.c). *Financing water and sanitation*. Retrieved August 2024, from https://www.unwater.org/water-facts/financing-water-and-sanitation

USAID. (2024). *Agriculture and food security*. Retrieved August 2024, from https://www.usaid.gov/democratic-republic-congo/agriculture-and-food-security

Villiers, A. T. (2011). Water security and conflict: A complex relationship. *Water Policy, 13*(1), 1–11.

Watson, N., Shrubsole, D., & Mitchell, B. (2019). Governance arrangements for integrated water resources management in Ontario, Canada, and Oregon, USA: Evolution and lessons. *Water*, 11(4), Article 663.

Wilkenfeld, P. D. (2004). Water conflicts: The new security agenda. *Journal of Peace Research, 41*(4), 409–422.

Wolf, A. T. (2007). Shared waters: Conflict and cooperation. *Annual Review of Environment and Resources, 32*(1), 241–269. https://doi.org/10.1146/annurev.energy.32.041006.101434

World Bank. (2017). *Wash poor in a water-rich country: A diagnostic of water, sanitation, hygiene, and poverty in the Democratic Republic of Congo*.

World Bank. (2020). *Level of water stress: Freshwater withdrawal as a proportion of available freshwater resources*. https://data.worldbank.org/indicator/ER.H2O.FWST.ZS

World Bank. (2022a). *Water and sanitation for all: Global tracking and learning*. https://www.un.org/sustainabledevelopment/water-and-sanitation/

World Bank. (2022b). *Changing social norms and values to end widespread violence against women and girls in DRC*. https://blogs.worldbank.org/en/africacan/changing-social-norms-and-values-end-widespread-violence-against-women-and-girls-drc

World Bank. (2023a). *Poverty & Equity Brief, Africa Eastern & Southern: Democratic Republic of Congo*. https://databankfiles.worldbank.org/public/ddpext_download/poverty/987B9C90-CB9F-4D93-AE8C-750588BF00QA/current/Global_POVEQ_COD.pdf

World Bank. (2023b, November 15). *Supporting drinking water access, a key to progress in the Democratic Republic of Congo (DRC)*. https://www.worldbank.org/en/news/feature/2023/11/15/supporting-drinking-water-access-a-key-to-progress-in-afe-1123-democratic-republic-of-congo-drc

World Bank. (2024a). *World governance indicators*. Retrieved August 2024, from www.govindicators.org

World Bank. (2024b). *Worldwide governance indicators: WGI table*. https://databank.worldbank.org/reports.aspx?Id=ceea4d8b&Report_Name=WGI-Table17

World Bank. (2024c). *GDP growth (annual %)—Congo, Rep.* https://data.worldbank.org/indicator/NY.GDP.MKTP.KD.ZG?end=2023&locations=CG&start=1961&view=chart

World Bank. (2024d, April). *The World Bank in DRC*. https://www.worldbank.org/en/country/drc/overview

World Bank & Global Water Security & Sanitation Partnership. (2024). *Navigating funding challenges for the WASH sector in DR Congo*. https://thedocs.worldbank.org/en/doc/dd99b720176a81d2243053bc3986cccd-0010012024/original/DRC-WASH-Infographic-English.pdf

World Health Organization. (2022). *Water, sanitation, and hygiene*. https://www.who.int/teams/environment-climate-change-and-health/water-sanitation-and-health

World Health Organization. (n.d.). *Human development index*. Retrieved August 2024, from https://www.who.int/data/nutrition/nlis/info/human-development-index

World Health Organization & UNICEF. (2017). *Progress on drinking water, sanitation, and hygiene: 2017 update and SDG baselines*.

World Health Organization & UNICEF. (2023, September). *WHO/UNICEF joint monitoring program for water supply, sanitation and hygiene (JMP)—Progress on household drinking water, sanitation, and hygiene 2000–2022: Special focus on gender.* https://www.unwater.org/publications/who/unicef-joint-monitoring-program-update-report-2023

World Health Organization & UNICEF-JMP. (2024a). *JMP household data.* https://washdata.org/data/household

World Health Organization & UNICEF-JMP. (2024b). *Rural and urban drinking water and sanitation service levels, 2015 and 2022.* https://washdata.org/data/household#!/dashboard/new

Worldometers. (n.d.). *Water use by country.* Retrieved September 2024, from https://www.worldometers.info/water/

World Resources Institute. (n.d.). *Baseline water stress.* https://www.wri.org/applications/aqueduct/country-rankings/?indicator=bws

Zareie, S., Bozorg-Haddad, O., & Loáiciga, H. A. (2020). A state-of-the-art review of water diplomacy. *Environment, Development and Sustainability, 23*(2), 2337–2357. https://doi.org/10.1007/s10668-020-00677-2

Zeitoun, M., & Mirumachi, N. (2008). Transboundary water interaction I: Reconsidering conflict and cooperation. *International Environmental Agreements: Politics, Law and Economics, 8*(4), 297–316. https://doi.org/10.1007/s10784-008-9083-5

Zhang, H. (2008). The analysis of the reasonable structure of water conservancy investment of capital construction in China by AHP method. *Water Resources Management, 23*, 1–18.

10

Ways Forward to Employ Decision Support Models in International Water Negotiations

Mohammadreza Shahbazbegian and Ariel Dinar

10.1 The Evolution of Decision Support Models Over Time

In an increasingly water-stressed world, transboundary water resource management presents complex international relations challenges (Dinar et al., 2007). Water flows across political boundaries create shared dependencies and potential conflicts among riparian states (Hensel et al., 2006). This necessitates sophisticated negotiation approaches that accommodate multiple stakeholders, competing interests, and the complex dynamics of shared water systems. Decision support models (DSMs) have emerged as powerful tools, offering structured frameworks for analyzing water management scenarios, evaluating trade-offs, and identifying solutions for diverse stakeholder interests.

DSM use in negotiations has evolved significantly over recent decades. Kersten and Lai (2007) note that negotiation support systems represent specialized decision tools designed to facilitate agreement processes among parties with potentially conflicting objectives. These systems have transformed from simple communication platforms to sophisticated analytical frameworks that model complex interactions, predict outcomes, and suggest compromises. According to Lim and Benbasat (1992), the theoretical foundations of these systems lie in their ability to reduce cognitive limitations, enhance information processing, and promote objective decision-making among negotiating parties.

Progression from general negotiation support tools to specialized water negotiation systems reflects the unique challenges of water-related conflicts.

Mohammadreza Shahbazbegian and Ariel Dinar, *Ways Forward to Employ Decision Support Models in International Water Negotiations*. In: *Decision Support Models to Assist International and Transboundary Water Negotiations*. Edited by: Mohammadreza Shahbazbegian and Ariel Dinar, Oxford University Press.
 DOI: 10.1093/9780197802601.003.0010

Kersten and Noronha (1998) argue that effective negotiation support systems must be tailored to the specific context and nature of the dispute. In transboundary water management, this specialization is particularly important due to the multifaceted nature of water conflicts, which involve quantity allocation, water quality, multi-sector needs, timing of flows, environmental protection, and development rights. DSM development specifically for international water negotiations has been driven by recognition of shared water resources' unique challenges, which has been discussed in Chapter 1 in more depth. Kronaveter and Shamir (2006) emphasize that water-specific negotiation support systems must integrate hydrological, economic, and political dimensions to effectively resolve international water resource disputes. The complexity of transboundary water systems—with interconnected surface and groundwater components, seasonal variations, and multiple-use characteristics—requires models that capture these dynamics while remaining applicable and meaningful to diverse decision makers.

The fluid nature of water and the fact that it is a shared resource necessitate specialized decision support approaches. Unlike territorial or trade negotiations, water negotiations must contend with hydrological connectivity, where actions in one part of the basin inevitably affect conditions elsewhere. Madani et al. (2014) demonstrate that effective water dispute negotiation support systems must incorporate sophisticated hydrological modeling alongside economic valuation and benefit-sharing analysis tools. Water negotiations are distinctively characterized by temporal dynamics sensitivity. Seasonal variations, long-term climate trends, and unpredictable extreme events create complexity, demanding dynamic modeling approaches. Lund and Palmer (1997) argue that water resource system modeling for conflict resolution must address both short-term operational decisions and long-term planning horizons, accommodating different stakeholder time frames.

The literature reveals a trend toward more sophisticated and integrative DSM approaches in water negotiations. Ofjord and Palmer (2002) highlight that computer models have become increasingly central to international water resources management and negotiation, offering scenario analysis, impact assessment, and visualization capabilities that enhance the negotiation process. These tools allow stakeholders to explore potential consequences of different management strategies before committing to specific actions, reducing uncertainty and building consensus around viable solutions. Early models, as described by Thiessen and Loucks (1992), focused primarily on technical optimization of water allocation scenarios but were limited in addressing the full spectrum of political, social, and environmental factors influencing negotiation outcomes. More recent approaches, such as Zagonari and Rossi's (2014) system for Tigris–Euphrates basin disputes between Iraq and Turkey, demonstrate comprehensive integration of hydrological, economic, and geopolitical factors. Their system explicitly addresses power asymmetries that often characterize transboundary water relations, where upstream states typically hold significant hydrological advantages over downstream neighbors.

Future trends likely to shape DSM evolution for international water negotiations include increasing availability of remote sensing data (Peter, 2004), real-time monitoring technologies, and big data analytics (Ibrahim et al., 2017). Osipov et al. (2016) highlight that modern decision support systems for international negotiations, such as those developed for the Arctic region, increasingly leverage these advanced data sources to provide more comprehensive and timely information to negotiators. Climate change impacts have further complicated DSM application in international water negotiations (Cooley & Gleick, 2011). Growing recognition of water's connection to other critical resources necessitates more integrative modeling approaches that address these nexus relationships. This systems perspective allows negotiators to identify potential synergies and trade-offs across different sectors, potentially expanding the solution space for water conflicts.

This book's chapters addressed sophisticated and integrative DSM approaches in water negotiations using methodologies and case studies. As highlighted in Chapter 8, climate change represents a critical factor that must be incorporated into contemporary water negotiation models. This incorporation allows negotiators to address current challenges and develop adaptive strategies for future conditions—essential for creating durable water agreements that can withstand changing hydrological conditions and evolving societal needs. The Helmand/Hirmand transboundary river case study in Chapter 7 shows how advanced system dynamics modeling can integrate hydrological, economic, and ecological variables to create collaborative decision-making platforms that transcend traditional confrontational negotiation strategies. The international water legal framework also shapes DSM development and application. Chapter 6 highlights how international legal instruments—including the 1997 Watercourses Convention and the 1992 Helsinki Convention—provide important principles that must be reflected in negotiation support tools. Data exchange obligations, monitoring, and establishment of joint institutions create both requirements and opportunities for cooperative decision support systems development. Institutional aspects of water governance represent another critical dimension for modern DSMs. Lotov (1998) emphasizes that computer-based support for water resource system environmental rehabilitation planning and negotiation must be embedded within appropriate institutional frameworks to be effective. This insight is echoed in contemporary research, such as Chapter 5's analysis of trust and cooperation in the Helmand River basin, which underscores that technical tools alone are insufficient without corresponding institutional mechanisms for trust-building and agreement implementation. DSMs for water negotiations have increasingly emphasized participatory approaches and stakeholder engagement. Newer methodologies, such as the WOSCIM framework presented in Chapter 9 for the Congo basin, emphasize participatory processes that engage diverse stakeholders in decision support tool development and application, recognizing that effective water governance requires both technical optimization and social legitimacy. Multi-criteria decision analysis (MCDA) integration represents another important advancement in water negotiation DSMs. As demonstrated in Chapter 4's analysis of transboundary water resource management of conflict resolution, MCDA provides a structured approach for evaluating complex trade-offs among competing objectives—particularly valuable in water negotiations where decision makers must balance economic, environmental, social, and geopolitical considerations. Innovative methodological approaches, such as Chapter 2's Smartsettle Infinity system, offer promising new directions for water negotiation support. The simulation-based methodology demonstrates the potential for dynamic preference modeling, intelligent suggestion generation, and multi-party optimization to facilitate consensus-building around efficient solutions, moving beyond traditional zero-sum conceptualizations. Conceptual innovations are also expanding the theoretical foundations of DSMs for water negotiations. Chapter 3's painted water theory represents an important contribution, offering a framework for categorizing water into different classes based on negotiability status. By distinguishing between water capturing and water demand, this approach helps bridge the gap between politically motivated hydraulic missions and actual water needs.

We discuss now ways forward for applying DSMs in international water negotiations and exploring room for their development through four critical contexts. First, we examine the role of river basin organizations (RBOs) as institutional frameworks that can effectively implement and coordinate DSM applications across political boundaries. Second, we explore the integration of DSMs within various water diplomacy tracks, from formal governmental negotiations to informal stakeholder dialogues. Third, we assess how international water conventions provide both normative guidance and practical opportunities for embedding decision support tools within transboundary legal frameworks. Finally, we investigate how emerging technologies—including remote sensing, artificial intelligence, and blockchain—are transforming the capabilities and applications of DSMs in shared water governance. By examining these four interconnected contexts, this chapter aims to provide a comprehensive roadmap for harnessing the full potential of DSMs to foster cooperative and sustainable management of transboundary water resources in an increasingly complex and water-stressed world.

10.2 Four Essential Elements Influencing DSMs in Future Global Water Negotiations

10.2.1 Institutional Innovation: RBOs and Next-Generation DSMs

The relationship between DSMs and RBOs represents a critical nexus where technical tools and institutional frameworks can mutually reinforce each other to advance transboundary water negotiations. When effectively synchronized, these elements create powerful synergies that enhance the management of shared water resources beyond what could be achieved independently.

RBOs provide the essential institutional foundation that enables DSMs to reach their full potential. As Schmeier (2015) demonstrates, well-structured RBOs create the organizational stability and technical capacity necessary for taking initiative. This can be developing sophisticated decision support tools. This institutional backing ensures continuity in model development, validation, and refinement over time—a crucial factor given the long-term nature of transboundary water challenges. When DSMs are embedded within RBO frameworks, they benefit from consistent funding, dedicated technical staff, and organizational legitimacy that external models often lack. This institutional home allows DSMs to evolve from short-term project-based tools to permanent fixtures in basin management. As evident in Chapter 6, these institutional arrangements align with the requirements of international water law instruments such as the 1997 Watercourses Convention and the 1992 Helsinki Convention, which emphasize the establishment of joint institutions as essential components of transboundary water cooperation.

Conversely, advanced DSMs significantly enhance RBOs' capacity to fulfill their mandates. By providing rigorous analytical capabilities, DSMs strengthen RBOs' position as knowledge brokers and neutral facilitators in transboundary negotiations. This enhanced credibility enables RBOs to more effectively mediate between competing national interests and advocate for basin-wide perspectives. The scientific legitimacy conferred by sophisticated DSMs empowers RBOs to propose innovative solutions that might otherwise face resistance from individual riparian states. Chapter 7 illustrates this dynamic through its interdisciplinary DSM based on system dynamics for the Helmand/Hirmand transboundary river, demonstrating how advanced modeling can transform hydropolitical discourse by providing a platform for collaborative decision-making that transcends traditional confrontational negotiation strategies.

The iterative feedback loop between DSMs and RBOs creates opportunities for continuous improvement in both domains. As DSMs generate insights about basin dynamics, RBOs can adapt their institutional structures and strategies accordingly. Simultaneously, evolving RBO priorities and stakeholder concerns inform the ongoing development of DSM capabilities and applications. This mutual adaptation fosters a dynamic relationship where technical tools and governance frameworks co-evolve to address emerging challenges. For instance, as DSMs identify new vulnerabilities related to climate change impacts, RBOs can establish specialized working groups or protocols to address these concerns, which in turn shapes future modeling priorities. Chapter 8's examination of the Colorado River basin underscores this point, showing how DSMs can assess the value of cooperation under changing climate conditions, providing essential information that guides institutional responses to evolving hydrological realities.

Joint capacity development initiatives represent another dimension where DSMs and RBOs can enhance each other. When RBOs invest in building technical expertise among their staff and stakeholders to develop and use DSMs, they simultaneously strengthen their own institutional capabilities and the quality of the models. This shared capacity-building creates a virtuous cycle, as Katz (2025) indicates that enhanced technical understanding among stakeholders leads to more sophisticated model demands, which in turn drives innovation in DSM development. This co-evolution of technical and institutional capacity is particularly valuable in regions with limited resources, where investments must yield multiple benefits. The water security–oriented framework presented in Chapter 9 exemplifies this approach through its participatory methodology that builds capacity among stakeholders while generating robust water security assessments.

Data governance provides a particularly important area for DSM–RBO synchronization. RBOs can establish protocols for data collection, validation, and sharing that serve as the foundation for credible DSMs. As Othoche (2021) highlights, standardized data management systems implemented through RBOs create the consistent, reliable information streams necessary for sophisticated modeling. Simultaneously, the specific data requirements of advanced DSMs can guide RBOs in prioritizing monitoring networks and information systems. This alignment ensures that data collection efforts are targeted toward the most decision-relevant parameters, optimizing limited monitoring resources. Chapter 6 reinforces this connection by emphasizing that exchange of data between riparian countries, complemented by monitoring obligations, forms the cornerstone of cooperation under international water law.

Communication pathways between technical experts and policymakers can be significantly enhanced when DSMs and RBOs are effectively synchronized. Lee et al. (2007) emphasize the importance of user-friendly interfaces in promoting the acceptance and utilization of negotiation support systems. When RBOs incorporate DSM outputs into their regular reporting and decision-making processes, they create institutionalized channels for translating technical insights into policy guidance. These formalized communication pathways ensure that model results meaningfully inform negotiation processes rather than remaining isolated within technical domains. Chapter 2's exploration of the Smartsettle Infinity system demonstrates the potential of advanced interfaces to facilitate consensus-building among stakeholders with divergent interests.

Trust-building represents a fundamental challenge in transboundary water cooperation that the DSM–RBO relationship can help address. As highlighted in Chapter 5, establishing trust is the foundation for sustainable cooperation between co-riparian states. The combination of transparent DSMs and inclusive RBO processes can create conditions that foster trust even in historically contentious basins. When stakeholders jointly participate in model development through RBO-facilitated processes, they develop a shared understanding of system dynamics and challenges. This participatory approach, as demonstrated in Chapter 9's application of the WOSCIM framework in the Congo basin, helps bridge gaps among riparian states and advances inclusive water management practices.

The conceptual innovations presented in Chapter 3's painted water theory offer promising directions for enhancing the DSM–RBO relationship. By categorizing water into non-negotiable, negotiable, and unnegotiable classifications, this framework helps bridge the critical gap between politically motivated hydraulic missions and actual water needs. RBOs can utilize this conceptual approach to structure more productive negotiations around realistic water allocation scenarios, while DSMs can operationalize these distinctions through quantitative modeling. This integration represents a significant advancement in reconciling technical water management tools with complex hydropolitical realities.

Looking forward, the most promising advancements in transboundary water management will likely emerge from deliberately designed synergies between DSMs and RBOs. By recognizing these entities not as separate tools but as complementary elements of an integrated approach, stakeholders can harness their combined potential to address the complex, multifaceted challenges facing shared water resources. This holistic perspective acknowledges that effective water diplomacy requires both sophisticated analytical capabilities and robust institutional frameworks, working in concert to promote sustainable and equitable outcomes across international boundaries. Chapter 4's discussion of MCDA for conflict resolution further supports this conclusion by demonstrating how sophisticated analytical frameworks can be embedded within appropriate institutional contexts to address the dialectical nature of water conflicts.

10.2.2 Diplomatic Bridges: Integrating DSMs Across Water Diplomacy Tracks

The evolution of water diplomacy from traditional state-centric approaches toward multi-track frameworks represents a significant paradigm shift in how transboundary water conflicts are addressed and resolved. This transformation has profound implications for the development and deployment of DSMs as tools for facilitating cooperation across international waterways.

Multi-track water diplomacy recognizes that meaningful engagement must occur at multiple levels simultaneously to achieve sustainable outcomes. As Yasuda et al. (2020) explain, *Track 1* diplomacy refers to official negotiations between governments, whereas *Track 2* includes participation from academic institutions and think tanks. *Track 3*, on the other hand, involves civil society organizations and local communities. This multilayered approach demands that future DSMs be designed with sufficient versatility to serve the distinct needs and capacities of actors across these various tracks. Models that were once developed exclusively for technical experts in government ministries (Track 1) must evolve to become accessible to a broader range of stakeholders, including civil society representatives who may lack specialized technical training but bring valuable contextual knowledge to the negotiation process. This need for stakeholder inclusion aligns with the approach described in Chapter 9, which presents the WOSCIM framework that emphasizes participatory engagement in transboundary water management.

The inclusion of non-state actors in water diplomacy creates new opportunities for DSMs to incorporate diverse knowledge systems and values. According to Yasuda et al. (2020), in the Brahmaputra basin, local communities have accumulated generations of ecological wisdom that has often been overlooked in formal decision-making processes, which are primarily led by technical experts. Future DSMs that can integrate this traditional ecological knowledge alongside conventional scientific data will be better positioned to generate solutions that are both technically sound and socially acceptable. This integration requires not only methodological innovations in modeling approaches but also substantial shifts in how model developers engage with knowledge holders across different diplomatic tracks. Chapter 4 offers potential methodological frameworks for incorporating these diverse perspectives, particularly through its dialectical model that recognizes the complex interplay between humans and natural systems.

Intercultural communication emerges as a critical consideration when DSMs operate across multiple diplomatic tracks. Yasuda et al. (2020) observe that variations in communication approaches and specialized terminology among government representatives, scholars, and local stakeholders often hinder effective discussions in the Brahmaputra basin. Next-generation DSMs must therefore incorporate visualization tools and user interfaces that can effectively communicate complex hydrological concepts across cultural and educational divides. Models that rely exclusively on technical jargon and conventional scientific visualizations will increasingly be seen as insufficient for supporting the inclusive dialogue that multi-track diplomacy demands. Chapter 7 demonstrates how interactive visual dashboards can bridge communication gaps between stakeholders, enabling collaborative exploration of complex water allocation scenarios.

The temporal dimensions of multi-track diplomacy have significant implications for DSM design and implementation. Track 1 diplomatic processes typically operate within political time frames dictated by electoral cycles and formal negotiation schedules, while Track 3 engagement with local communities requires longer-term relationship-building and trust development. Future DSMs must therefore be capable of producing both rapid analytics to support immediate decisions in formal negotiations and longer-term scenario analyses that inform sustained dialogue across all diplomatic tracks. Chapter 5 illustrates how decision support frameworks can address these temporal challenges through systematic cost–benefit analysis approaches.

Power asymmetries between actors in different diplomatic tracks present particular challenges for DSM implementation. Technical capacity imbalances between upstream and downstream states in a transboundary basin are further complicated by disparities between government agencies and local communities (Shabazbegian & Noori, 2022). Next-generation DSMs must incorporate design features that explicitly address these power imbalances, potentially through tiered interfaces that provide different levels of analytical complexity for users with varying technical capacities. Models that require advanced technical expertise to operate effectively risk reinforcing existing power disparities rather than facilitating more equitable dialogue across diplomatic tracks. Chapter 3 provides a particularly relevant framework for addressing these power dynamics by distinguishing between different categories of water claims and helping to focus negotiations on areas where genuine flexibility exists.

The legitimacy of DSMs across multiple diplomatic tracks depends increasingly on transparent model development processes. Stakeholders involved in various sectors of a transboundary basin may show doubt regarding "black box" models that have been created without their involvement or comprehension. This observation suggests that future DSMs must be developed through participatory processes that engage representatives from multiple tracks throughout the model design, calibration, and validation phases. Models developed exclusively by technical experts without broader stakeholder engagement will likely face legitimacy challenges when deployed in multi-track diplomatic contexts, regardless of their technical sophistication. Chapter 6 underscores this argument by highlighting how international water law increasingly emphasizes data exchange and joint monitoring as foundations for legitimate cooperative water management.

Looking ahead, the most promising frontier for DSMs in water diplomacy lies in their potential to create a shared understanding across diplomatic tracks. The greatest value of multi-track water diplomacy is its ability to foster dialogue between constituencies that would otherwise remain isolated from each other. Next-generation DSMs can serve as boundary objects that facilitate this cross-track dialogue, providing a common reference point around which diverse stakeholders can organize their discussions. Models designed with this boundary-spanning function in mind will prioritize accessibility and transparency alongside technical rigor, creating tools that genuinely enable cooperative problem-solving across the full spectrum of water diplomacy tracks. Chapter 2 exemplifies how advanced negotiation support tools can help parties identify mutually beneficial solutions that might otherwise remain undiscovered in complex multi-issue water negotiations.

As water diplomacy continues to evolve toward more inclusive, multi-track approaches, DSMs must similarly transform from purely technical tools into platforms for collective learning and dialogue. This evolution will require significant innovations in both technological capabilities and engagement methodologies, ultimately producing a new generation of decision support tools that are as socially sophisticated as they are technically advanced. Chapter 8 demonstrates how this evolution can yield quantifiable benefits, showing that the value of cooperation increases as environmental pressures intensify—a finding with important implications for multi-track water diplomacy efforts worldwide.

10.2.3 Legal Foundations: Embedding DSMs Within International Water Conventions

The evolving landscape of international water law, particularly the progression from the Helsinki Rules to the UN Watercourses Convention and the Berlin Rules, offers critical insights into how legal frameworks may shape the development and implementation of DSMs for transboundary water negotiations in the coming decades. These legal instruments provide the normative foundation upon which technical tools like DSMs must be built to ensure their legitimacy and effectiveness in international contexts.

The trajectory of international water conventions reveals a gradual shift from general principles toward more specific procedural obligations and substantive rights. As Salman (2007) observes, "The UN Watercourses Convention builds on the Helsinki Rules and establishes more detailed procedures for notification of planned measures and for the settlement of disputes." This evolution toward greater procedural specificity creates both opportunities and challenges for DSMs. On the one hand, clearly defined procedural requirements provide a structured framework within which DSMs can operate, ensuring that model outputs feed into established notification and consultation processes. On the other hand, these procedural obligations necessitate that DSMs be designed with sufficient flexibility to accommodate the diverse legal contexts and varying levels of compliance across different basins. Chapter 6 extensively examines this relationship between international water law and DSMs, highlighting how legal frameworks provide essential requirements for data exchange and monitoring that directly support DSM implementation.

The principle of equitable and reasonable utilization, a cornerstone of international water law, has profound implications for the design of future DSMs. Salman (2007) highlights that the Berlin Rules uphold the principle of equitable utilization established by the Helsinki Rules, while also prioritizing the duty to avoid causing significant harm. Models that can quantitatively assess trade-offs between development benefits and environmental or social harms will become increasingly valuable as riparian states seek to balance these competing objectives within the framework of international law. Chapter 8 demonstrates how DSMs can quantify the benefits of cooperation under climate change scenarios, providing exactly the kind of trade-off analysis needed to implement equitable utilization principles.

The obligation to exchange information and data, which has become progressively more explicit in successive water conventions, directly supports the fundamental requirements of DSMs. According to Salman (2007), the UN Watercourses Convention encompasses comprehensive regulations regarding the consistent sharing of data and information, as well as the requirement to notify about proposed actions. These legal obligations create a foundation for the data-sharing mechanisms that are essential for robust modeling. Future DSMs will need to be designed to accommodate and leverage these legally mandated information flows, while also addressing the inevitable gaps and inconsistencies in data availability across international boundaries. Chapter 6 specifically addresses how the exchange of data is a primary obligation under international water law, serving as the foundation for implementing more substantive obligations like equitable utilization and the no-harm rule.

The emerging emphasis on public participation in international water law, particularly evident in the Berlin Rules, suggests that future DSMs will need to incorporate stakeholder perspectives more explicitly. Dellapenna (2006) notes that the Berlin Rules incorporate more comprehensive regulations regarding public involvement compared to earlier versions, highlighting an increasing acknowledgment of civil society's importance in the governance of water resources. This trend indicates that next-generation DSMs will need to move beyond purely technical considerations to incorporate diverse value systems and traditional knowledge. Participatory modeling approaches that engage stakeholders throughout the model development process will likely gain prominence as tools for implementing the public participation provisions of evolving water conventions. Chapter 9 exemplifies this participatory approach, demonstrating how water security assessments can integrate stakeholder perspectives to enhance the legitimacy and effectiveness of transboundary water management.

Environmental protection provisions have also grown more prominent in successive water conventions, with the Berlin Rules placing particular emphasis on ecological flows and ecosystem needs. This evolution suggests that future DSMs must enhance their capacity to model ecological processes and ecosystem services. Models that can quantify the environmental implications of different allocation scenarios will become essential tools for implementing the environmental protection obligations embedded in international water law. Salman (2007) notes that the Berlin Rules include a dedicated chapter on protecting aquatic environments, underscoring the increasing importance of environmental considerations in water management. Chapter 4 offers methodological tools that can help integrate these environmental considerations into DSMs, particularly through its dialectical model that acknowledges the complex relationships between human systems and natural environments.

The settlement of dispute provisions in international water conventions provides a framework within which DSMs can contribute to conflict resolution. Salman (2007) points out that the UN Watercourses Convention outlines specific mechanisms for resolving disputes peacefully, such as the use of fact-finding commissions. In this context, DSMs can serve as technical tools to support fact-finding exercises, providing objective analyses that inform mediation and arbitration processes. Future DSMs will likely be designed with specific capabilities to address the evidential requirements of international water dispute resolution mechanisms, with particular attention to transparency and reproducibility of results. Chapter 2 demonstrates how sophisticated negotiation support tools can play a crucial role in resolving disputes by assisting parties in uncovering mutually advantageous solutions that may otherwise go unnoticed in intricate water allocation conflicts.

As we move forward, the relationship between international water agreements and demand-side management strategies will progressively develop alongside advancements in both legal frameworks and technological innovations. The trend toward more comprehensive, specific, and environmentally conscious legal instruments suggests that DSMs will need to become increasingly sophisticated in their ability to model complex socioecological systems while remaining accessible to diverse stakeholders. Chapter 3's painted water theory offers a promising framework for addressing this challenge by differentiating between categories of water claims and helping focus negotiations on areas where genuine flexibility exists within legal constraints. As DSMs become more deeply embedded in legal and institutional frameworks, their design must carefully balance technical rigor with practical applicability to ensure they effectively support the implementation of international water law principles in an uncertain future. Chapter 7 demonstrates how this balance can be achieved through interactive visualization tools that make complex hydrological relationships accessible to diverse stakeholders while maintaining scientific integrity.

10.2.4 Digital Frontiers: Emerging Technologies Reshaping Water Negotiation Tools

The emergence of sophisticated technologies has fundamentally transformed the landscape of DSMs for international water negotiations. As transboundary water management becomes increasingly complex due to climate change, population growth, and competing demands, technological innovations offer unprecedented opportunities to enhance the efficacy and acceptance of DSMs as negotiation tools.

Advanced computational capabilities have enabled the development of more sophisticated hydrological models that can simulate complex river basin dynamics with greater accuracy. These advancements enable parties to explore a wider range of scenarios and their implications, facilitating more informed decision-making during negotiations. Such scenario-based approaches are exemplified in Chapter 7, where system dynamics modeling provides a dashboard for stakeholders to simulate complex water allocation scenarios in the Helmand/Hirmand River basin.

Remote sensing technologies and Earth observation systems have revolutionized data collection for transboundary waters. According to Othoche (2021), satellite monitoring systems have addressed the conventional issues of data asymmetry by granting riparian states equal access to essential hydrological information, which fosters trust and transparency during negotiations. This democratization of data access represents a significant step forward in addressing power imbalances that have historically hampered transboundary water negotiations, particularly in regions where ground-based monitoring networks are sparse or inaccessible. Chapter 6 emphasizes this point by highlighting that international water law instruments specifically call for data exchange and monitoring obligations as fundamental steps toward cooperative water management.

Artificial intelligence (AI) and machine learning algorithms are increasingly being incorporated into DSMs to enhance their predictive capabilities (Sarkar & Jha, 2025). These technologies can identify patterns in complex datasets and generate insights that might elude human analysts. By processing vast amounts of historical and real-time data, AI-powered DSMs can provide more accurate forecasts of water availability and demand, enabling negotiators to anticipate and plan for future scenarios with greater confidence. Chapter 8 demonstrates the value of such predictive modeling in the Colorado River basin, where climate change scenarios are incorporated into decision support frameworks to assess cooperation benefits under changing conditions.

User interface design has emerged as a critical factor in the acceptance and utilization of DSMs. Lee et al. (2007) emphasize that the adoption of negotiation support systems by decision makers is greatly affected by their perceived utility and user-friendliness. As technological capabilities advance, attention must be paid to creating intuitive interfaces that allow negotiators with varying levels of technical expertise to effectively engage with the models. Visualization tools that translate complex data into accessible formats are particularly valuable in this context, enabling stakeholders to grasp the implications of different policy options without requiring specialized knowledge. Chapter 2 illustrates this principle through its exploration of Smartsettle Infinity, highlighting how advanced negotiation support systems with intuitive interfaces can facilitate collaborative negotiations among riparian states.

Blockchain technology offers promising applications for enhancing transparency and accountability in the future negotiation support system (Witt et al., 2025) as well as water agreements (Huseynov & Mitchell, 2024). By creating immutable records of water allocation decisions and monitoring data, blockchain can help build trust among riparian states and ensure compliance with negotiated agreements. Blockchain technology could have enhanced Chapter 5, which conceptualizes trust using a cost–benefit decision-making framework in the context of the Helmand River basin.

Virtual and augmented reality technologies present innovative ways to visualize the impacts of water and environmental management decisions. These immersive technologies can help negotiators and stakeholders experience potential future scenarios, making abstract concepts more tangible and facilitating more empathetic decision-making (Levchenko et al., 2021). As transboundary water negotiations often involve balancing competing interests across multiple sectors and communities, these technologies can play a valuable role in fostering mutual understanding and identifying win–win solutions. Chapter 4 aligns with this approach, offering frameworks for resolving conflicts between different water users and riparian countries.

All in all, technological advancements are poised to significantly enhance the role of DSMs in international water negotiations. However, as Othoche (2021) cautions, technology by itself is not enough; effective implementation necessitates suitable institutional structures, the development of skills, and authentic political commitment. The challenge lies in harnessing technological innovations while ensuring they remain accessible, equitable, and responsive to the complex sociopolitical contexts in which water negotiations take place. Chapter 9 exemplifies this holistic approach, integrating technological tools within broader frameworks that promote water security through inclusive, evidence-based decision-making processes.

10.3 Conclusion and Ways Forward

DSMs have evolved significantly from simple communication platforms to sophisticated analytical frameworks capable of modeling complex transboundary water interactions. This evolution reflects the increasing recognition of water's unique characteristics as a shared, fluid resource that demands specialized negotiation approaches. As demonstrated throughout this chapter, the four essential elements examined—institutional frameworks through RBOs, multi-track water diplomacy, international legal instruments, and emerging technologies—collectively provide a comprehensive roadmap for the future development and implementation of DSMs in international water negotiations.

The synergistic relationship between DSMs and RBOs represents a powerful nexus for advancing transboundary water cooperation. Chapter 7's interdisciplinary DSM based on system dynamics for the Helmand/Hirmand transboundary river clearly demonstrates how advanced modeling transforms hydropolitical discourse by providing collaborative decision-making platforms. Similarly, Chapter 8's examination of the Colorado River basin shows how DSMs can assess cooperation value under changing climate conditions, guiding institutional responses to evolving hydrological realities. When effectively synchronized, these elements create institutional stability and technical capacity that allows DSMs to evolve from project-based tools to permanent fixtures in basin management.

The transformation of water diplomacy toward multi-track frameworks necessitates corresponding innovations in DSM design and implementation. Chapter 9's framework exemplifies this approach through its participatory methodology that builds capacity among diverse stakeholders while generating robust water security assessments. Chapter 5's trust-building framework further illustrates how DSMs must address power asymmetries and facilitate cross-cultural dialogue to be effective across diplomatic tracks. The conceptual innovations in Chapter 3's painted water theory offer a valuable framework for categorizing water into different negotiability classes, helping bridge the gap between politically motivated hydraulic missions and actual water needs.

International water law provides the essential normative foundation upon which effective DSMs must be built. Chapter 6 extensively examines this relationship, highlighting how legal frameworks provide essential requirements for data exchange and monitoring that directly support DSM implementation. Chapter 4's MCDA for conflict resolution demonstrates how sophisticated analytical frameworks can be embedded within appropriate legal contexts to address the dialectical nature of water conflicts. These chapters collectively illustrate how the evolution from the Helsinki Rules to the UN Watercourses Convention and Berlin Rules shapes DSM requirements and applications in transboundary settings.

Emerging technologies offer unprecedented opportunities to enhance DSM effectiveness in water negotiations. Chapter 2's exploration of the Smartsettle Infinity system demonstrates how advanced interfaces can facilitate consensus-building among stakeholders with divergent interests. Chapter 7's interactive visual dashboards showcase how technological innovations can bridge communication gaps between stakeholders, enabling collaborative exploration of complex water allocation scenarios. These technological advancements must be implemented within appropriate institutional frameworks, as underscored by the participatory approaches advocated in Chapter 9.

Future progress in transboundary water management will likely stem from the intentional incorporation of these four critical components. The case studies presented throughout this book—from the Helmand/Hirmand River basin (Chapters 5 and 7) to the Colorado River basin (Chapter 8) and the Congo basin (Chapter 9)—provide practical illustrations of how DSMs can be tailored to specific contexts while adhering to universal principles of effective water governance. These real-world applications demonstrate that DSMs are not merely technical artifacts but dynamic interfaces between science and policy, helping translate hydrological realities into politically feasible agreements.

As climate change intensifies water security challenges worldwide, Chapter 8's focus on climate adaptation strategies illustrates how DSMs will become increasingly valuable for shaping a more inclusive negotiation, depending on the climate change scenario. The innovative methodologies presented in Chapter 2's simulation-based approach and Chapter 4's dialectical model offer promising new directions for water negotiation support, moving beyond traditional zero-sum conceptualizations toward optimization and cooperation. By embracing the multifaceted approaches outlined throughout this book, the international community can advance water diplomacy toward genuine cooperation that benefits all riparian states and the ecosystems upon which they depend.

The overall contributions of this book demonstrate that effective DSMs require both sophisticated technical design and thoughtful implementation within appropriate institutional, diplomatic, and legal frameworks. By integrating these lessons across disciplinary boundaries, future applications of DSMs in international water negotiations will be better equipped to address the complex challenges of managing shared water resources in an increasingly water-stressed world.

Perhaps future DSMs will recognize that transboundary water negotiations are fundamentally about people—their needs, values, fears, and aspirations. By designing models that facilitate genuine dialogue across cultural, disciplinary, and institutional boundaries, we can harness the full potential of decision support tools to promote international water negotiation.

References

Cooley, H., & Gleick, P. H. (2011). Climate-proofing transboundary water agreements. *Hydrological Sciences Journal, 56*(4), 711–718.

Dellapenna, J. W. (2006). The Berlin rules on water resources: The new paradigm for international water law. In R. Graham (Ed.), *World Environmental and Water Resource Congress 2006: Examining the confluence of environmental and water concerns* (pp. 1–10). American Society of Civil Engineers.

Dinar, A., Dinar, S., McKinney, D. C., & McCaffrey, S. C. (2007). *Bridges over water: Understanding transboundary water conflict, negotiation and cooperation* (Vol. 3). World Scientific Publishing Company.

Hensel, P. R., Mitchell, S. M., & Sowers, T. E., II (2006). Conflict management of riparian disputes. *Political Geography, 25*(4), 383–411.

Huseynov, F., & Mitchell, J. (2024). Blockchain for environmental peacebuilding: Application in water management. *Digital Policy, Regulation and Governance, 26*(1), 55–71.

Ibrahim, I. A., Brown, R. D., & Truby, J. (2017). Big data analytics and its impact on basin water agreements and international water law: A study of the Ramotswa aquifer. *University of Pennsylvania Journal of International Law, 73*, 101.

Katz, D. (2025). The technological transformation of transboundary water management. In D. Katz (Ed.), *World scientific handbook of transboundary water management: Science, economics, policy and politics: Vol. 2. Tapping technologies: Therole of technological change in transboundary water management* (pp. 1–10). World Scientific Publishers.

Kersten, G. E., & Lai, H. (2007). Negotiation support and e-negotiation systems: An overview. *Group Decision and Negotiation, 16*, 553–586.

Kersten, G. E., & Noronha, S. J. (1998, October). Negotiation support systems and negotiating agents. In N. Ferrand (Ed.), *Modeles et systemes multi-agents pour la gestion de l'environnement et des territoires, actes du colloque SMAGET* (Vol. 98, pp. 349–357). Cemagref Éditions.

Kronaveter, L., & Shamir, U. (2006). Negotiation support system for resolution of disputes over international water resources. In A. Castelletti & R. Soncini-Sessa (Eds.), *Topics on system analysis and integrated water resource management.* Elsevier.

Lee, K. C., Kang, I., & Kim, J. S. (2007). Exploring the user interface of negotiation support systems from the user acceptance perspective. *Computers in Human Behavior, 23*(1), 220–239.

Levchenko, A., Ivanov, V., & Taratukhin, V. (2021). Virtual reality–built prototype as a next-gen environment for advanced procurement reporting and contract negotiation. In *International Conference for Information Systems and Design* (pp. 90–106). Springer International Publishing.

Lim, L. H., & Benbasat, I. (1992). A theoretical perspective of negotiation support systems. *Journal of Management Information Systems, 9*(3), 27–44.

Lotov, A. V. (1998). Computer-based support for planning and negotiation on environmental rehabilitation of water resource systems. In D. P. Loucks (Ed.), *Restoration of degraded rivers: Challenges, issues and experiences* (pp. 417–445). Springer.

Lund, J. R., & Palmer, R. N. (1997). Water resource system modeling for conflict resolution. *Water Resources Update, 3*(108), 70–82.

Madani, K., Rouhani, O. M., Mirchi, A., & Gholizadeh, S. (2014). A negotiation support system for resolving an international trans-boundary natural resource conflict. *Environmental Modelling & Software, 51*, 240–249.

Ofjord, G. D., & Palmer, R. (2002). Use of computer models in management and negotiation of international water resources. In S. Castelein (Ed.), *From conflict to co-operation in international water resources management: Challenges and opportunities* (pp. 178–189). UNESCO.

Osipov, G. S., Dmitriev, M. G., Smirnov, I. V., Danik, Y. E., & Ananyeva, M. I. (2016, June 30–July 6). The concept of the decision support system for international negotiations in the Arctic region. In *International Multidisciplinary Scientific GeoConference: SGEM* (Vol. 1, pp. 461–467). STEF92 Technology Ltd.

Othoche, B. (2021). Exploring technologies for sustainable transboundary water resource management in the era of climate change: A case for the Nile River basin riparian states. In A. M. Melesse, W. Abtew, & S. A. Moges (Eds.), *Nile and Grand Ethiopian Renaissance Dam: Past, Present and Future* (pp. 181–193). Springer.

Peter, N. (2004). The use of remote sensing to support the application of multilateral environmental agreements. *Space Policy, 20*(3), 189–195.

Salman, S. M. (2007). The Helsinki Rules, the UN Watercourses Convention and the Berlin Rules: Perspectives on international water law. *Water Resources Development, 23*(4), 625–640.

Sarkar, S., & Jha, P. K. (2025). Application of AI/ML in water resource management to resolve transboundary water conflict. In A. Nanda, P. K. Gupta, V. Gupta, P. K. Jha, & S. K. Dubey (Eds.), *Navigating the nexus: Hydrology, agriculture, pollution and climate change* (Vol. 1, pp. 431–455). Springer Nature.

Schmeier, S. (2015). The institutional design of river basin organizations—Empirical findings from around the world. *International Journal of River Basin Management, 13*(1), 51–72.

Shahbazbegian, M., & Noori, R. (2022). Hydropolitical system archetypes: Feedback structures, physical environments, unintended behaviors, and a diagnostic checklist. *Hydrology, 9*(12), Article 207.

Thiessen, E. M., & Loucks, D. P. (1992). Computer assisted negotiation of multiobjective water resources conflicts. *JAWRA: Journal of the American Water Resources Association, 28*(1), 163–177.

Witt, J., Schoop, M., & Knaus, K. (2025). Opportunities and challenges of blockchain technology for negotiation support systems. *Group Decision and Negotiation, 34*, 373–403.

Yasuda, Y., Hill, D., Aich, D., Huntjens, P., & Swain, A. (2020). Multi-track water diplomacy: Current and potential future cooperation over the Brahmaputra River basin. In S. Ho (Ed.), *A river flows through it* (pp. 159–181). Routledge.
Zagonari, F., & Rossi, C. (2014). A negotiation support system for disputes between Iraq and Turkey over the Tigris–Euphrates basin. *Journal of Hydrology, 514*, 65–84.

Index

Tables and figures are indicated by an italic *t* and *f*.

D